P9-DBI-555

MARIE ANTOINETTE.

MY SCRAP-BOOK

OF

THE FRENCH REVOLUTION

EDITED BY

ELIZABETH WORMELEY LATIMER

AUTHOR OF "FRANCE IN THE NINETEENTH CENTURY," "RUSSIA AND TURKEY IN THE NINETEENTH CENTURY," "ENGLAND IN THE NINETEENTH CENTURY," "EUROPE IN AFRICA IN THE NINETEENTH CENTURY," "ITALY IN THE NINETEENTH CENTURY," "SPAIN IN THE NINETEENTH CENTURY," ETC.

THIRD EDITION

CHICAGO
A. C. McCLURG AND COMPANY
1899

NOTE.

OF this book I am simply the compiler, — unless, indeed, I may call myself the translator of such parts as have been derived from French sources. I collected the material two years since, when giving parlor lectures on the French Revolution; and much that then passed into my scrap-drawer seemed to me too interesting to be confined to small circles of ladies who gathered round me with their crochet-work or embroidery. I have, therefore, collected my "Scraps" into a book for general reading.

Thomas Waters Griffith, whose reminiscences begin this volume, was the uncle of my husband, Randolph B. Latimer. He wrote several books concerning the early history of Baltimore and Maryland, and left behind him a manuscript volume of his personal reminiscences. With that portion of it which contains a narrative of his residence in France during the Reign of Terror and the rule of the Directory I have begun this volume. After his return from France, he was sent by the government at Washington to report on the condition of the Island of Hayti. He was a strong Federalist, and has left a minute account of riots in Baltimore in 1812, when the offices of a Federalist newspaper were attacked by a so-called "patriotic" mob. Louis XVIII., in 1816, sent him the Cross of St. Louis, in recognition of the services he had rendered to *émigrés* during the Reign of Terror. He was also made a Freemason during his residence in France. I have a parchment containing a certificate of his initiation into the order, in the second year of the Republic.

I was a subscriber to the Literary Supplement of the Paris "Figaro" for twenty years. During the years 1893, 1894, and 1895, the centennial anniversary of terrible scenes in the Reign of Terror, this paper published valuable articles on the subject as the one hundredth anniversary of each event arose. These monographs, I think, cannot but be found interesting by many of my readers.

I have tried to keep in mind in all my writings the motto, *Suum cuique*, and to claim no more credit than what is fairly my due.

In conclusion, I would like to acknowledge my obligations in this book — and the obligations of a lifetime — to "Littell's Living Age." Living, as I have done, in the country, I could not without its assistance have kept in touch with foreign magazine literature. In 1841, Mr. Robert Walsh, then United States Consul in Paris, and at that time one of America's leading literary men, showed me an early number of the "Living Age," saying, "This publication will prove of immense value to all classes of readers in our country." I have a complete copy of the "Living Age" from 1848 to the present day, — nearly two hundred volumes, each containing more than six hundred pages. To me it has been of inestimable value in my work, and to the children in my family an education.

The "Scraps" in this volume are not, I think, accessible to the public without research, with the exception of two or three taken from Carlyle's "French Revolution." I inserted them as links between events which I thought needed some connection; and who can paint in a few brief words a picture like Carlyle? His rugged style lends point and picturesqueness to his narratives, and, as Victor Hugo says, "*fait penser*." Nevertheless, in these extracts I have taken the great liberty of slightly modifying the language. If Carlyle were living, I am afraid he would be angry with me. I saw him angry once (not with me), and should have been afraid to provoke him again to anger. But my excuse for my presumption is that the introduction of a few pages of pure Carlylese into the midst of a work written in a wholly different style, though by a variety of authors, would have produced in parts of my book a sort of dislocation. Perhaps I had no right to substitute "frenzied" for "fremescent," and so on; for, indeed, the word "frenzied" has not half the force of "fremescent." But the one is our every-day English; the other, not.

E. W. L.

BONNYWOOD, HOWARD CO., MARYLAND,
August, 1898.

CONTENTS.

Book I.

REMINISCENCES OF AN AMERICAN GENTLEMAN RESIDENT IN PARIS FROM 1791 TO 1799.

CHAPTER PAGE

I. THOMAS WATERS GRIFFITH: HE GOES TO FRANCE . . 9
II. AUGUST AND SEPTEMBER IN PARIS IN 1792 27
III. HIS IMPRISONMENT IN THE REIGN OF TERROR . . . 43
IV. LIFE IN PARIS UNDER THE DIRECTORY 58

Book II.

FRANCE BEFORE THE REVOLUTION.

I. IMPRISONMENTS AND ESCAPES OF LATUDE 70
II. A PEASANT'S VIEW OF THE REVOLUTION 107
III. PARIS IN 1787 116
IV. COURT LIFE AT VERSAILLES ON THE EVE OF THE REVOLUTION 130

Book III.

THE COLLAPSE OF FRENCH ROYALTY.

I. THE FLIGHT TO VARENNES 144
II. COUNT AXEL FERSEN 164
III. AUGUST THE TENTH AND THE SEPTEMBER MASSACRES 172
IV. THE PRINCESSE DE LAMBALLE 184
V. THE KING 198
VI. MARIE ANTOINETTE AND ROBESPIERRE 223
VII. CLOSING SCENES IN THE LIFE OF MARIE ANTOINETTE 232

Book IV.

THE REIGN OF TERROR.

CHAPTER PAGE
I. Marat 244
II. Danton 277
III. The Feast of the Supreme Being 290
IV. The Fall of Robespierre 308
V. A Chapter of Episodes: —
i. Robespierre as a Poet 324
ii. Robespierre's Private Life with the Family of Duplay 325
iii. The Revolutionary Calendar 335
iv. "Which?" By François Coppée 342
v. Dogs in the Revolution 343

Book V.

THE CLERGY OF FRANCE DURING THE REVOLUTION.

I. Exiles for Conscience' Sake 348
II. A Conventional Bishop 355
III. A Protestant Pastor 362

Book VI.

LAFAYETTE AND HIS FAMILY.

I. Lafayette's Career 373
II. Deaths of the Ladies of Madame de Lafayette's Family 390

Book VII.

LOUIS XVII.

I. The Dauphin in the Temple 401
II. Historic Doubts as to the Fate of Louis XVII. 408
III. The Lost Prince 421

Index 443

LIST OF ILLUSTRATIONS.

MARIE ANTOINETTE . . . . *Frontispiece*
THOMAS WATERS GRIFFITH . . . . *To face page* 10
GOUVERNEUR MORRIS . . . . „ „ 22
THOMAS PAINE . . . . „ „ 50
JAMES MONROE . . . . „ „ 56
CHARLES MAURICE TALLEYRAND . . . . . . „ „ 60
CHARLES COTESWORTH PINCKNEY . . . . . . „ „ 66
HENRI MASERS DE LATUDE . . . . „ „ 70
MADAME DE POMPADOUR . . . . „ „ 90
MADAME NECKER . . . . „ „ 102
LOUIS XVI. . . . . „ „ 132
DUCHESSE D'ANGOULÊME AND THE DAUPHIN . „ „ 146
MARIE ANTOINETTE . . . . „ „ 154
COUNT AXEL FERSEN . . . . „ „ 164
MADAME ELISABETH . . . . „ „ 174
PRINCESSE DE LAMBALLE . . . . „ „ 184
LOUIS XVI. . . . . „ „ 198
MARIE ANTOINETTE LEAVING THE TRIBUNAL . „ „ 232
MARAT . . . . „ „ 244
CHARLOTTE CORDAY . . . . „ „ 262
DANTON . . . . „ „ 278
ROBESPIERRE . . . . „ „ 308
HENRI GRÉGOIRE, BISHOP OF BLOIS . . . . . „ „ 356
JEAN PAUL RABAUT . . . . „ „ 362
LAFAYETTE . . . . „ „ 374
MADAME DE LAFAYETTE . . . . „ „ 380
LOUIS XVII. . . . . „ „ 402
DUCHESSE D'ANGOULÊME . . . . „ „ 416
REV. ELEAZER WILLIAMS . . . . „ „ 422

MY SCRAP-BOOK

OF

THE FRENCH REVOLUTION.

BOOK I.

REMINISCENCES OF AN AMERICAN GENTLEMAN RESIDENT IN PARIS FROM 1791 TO 1799.

I. THOMAS WATERS GRIFFITH: HE GOES TO FRANCE.
II. AUGUST AND SEPTEMBER, 1792.
III. HIS IMPRISONMENT.
IV. LIFE IN PARIS UNDER THE DIRECTORY.

CHAPTER I.

THOMAS WATERS GRIFFITH: HE GOES TO FRANCE.

THOMAS WATERS GRIFFITH, who was born in Baltimore in 1767, and died in the same city in 1834, left behind him several printed books of which he was the author, many papers and letters of historical interest, and a copious account of fifty years of his own life, eight years of which time he passed in France during the stormy days of the French Revolution. As a merchant resident in Havre, and subsequently U. S. Consul at the same port, he had it in his power frequently to favor the escape of *émigrés*; and Louis XVIII., in recognition of these services, sent him the Cross of St. Louis in 1816. Mr. Griffith says little, however, of such things in his Journal. In 1799, during the disputes between the United States and the Directory, he quitted France, to which country he never returned. He was afterwards sent on a mission to Hayti, of which he has given an interesting account in his Journal. The manuscript ends in 1821, after which time he led till 1834 an uneventful life as a public-spirited and useful citizen of Baltimore.

That my readers may know what manner of man was this young eye-witness of the French Revolution, from the autumn of 1791 to 1799, I here introduce his Revolutionary experience by a few extracts concerning his early life in the first pages of his Journal. It begins thus: —

The Proprietary of Pennsylvania had taken so much pains to cultivate the place of his first settlement in that province that the population soon increased by immigration. Early in the eighteenth century came out a colony of Welsh Baptists from England, who took up a considerable body of land on the head waters of Christern Creek. They had brought with them their own pastor, the Rev. John Griffith, my great-grandfather, and they at once erected a brick church, and set aside land for its support. The colonists retained their habits of industry and honest simplicity. They were a rural population fifty miles distant from the port of Philadelphia, and they long preserved their native (Welsh) language, in which indeed I have often heard them converse with fluency and pleasure.

My father, Benjamin Griffith, when he had acquired a small capital, settled down in Baltimore, and married Rachel, daughter of Thomas Waters, who was also of Welsh extraction. I was the only child of this marriage, my young mother dying in Baltimore shortly after my birth. I was then sent as soon as possible to the care of my grandparents in Chester Co., Pennsylvania, who lived within sight of Valley Forge. In those days imported convict servants were employed in Maryland, and an Irish girl of this description was sent to take charge of me in Pennsylvania. Such servants were often persons of the worst character, who brought crime and disorder into peaceful families. My nurse was of this description, and her conduct towards me, her unfortunate charge, betrayed such criminal designs that my protectors got rid of her as soon as possible. Not long after, she was tried for murder at Chester, convicted, and executed.

THOMAS WATERS GRIFFITH.

My father married again and had a large family, two daughters[1] and five sons. I take pleasure in reflecting on the respect my ancestors had acquired by their uniform integrity, and their religious and benevolent deportment. My father, Benjamin Griffith, was an outspoken enemy to British taxation, and when our Revolutionary troubles broke out, and troops were raised in Baltimore and Pennsylvania, he at once volunteered his services, while his family was moved from Baltimore to a place of safety.

When in 1776 the British army passed within two miles of my grandfather's house, and halted a day or two south of the Valley Forge, I well remember the appearance of the Hessians, who came looking for Colonel Denvers, who had married my aunt. Not only did they plunder our house and barn, but they went so far as to put a halter round my grandfather's neck, alleging that he would not tell them where the rebel colonel was. This, in fact, he did not know, the colonel being at that time at the American headquarters then moving from place to place in advance of the enemy. To Mrs. Denvers and her infant boy (who they knew was named George Washington) they were civil enough; and also to myself, although I was not a little alarmed at their strange language and long whiskers. I thought them savages, and very dreadful. When scouting parties came it was necessary to spread before them quantities of bread, butter, cheese, and such drinks as the house afforded. The foraging parties gave out that all they took should be paid for in Philadelphia, and my grandfather took their receipts, but nothing was ever received.

Not long after the British left to occupy Philadelphia, the same ground was occupied by American troops; and Colonel Denvers' house became the headquarters of General Potts, whose orderly conduct and social manners made him a great favorite among us.

After the battle of Germantown, in which my father served with the Baltimore troop, he was sent to bring back to Baltimore the remains of his commander, General Cox, whom he

[1] The younger daughter married, in 1813, Randolph Wallace Lati mer of Baltimore. — E. W. L.

had interred upon the battlefield. He took this opportunity, as I was then ten years old, of reclaiming me from my grandparents, and took me home to be placed under the care of his second wife, who was my mother's cousin.

I missed, however, the freedom of country life, and pined for the farm of my grandfather. But thus it happened that I was spared all sight of the sufferings of the Revolutionary army in the terrible winter of 1777-78, when, half-naked and half-famished, our soldiers encamped during the bitter winter months between the Heights looking down on Valley Forge and the Schuylkill.

It was the year 1776, and I was sent to school in Baltimore, but I often changed my teachers, who were forced to give up teaching for various causes; one, — Mr. Laurence Bathurst, who was a good man and an excellent instructor, — because he was a Roman Catholic. At that time nothing was taught in those schools but English reading, writing, and ciphering, and there was a great scarcity of teachers of any kind. It was a fortunate circumstance, I think, for the establishment of free institutions in the United States that the state of society at that period was rather patriarchal than refined. Children were under great restraint to parents; their manner of living was plain; their desires limited; and the rules of justice, with the fear of God, were implanted in the youthful mind by the general use of the Bible and Testament as reading-books in the schools.

When I had attained the age of fourteen I was sent to a superior school in Delaware. The whole yearly expense of my boarding and tuition was about eighty dollars. The fare was very scanty, but we had at least some tea and sugar after the French alliance and the change of the currency from paper money to specie; whereas before that our diet was confined to bread and milk, or other plain food, to which no doubt I owe a length of days which my infancy by no means promised, and certainly a disposition to be thankful for any kind of sustenance a bountiful Creator may provide for me.

At this school I made progress in learning, and was held to have had success in elocution, so that Governor Van Dyke of Delaware, who was present at one of our school celebrations, had the complaisance to advise my being kept at school and placed where I might study law as my profession. But a year or two later, when an offer was made me of going into the office of a relative who was a Baltimore lawyer, my father told me plainly (being moved thereto, I think, by the strict religious opinions of his wife) that in his opinion the profession was not compatible with Christian duty. There can, I think, be no doubt that some professions afford less security against temptation than others, and perhaps that of the law is the worst in this respect. Still, some lawyers have been called honest, and it depends on any man under Divine Providence to guard himself, and make his profession honest and even honorable so far as depends on himself.

At the school in Delaware we had occasional private theatricals; on one occasion I acted Marius in Addison's play of "Cato," and the Mock Doctor in an after-piece. The news of the surrender of Lord Cornwallis was celebrated by burning thirteen tar barrels elevated on poles in our school-yard.

I was taken at sixteen from that school,— alas! too young; but my father had not abandoned the idea of completing my education. An intimacy had sprung up between himself and some French officers during their stay in Baltimore, and this induced him to wish that I should acquire the French language. He had indeed promised M. Louis, Commissioner-General, who had been quartered in his house in 1781, to send me to France, and put me under his care. I was therefore placed at a school where I could learn French, and in 1783, peace being restored with the acknowledgment of American independence, a sudden impetus was given to commerce, building, and general improvement in Baltimore. My father filled several of the municipal offices, and I was placed in a counting-house to learn book-keeping. But my father, wishing to open for me a more extensive field of improvement, sent me to Philadelphia to be placed in the counting-house of Mr. John Field. He was a member of the Society of Friends, and expressed himself "willing," as he said, "to take the youth;" but he demanded a premium of eight hundred dollars. This my father, with his large family by his second wife, was unable to pay. All my life I have been somewhat anxious to be smartly dressed, and my appearance, as I heard afterwards, was in part the cause of the high premium demanded, for Mr. Field observed that from my looks he was led to consider my father as a wealthy man; and that, dress as I might, I should have to make fires and sweep out the store for some time. To this I should have offered no objection, but the sum asked for my premium was too great. I was therefore placed in Baltimore with a merchant recently arrived from Liverpool.

Besides attending to business in a way which I was led to believe was wholly satisfactory to my employer, I found time to take lessons in French, dancing, and psalmody, also in instrumental music for a short time; but the latter was particularly discouraged by my employer, who took occasion to say in my presence that a good merchant and a good musician could not be combined in the same person. Therefore my fiddle was laid aside with the approbation of my father, although he was particularly fond of music. He was always consulted by me in matters of amusement as well as business, and his will was ever a law to me, not only from the awe inspired by his occasional rebukes, but from the gratitude ever due to an affectionate and prudent father. He was at that time much influenced by his wife, who had recently joined the Baptist communion. My father greatly revered the character of an open professor of religion, though he never embraced it himself. He cheerfully hired seats in the Episcopal and Presbyterian churches, until about this time a stated minister was procured for the Baptist Society. I had myself been baptized in my infancy by the rector of St. Paul's Church. I had not, however, at the period of which I write, formed any decided religious sentiments, but was induced from a slight knowledge of classical literature rather to incline to the theology of heathenism. This tendency to skepticism was probably stimulated by the suspicions of my father, who at this time exhibited much anxiety concerning my religious opinions. I did not, however, relax in my attendance on public worship, nor allow the slightest want of respect to appear in my conduct towards religion and its professors.

When I attained my twentieth year and received a clerk's salary, I was eager to pursue my acquaintance with foreign languages, and boarded first with a German, afterwards with a French family. I made one observation which I think I have never seen elsewhere; namely, that there are in these languages no terms of swearing exactly corresponding to our English cursing.

I occasionally looked into Mr. Murphy's Circulating Library, but I did not subscribe. My father's collection of books was limited, chiefly divinity. I read with great interest Hume's "History of England" and the "Spectator." To this last I was indebted for the general knowledge of manners with which I commenced life. I also belonged to a debating society of young men as little advanced as myself, and became a member of the first Abolition Society, at this time started in Baltimore, and in its establishment I took much interest.

The people of Baltimore, during the first years that succeeded the war, grew faster in wealth than in discretion. In the course of three years a reaction came. The country was exhausted of capital to pay for excessive importations. Each State was seeking relief for itself, and great fears were entertained lest we should be subject to taxation in passing from one State to another. People of property were compelled to reduce their expenses, and the working classes were destitute of employment. The Treasury of the Union was empty, and could not be replenished by funds from the States, for the States had relied on duties collected in their ports; these daily diminished, and public creditors were either put off or paid in some States by a further issue of paper, — an expedient that afforded only temporary relief. But there was little of this paper in circulation. Baltimore had been without a bank until nearly this period, and all large payments were made in bags of heavy coin.

Under these circumstances my employer diminished as

much as possible his expenses; and, unfavorable as the times were, I embarked in business on my own account. My capital consisted only of my savings; but my character for integrity and industry stood me in good stead, and on the whole I succeeded far better than could have been expected. I also, about this time (1790), began to send communications to the newspapers. My opinions were those of a Federalist; and it is with some pride I can add that the same political principles have been my guide and standard throughout life.

I had occasionally visited my respected grandfather, who was living in Philadelphia; also New York and Alexandria, with a desire to find one of these places suitable for my future business; but I finally concluded on going to France and establishing myself in one of the French seaports, where I could receive consignments from America.

This determination was greatly strengthened by the admiration with which at that time (1790) I viewed the first steps taken in France towards the establishment of a free government, — a sentiment in which, it may be said, every man in America partook at that period, including my aged grandfather.

Although Mr. Adams had forcibly pointed out the dangers that might arise from uncurbed democracy, and our own General Government had been modelled on his principles, the true position of things in France was not even suspected in America; indeed, every act of the Constitutional Assembly was enthusiastically admired. There was no republication in America of the speeches of the more conservative members, which might have corrected our ignorant enthusiasm; while the splendid declamations of Mirabeau, which were all reprinted, made us think that Frenchmen were fitted for a government more liberal than our own.

Personal attachment to Louis XVI. was, however, very general in the United States, for the services he had so lately rendered us; and many no doubt thought it likely that a British Constitution, with a limited monarchy, would be the blessing France would derive from the Revolution. The violent acts of revenge which were committed against families residing in *châteaux* in the country were not fully known to us; and by this time they had partially ceased, the great body of the nobles having emigrated. The converting of the immense tracts of land held by the clergy and the monks to the relief of poor *curés* and their parishioners, long oppressed by taxation, was approved by our own people, many of whom looked on these things as a repetition of what had been done in England in the days of the Reformation by our ancestors.

My grandfather spoke often of the three wars in which England had been engaged with France during his lifetime, one of which, if not two, had brought strife to his own door; and though he devoutly prayed that peace should pervade the whole earth, he foresaw, as he often told us, that before his death he should see another war.

During my frequent visits to Philadelphia I had seen among my relatives a young lady who was my cousin by the mother's side, and who was about two years younger than myself. She appeared to me more charming than any other, and she seemed inclined to favor my partiality. She maintained a regular correspondence with me, until at last I conceived that I had only to ask to obtain her hand. I felt I could not be happy without her. This it was that induced me to dispose of my business in Baltimore in order to fix myself in Philadelphia.

In Philadelphia I persevered in my attentions to my cousin until I discovered that she was actually engaged (and had been so for some time) to another gentleman. This, though perhaps a fortunate thing for a young man in my circumstances, wounded my self-love and in every way did me an injury. Possibly my vanity may have led me to put flattering constructions on a woman's mere politeness, though I still think it was not excusable in my fair cousin to continue such a correspondence after an engagement without an avowal of it; nor do I think she was justified in soliciting my influence with her parents in favor of my rival. This did not reconcile me to my disappointment. All further intercourse ceased from that moment;[1] and as absence and new faces were most likely to obliterate the recollection of her attractions from my mind, I decided, as I have said, to seek my fortunes in France, taking leave of my relatives, and especially of my dear and aged grandfather, who parted from me with much solemnity, warning me to be careful, sober, and just in my transactions; to put my trust in God; and to remember that if (as he said) the rolling stone should gather no moss, there was always a home for me under his roof in Philadelphia. As for me, the tears rushed down my cheeks as from the eyes of a child six years old.

Georgetown, in the District then laid out for the seat of our General Government, being the best place in which to purchase good yellow tobacco, I went there, and embarked seventeen hogsheads in the hope of making something by them, and I sailed with them in the ship "George," Captain Wildes, belonging to Mr. Theodore Lyman of Boston, at the latter end of August, 1791.

Before the ship had been long at sea the necessity of a superintending Providence impressed itself upon my mind, and I forever ceased to consider it a matter of indifference whether there were twenty gods, or the One God.

Our passage was boisterous and tedious. Anxious to learn the situation of affairs in Europe that I might judge of my future prospects, I persuaded the captain to land me at Dover, whence I went on by a night coach to London.

In London, besides attending to my business, I did the usual sight-seeing, catching a glimpse amongst other things of King George III. as he skipped into his carriage, and was amazed by the rapidity of his movements.

In London an American gentleman associated in the shipping business at Havre, with Mr. Francis Taney, proposed to me to assist them for a while. I was glad to accept this offer, but I knew I could not be very useful to them, nor prosecute my intention of establishing myself in France,

[1] The miniature of this lady now hangs over my mantel-piece. It was taken from his pocket-book after his death, fifty years after the cruel disappointment he has here recorded. — E. W. L.

until I had acquired a more familiar knowledge of the language of the country than I had been able to obtain by reading and translating "Télémaque."

Although it was the close of 1791, and the Revolution was well on its way in Paris and its surrounding provinces, Normandy was not very much disturbed. Havre was still garrisoned by several Swiss regiments, the officers of which were very accomplished, and maintained excellent discipline; but the National Guard, lately established, performed some duties, and as every one was obliged to serve in this new militia, if called upon, I did not find myself exempt, and had to engage a substitute from time to time.

After staying some weeks in Havre, I decided to go to Bolbec, about twenty miles distant from it on the Paris road, where a respectable school was kept by a priest, still unmolested, in an old abbey. Most of the scholars were the young sons of West Indian planters.

I found the landscape in Normandy rural and pleasing. The highways were excellent. The country was studded with farmhouses surrounded by apple orchards. I saw, too, young children leading cows to pasture by the wayside. But I was surprised to learn that no butter was made to sell.

Bolbec had a cotton factory, for Normandy is manufacturing as well as agricultural. I found there a young gentleman from Boston of the Russell family, who, like myself, was boarding in this quiet village for the sake of learning French. We were received into the house of a surveyor who occupied part of the old abbey, and we paid at the rate of $260 a year for board and instruction, the young ladies of the family undertaking the latter, though we also hired the services of a master.

I made such progress that at the end of two months I was able to return to Havre; and from that time I was able to speak and write French almost as if it were my native language.

Many of the characteristics of the Normans are no doubt derived from the blood of their Norse ancestors. Amongst the French they are distinguished by their sagacity and love of cider, to which the climate, being colder than most other parts of France, may incline them. I found them a plain, industrious, frugal people, clad as their ancestors, it was said, had been from time immemorial, in drab cloth, broad-brimmed hats, and wooden shoes. The females owe to the climate the fairest complexions in France. They all wear pyramidal caps, of muslin or lace, with lappets hanging down the back. Their weddings are almost as solemn as their funerals. They go to church in pairs, youths and girls; but on their return the friends of the bridal couple keep open house with feasting and dancing for many days.

The poultry, fruit, and meats of Normandy are excellent; fish and oysters also are procured from the British Channel. Normandy left to itself would never have become revolutionary. Its people were conscious of no intolerable oppression.

So far the events in Paris had been to the quiet inhabitants of Bolbec little more than mere news. It will be recollected that in the summer of 1791 Louis XVI. had been stopped near the frontier at Varennes in an attempt to fly from France, and that he was brought back to Paris. There the uncertainty felt as to his real views was the cause of suspicion. Doubts marred the enjoyment that the nation had begun to take in the Constitution and the new state of things.

News of the flight to Varennes, which took place June 21, had not reached America at the close of August, when I began my voyage, so that I was quite ignorant of what had so materially changed the face of affairs. I began to find it difficult to form any opinion concerning the Revolution in progress. On this subject I found my two most intimate French acquaintances — the surveyor and the abbé — at variance, but with this difference: the surveyor was boisterous and outspoken enough, while the abbé was afraid to say much, even to Russell and myself, because we were not subjects of a monarchy. With my friends at Havre I continued to hope for the success of the liberal principles intended to be established by the new Constitution, without reference to a republican form of government, such as had been established in our own country. And these appeared to be the sentiments of the merchants and people with whom I associated.

At Havre and at Bolbec I accompanied my friends to church, for, in whatever language God was worshipped, the place was sacred to me; and I thought I gained in piety by my presence there, though I was ignorant of what I heard, the service being in Latin everywhere.

The commerce of Havre was chiefly with the West Indies, including formerly much of the trade in unfortunate Africans. Its population was about 30,000. It had two churches and a small theatre.

In the spring of 1792 I left Havre for Paris, intending to establish myself in the south of France, the place to be determined by what I might see in the capital. War had by this time been declared between France, Germany, Austria, and Prussia. Louis XVI. had boldly rejected laws which would have deprived him of the means of performing acts of charity, but now felt himself compelled to sanction war against his own brothers.

In Paris I went to lodge in a hotel, rather retired, in the Rue Guénegard. I waited at once on Mr. Gouverneur Morris, the American minister, and met there, among others, Commodore John Paul Jones, Joel Barlow the poet, James C. Mountflorence, and several more Americans. I also met the Count d'Estaing, Saint John de Crèvecœur, Esq., formerly consul of France in New York, and his son Otto, M. Ray de Chaumont and his lady, formerly Miss Cox of Philadelphia, and Madame de Lafayette, with some of her family, but the marquis was already at the head of an army on the borders of the Rhine.

Commodore Paul Jones died in Paris soon after my arrival there; and I, with the American gentlemen I have named, and a small deputation from the National Assembly, attended his funeral. His interment took place in one of the common cemeteries of the town. There was no priest, nor any funeral service, but a few soldiers fired a volley of muskets in honor of the naval hero over his grave.

My stay in Paris was prolonged by my great interest in the stirring events of the time, until my finances became low, when, remembering how much my country owed to France for her aid in resisting England, I began to consider a plan for joining the army under General Lafayette. I looked with admiration on the services the general had rendered to the cause of liberty, both in my own country and in France. I was moreover influenced by Major Mountflorence, who had served in the North Carolina Line. I therefore agreed with that gentleman that we should consult with Mr. Morris, our minister, and, if agreeable to him, go to camp with recommendations that he might furnish us to General Lafayette, and obtain suitable employment in the French army, under his command, if possible. But Mr. Morris, though he had not been much longer in France than either of us, filled a post, and occupied a station, which enabled him to appreciate the state of public affairs, and see further into futurity than ourselves; besides which, genius and judgment he was known to possess.

When we made our plan known to him, he politely tendered us the letters for Lafayette, but advised us most earnestly to decline them for a few weeks, declaring prophetically that the Constitution would be crushed, and the marquis be overthrown with the king at the same time. This counsel alarmed Major Mountflorence as well as myself. We agreed to postponement, and never again thought of joining an army towards which the marquis had been accused of treachery, and from which at last he was forced to fly, having risked his life in Paris to resent insults to the king on the 20th of June preceding.

The blood of the Count d'Estaing, Count Dillon, Count Beauharnais, Baron Custine, and others whose names are recorded in the annals of our struggle for liberty, was subsequently basely shed. They were all men to whom the American people owe eternal gratitude. In France Louis XVI. had by this time (July, 1792) excited feelings not only of distrust but enmity; but Americans thought tenderly of Louis XVI., precipitated from his throne, — that throne from which

GOUVERNEUR MORRIS.

he had secured the independence of our country, after having impoverished his treasury and risked his future in our cause.

I was a spectator in 1792 of the celebration of the taking of the Bastille on the 14th of July, 1789, three years before. The celebration took place both on the site of the demolished fortress and at the Champ de Mars. At the latter place the patriotic king was very coldly received, and the name of Lafayette was hailed with terms of reproach. The Emperor of Austria excited no fear in Paris, but recollections of the treaty made by several sovereigns at Pillnitz, and the mysterious conduct forced upon the king, while he was held almost as a prisoner after the return from Varennes, produced no little anxiety for the future, to get rid of which the populace was ready to join in whatever movements the leaders of the Revolution might suggest. It was not at this time, nor indeed during the former period of the Revolution, in the power of King Louis to have upheld the monarchy, nor to have prevented the coming horrors, even had he been the most military character of the age, and as little disposed to protect the rights of others as were the Revolutionary governments which came after him. The people were not disposed to unite with the privileged classes, but they might have been compelled to do so if the nobility and clergy had voluntarily abandoned their feudal privileges, which were oppressive on the middle class as well as the inferior orders, and had united themselves in an upper House, — a House of Peers. They would then have gained over or neutralized the middle class, and have prevented the populace from working its will, thus producing a salutary reform without violence or bloodshed. Certainly this would have been the case had they taken the initiative before the destruction of the Bastille, — nay, possibly, even before the removal of the king to Paris by the populace on Oct. 6, 1789. But after the masses had become interested, as they thought, in the extinction of everything above them, and had ascertained the effective power of their numbers, no mortal wisdom could have stopped the wheels of the Revolution. Themselves only, and a very few of them, gorged with the blood of the moderate party in May, 1794, alone could have brought about a counter-revolution. Yet even then soldiers organized to put down massacres always trembled for their lives in the event of their own success.

The factions of Orléans, of Pétion Mayor of Paris, of Brissot, who was of the Philosophical School, of Collot d'Herbois the comedian, and of Danton and Robespierre (who wanted nothing less than control of the government), prepared for an attack which they had planned on the palace, by calling to Paris in the summer of 1792 detachments of ignorant provincials, who were told, and made to believe, that they would receive in the capital complete military equipments, and be marched to the frontier. Such of them as had arrived in Paris by July 14, 1792, received the name of Fédérés. They attended the celebration of the day, with the whole body of the National Guards of Paris and a few regular troops. The king and his ministers were to renew their declarations of fidelity to the Constitution on the Champ de Mars on that occasion.

I witnessed this act, if it could be said to be "witnessed" by one among a hundred thousand spectators standing upon earth banks at least two hundred yards from the platform erected in the centre of the amphitheatre for the different members of the government and high officers of the city, civil and military. The king was but coldly received; and General Lafayette had already become so obnoxious to the populace that his name was freely contrasted with that of the Mayor Pétion. To me it was exceedingly mortifying to find that such a man as Pétion had supplanted Lafayette in the confidence of the majority of the populace, not only on his own account, but because it was an evidence of a disposition to disparage early and devoted patriotism, and exhibited a disposition incompatible with those principles on which the Constitution was founded, or the existence of any permanent government derived from the people could be based.

Nevertheless the general made one last effort to save the government, by coming from camp to testify his horror of the insults offered to the king, and to advise such measures as might avert another 20th of June. But his influence as a patriot, which could have dispersed a mob in 1789, proved now unavailing, and it was scarcely known he was in Paris till he was gone.[1]

Some days after this I went to a public dinner given by Santerre, an officer who was afterwards Commandant of the National Guard, to the Fédérés, on the Place de la Bastille, of which State Prison there still existed some remains. The men all thought that they were to be marched to the frontier as soon as a sufficient number of volunteers could be collected, and in fact they were soon joined by two or three regiments from Marseilles under an officer called Westermann. These men brought with them the celebrated Marseilles Hymn, first heard in Paris when sung by them. They had committed many acts of violence upon their route, and brought with them far other views than those announced by the air. They came prepared for revolution.

I was standing on the steps of the Church of St. Eustache when they filed past with their arms and baggage. Suddenly I was told in a very peremptory manner to take off my cockade, which was made of ribbon, as were other cockades worn by many citizens. I could not imagine how it could offend them, since to be without a cockade was a sign of sympathy with royalty, which no one would have ventured to exhibit. I was at last kindly told by other spectators near me that I must get a worsted one, like a soldier, silk being considered too aristocratic by these advanced radicals.

Some of the National Guard in the part of the city inhabited by the more wealthy and more loyal citizens encountered the Marseillais in the Champs Élysées, and not being so ready to submit to dictation as I had been, a fight ensued, in which some lives were lost. After this, in order to protect the Royal Family in the Tuileries from the daily insults of such pretended patriots, the palace was represented as national property, and the terraces of the gardens

[1] For a further account of Lafayette see Book VI., Chapter I.

were encompassed with tricolored ribbons, instead of guards. The tricolor ribbon was respected, and the mob was thus excluded from the plots of ground immediately under the windows of the palace.

The Hall of the Legislative Assembly was a wooden building which had been erected for a riding-school. It stood on the north side of the garden of the Tuileries, and was separated from it by a terrace thirty feet wide. The hall contained a gallery for spectators, which was daily frequented to overflowing by men and women of the worst description. It was the policy of the leaders of the factions to gratify these people by bold and false accusations of the government and every person the government employed. These stories they knew would obtain general circulation, with additions, through such auditors. It was in this place that the gravest suspicions were thrown out against the fidelity of the king and the virtue of his consort. With the same treacherous view General Lafayette was slanderously charged with having poisoned some of his soldiers about this period; but he had still a sufficient number of friends in the Legislative Assembly to procure a Committee of Investigation, which, after visiting the camp, reported that, if any of his soldiers had been poisoned, it was caused by stained glass from windows in a church in which a quantity of provisions had been stored. And that ended the matter.

Hearing some individuals of the kind I have mentioned as frequenting the gallery of the Legislative Assembly, repeating to other persons who were walking on the terrace of the garden of the Tuileries that overlooks the river, these refuted charges, I ventured to explain the circumstances. I was hooted at, and thought it prudent to retire for safety.

CHAPTER II.

AUGUST AND SEPTEMBER IN PARIS IN 1792.

ALTHOUGH the Municipal Government of Paris had petitioned for the suspension or removal of Louis XVI., and their petition had produced no action on the part of the Assembly, it was very evident that his removal or dethronement would soon be attempted by force.

Early on the 9th of August, 1792, the tocsin was rung in the eastern part of the city, and in the suburbs; and the National Guard was assembled at the bridges and other stations, while the Swiss Guard received orders to defend the palace with a detachment of the National Militia. At the same time, gentlemen attached to the royal family and Constitution went to the palace, prepared for what might happen. This was sanctioned by officers of the Department of the Seine, as well as by the Municipal Government, and indeed by a majority of the Legislature. Some members, however, plotted very successfully to detain many of the Swiss Guard at their barracks in the country,[1] leaving only about eight hundred of the Guard at the palace under Major Bachman, who, with the National Guard (there were at that time no regular troops in Paris), were under the command of M. Mandat.

I went at nightfall with Mr. Corbin, a young gentleman from Virginia who had lately become my fellow-lodger, to ascertain in the streets what was likely to happen. We went first to the Jacobin Club, the seat of the chief faction. It

[1] We *now* know that the larger part of the Swiss Guard was detained at Courbevoie on the Seine, to serve as escort to the king and his family, who, it was hoped, might take advantage of arrangements made to effect their escape. — E. W. L.

was at the old convent of the Jacobite monks. Then we went to the Place du Carrousel, on the east front of the palace. The Hall of the Jacobins, into which we were admitted, — for we had disguised ourselves as Fédérés, — contained a few other such volunteers. Some private letters from soldiers in the camp were read; and it was declared during the debate that the mob waited only for the legislators to lead it on, to commence an attack on the palace; also, that even then the Sections were assembled at their several Section-houses.

The king's guards were under arms in the Carrousel when we quitted the Jacobin Club late at night, and we felt persuaded that with these men at their posts, the assailants, if they did attack, would be repulsed.

By eight o'clock in the morning, however, the crowd of Fédérés and rabble had so swollen that the mob began the attack by a discharge of artillery on the guards within the Carrousel. I was not awake until I heard the reports of the cannon; for I had not retired until morning, having passed the night in the streets. I rose immediately, and proceeded to the Quai opposite the Louvre, where I saw as much of the contending parties as I could have done from any place in the city. I could not, however, see the Swiss or others stationed behind or within the palace.[1] Danton and his coadjutors had forced the city authorities to give up their scarfs of office and resign their commissions to them. Placing the mayor under arrest, they assumed his functions, ordering the National Guard to "dismiss," and M. Mandat, their commander, to repair to the Hôtel de Ville. There, when he appeared, he was instantly murdered.

The officers of the National Guard, being thus left without a head, became confused, and the men left their posts for their homes. Scarcely one man in uniform appeared among the mob, who had compelled many private individuals, and even strangers, to join them. Among these was one of my

[1] For an account of what was going on within the palace, see a subsequent extract in this book from Carlyle's "French Revolution."

friends, a young doctor from Annapolis, who lodged at the southeastern extremity of the city. They furnished him with a pike.

The Swiss Guard at the palace continued to fight after the royal family had been escorted by a deputation from the Assembly to the Hall of Legislation, for they had not received the order given by the king to cease firing; and they actually drove the rabble to some distance in every direction. The mob, however, after reinforcements had arrived, rallied and got possession of the palace, after killing most of the Swiss and many of the National Guard, besides private gentlemen. This they were better able to effect because some of the National Guards, who were enraged at seeing men in the mob wearing their own uniform, united with the Swiss, and, being fired on, seemed under some necessity to take part to save themselves.

After pillaging the palace for a few hours, and conducting about two hundred Swiss to prison, the mob retired; and the city became suddenly more quiet than it had been for weeks before.

My friend Mr. Corbin, after we had viewed the flames which were set to the barracks in the Carrousel, on meeting some of the rabble patrolling, and others with heads upon pikes, became alarmed. The insurgents not having had time to mature their plans of vengeance, the gates of the city remained open; so he departed for Havre that same day. I accompanied him in a hackney-coach across the river to the stage office. Our hack had just brought a wounded lodger to our house who had escaped from the palace. Few carriages were to be seen on the streets except those conveying public characters, and the one we procured demanded double the usual fare.

The gentlemen who had devoted themselves to the king and Constitution by becoming members of the Cabinet were arrested, and were soon after tried and executed. Clermont-Tonnerre, and perhaps some others who had opposed the Revolution, were assassinated in the streets. It was indeed certain death to appear well dressed; and the Swiss soldiers, whose uniform was scarlet, could not find refuge or safety anywhere but in prison.

Notwithstanding these untoward circumstances, I traversed the field of battle and made my way into the palace, where the pavement was stained with blood. I was there, indeed, before all the bodies of the dead had been removed.

The public were not permitted to know how many fell on either side; but as several hundred Swiss had spent their ammunition before they died or surrendered, the whole number of victims must have amounted to several thousand.

Entering the gallery of the Assembly, which was filled with even worse-looking people than usual, I saw for the first time Louis XVI. and part of his family, in a box used by the reporters. The king was short and robust, of a countenance mild and pleasing; the queen tall, graceful, and handsome; the king's sister plain, but dignified; and the children delicate and interesting. None of them manifested any idea of the horrid fate which awaited them, but seemed willing to conciliate the members by their condescension, — without any effect, however, at least upon my neighbors in the gallery; one of whom (and a female, too) did not hesitate to call the prince *a bastard, and no better than his mother.*

Returning the next day to the vicinity of the Hall of the Assembly, I saw the unfortunate royal family set out in carriages for the Temple, which was formerly a royal castle, but by this time converted into a prison. It was situated in a remote, but thickly settled, part of the city.

Wishing my friends in America to be acquainted with these acts, beginning with what I had seen of the reception of the king at the Champ de Mars, — events which terminated the Constitution and the Constitutional Monarchy, — I printed an account of them in 1795, and sent all the copies to America.

After I had seen the things I have described, I went to wait on Mr. Gouverneur Morris, our ambassador. I found at his house a number of gentlemen and ladies, who from former intercourse with America, and in many cases services rendered to the United States, considered themselves entitled to protection in the hotel of the minister. Mr. Morris had had no communication with the authorities, nor had he even been in the streets from the commencement of the insurrection, and he expressed some surprise at the disguise I had assumed to avoid giving offence to the populace. After he had received my explanation and had learned my views of the situation, he took me into the adjoining room, and there stated to me in the following terms, as nearly as I can recollect: "The persons you have seen, six or more individuals, who have rendered services to our country, or are related to such persons, consider themselves in danger in their homes, and have taken refuge in my house. Whether they will be disappointed of safety here I cannot tell. I call you to witness, Mr. Griffith, if my protection of these persons should become a matter of reproach to me, here or at home (and I have reason to expect it will, from what I have already experienced), that I did not invite them to come, but that I will not put them out now that they are here, let the consequences be what they may." A determination which I considered fully justified as much by patriotism as by private feeling. And so I expressed myself to the minister.

The frightful massacres that in three weeks followed the insurrection of the 10th of August were precipitated by the manifesto issued by the Duke of Brunswick, and the approach of the Prussian army to Paris. There was a widespread apprehension that French generals would betray the nation. Such a report was diligently circulated by the Revolutionists in the Assembly, and sustained by inferior officers in the army who wanted promotion. The population of Paris, greatly excited, was ready for insurrection, fearing which, many respectable citizens set out for the French camp to establish a character for patriotism, and place themselves above suspicion. By this they also hoped to place their families under the protection of the Revolutionists. This seriously diminished the number of well-disposed citizens in Paris who might have been the king's defenders.

For some time after the 10th of August the gates of Paris were closed, and no one was permitted to leave the city, as it was intended to hunt out and take vengeance on a number of persons who, from their rank in life, their profession, their talents, or their political sentiments, were obnoxious to the insurgents. Members of the late Cabinet, who, from devotion to the Constitution or the king, had recently accepted office, were the first victims, and some were murdered in the streets without the formality of a trial; others were crowded into the common jails to be massacred collectively.

It was on September 2, when several hundred priests of all ages, and gentry of all ages and both sexes, had been thus collected, that the leaders were selected, the judges and executioners were chosen, and a band of hardened villains were sent to the prison of La Force, to the Abbaye, and to others to commence their fiendish operations.

I was tempted to go to the Abbaye, but was stopped by my landlord, a most worthy citizen, who, returning himself when he found it was no longer safe to look on, brought me back to the hotel, which was not very far from the Abbaye. Many thousands of the citizens of Paris remained ignorant of the horrors then enacted within its walls, until they saw the remains of slaughtered men and women paraded through the streets.

I myself was at dinner on one of those days with Messrs. Mountflorence and Anderson in the Rue St. Honoré, nearly opposite the Palais Royal, then the residence of the Duc d'Orléans, when we were roused from table by a noise in the street, and going out saw the head of a female borne upon a pike, and the fragments of a human body dragged through the gutter by a few miserable wretches who appeared infuriated by intoxication and joy. Upon inquiry we found that these were the lifeless remains of the young and beautiful Princesse de Lamballe, whose flowing hair had been fashionably dressed after her head had been severed from her body. The head was pushed into the faces of passers-by upon the street; even into carriages containing others of her sex, who, as may be supposed, were for the moment deprived of their senses.

Elated by their success on the 10th of August, excited by the defection of Lafayette, and terrorized by the loss of Longwy and Verdun, strong posts which had been captured by the Prussians, a Revolutionary Government set itself up at the Hôtel de Ville, Robespierre acting as president, Collot d'Herbois and Billaud-Varennes being secretaries. The massacre of the prisoners had been by them determined on. The volunteers were crying out for the heads of their enemies before they could venture, as they said, to march against the enemy, and leave their wives and children behind.

Before this I had visited Versailles, about twelve miles from Paris, from which the king and royal family had been compelled to go to Paris (Oct. 6, 1789) about three years before. It was said that Lafayette, commanding the National Guard, had not duly protected these persons, and that he should have done more, nine weeks earlier, to prevent the shedding of blood after the taking of the Bastille. I found the residence of the king most splendid. It had not, when I saw it, suffered the dilapidation to which it afterwards became a prey.

I went also to St. Denis, a small town six miles east of Paris, in the cathedral of which had been deposited the corpses of kings, and of distinguished soldiers. The tombs when I saw them had been all plundered to obtain lead for munitions of war. I recollect seeing no grave but that of Turenne undisturbed; his remains were afterwards removed. I saw his tomb with those of Voltaire, Rousseau, and Mirabeau in the old Church of Ste. Geneviève, called by the Revolutionists the Pantheon, and dedicated, as its inscription said, "to the memory of the great men of France by their grateful country."

It was about this same time that the city government ordered the demolition of the statues of the sovereigns of France standing in different public places, — even that of Henri IV., on the Pont Neuf. This statue was equestrian and bronze. I happened to be a witness of the outrage. Workmen filed the legs of the horse, and, with a long rope at the neck of the king, brought the whole down with a tremendous crash. The same spirit effaced the initials and the insignia of the kings from off the palaces and public buildings, and obliged individuals to remove all armorial bearings from their houses and carriages.

The horrors of the months of August and September and the loss of rest had thrown me into a slight fever, and the further outrages I witnessed determined me to leave Paris. Therefore, a few days after the gates were opened, I set out with a passport from Mr. Morris, our minister, duly countersigned, in company with a fellow-lodger named Coulanges, who had obtained an English pass from some friend, and who, as he had been living in the king's palace on the day of battle, thought it necessary to take an indirect road to reach his home near Rouen in Normandy.

Until then I had usually travelled unaccompanied by friends or acquaintances, and in the public diligences. The diligence is a heavy vehicle having room inside for six passengers and in front the coupé, which holds three more,[1] also a covered seat on the top for one beside a guard, called the conductor, who takes charge of the baggage and goods contained in a basket behind.

The conductor overlooked the change of horses and the conduct of the postilions, who ride on one of the four or six horses, booted in iron or steel. The horses are furnished, as those for private travelling carriages are, at the post-houses, usually about six miles apart. The horses belong to private individuals, who purchase from the government the privilege of furnishing them. The diligence travels at the rate of about four and one half miles an hour, but the two-wheeled carts conveying the mail go about six miles per hour. Both take charge of valuable effects, of which they guarantee the amount, if paid for at the stipulated premium.

[1] The diligences of this period seem to have had no *rotunde*, a compartment behind which carried four passengers. Fifty years later the baggage was placed on the top and covered by a tarpaulin.

M. de Coulanges and I now hired a light carriage, and took a roundabout route for Versailles. In the evening we saw the fire made for burning the clothes of the prisoners from Orléans who had been brought to Versailles to be massacred that day.[1] We had met on the road some of the murderers in wagons lighted by torches, and bearing the heads of several victims as trophies, or rather as evidence of their claims upon their employers at the capital. It was known that some obnoxious gentlemen had been collected at Orléans before the dethronement of the king. Orléans was thought to be a place where they might be constitutionally tried; but no suspicion had been entertained by me or my companion, or indeed by the citizens of Paris, I believe, besides those accessory to the horrid scene, of what was to be enacted at Versailles on Sept. 9, 1792, or that travellers on that road would be saluted, as we were that evening, by such cannibals, and compelled, as was usual on such occasions, to shout applause for their gratification.

So little disposed to follow the example of the people in Paris were the people in the provinces (now the departments) that there were at first only a few victims in the southern towns of France. To excite the country to deeds of violence, it was always found necessary to send out professional incendiaries.

It has been advanced by some, that if the morals of the French people had not been neglected by the clergy, a disposition to countenance such horrors could not have existed. But experience does not often make people wise, much less precept, and it is not given to man to convert the hearts of sinners. Infidelity had been for fifty years in the very air of France. The *curés* at least — whatever may have been the case with the higher clergy — were, in general, so virtuous and so zealous that a very great majority of people who had arrived at mature life (perhaps nine tenths of them) refused to abandon the Sabbath, or join in the worship of the new gods and goddesses. They remembered their priests with gratitude, and trembled at

[1] For an account of this atrocity, see a subsequent chapter.

offences which violated the commands of the true God, — the God of their fathers.[1]

After having been refused admittance to several public houses in Versailles on the night of September 9 which followed the massacre, we wandered about the city seeking a place to sleep. The city seemed deserted. We saw neither man nor woman until, late at night, we were kindly received by a private family to whom M. de Coulanges was known. The next day we continued our journey to the bank of the Seine, below St. Germains; going thus, as it were, across country, that we might not be suspected of coming from the capital. We also, by way of precaution, quitted our carriage and hired a boat, proceeding alternately by land and water till we reached the city of Rouen.

There M. de Coulanges stopped at a friend's house, bidding me adieu in terms which plainly implied that he never expected to see his fellow-traveller again; which in fact was the case, nor do I know what became of the unfortunate man, who probably joined his amiable wife and daughter in Normandy, and I trust escaped the vigilance of his enemies, since Normandy was not distinguished by such acts of violence as other parts of France soon after exhibited.

It is my conviction that the population of Paris was as well informed, and had as correct principles, both as to politics and morals, as the same number of people in any place on the surface of the globe, but the Revolution had attracted thither *philosophes* and turbulent spirits from every country, and these were the more ferocious because they had no personal interest in the welfare of the nation. Uniting themselves with a few Frenchmen of the same general character, they became the employers of all the desperate villains ever to be found in any populous city. Until the disorders of the Revolution, no people had appeared more contented than the French with the rational liberty they were beginning to enjoy under their new constitutional government. But as soon as both king and Constitution

[1] See an account of the French clergy exiled to England, in a subsequent chapter.

were overthrown, the real patriots — the men whom France and the world looked up to for the support of liberal principles — speedily became victims of the anarchy which followed.

Duly appreciated, there is in every society a great disproportion between the wise and the weak. Even in Paris there were probably fifty ignorant persons for one possessing knowledge.

I reached Havre in safety, after the perils of my journey from Paris to Rouen, and resumed commercial speculations, chiefly in tobacco, with my friend Taney, who had married into a French family, — that of M. Govain.

I was in Havre during the month of January, 1793; in other words, during the time of the trial and execution of the king. Shortly before war was declared against France by England, I went to London for the purpose of attending to the purchase and shipment of tobacco.

Whilst in London I attended some of the debates in Parliament, and had the satisfaction of hearing Messrs. Fox, Pitt, Burke, Dundas, and Sheridan speak on the declaration of war contemplated against France. In that country, the Royalists and Moderates having been entirely put down, the factions in the convention were determined, as they said, to endure nothing but a republican constitution, and, having killed their own king, carried their revolutionary warfare into every country subject to a different form of government.

Although the interest elicited by all this in the British House of Commons was calculated to bring out all the eloquence and talent of the British Senate, I did not think at the time, nor do I now believe, that it surpassed what I had heard not long before in our American Congress, from Ames, Madison, Smith of Carolina, Vining, and some others, on the far less interesting subjects of internal taxation, banking, etc. The speech of Mr. Burke was calculated in my opinion to make the greatest effect, but he wanted at that time personal influence, for his desertion of the Opposition lost him his friends on that side, and he had not been long enough a supporter of the administration to obtain confidence from its friends outside the walls of the Parliament House.

The people of England had been at first much pleased at the prospect that the French would model their government after that of Great Britain, but the execution of King Louis had disgusted them generally, and great pains were taken to manifest their attachment to King George on every occasion.

I was nearly pressed to death descending the steps into the pit of Covent Garden Theatre (Drury Lane having been destroyed by fire) on a night when the king was to be present, but I obtained a good seat, and was much gratified. The boxes were crowded by ladies elegantly dressed, and I thought them all beautiful, as they certainly were in respect of complexion, compared with our ladies in America; but both American and French ladies have advantages of person and expression of countenance over those of England.

The king showed the greatest delight at every lively incident the play afforded, and heard the national air, "God Save the King," in full chorus, until he was tired, and waved his hand. Kemble, Palmer, Johnson, and Quick, Mrs. Siddons, Mrs. Crouch, Mrs. Esten, and Mrs. Jordan were the performers.

After a pleasant and advantageous visit to England, where I made the acquaintance of many Americans settled in London, I embarked with my tobacco on a small American craft, which took some time to make the voyage to Havre, as she grounded repeatedly before getting clear of the Thames. My venture, however, proved very successful, and I made a second voyage to England. By this time war had been declared; and the American captain of the scow in which I sailed landed me near Dungeness, for the sake of despatch, and to avoid the formalities which a state of war had introduced in the admission of passengers from France. But the vigilance of a guard upon the beach had nearly produced some unpleasant difficulties. I was followed closely into a smuggler's hovel, and was protected from arrest only by the courage of my host; the red-coats insisting that I was a Frenchman, and the other insisting that I was no more a Frenchman than any of themselves. He afterwards engaged himself to carry my valise to Romney, which was the first post town beyond the Downs — or sands.

My report of the tobacco market in France was so encouraging that other American merchants in London and Liverpool joined in shipping a considerable quantity to our Havre house. Orders in Council were obtained to permit the departure of our vessels with their cargoes, but I was not taken before the Secretary at the Foreign Office to be examined on the state of affairs in France, as was usual in such cases. This voyage also yielded our concern a very handsome profit, and my share placed me in a more independent position than has ever been my lot before or since. Mr. Taney effected a sale of the tobacco to the Government itself for the use of the French army and navy, which, as usual, received rations of the article, and had been likely to come short of supplies, when a close blockade of the French ports should be carried into effect.

Before leaving London I joined my countrymen on the Fourth of July, 1793, to celebrate our independence by a dinner at the London Tavern, Bishopsgate Street. At this dinner there were about eighty gentlemen, including several London merchants who were attached to the United States by the interest they had in our trade, and regard for the sage republican principles of our citizens. This dinner, not accompanied by music or any outdoor exhibitions, cost us a guinea apiece.

Boston vessels before the blockade continued to enter the port of Havre; but French merchants had abandoned the ocean altogether, and it was lamentable to see their fine ships crowding the docks, never again to be sent to sea.

About this time I abandoned all idea of establishing myself at some port on the Mediterranean. As time went on, Mr. Taney became alarmed at the situation of affairs in France, both commercial and political, and, contemplating a return to America, purchased of the Count d'Estaing the lands presented him by the State of Georgia. To receive the money due by the Government for its purchase of tobacco, and commence Mr. Taney's payments to the count, I again went to Paris; but preferring to take a passport from the municipality of Havre, to whom my American citizenship was well known, I left behind me that of the American minister, because it was no longer of recent date.[1]

Affairs in France had grown from bad to worse during the first nine months of the year 1793. I had been away from Paris about a year when I returned to it. The debates in the Assembly afforded no evidence of any approaching settlement of the Government; the paper money was falling in value; and every citizen between the ages of eighteen and twenty-five was liable to be marched to the frontier to oppose the Allies, or to the West to fight Frenchmen. In its paper money, however, and in its conscription, consisted the strength of the French Revolution. But before that period France had long been a first-rate military power. A love of glory animated the officers, all descendants of the old nobility, who kept the soldiers under them in strict subordination. The Revolution stimulated a strong desire for promotion in the subalterns and non-commissioned officers, many of whom became colonels and generals, while a desire for plunder stimulated all ranks in the army, from officers high in command to private soldiers. Thus the battle of Jemappes was successfully fought by a commander who had never been heard of before, and the Prussians and Austrians were discouraged and checked, being driven beyond the Rhine by other generals of equal previous obscurity. These acts of national prowess emboldened the Revolutionary leaders in Paris. In their first fright, when the Prussians were advancing on Paris in the summer of 1792, they committed the horrors of the prison massacres, and then, to proclaim themselves to all the world as republicans, they proceeded to execute their king. Their persecution of the clergy, and of all who did not join with them or applaud them, was the signal for civil war, which broke out in the West and South

[1] It is highly probable that this passport was lent to some escaping *émigré*, which would account for Mr. Griffith's subsequent reluctance to apply to Mr. Morris. The narrative, however, is careful to conceal this, — if it was so. — E. W. L.

of France, in June, 1793, and which continued with occasional intermissions from that time, until the people were prepared, by the imperial despotism of Bonaparte and his adherents, for the peaceful reign of Louis XVIII.; to which the soldiery, still longing for spoil, were the last to assent.[1]

Elder brothers, lest they should be called on themselves to go to the frontier, urged their juniors to go to camp in obedience to the infamous law of the conscription, which entailed tremendous penalties on parents if their sons should desert, so that more than a million of Frenchmen were in the field by the second campaign.

No treachery to the nation or to a constitutional government was intended by the people of Lower Normandy or of Provence, on whom cruel vengeance was taken; nor can the name of Chouan be any disgrace to men of Brittany or Anjou; while the deplorable fate of Charette, Stofflet, Lescure, Larochejaquelein, Sombreuil, Broglie, Coster, and Georges Cadoudal must excite the sympathy of Frenchmen while gallantry and self-devotion receive plaudits everywhere.

Soon after I arrived in Paris, I went out to Mont Calvaire, a few miles from the city, to deliver a letter to M. de Sulenef, whose son had lately purchased lands in Tennessee, and had embarked from Havre. I was observed by the village officials with a suspicious eye, and thought by them to be an Englishman liable to arrest. Accordingly I was arrested the same night while in bed, and sent under charge of a gendarme to the Committee of Public Safety, then composed of David, Vadier, and others. I was able to save myself from being tied and dragged after the mounted guard by hiring a cabriolet for both of us to ride in. This took place on Oct. 17, 1793, the day after the execution of Queen Marie Antoinette.

I had seen that unhappy lady the day before carried in a cart, as I stood upon the Boulevard, where it joins the Rue

[1] Mr. Griffith was a warm adherent of the Restoration; and to him Napoleon Bonaparte never ceased to be the "Corsican monster." His reminiscences reflect the feelings of his party in his lifetime. — E. W. L.

St. Honoré; through this street she came, and down by the Church of the Madeleine, to which place her remains were brought for interment within sight of the place of execution. Misled by the basest slanders, a populace who on her arrival in France, twenty years before, had hailed this princess with admiration, upbraided her with the most vulgar epithets as she went to execution. She was but thirty-eight, and possessed of personal charms unequalled at her time of life. Perfectly resigned to a fate she had anticipated, abandoned apparently by every human friend, she was sustained by heaven and viewed her enemies with the calmness and dignity of a saint.[1]

The king had been conducted to the same scaffold only nine months before, with a numerous and splendid escort, but Marie Antoinette, no less a queen, was surrounded by the rabble. Louis was conveyed in a handsome coach, and in court-like dress, accompanied by his own confessor; while she, attired in a plain white robe and cap, was seated beside a religious instructor unknown to her, in a common cart, her back to the driver, like the vilest convict, and no one dared to utter a prayer or breathe a sigh on her behalf, but at the risk of his life. I was actually forced away from a situation which would have commanded a full view of the guillotine had I remained, to avoid being discovered in a state of agitation. But it was only to see the victim, and not to witness the execution, that I had gone there.

Both the 21st of January and the 16th of October were days of mourning with all the respectable part of the inhabitants of Paris, and many, to testify their grief at what was passing, assembled in the remotest parts of their houses to bewail together what none of them could prevent. The Princess Elisabeth followed her brother and sister to the same block. This princess, sister of the king, had lived estranged from the world in some measure by her piety, as I heard Mr. Morris feelingly declare, and had been an object at which even the tongue of slander had never lisped a reproach.

[1] See a subsequent chapter on the queen's imprisonment and execution.

CHAPTER III.

HIS IMPRISONMENT IN THE REIGN OF TERROR.

I RETURN now to my own arrest. The Committee of Public Safety was too much engaged to examine me when I was first brought into Paris, and the guard who had arrested me was told to bring me in the evening.

I spent the day accompanied by this guard in calling to inform some friends of the predicament in which I found myself, little doubting, however, that I should soon be discharged.

Late in the evening I was examined by two members of the Public Safety. They were ignorant that Great Britain ever permitted commercial intercourse with enemies upon any terms; and although they were told that the policy of the English government induced it occasionally to exchange with any people, friend or foe, an article of luxury like tobacco, with which they were overstocked, for money or for other raw material, they would not understand how, by thus disposing of American produce shipped to Englishmen as a remittance, they obtained payment of debts due them by Americans. Such intercourse, however, I told them was only permitted to neutrals, such as I was, and my tobacco had not only been sold for the use of the French army and navy, but that to obtain payment from the French Government was the principal cause of my visit to the capital. They then inquired for my American passport, and on being told that I had left it at Havre, on receiving that of the Municipality, they affected to doubt the authenticity of the latter, or hinted that it might have been obtained by some imposition or corruption. They therefore sent me to an old convent called the Madelonettes, which had been fitted up as a public prison, my detention, as they stated, being a measure for the public security.

Arriving at the prison late at night, I was immediately left in a room on the ground-floor with a number of indifferent characters, without light, or any other accommodation than a mattress on a guard-house bedstead; but I was permitted on the morrow to join the prisoners above stairs. There I found the late minister, Latour du Pin, and a number of the first characters in France, besides some of the best performers in the late Royal Theatre, — all together about three hundred males, crowding the house excessively. In two or three days, however, I was put into a small room on the second floor, which in France they call the first story. I was then admitted into the Hall, and allowed to communicate with the other prisoners in the daytime. I was supplied with good bedding, bread and water, and any other convenience or refreshment I chose to pay for. Monsieur M. A. Govain, brother-in-law to Mr. Taney, and then a conscript, happening to be in Paris, called at the Madelonettes, and undertook to direct my passport to be brought from Havre and to execute any commissions for me in the city.

It was not till I found myself separated from this friend by bolts and bars, and obliged to converse with him from my window upstairs, that I realized the feelings inspired by imprisonment. I saw in many of my companions — who, being natives of France, were liable to every persecution — all the resignation which good sense and an innocent conscience could inspire. Some, indeed, giving themselves up to their fate, exhibited a degree of contentment which their hope of future reward alone could justify; others alarmed us by their joyous manifestations of indifference,— exhibiting that feeling in songs and concerts of music, till even the keeper of the house, who fully appreciated the malice of the population outside, dreaded lest he should be visited by reproach, or some violent attack result in the destruction of his charges.

Such conduct on the part of men whose lives were in jeopardy might induce a hasty conviction that the French are essentially a vain, visionary, and fickle people; but more reflection would, I should think, produce a contrary effect. Resignation, patience, and resolution I have found, I may almost say, uniform traits in the French character. I passed seven years in France, observing the minute actions of individuals; but others might draw the same conclusion from their performance of literary works requiring the devotion of a whole lifetime, the public improvements which have been carried on from one generation to another, and the perfection to which the French have brought many of the arts and sciences. My fellow-prisoners considered themselves already beings of another world. The degradation of their country was death to them, and they had no desire to prolong life on the terms by which it was held by others.

Becoming at last somewhat impatient, I ventured on the 29th Vendémiaire (October 20) to address our minister, Mr. Morris, though I had not yet received my passport from Havre, informing him of the circumstances of my arrest, etc.

Mr. Morris's answer, dated October 21, declined to attempt any interference until the passport was produced or satisfactorily accounted for; but as the letter is at once an evidence of Mr. Morris's official integrity as an American minister, and his skill in using the opportunity to counteract the suspicions the French Government had thrown out against him, as leaning towards the English with partiality, I give it as I received it. The letter, of course, was to be read by the prison officials before it was delivered to my hands, and was written in the following words: —

MONSIEUR, — Je suis bien fâché de voir par la vôtre, du 29, que vous êtes détenu prisonnier. Je crois que si vous aviez gardé mon certificat ce malheur ne vous serait pas arrivé. Il me paraît très possible qu'une autre personne en soit le possesseur, et dans ce cas cette personne vous représentera dans le monde comme vous représentez cette personne dans la prison. La Nation Francaise accorde aux citoyens des États Unis une protection plenière, mais il ne faut pas en abuser; et c'en serait un abus de demander votre liberté avant que je n'ai la certitude que le certificat que je vous ai donné ne soit pas à la protection d'un Anglais, ou autre étranger, ou personne suspecte.

J'ai l'honneur d'être, monsieur, votre très humble serviteur,

GOUVERNEUR MORRIS.

In this letter there is nothing to flatter me, but I give the contents entire to show the perversity of things engendered by the Revolution, and not to lose an opportunity of holding up to public gratitude, as far as depends on me, the slighted memory of a statesman by whose attention I was honored, who was one of the founders of our Republic, and would have been a credit to any nation.

On October 24 I sent to the minister my passport, and on the 27th the Secretary for Foreign Affairs presented to the Committee of Public Safety his demand for my discharge, while the same day I wrote myself to the Committee. But Robespierre and his agents were too much occupied with hunting up victims for the Revolutionary Tribunal to pay attention to me, or to the minister. Nor was more attention paid to a petition got up by Americans in my behalf, and signed by Mr. F. L. Taney, Joel Barlow, Mark Leavenworth, James Jones, and Thomas Ramsden; unless it were to transfer me, with about twenty others, — old men and foreigners, against whom there were no specific charges, — to the old Scotch College in the Faubourg St. Marceau, where we could see our friends and enjoy other privileges not known in common prisons.

Having copied the first letter of Mr. Morris in justice to him, I copy another in justice to myself.

À PARIS, Déc. 31, 1793.

MONSIEUR,—J'ai reçu votre lettre du 1er Nivose. J'ai reclamé votre liberté à plusieurs reprises, et je suis persuadé que le Ministre y a fait attention. La dernière fois que j'ai eu l'honneur de le voir il m'a dit que le délai dont je me plaignais devait être attribué à la multiplicité des affaires qui occupent la Committee. Je viens de lui répéter mes instances, en demandant qu'on m'instruisse au moins des causes de votre détention. Dès que j'aurai reçu une réponse quelconque je vous l'acheminerai. Je suis très sensible à votre malheur, et je ne négligerai rien qui puisse dépendre de moi pour le soulager. J'ai l'honneur d'être, monsieur,

Votre très humble serviteur,

GOUV. MORRIS

Colonel Swan of Boston, who had distinguished himself by some well-written letters to the Marquis de Lafayette, which were printed, was approached by some of my friends; but it was indirectly hinted to that gentleman by some in power, that if I was in prison the best service he could render me was to let me be forgotten, for fear of worse. The same cause prevented him from signing the petition, which with this, and one other exception, contained the name of every one of my countrymen who ventured to remain in Paris.

The transfer from the Madelonettes to the old Scotch College was made in hackney-coaches, our guard gendarmes. Four prisoners, tied two and two, were in each coach; but as I happened to be one of the last, our guard concluded enough were secured, and in this way I escaped the ignominy.

We were fairly told that we were to receive great indulgences, but the old French gentlemen had no little suspicion that we were actually going to some obscure place to be murdered; and it may be said that the information given us by our guard, while passing through the more populous parts of the city, was not reassuring. We were told that should we attempt a flight they had only to call upon the citizens, and they would soon prevent our attempting it a second time.

At the new prison we had free intercourse with each other, night and day, and the air of a spacious garden. Amongst my chamber companions was an Irish priest of the name of Kearney, an excellent scholar and a benevolent man, under whom I completed my French studies, and from whom I afterwards received very agreeable attentions.

There were in the house about eighty gentlemen, and it happened that the adjoining house was the English Nuns' convent, also converted into a prison for about one hundred ladies. The gardens were separated by a high wall, and we could not enjoy the conversation of the ladies; but we did not fail to visit our belvedere daily, and they their garden, from whence we could see one another, and thus be gratified with part of the pleasure society affords. Among the prisoners at the Scotch College were Sir Robert Smith, Mr. Churchill, son of the English poet, and a Mr. Cameron of the ancient Scotch loyalists, besides Mr. Kearney, the Irish priest. All these had the good fortune to survive the rigor of Robespierre. This was not the case with all my companions at the college. One young man from Manchester, with some Frenchmen, was conducted forth and executed for attempting to make his escape, — as I understood, — but perhaps only to make up the daily number of one hundred and fifty victims, on whom the tyrant exercised his vengeance just before his fall.

The prisoners in Paris were supplied with bread, fuel, mattress, and sheets; all other articles of necessity or comfort we found for ourselves. Those among us who had no means were supplied by those who had. By sending to market we lived at small cost, — my expenses from the depreciation of currency not amounting in our money to more than fifty cents a day, including the contribution alluded to. Paper money was plenty enough, but the uninterrupted continuance of all the machinery of municipal government is matter of astonishment. While all the superior posts in the administration were either in a state of continual change, or wholly suspended, the inferior officers, jailers and so forth, kept their places. They did not approve the state of things, but they dared not abandon their duties, especially in the prisons, so well did they and their employers know that complete barbarism would have taken their place, had they resigned their posts into Revolutionary hands.

In the convent of English Nuns were the wives and daughters of several noblemen, and a number of other young, beautiful, and respectable ladies of good families. The only difference in the treatment they received and ours was that they could obtain permission to make visits in the city; but this indulgence was of little use to them. Their relatives were already murdered, in foreign countries, or in other prisons.

During our confinement in the college, the British and

Spaniards were forced to abandon Toulon, which had been given up to them by the persecuted part of its inhabitants; and the event was signalized by demonstrations of real or feigned joy among the prisoners, who were furnished about the same time with evidence of hostile feeling towards them on the part of the populace. To sustain the influence of the sanguinary party then in power, the bust of Marat, who had been assassinated some months before by Miss Charlotte Corday, was paraded through the streets, followed by a procession of some thousand people. When it passed the college, the prisoners judged it advisable to appear at the windows, and there exhibit signs of commendation. These were approved by some, but others in the procession considered our zeal officious; and in the confusion there arose no little apprehension that we might be assailed and promiscuously murdered.

I believe that most of those I left in the Madelonettes became victims; but only a few young men, who attempted an escape by means of rope-ladders after I left the Scotch College, were executed or brought to trial. However, the length of my confinement and too close association with some of my fellow-prisoners broke down my health, and brought on me a complaint from which I suffered for many years after.

Towards the middle of January, 1794, Messrs. Jackson and Francis of Philadelphia, and Mr. Joseph Russell of Boston, came over from England; but one of them having taken charge of some letters from *émigrés* to their friends, it was found that one of these letters contained counterfeit *assignats*, and the gentlemen were all escorted to Paris to be examined by the Committee of Public Safety. As Republicans, they had expected very different treatment. Jackson, who had been in the American army, was not easily put off his guard, but, assuming the uniform and address of an officer lately attached to General Washington's staff, obtained his audiences at discretion, and prevented the imprisonment of himself and his companions by an explanation of the incident in a style of energy and innocence.

About the same time, partly, I believe, from more correct views of our national feeling towards France, obtained through Mr. Jackson, and partly from returning confidence in our minister (at least in his official acts), the Committee of Public Safety took up my business, and in January, 1794, ordered my release without any explanation or apology, or any more ceremony than had been exhibited at the time of my arrest. By some accident the order was discovered by Mr. Ramsden; and he, in a very friendly manner, took charge of it, and brought it to the prison lest there should be some miscarriage, and I should not have the benefit of it.

The day after my release I joined Mr. Barlow, Major Jackson, and other Americans in a petition which they, with leave, presented to the National Convention, praying for the release of Thomas Paine as a citizen of the United States, he having been lately imprisoned as a British subject. Mr. Paine's "Rights of Man" had, with his former writings, induced the French to believe that he would be an acquisition in forming their government, and he became a member of the Assembly, though he was unable to deliver his sentiments in the language of the country. It was an axiom with him that all men were sufficiently wise to discover their own interests; and as every man had an interest in his own liberty, the French must be prepared to enjoy a free government. Therefore he supported the declaration of September, 1792, that France should abolish royalty and establish a republic. But being destitute of any revengeful motive in the case of King Louis, Paine had not joined in voting for his death, and thus excited the suspicions of his colleagues, who sent him to prison on the first opportunity. There, possibly to conciliate those who professed atheism, he prepared his pamphlet on the "Age of Reason;" but he was miserable under the continual apprehension of being murdered, and bitterly accused the leaders in the Convention of plotting his death.

The President of the Convention told us that the government considered Paine, who was born in Great Britain, sub

THOMAS PAINE.

ject to the laws relating to countries with which France was at war, but that, appreciating our motives, our petition would be referred to the Committee of Public Safety. He then invited us to the honors of the Session, which meant seats within the bar. But not a few members hissed during the reading of parts of our memorial, in which Paine's attachment to republican principles was asserted.

At the head of the committee to which our petition was referred was the noted Robespierre, a dissatisfied member of the bar of Artois, who had been a member of the first or Constituent Assembly. He was assisted by Carnot, Barrère, and others.

It is hardly necessary to say that by this time everything like style or gayety of dress was abandoned, both by natives and foreigners. Pantaloons, short boots, round hats, and cropped hair were altogether fashionable among gentlemen; but ladies of rank or fashion were entirely shut up, or, if they appeared in public, were so disguised as to be unknown.

The halt of the Prussian army under the Duke of Brunswick, after his threatening proclamation had stirred up the fury of the French, may have been due to the critical situation of the king and queen, but I have never been able to understand why the British minister withheld from the insurgents in La Vendée and Brittany aid that he could well have despatched to them, after the destruction of the French fleet by Lord Howe. In my opinion such aid would have far better helped the cause of England and her allies against France than the subsequent war in the Peninsula. That Mr. Pitt should have doubted of success at this time and in this manner has always given me surprise, though I cannot accuse him of duplicity, as was done by the French Royalists.

As I considered that the partiality of my countrymen towards a republican form of government had led them to mistake the character of the French Revolution, I could not but see, in the declaration of neutrality made by General Washington, more magnanimity than in the scanty help afforded by England to check the effusion of innocent blood, and prevent a generation of men and women from being delivered over to anarchy.

It is probable that, but for the divided state of public feeling at that day in America on the subject of the French Revolution, the President would have declined to send a minister to France when the government of the Reign of Terror demanded the recall of Mr. Morris; nor would our government have solicited another minister from France to replace Genet, the incendiary who had insulted General Washington and our whole nation. Our conduct on this occasion countenanced the regicides, and encouraged their successors to make war on the United States four years later, in 1798.

When, after the recall of Mr. Morris, Mr. Monroe arrived in France, he found himself the only representative of any foreign power. The smallest republics in Europe evinced their displeasure; the American confederacy alone courted the friendship of Genet's employers, who in the end plundered the people who thus had countenanced them.

Mr. Monroe, on his arrival in Paris, finding that many of the miscellaneous duties that fell on Mr. Morris could be equally well performed by a subordinate, procured the appointment of a chargé d'affaires. He arrived in time to witness the overthrow of Robespierre, — a man whose tyrannical acts were supported, if not often suggested, by some of his colleagues. These men suggested atrocities, and the members of the Legislative Assembly submitted to such acts through fear, until their own persons were threatened; and then, seeing no other relief than through the overthrow of the Jacobin leaders was to be expected, they gathered courage from despair, and, making a virtue of necessity, they called to their aid a class of the population they had long oppressed, and a counter revolution was effected, with little difficulty and almost without bloodshed.

Soon after my release I returned to Havre, where I found Mr. Taney preparing to embark for America. He had been arrested by order of the government a few days before; and although he had been speedily released, he dreaded worse.

The American ship "Caroline," about this time, with specie, the proceeds of our last venture in tobacco, on board, was captured by H. M. Frigate "Thetis," Captain Lord Cochrane, and a suit for the recovery of our money was instituted, which made it desirable I should again visit England. My health had been much broken by my imprisonment, and I received at Havre the most kind care from Mrs. Taney, and her father, M. Govain. Madame Govain had been most anxious for my conversion to the Catholic faith, while faiths were still respected; but now that her *curé* had fled, it was a consolation to find in me a Republican and a Christian. The churches in Havre being at this time closed, many conscientious persons wandered into paganism, and my own servant seriously inquired of me whether there was, or was not, a God. To which I ventured to reply that religion was a blessing, and ought to be a guide, and at all events it was safe to believe in it.

At this time it was not possible for a person of noble descent, estate, or connections, to remain in France with safety, and the few who had so far escaped, were flying in all directions. I had the happiness to embark at Havre on board a neutral vessel, the beautiful and accomplished Countess de Fontange, whose husband had entered the Spanish army; nor was she the only person to whom I rendered similar services, but these mostly took refuge in the United States.

In July, 1794, I thought it best to repair to London and watch over our interests in the Court of Admiralty. I therefore embarked on board a small Swedish vessel I had freighted, for Hamburg, intending to proceed from thence to England. We ran the blockade successfully, after a dangerous and tedious passage, and I landed at Gluckstadt, a small town in Holstein, where I was at once suspected to be a Frenchman, but, as my papers were all in order, I was ordered to proceed the next day to Hamburg.

Hamburg had been long respected by European belligerents as one of the Free Cities, but no respect was paid to it by the French, who not only entered it, but plundered it; so that nowhere had the Allies more ready supporters than the Hamburghers. When the French overran Germany, this long-prosperous Free City was made to pay dearly for its wonted neutrality, in forced seizures and loans, until finally, by the anti-commercial system by which Bonaparte endeavored to cripple England, her merchants were shut out from the ocean, and whatever the Revolutionary armies had left became the spoil of the French Emperor's generals.

At Hamburg I found Mr. Barlow and some other Americans, who no longer considered themselves comfortable or safe in France, and I became personally acquainted with Mr. Parrish, the United States consul, and M. Goddeffroy, my former correspondent.[1] At a dinner at his hospitable house, where there were many foreigners, I remarked that his accomplished daughters conversed with each stranger in his own tongue, with perfect ease and facility.

I took my passage to England in a packet, in which I crossed the North Sea in four days. The weather was sufficiently moderate to enable the crew to cast a net and to catch an abundant supply of fish and oysters. The oysters, however, were so much impregnated with a coppery taste as hardly to be eatable, which taste is common to all the oysters on the European coasts, so that they are at first very unpalatable to an American.

I took lodgings in London, where I spent the winter (1794–95); but I was nearly all the time confined to the house, indebted to my landlady for her kind care, and for society to such Americans as found leisure and inclination for friendly offices. This is a form of charity which too many worthy people overlook, while they daily perform other acts of benevolence.

While I was thus confined to my lodgings I was appointed, as I afterwards learned (for the commission was dated Dec. 18, 1794), consul of the United States for the port of Havre-Marat, as it was then called, instead of Havre de

[1] The house of Goddeffroy & Co. now carries on an immense business with islands in the Pacific, and is greatly interested in the affairs of Samoa. — E. W. L.

Grace. I received some copies of the Laws addressed to me as consul, from the Department of State at Washington, three years after, and a duplicate of my commission was furnished me on my return to America; but such were the uncertainties of the post-office service at that period that my commission never reached me, though I fulfilled the duties of consul at Havre, and the authorities accepted me as such. I subsequently inquired of Mr. Monroe whether such a document had come into his hands. He answered that no such paper had been received by him, and added, "But such was the favorable opinion that I formed of your character and conduct that I am satisfied that your appointment would have been agreeable to me."

While I was in London one of the chief actors was hissed off the stage at Drury Lane because he made his appearance with short hair, thus marking, as the audience supposed, his sympathy with the French and their Revolution. But the Prince of Wales (inclined to side with Mr. Fox in his opposition to the tax on hair powder) adopted the crop, and it became fashionable in England soon after.

My business with the Admiralty Court being happily settled, I left England for France in company with Mr. John Field of Philadelphia, and Mr. Waldo of Boston, who were about going to Paris, France having become more settled after the unexpected fall of Robespierre. I joined them in a postchaise and four for Margate, April 5, 1795.

That being the day on which the Princess Caroline of Brunswick was expected to arrive, the road was crowded, the simple ones supposing that the Prince of Wales would come with speed to greet his bride. We did not pass without observation, especially as a very well-dressed black servant of Mr. Waldo was mounted behind the carriage. In the midst of a solitary wood we met a coach and six, containing no less a person than Mr. Pitt, returning, without attendance, from a visit to one of the Cinque Ports, of which he was warden. He was a tall, thin, serious-looking gentleman in black. I was surprised to see the first minister of state thus travelling alone, and without a guard.

In consequence of the fall of Robespierre, July 27, 1794, I began to consider the establishment of rational liberty still possible in France. Robespierre was a middle-aged man of good person, wore spectacles, and was attentive to dress. From some proofs of candor and disinterestedness, — from his absence on the 10th of August, — and from the fact of his saving the lives of the seventy-two protesting Deputies, and restoring the belief in a future state, I am inclined to think that he had been pushed forward by a current which was irresistible.[1] He was a man not endowed with much courage; but if he could have put down his rivals, his government might have been at least as mild as that to which the French submitted their necks soon after. His former accomplices, Billaud-Varennes, Collot d'Herbois, and Tallien, became his accusers to save themselves, and few adhered to him when attacked.

We landed at Dunkirk, a place famous in history, where I instantly discovered the happy change produced by the downfall of the late government. The churches were now open for worship, and the richer classes seemed to vie with the humbler in showing their devotion. All countenances were brightened. Each class seemed disposed to acts of civility and kindness.

Mr. Monroe, who had recently arrived in Paris, to replace Mr. Morris as minister of the United States, had been well received by the more just and temperate Committee of the Convention. The American character became everywhere treated with respect.

At Amiens I took leave of Messrs. Field and Waldo, who were going direct to the capital, while I hastened across country to Havre. The road from Calais to Paris was ornamented with two rows of forest trees, about thirty feet from tree to tree; but, for the safety of travellers, no forest or grove of trees is suffered to stand within twenty or thirty yards of the main road.

In the cultivation of the land and in their manners, I saw little difference between the people of Picardy and those of

[1] See Book IV., Chapter IV.

JAMES MONROE.

Normandy; and the peasantry throughout France, in those parts where they cultivate the grape, or raise grain, or follow grazing, are, as I saw them, sober, plain, and pious. I had indeed many opportunities of mixing with them, especially in those evening dances of the villagers, in which I often joined with heartfelt pleasure. I saw much of them, too, while engaged in their various occupations.

Their landlords were never so obnoxious to them as the unequal tax on salt, and the forced labor required of them on the roads. Much of the best soil was held by the regular clergy; but as these fathers spent their lives among the villagers, and employed the industrious, besides ministering to the wants of the afflicted, it may be doubted whether the sale and division of their domains will add to the enjoyment, real happiness, or contentment of the peasantry, although many peasants of course will become more independent in their persons and property than formerly.

CHAPTER IV.

LIFE IN PARIS UNDER THE DIRECTORY.

WHILST I was absent in England during the greater part of the year 1794, the affairs of Mr. Taney had been far from prospering. The fall of the markets, the seizure of some of his shipments, and, above all, the delay of the Government in paying for the tobacco purchased from him proved his ruin.

To obtain some settlement from those in power after the fall of Robespierre, I again went to Paris before the end of April, 1795; and as the strict English blockade had destroyed the trade of Havre, I never returned to it again.

Before I left London I had been recommended to several French emigrants as a person to whom they might confide letters; amongst others, M. Cazalès, the late eloquent and intrepid opponent of the Revolutionary measures of the Constituent Assembly. He called on me, and, besides his own letters of a private nature, tendered me a polite introduction, which I accepted, to his friend M. de Nanteuil of the Place Victoire, formerly one of the farmers of the diligences. This proved to be one of the most fortunate circumstances of my life; for to this gentleman and his amiable family was I indebted for the greatest pleasures of the ensuing four years, — being the happiest portion of my life during my absence from America.

At the same time that Mr. Monroe, our new ambassador, reached Paris, came three friends of mine from Baltimore, — Captain Barney, Mr. J. H. Purviance, and Mr. Henry Wilson; besides Mr. Skipwith, Mr. Monroe's secretary, and a number of Americans from other places. By the aid of Mr. Skipwith and my friend Major Mountflorence, also attached to the embassy, I succeeded in obtaining an acknowledgment of the claims with which I was intrusted, including my own, and some payments were made in depreciated money; but the major part remained unpaid until, by the cession of Louisiana in 1803, the American Government assumed most of the debts.

By Mr. and Mrs. Monroe I was received and treated in a most friendly manner. The minister, contemplating a residence of some time in Paris, and tempted by the low price of property, purchased a very handsome villa within the walls of the city, to the west; where he and his lady, then young, beautiful, and affable, entertained at sumptuous dinners numerous parties of Frenchmen and Americans, besides giving a magnificent fête, long remembered, on the Fourth of July, 1795, soon after the installation of the new embassy. The only child of Mr. and Mrs. Monroe, a young daughter, was sent to Madame Campan's boarding-school at St. Germain.

Nothing could have given me so much pleasure as the great change I found in Paris after my return to it in April, 1795. The excluded members of the Convention — nearly seventy in number, and those the best — had resumed their seats. The Jacobin Club was suppressed. The princess royal had been sent from the prison where she had lived, bereaved of her parents, to the palace of her uncle at Vienna; the guillotine was put down, and there was an end to the infamous Revolutionary Tribunal.

At Mr. Monroe's I met, besides Thomas Paine, — whom Mr. Monroe charitably lodged and boarded for some time after obtaining his release from prison, — my countrymen, Messrs. Barlow, Eustis, Putnam, Barney, Codman, Waldo, Sands, and Higginson; besides Colonel Humphries, our minister, on his way to Spain; Kosciusko, the Pole, who served in our War of Independence, and many others. I met also most of the officials or founders of the new government, including the Abbé Grégoire,[1] who retained his fidelity to the Catholic faith, and deserved the bishopric he got, while Gobel, the Diocesan of Paris, basely abandoned

[1] See Book V., Chapter II.

the Church. I met, too, M. Mercier, author of a facetious but just picture of Paris; and Cambacérès, then occupied in a compilation of Laws which was afterwards designated the Code Napoléon. With Napoleon he was subsequently associated as one of the three Consuls. There were also Lanthenas, Jean de Brie, and Boissy d'Anglas, conventionalists, men who sincerely labored to establish a republican form of government, — of the practicability of which neither they nor Mr. Monroe seemed to entertain any doubt. I also saw there the Count de Ségur, M. Volney the traveller, and many others. But Sieyès, the wily Talleyrand, and others of that stamp, affected to shun places of conviviality and the society of foreigners.

It will be allowed that in such company I had great opportunities for improvement, and also that it may have been hard for a young man to withstand contamination from the erroneous religious and political opinions that many of these gentlemen entertained.

The man who afterwards became First Consul was not commonly spoken of till made chief of the Army of Italy. He was the offspring of a species of gentry in Corsica, whom it was the policy of France to conciliate at the time he was educated at the Military School at Brienne. He was a demagogue from infancy, and first signalized himself at Toulon in 1793. Under Barras he also put down the Sections, 13th Vendémiaire (Oct. 4, 1794).

The Jacobins, alarmed, after the fall of Robespierre, by the condemnation of Fouquier-Tinville, the Public Prosecutor of the Revolutionary Tribunal, attempted to regain their authority in the May following, and for a while succeeded, after killing in an *émeute* the member Féraud; but their adherents were repulsed, the assassin of Féraud was arrested, and at once condemned to death. When carried, however, to the Place de Grève, where executions at that time took place, he was rescued from a few cowardly gendarmes by a small party of the populace, and hidden in the Faubourg St. Antoine. As I had never witnessed an execution by the guillotine, I took this opportunity to go to the Place de Grève

CHARLES MAURICE TALLEYRAND.

with my friend Purviance, and was present at the rescue, which commenced by a few boys crying, *Grâce! Grâce!* The Convention, however, ordered the Faubourg St. Antoine to be besieged, and, after two or three days of commotion, the city was restored to quiet by the surrender and execution of the murderer.

While Thomas Paine was lodged in our ambassador's house, Mr. Monroe informed me that he was writing a most abusive letter to General Washington, and asked me to see him and persuade him to have it suppressed, as he himself had in vain endeavored to do. This I did, but all in vain; for Paine thought himself slighted by our Government, which had not demanded his release without waiting for his solicitation. He was, like many other geniuses advanced in life, both vain and obstinate to an extreme degree.

When Mr. Monroe was recalled in 1796, the Americans in Paris, who had received many services and civilities from him, and who had no knowledge of the objectionable communications that had passed between himself, his own and the French Governments, united in addressing him a complimentary letter, which he affixed to his defense on his return to America, and which was the innocent cause of some little coolness on the part of friends at home to some of the signers, including myself. Although I always differed with Mr. Monroe's general politics, I do not reproach myself with signing this testimony to his private worth and public services.

On my former visits to Paris I had always lodged at public hotels or inns, where I met other Americans or strangers; but being desirous of forming French acquaintances to the exclusion in some measure of other society, I took the liberty to ask my friend M. de Nanteuil, after I had been introduced to his lady and his family, which consisted of two amiable young daughters and a young son, if I could live with them. But he very cordially informed me that the customs of the country would not allow parents who had unmarried daughters in the house to admit gentlemen on the footing I proposed, but that I might consider his house like a home, so far as to call and take meals with them whenever I found it convenient. I was even urged to bring with me American friends and others at discretion. I was also introduced into the family of M. de Nanteuil's younger brother, who had an elegant little villa at Rhony, the same that had once been the residence of the Duc de Sully. There I was present at many pleasant parties, and passed many happy days. I became acquainted and was often in company with Madame Tallien, who was certainly, though aged about thirty,[1] and the wife of a second husband, one of the most elegant and accomplished women of the age, as she was that one of all her sex who most contributed to serve humanity by her influence over the monsters who had usurped the government of her country. I also knew Madame Recamier, the young and amiable wife of the banker of that name, who was universally considered the beauty of Paris for several years. She was not so tall as Madame Tallien and more portly; both had black eyes and hair.

In the circle of young ladies, nearly all of whom were schoolfellows, having been together at the establishment of Madame Campan, I met Mademoiselle Oulot, who became the wife of General Moreau, Mademoiselle Agläé Anguié, who in 1807 became the Princesse de la Moskowa, wife of Marshal Ney, and Mademoiselle Hortense de Beauharnais, who was the step-daughter of Bonaparte, and became Queen of Holland. They were all rivals in accomplishments then, and all have since experienced the most painful reverses. Among all the young ladies whom I knew in France, Mademoiselle Anguié, whose fate was the most deplorable, united the greatest charms of person and mind, and pleased me most. This young lady's father had suffered his share of Revolutionary malice. Her mother had died by violence; her aunt, Madame Campan, had been driven from the chamber of the queen to keep a boarding-school; while her uncle, M. Genet, had rendered himself obnoxious to the American people, and was proscribed at home. Yet these afflictions, though

[1] Mr. Griffith is mistaken; she could not have been more than twenty-four, having been born in 1773.

far inferior to what she must have suffered in later life from the execution of her husband, Marshal Ney, gave her a sort of pensive modesty, which, at her age and with her great beauty, made her exceedingly attractive.

When Bonaparte assumed the extraordinary task of making matches between his generals and ladies who possessed a certain fortune, he presented Mademoiselle Anguié to Ney, and is said to have declared that he had selected "the fairest of the fair for the bravest of the brave."

I was long enough privileged to be intimate in French society to assert, contrary to the statements of many travellers, that the chances of happiness in marrying among the French are as great, or nearly so, as they are anywhere. This will not appear so extraordinary when it is considered that young ladies in France always received their education in some convent, and were afterwards much restricted in their intercourse with the other sex. They come into society without any former impressions or partialities, and, when their parents form suitable connections for them, will generally attach themselves to their husbands and their domestic duties, unless the husbands become libertines, or the fascinations of fashionable or court life overcome their religious principles.

Although in other countries young ladies are permitted a more general intercourse, how seldom does it happen that they obtain in marriage the man they most admire! They are not at liberty to solicit for themselves; but in France their parents will often seek for them the object of their preference.

I lived in furnished apartments in the Rue Richelieu at one time and in the Rue St. Roch, afterwards with Mr. J. H. Purviance, private secretary to Mr. Monroe; but I was generally alone. I kept a cabriolet, or gig, and a servant, a native of Cologne, who was my hair-dresser, valet de chambre, and footman, and who prepared my breakfast. If I was not engaged abroad, I dined at a restaurateur's; that is, one of those splendid cook-shops with which the capital of France abounds. I partook of all public amusements, and was frequently in the streets till daylight, without ever receiving the slightest injury or insult from individuals.

One of my country excursions was to Daumartin, a villa which had been purchased by my friend, Mr. Richard Codman, of Boston. The castle, erected probably a thousand years before, presented only piles of stone and mortar, which seemed to adhere as one mass and to be capable of resisting all attacks another thousand years.

To counteract the excitement in France against the United States in 1797, I wrote an answer to a remark in the correspondence of the ambassador Fauchet, relative to the influence of British trade in America. The title of my pamphlet was, "L'Indépendence absolue des États Unis de l'Amérique prouvée par l'État actuel de leur Commerce," etc. Its style was corrected by a French friend, M. Billocq. I also published articles in the French newspapers for a similar purpose.

The Revolutionary armies under Dumouriez, Pichegru, Jourdan, Hoche, and Moreau, aided by the sympathy of foreign populations and the want of a common feeling among the allied sovereigns, had enabled the French Government to procure peace with Spain, Prussia, Switzerland, and Holland. Soon after the fall of Robespierre, Bonaparte carried his victorious arms through Italy, and even to the neighborhood of Vienna. The British Government was left almost alone, and authorized Lord Malmesbury to enter into negotiations at Lisle; but the Directors and the leading men in the Assembly became uneasy at the prospect of a general peace. They overthrew their opponents on the 18th Fructidor (Sept. 4, 1797) by calling in the military under Augereau, and broke off the negotiations, sending Bonaparte to Egypt to conquer other colonies in place of those they had lost in America; and considering themselves destitute of any further interest in the neutrality of the United States, they began at once to plunder the Americans, and their government used the most insulting language to our own.

Having very weak eyes from infancy, I now attempted the use of spectacles before I was twenty-four, and to that, and perhaps to the use of Rapparee snuff (begun then also), I may impute the preservation of my sight, using my spectacles only for reading; but a miniature painter whom I employed at this time to take a likeness of me for my father, discovered that my left eye was defective, being in part permanently covered by an eclipse.

Mr. Monroe was recalled in the fall of 1796, and General Pinckney was sent out to obtain some restoration of harmony. This venerable American officer and patriot was indignantly rejected by those self-created despots (the members of the Directory), and it became necessary to satisfy our people, who could not credit the horrid acts of pretended republicans. Another embassy was therefore sent: Gerry, Marshall, General Ellsworth, and Messrs. Davis and Murray. While these ambassadors of peace were on their way, American property was subject to many risks, and our persons were in danger. Mr. Skipwith, our consul, was obnoxious at Havre, and he was obliged to retire; so also in Paris was Major Mountflorence, his late assistant.

My own health requiring change and care, I spent some time in 1798 at Passy, and perhaps avoided molestation by doing so. As if the Directory feared that personal outrages on Americans should not be understood, they passed a decree enjoining foreigners (meaning particularly Americans) to leave the city and the country, within a very short period, unless they obtained *a card of hospitality;* that is, a permit to prolong their stay from week to week. In consequence of this decree, Paris was almost deserted by Americans, but my commercial concerns would not admit of my departure, and I was arrested several times, because I had not taken care to renew week by week my *card of hospitality.*

As if enough had not been done to open the eyes of Americans, the Directory sent an army into the Swiss Cantons, and compelled those brave and ancient republican allies to put themselves under French protection.

I endeavored to become attached to the Dutch embassy, but Mr. Murray had engaged Mr. I. Henry as his secretary; however, after all official characters had left Paris, I became the medium through which he transmitted American official despatches to the French minister for foreign affairs.

When I published my Defence of the Independence of the United States (of which I have already spoken) I sent copies to MM. Rœderer, Anguié, Dupré, and others; also to M. Talleyrand, the minister, who in a note of thanks replied that, if I had not proved what I proposed, I had abundantly shown that it was the interest of the United States to cultivate a good understanding with the French nation.

The corrupt conduct of this artful man, while minister for foreign affairs, and the energy with which our government exposed his intrigues, together with reverses to the French arms in Italy, and the destruction of the French fleet on the coast of Egypt, first compelled the Directory to renew amicable negotiations with the United States, which they would gladly have extended to Great Britain. Then came their final overthrow in 1799 by the military party.

I took an opportunity once to ask M. La Forest, who had been French consul at Philadelphia, and was then chief clerk in the Foreign Department, how he could reconcile it to his conscience to serve such wicked rulers. To which he pleaded poverty as his excuse, but also declared that greater evils might have taken place but for the influence of M. Talleyrand.

While the relations of the French Government with America continued unsatisfactory, nothing profitable could be done by an American in France. Messrs. Pinckney and Gerry had gone home, and the hostility of the French Government to all Americans who remained in Paris was apparent in many ways. I therefore determined to return home, and, when things should improve, attempt to obtain a more profitable situation than that of consul at Havre. That a change would take place before long I did not doubt. The people had long since become tired of strife and of the many shifting changes in their Government; and some Revolutionary leader had to be sought on whom power and authority should devolve sufficient to defend the country

CHARLES COTESWORTH PINCKNEY.

externally and maintain peace in the interior. For this they chose a person who, being a foreigner, entertained no partiality for any district of the country, nor any class of people, and yet was committed to the Revolution. To Napoleon Bonaparte the nation submitted, with few exceptions, as cordially as if he had been born their king, for the French, like other people, will go from one extreme to another, and, after contending with great zeal for some particular object until they are exhausted, will become so relaxed and indifferent as to appear better contented without it.

Before I left Paris in July, 1799, it was known that the government of France had been offered to Moreau, Hoche, and some other military commanders. People were then ignorant that Bonaparte was on his way from Egypt, and there was a general feeling that the king would be restored, and universal peace take place immediately.

In the course of my exertions to provide for myself in the future in case I should never receive the money that was due me from the French Government, I purchased for a large sum in *assignats* a hotel in the Rue de Richelieu. Upon the fall of this paper money I sold the same property for payments in specie, of course at an enormously reduced price, but one nevertheless that would have left me a considerable profit. Before the payments were all due, however, the new paper money called *mandats* was created, which, like assignats, fell in value as soon as it appeared, but, having been made legal tender, my purchaser took advantage of it, and thus my hopes of a successful speculation in real estate cost me dear.

As no passage direct for America could be obtained in France in 1799, and as I was desirous to see Bordeaux, I determined to proceed home by Spain. I procured a passport from Mr. Skipwith, indorsed by the minister for foreign affairs, to be countersigned by the resident Spanish minister and head of the Department, when I should have deposited my *card of hospitality*.

Fully impressed with the idea that I should soon be in France again, I did not feel that regret I otherwise should have done at parting with my inestimable friends. I even entertained hopes of seeing again General Decoudray, who, a bachelor, and at the age of eighty, entertained in the most agreeable manner large parties of gentlemen, of whom I was one. He inhabited an ancient castle of his family at Brie. He was sincerely beloved by his tenantry, and even in the days of party violence the castle gate served only as a common door, the moat was dry, and the battlements without a guard. From a pleasure house in the park we could see a distant castle, once the residence of La Belle Gabrielle. Some anecdotes relating to that amour of the Great Henry were told us as family traditions, and the general had in his town house in the Place Royale two chairs that had served the happy couple, as he said.

I took charge of some letters from Madame de Lafayette to General Washington, and from M. Leroy to Mr. Adams and Colonel Hamilton. At the moment I was stepping into the diligence, that gentleman told me in a whisper that our friends in America might be certain of a speedy revolution in the government of France.

My servant, Louis Monnard, being a native of Cologne, and liable to the conscription, was very desirous to leave France, but could only do so by obtaining the security of some friends for his return.

We passed through a fine arable country on the banks of the Loire, to Orleans; thence by Blois to Tours, and so on to Bordeaux; there I hired a light carriage, and crossed the sands to Bayonne. The Landes, as they are called, present a surface almost bare, and the people appear to live on the produce of their pine timber, and on flocks of sheep, which the shepherds watch and drive mounted on stilts, while they spin tow or flax by hand. I lived upon the road on the thighs of geese, smoked like bacon. However, as I approached Bayonne, the country improved.

At Bayonne I hired mules, and a guide to conduct me over some small spurs of the Pyrenees into Spain. The guide proved to be a girl of twenty-two, daughter of the man who owned the mules. It seems that the commandants of the French and Spanish guards on the frontier treated the Biscayan women with much confidence; and although I was not permitted to see my baggage, I do not believe that anything was even opened.

When I reached San Sebastien, having happily got out of France, I found in the harbor several American ships armed, manned, and furnished with letters of marque against the French.

The first vessel sailing for America was a small schooner bound to New York, and its commander, Captain Palmer, taking me as a passenger, we sailed early in August, 1799. We made two or three narrow escapes from vessels which we supposed to be British cruisers. At one time there were two which we did not discover till quite near us. At another time a frigate by press of sail got within gunshot of us after a day's chase; but as we were in the act of coming to, she carried away her fore-topmast, which emboldened us to cheer and fill our sails again.

We finally lost sight of her, to the great joy of our captain, for his vessel and his cargo of French goods actually belonged to French merchants in New York; and if he did not lose all, he would at least have been sent to England and detained at great expense.

On September 20 we made the Highlands, but too late in the day to pass Sandy Hook, and, not to be obliged to tack at a critical season between Long Island and the Jersey Shore, Captain Palmer stood out to sea till the next day, when we reached New York.

We heard from the health officer, who made no difficulty in letting us go up to the city, that yellow fever, that fatal disease which several times during my absence had visited my country, was now raging in New York so terribly that almost all the inhabitants had quitted the city.

BOOK II.

FRANCE BEFORE THE REVOLUTION.

I. Imprisonments and Escapes of Latude.
II. A Peasant's View of the Revolution.
III. Paris in 1787.
IV. Court Life at Versailles on the Eve of the Revolution.

CHAPTER I.

INTRODUCTORY REMARKS ON BOOK II.

THE French Revolution of 1789 was not primarily a revolt of the peasantry. All over France, indeed, the salt tax, or *gabelle*, and the *corvée* (or forced labor on the roads) were held to be sore grievances by the rural population; but in Northern, Western, and Southern France the peasants were unfavorable to the Revolution, and it required a great deal of Revolutionary "mission work" to stir them up against their clergy and their nobles. It was not so in Central France, or in Lorraine, — a province that had not long been annexed to the French crown. Lorraine had been burdened by all sorts of feudal exactions imposed upon the country by its semi-German rulers, and even after its annexation to France in 1766, some of its nobles retained what was called *office et seigneurie*, which gave them jurisdiction, and even the power of life and death, in certain townships and villages.

The Revolution in its earlier stages, before the roughs of Paris learned their power and took the upper hand stimulated by a large foreign anarchic element, was the offspring of a sense of oppression that pervaded the intelligent classes. The nobility, especially the cadets of noble houses, dreaded personal oppression by the crown, — above

HENRI MASERS DE LATUDE.

all, its *lettres de cachet*, distributed with a strange recklessness in all directions; the professional class felt bitterly its exclusion from all careers of honor. No man could rise in life without his quarterings; he might gain wealth, but place, power, and social consideration were denied him. In the army and navy the officers were all nobles, and those who could not exhibit a certain length of pedigree without a flaw were called *officiers bleus* and socially ostracized by their comrades. A desire for "liberty" was in the air. It pervaded all classes, it was stimulated by the *fin du siècle* literature of that day, and, above all, by sympathy with American ideas brought back to France by young French officers who had served under Washington in our War of Independence.

The queen and her court party shook off the fetters of court etiquette for the enjoyment of liberty at the Trianon. Liberty of opinion, liberty of action, freedom from the bonds which shackled every free movement in every man's daily life, was the aspiration of many millions of hearts in France for ten years before the cry arose for reform in the finances, and for the assembling of the States-General. The iron had entered into every man's soul who belonged to the cultivated classes; but the movement did not affect the peasantry until the desire for plunder took possession of them, and in Central France they burned the châteaux of their lords.

What the terrors of the Bastille were we may learn from the narrative of Latude; what the Revolution effected for the peasantry has been told by MM. Erckmann and Chatrian, who wrote down their narrations from the lips of ancient actors in these stories;[1] and how Paris and Versailles on the verge of the Revolution looked to the gay, the young, and the careless, we may read in the narrative of two young

[1] There is no better picture of the Revolution and peasant life before the Revolution than may be found in George Sand's charming story of Nanon; of which the "Christian Union" said, when a translation of it appeared in 1886, published by Messrs. Roberts, that "it was like the Pastoral Symphony in prose." — E. W. L.

men of the middle class who came up to the capital on a frolic on the eve of the outburst of the great volcano.

I have added a paper, also translated from the "Supplément Littéraire du Figaro," in which a modern reporter feigns to give us his impressions of Paris and court life at the same date.

IMPRISONMENTS AND ESCAPES OF LATUDE.[1]

Henri Masers de Latude was born March 23, 1725, near Montagnac in Languedoc, in a castle belonging to his father, the Marquis de Latude, Knight of the order of St. Louis, Lieutenant-Colonel of the dragoons of Orleans, and at the time of his death (which took place during his son's imprisonment) the king's lieutenant at Sedan.

Henri de Latude, a younger son, and by a second marriage, was well educated with a view to his becoming an officer and a courtier; but from some slight hints in his story, we judge that he made more enemies than friends at Montagnac in his early years.

A taste he had for mathematics led his father to get him an appointment as a supernumerary officer in the Engineers, under an old friend of the family, then serving at Bergen-op-Zoom; but the peace of 1748 cut short his military career, and he repaired to Paris to push his way in life, and to improve his education.

At that time Jeanne Antoinette Poisson, Marquise de Pompadour, had reigned about three years over Louis XV., over France, and almost over Europe. She had resented Frederick the Great's refusal to receive her compliments through M. de Voltaire, by a declaration of war, and had forced the Empress Maria Theresa, staid wife and good mother, to address her as "my cousin." Her reign lasted in France for nineteen years. Latude, with all his wrongs, has painted her in no darker colors than history. The woman was possibly no worse than her generation, but on her was visited the nation's sense of oppressions, evils, and

[1] By Mrs. E. W. Latimer. Published in "Littell's Living Age," Feb. 17, 1883.

abuses; and this exasperation, before the century was out, was to culminate in the Revolution.

The difficulty of approaching this lady, who was the fountain of all favor, both in camp and court, seems to have inspired more than one young simpleton with projects as dishonorable, ill advised, and ill laid as one conceived and carried out by Latude. He addressed a package to Madame de Pompadour into which he put a powder perfectly harmless. Then he hastened to Versailles, and requested an audience. Having procured it, he informed her that in the garden of the Tuileries he had overheard a project formed by two men to poison her; that he had followed them to the general post-office, where they had deposited a letter; this letter he believed to be for her, and to contain a subtle poison.

Madame de Pompadour expressed the utmost gratitude for his zeal, and offered him upon the spot a purse of gold, which he declined, saying he only aspired to her patronage and protection. Madame de Pompadour, however, was a shrewd woman. She made him write down his address, which he did, without reflecting that on the envelope of his package he had not disguised his handwriting. He therefore returned to his own lodging exulting in the success of his *ruse*, and dreaming of future advancement in the court and army.

Madame de Pompadour at once obtained her letter from the post-office, and tried the effect of the powder it contained on several animals. As these were none the worse for taking it, she compared the handwriting on the cover with Latude's. He was detected at once, and forthwith was waited upon by an agent of police, who hurried him into a *voiture de place*, and set him down about eight o'clock in the evening of April 27, 1749, in the courtyard of the Bastille. He was taken into the Chamber of Council, and there found the prison authorities awaiting his arrival. Here they stripped him and took from him all his money, papers, and valuables. His clothes were retained for further search, and he received in exchange some miserable rags, which, as he phrases it, "had been watered by the tears of other unfortunate prisoners." This ceremony was at the Bastille called *faire l'entrée d'un prisonnier*. They then made him write his name, and the date of his arrival, in the prison register, after which they conducted him to a room in one of the towers, into which they locked him.

Berryer, the lieutenant (or, as we should say, the minister) of police, was sent next morning to interrogate him. When Latude had told him exactly what he had done and the motives that prompted him, Berryer replied that he saw nothing in his action but a piece of youthful folly. He promised to intercede with the Marquise de Pompadour, and did so; but the incensed favorite could not be brought to consider the offence "a young man's indiscretion," and emphasized her intention to keep him in strict and solitary confinement. M. Berryer, however, ordered that he should have every indulgence, and even the society of an English spy, a Jew named Joseph Abuzaglo, betrayed by the opening of his letters in the post-office. But these companions in misfortune only increased each other's despair.

Abuzaglo had a wife and children, ignorant of his fate, with whom he was denied any communication whatever. He had, however, a supposed patron in the Prince de Conti, who he expected would exert himself in his behalf; and he and Latude made mutual promises that whoever was first released should spare no pains to procure the liberation of the other. These vows must have been overheard by their jailers. One morning, about four months after Latude's arrest, three turnkeys entered their chamber, one of whom informed Latude that the order for his liberation from the Bastille had come. He took an affecting leave of Abuzaglo, promising to remember their agreement; but no sooner was he outside the double door of his late dungeon than he was informed that they were going to remove him to Vincennes.

Abuzaglo a short time after regained his liberty; but, believing Latude to be already free, and outraged by his total inattention to his promises, he took no steps in his behalf.

Latude, in his new prison, fell dangerously ill. Kind

M. Berryer still watched over him. He assigned him the most comfortable apartment in the castle of Vincennes, with a window that commanded a superb view of the surrounding country. It was now that the ardent, scheming spirit of Latude began first to conceive the idea of an escape. A poor old priest had been confined in the castle many years, on a charge of Jansenism. He was permitted to teach the children of one of the turnkeys, and to receive frequent visits from an old friend, the Abbé de St. Sauveur. For two hours every day Latude was allowed to take exercise in the garden of the castle, always attended by two turnkeys. Sometimes the elder turnkey waited in the garden while the younger went upstairs to unlock the prisoner's door. Latude began by making a practice of running downstairs in advance of his attendant, who always found him conversing with his fellow-turnkey within the garden door.

One evening the bolts were hardly withdrawn when Latude rushed downstairs, closed the outside door, and fastened it upon the younger man. How he settled with the elder he does not tell. After that he had to pass four sentinels. The first was at a gate which led out of the garden, which was always closed. He hurried towards it, calling out eagerly, "Where is the Abbé St. Sauveur? The old priest has been waiting for him two hours in the garden!" Thus speaking, he passed the sentinel. At the end of a covered passage he found another gate, and asked the sentry who guarded it where the Abbé St. Sauveur was. He replied he had not seen him, and Latude hurried on. The same *ruse* was successful at the other two posts. Latude was free, after twelve long months of captivity, — four in the Bastille and eight at Vincennes.

He hurried to Paris across country, and shut himself up in furnished lodgings. Will it be believed that the man who had planned and executed so audacious an escape could think of no better mode of retaining his liberty than to draw up a memorial to the king, "speaking of Madame de Pompadour with respect," and expressing regret for his past conduct? He ended by giving his address in Paris; and then, having intrusted this document to one of the physicians of the court, he waited impatiently for an answer.

Throughout the narrative we are struck by the extreme ignorance or indifference of this young man of quality respecting the outside world. To him France, or rather Paris and Versailles, seem to have contained the whole human family, — or at least all that portion of it with which alone it was possible for a man of his position to hold civilized intercourse.

In a few days his retreat was visited by another agent of police, who reconducted him to the Bastille. In spite of the good offices of M. Berryer, in spite of the promise made him on his arrest that he should be set at liberty if he would reveal the exact manner of his escape, he now changed his former comforts for a dungeon. This place was lighted by a loophole which admitted some faint rays of light, and M. Berryer ordered him to be supplied with books and writing materials. This indulgence proved his ruin. Hotheaded and imprudent, he could not refrain from writing on the margin of one of the volumes furnished him a coarse squib upon his persecutress, such as few women of her condition could have been expected to forgive: —

> "Unblessed with talents, unadorned with charms,
> Nor fresh nor fair, a wanton can allure
> In France the highest lover to her arms.
> As proof of this, behold the Pompadour!"[1]

Latude was not aware that every book was carefully examined after it had been in the hands of a prisoner. His wretched verses were no sooner found than they were pointed out to the governor, who forthwith carried them in person to Madame de Pompadour.

> "Hell hath no fury like a woman scorned."

In her first paroxysm of rage she sent for M. Berryer.

[1] "Sans esprit, et sans agréments,
Sans être ni belle ni neuve,
En France on peut avoir le premier des amants;
La Pompadour en est la preuve."

"See!" she cried, stammering in her excitement; "learn to know your *protégé*, and dare again to solicit my clemency!"

For eighteen months after this the compassionate Berryer left poor Latude unsolaced in his dungeon; at the end of that time he had him removed to a more comfortable apartment, and offered him the companionship of a servant if he could procure one to share his captivity. Persons confined under a *lettre de cachet* could sometimes obtain this favor on condition that the servant should share the imprisonment of his master until the death or pardon of his principal released him from his obligation.

Pierre Cochar, the young man whom the family of Latude succeeded in inducing to share the solitude of their kinsman, soon broke down under the horrors of captivity. He pined, he bewailed his engagement, and at last fell ill. In vain his master implored his release from prison. He was only carried from the cell when in his dying agony.

The three months of imprisonment which killed Cochar were the three least intolerable months in a captivity of thirty-five years suffered by his unhappy master. M. Berryer, unwearied in his kindness, next procured him the society of another prisoner, young, enthusiastic, talented, and full of spirit, who had already languished three years in the Bastille under a *lettre de cachet*. He had written to Madame de Pompadour, "pointing out the odium in which she was held by the public, and tendering advice as to how she might recover the good opinion of the nation while retaining the confidence of the king."

This young man was named D'Alègre; and towards him, as towards Latude, Madame de Pompadour had sworn undying vengeance. Penetrated with the conviction that only her death or her disgrace could end their misery, Latude was maddened into energy, D'Alègre reduced to despair. The former planned, and both together executed, the most daring escape known in prison annals. It was out of the question to attempt to get out of the Bastille by its gates. "There remained," says Latude, "no other way but by the air." In their chamber was a chimney, the flue of which came out at the top of the tower; but, like all those in the Bastille, it was filled with iron gratings, the bars of which were hardly far enough apart to let the smoke pass upward. From the top of this chimney to the ground was a descent of two hundred feet. The *ground*, however, was a deep moat, commanded on its other side by a very high wall.

The two prisoners had no means of communicating with the world outside their prison. They had no implements, and no materials; only their bare hands, their education, and their manhood.

The first thing to be done was to get to the top of the chimney; or, to speak more correctly, they had to begin by discovering a place of concealment for any tools and materials they might find means to secure. Latude came to the conclusion that there must be a space between their floor and the ceiling of the chamber beneath them. In order to make sure of this he made use of an ingenious stratagem.

There was a chapel attached to the Bastille in which four little closets were arranged for any prisoners permitted to attend mass. This was a great favor, but it was enjoyed, thanks to M. Berryer, by our young men, and by the prisoner in No. 3, the room beneath theirs. Latude got D'Alègre to drop his toothpick case while going up the stairs, near the door of No. 3; to let it roll downstairs, and ask the turnkey to pick it up for him. While the man (who was still living in 1790) was so engaged, Latude contrived to get a hurried peep into the chamber. He measured it with his eye, and thought its height about ten (French) feet and a half. He then measured one step of the stairs and counted thirty-two of them up to their own apartment. This convinced him that there must be a considerable space between the ceiling of No. 3 and the floor of the room he and D'Alègre occupied.

As soon as he and his companion were shut into their own chamber, he threw himself on his friend's neck, exclaiming in a transport of delight, "We are saved!" D'Alègre naturally objected that they had no tools, and no materials. "Yes!" cried Latude, "in my trunk there are at least a thousand feet of rope!" In Languedoc, as still in Germany and in some parts of Scotland, the domestic life of woman-kind was simplified in those days by the practice of having the family washing done about three times a year. This necessitated enormous supplies of linen. Latude had been permitted to have his wardrobe sent him. He had thirteen dozen and a half of linen shirts, and towels, stockings, and night-caps in proportion. Part of this linen he had bought cheap from French soldiers after the plunder of Bergen-op-Zoom.

They had a folding table with two iron hooks, which fastened it to the wall. They managed to sharpen these hooks, and in two hours more had whetted part of the steel of their tinder-box until it made a sort of knife, which enabled them to fix handles to the hooks, which were to be used to get the gratings out of the chimney. Their first work, however, was to raise some tiles from the floor of their room, when, after digging about six hours, they ascertained that there was indeed a space of about four feet between their floor and the ceiling below them. They then replaced the tiles and proceeded to draw out the threads of their shirts, one by one. These were knotted together, and wound into two large balls, each of which was composed of fifty strands sixty feet long. Of these they next twisted a rope about fifty-five feet in length, with which they contrived a rope-ladder of twenty feet, intended to assist their work in the chimney.

For six months they labored to remove the iron gratings. An hour at a time was all each man could endure at this arduous employment, and they never came down without their hands and legs being covered with blood. The iron bars were set in exceedingly hard mortar, which they had no means of softening but by blowing water on it from their mouths, and it took a whole night to work away the eighth of an inch. When a bar was taken out they reset it loosely in its place again. Next they went to work on a ladder of wood, on which they intended to mount from the moat to the top of the wall, and thence to descend into the garden of the governor. It was from twenty to twenty-five feet long, and must have cost incredible labor. They next found that they would want blocks and pulleys, which could not be made without a saw. This saw they contrived out of their iron candlestick, and the remainder of the steel in their tinder-box. With their rude knife, their saw, and the iron hooks, they chopped and fashioned the firewood doled out to them. Their ladder had one upright, through which holes were pierced for the rungs. It was constructed in three pieces, mortised and fitted so that they could be put together at any moment. Each hole had its rung, and two wedges to keep it steady attached to it by a pack-thread. The upright was three inches in diameter, and the rungs projected about a foot on either side.

As each piece was finished, it was carefully laid away under the floor. They also made a pair of dividers, a square, and a carpenter's rule.

The prisoners were liable to domiciliary visits, though none were ever made them after dark. They therefore worked during the night, and had to be careful not to leave a chip or shaving to betray them. For fear they should be overheard when speaking of their project, they invented names for all their tools, and signs to put each other on their guard when threatened by any danger.

Their principal rope-ladder, which was to let them down from the roof of the Bastille to the moat, was one hundred and eighty feet long. When the Bastille was captured in 1789, it was found in the museum of the place, among the curiosities of the prison.

The roof of the Bastille, after they should have descended twenty feet from the tower in which they were confined, projected about four feet over the main building, and in order to keep the person steady who should be descending the rope-ladder, they made a second rope, three hundred and sixty feet long, which was to be reeved through a block for the fugitive to hold on by.

They continued to manufacture smaller ropes for various purposes, until they had almost fourteen hundred feet of rope, and two hundred and eight wooden rounds for their two ladders. These rounds were muffled by strips of their clothing.

Presuming them to have reached the moat, the next question was how to cross the wall, which was at all times lined with sentinels. They dared not risk the darkness of a rainy night, and were afraid of the torches carried by the Grand Round. They resolved, if necessary, to undermine the wall which stood between the moat of the Bastille and the Fosse of the Porte St. Antoine. For this purpose they needed an auger, and made it out of one of their bed-screws.

The day fixed for their escape was Wednesday, Feb. 5, 1756, seven years after the first imprisonment of Latude. They packed up a portmanteau, containing for each of them a change of clothes, and provided themselves with a bottle of cordial. In the afternoon they risked putting together their great rope-ladder. Happily no one looked in upon them, and they hid it under a bed. The gratings were already out in the chimney.

After supper their turnkey locked them in for the night, and the moment of escape had arrived. Latude was the first to climb the chimney. He had rheumatism in his arm, but was conscious of no pain under the influence of excitement. Choked by soot, and with his knees and arms excoriated, he reached the open air, and sent down a ball of twine to D'Alègre, who tied it to the end of a rope, to which was fastened their portmanteau. In this way they hauled up their various stores. D'Alègre came up last on the loose end of the rope-ladder. On looking over the roof of the Bastille they decided to descend from the foot of another tower, the Tour de Tresson, where they perceived a gun-carriage to which they could fasten the rope-ladder, and their block with the guide-line. Latude, with this line fastened to his body, went gently down the ladder, watched breathlessly by his companion. Notwithstanding all precautions, he swung fearfully. The remembrance of it, forty-five years after, made him, he says, shudder. At last he landed safely in the moat. D'Alègre lowered the portmanteau and other articles, for which a dry spot on the bank was luckily found. When these things were all down he descended, and found Latude up to his waist in water.

It was with much regret that they left their ropes behind them. Latude recovered them thirty-three years after, July 16, 1789, and they were publicly exhibited during the excitement that succeeded the destruction of the Bastille. It did not rain, and they heard the sentry treading his rounds about twelve yards from them, so that there was no hope of crossing the wall, for which they had prepared their wooden ladder. The alternative was to pierce it. The water was very cold, and there was floating ice upon its surface. They chose the deepest part of the moat, and for nine hours worked in water up to their arm-pits, diving when alarmed by the torches of the Grand Round.

At last through a wall four and a half feet thick, they made a hole wide enough to admit their bodies. They scrambled through into the Fosse St. Antoine, got out of this, and were rejoicing in their safety, when they fell into another drain whose situation had been unknown to them. It was only two yards wide, but it was very deep, and at the bottom were two feet of slime and mud. Latude fell in first, and D'Alègre on top of him. Vigorously exerting himself, however, Latude scrambled out, and dragged up his companion by the hair. As the clocks of Paris were striking five in the morning, they found themselves upon the highway.

Their first impulse was to embrace each other, their next to fall down on their knees and to return thanks to the Almighty. They then proceeded to change their clothes, but they were so exhausted that neither could have dressed himself without the assistance of the other.

Getting next into a hackney-coach, they were driven to the residence of M. Silhouette, chancellor to the Duc d'Orléans. He was away from home. They then took refuge with a tailor of Languedoc.

Here they remained concealed for nearly a month, while a search was set on foot for them in all directions. D'Alègre left first, disguised as a peasant, and went to Brussels (then the capital of the Austrian Netherlands), sending word back to Latude that he was safe, by some secret sign arranged between them.

Provided with false papers through the help of the good tailor, and the documents of an old lawsuit, Latude set out upon his journey to Brussels. He walked some leagues out of Paris and let the diligence to Valenciennes pick him up upon the high-road. The story that he told was that he was a servant going to Amsterdam to carry his master's brother some important papers. He met with several small adventures on his journey, and committed some acts of imprudence; for example, on passing the boundary between France and Austria (a wooden post, painted with lilies on one side and an imperial eagle on the other) he fell upon his face and kissed the dust, to the amazement of his fellow-travellers. Eleven years before he had passed part of a winter in Brussels; he was therefore well acquainted with its localities. On inquiring for his friend at the Hôtel de Coffi, in the Place de l'Hôtel de Ville, where he had planned to meet D'Alègre, he became convinced, from the hesitation and prevarication of the landlord, that evil had befallen his comrade. He therefore resolved to start at once for Antwerp. He was dressed like a servant, and travelled like one. In the canal-boat in which he took his passage, he found a chatty young Savoyard chimney-sweep and his wife, who related to him, as news of the day, the details of his own escape, and ended by informing him, that one of the two fugitives had been arrested a few days before, by the high provost of Brussels, who had sent him at once over the French frontier in charge of a French police officer. The Savoyard added that this story had been told him by the servant of an official who had charged him to keep the matter close, as they were anxious to secure the arrest of the other party. Greatly alarmed at what he heard, and full of solicitude for poor D'Alègre, Latude determined to break off from the Savoyard, and left him at the first stopping place, under pretence that he had taken the wrong boat for Bergen-op-Zoom. He pushed on alone on foot until he reached the Dutch frontier, quaking at every footstep; for the fate of D'Alègre proved that the Austrian Netherlands were no safe asylum.

He had had seven louis d'or (thirty-five dollars) when he left Paris, and this little sum was now exhausted. While trying to relieve his hunger on a canal-boat by some black bread and a salad of grass, he excited the compassion of Jan Seerhorst, who kept a sort of tavern in Amsterdam. This man took him under his protection and promised to introduce him to a Frenchman, who proved, however, to be from Picardy, and acknowledged little fellowship with a native of Languedoc; but Seerhorst, seeing the disappointment of Latude, took him to his own abode, where he slept with five other persons in a cellar.

Chance next threw our escaped prisoner in the way of a native of the same town as himself, named Louis Clergue, who gave him clothes, linen, and a comfortable chamber. On learning his story, he expressed great alarm lest the same power that had arrested D'Alègre in the Austrian Netherlands should extend to Holland. He proposed to get Latude a passport to Surinam, but the young man, made confident by the opinion of Clergue's friends that the States-General would never betray an unfortunate fugitive, decided to remain in Amsterdam.

The French ambassador at the Hague was already negotiating for his arrest. Among the records of the Bastille were found proofs that it cost the French Government upwards of forty thousand dollars to effect his recapture. Part of this money is supposed to have been spent in bribery.

June 1, 1756, as Latude went to a bank to receive a letter and remittance from his father, he was arrested in broad daylight, and dragged through the streets of Amsterdam with violence and blows, like a notorious criminal.

In vain Louis Clergue and his friends protested against the outrage. Latude was closely confined, and permission had been obtained from the Archduke Charles, the representative of Maria Theresa, to take him through Austrian territory. When this arrived, with a belt around his body to which his arms were pinioned, Latude began his journey under charge of Saint-Marc, a French agent of police who had arrested him.

Travelling with all kinds of tortures and indignities, Latude arrived at Lille. There he was fastened for the night to a deserter of nineteen, who was to be hanged next day, and who proposed that they should strangle each other. The next evening he reached the Bastille. Here Saint-Marc received a sort of ovation, and Latude was committed to a dungeon under charge of his former jailers, who had suffered three months' imprisonment for his escape.

In this dungeon, desperate and hopeless as his situation was, he still found something to cheer and occupy him. He made friends with the rats, numbers of which came hunting for food and lodging in his straw. The dungeons in the Bastille were octagonal. The one in which he was confined had loopholes eighteen inches wide on the interior, reduced to three inches by the time they reached the outer wall. There was no furniture in the dungeon, and the sills of the loopholes served for seat and table. Latude often rested his chained arms upon these slabs to lighten the weight of his fetters.

One day while in this attitude a rat approached him. He threw it a bit of bread. The rat ate it eagerly, and when his appetite was satisfied carried off a crust into his hole. The next day he came again, and was rewarded by more bread and a bit of bacon. The third day he would take food from Latude's hand. After this he took up his quarters in a hole in the wall near the window, and after sleeping in it two nights, brought to it a female companion. Sometimes she quarrelled with her mate over their food, and generally had the best of it, retiring to her sleeping place with the disputed morsel. On such occasions the old rat would seek refuge with Latude, and devour out of his mate's reach whatever was given him, with an air of bravado.

Soon, whenever dinner was brought in, Latude called his

family. The male rat would come immediately, the female more timidly. Soon appeared a third rat, very familiar and sociable, who no sooner felt at home than he proceeded to introduce seven others. At the end of a fortnight the family consisted of ten large rats, and subsequently of their progeny. They would eat off a plate that their human friend provided for them, and liked to have their necks scratched, but he was never suffered to touch one on the back. He gave them all names to which they learned to answer, and taught them tricks of various kinds. One of them, a female, was a remarkable jumper, and very proud of her accomplishment.

For two years Latude solaced his captivity by this strange society. One day he found a bit of elder in his cell, brought in in some fresh straw; and although his hands were manacled, he contrived, by the help of a buckle from his small-clothes, to fashion it into a flageolet. His attachment to this instrument was such that he never parted with it during his lifetime.

At last he bethought him of the advantage it would be to the French army if its sergeants as well as privates carried fire-arms, instead of the old-fashioned halberd, half pike, half battle-axe. He proposed to recommend this improvement to the king, hoping thus to direct his attention to himself. He was no longer allowed pen and paper. He had therefore to invent substitutes. His paper was made out of tablets of moistened bread, his pen was a sharp fish-bone, and his ink his blood.

When he had finished his memorial, he obtained permission to see Father Griffet, the confessor of the Bastille. From him he obtained writing materials, and in April, 1758, the memorial was presented to Louis XV.

The plan, being found beneficial to the service (as it increased the effective force by twenty thousand men), was carried out; but no notice was taken of Latude.

Three months passed, and he ventured on a new suggestion. This was to add a cent and a half to the postage of every letter, and use the proceeds as a fund to pension the widows of officers and soldiers killed in battle. This likewise was adopted, so far as the increased postage went; but the prisoner was still disregarded.

Among the papers found in the Bastille when it was sacked in 1789, was a letter from an oculist, Dr. Dejean, ordered about this time to examine Latude's eyes. Each prisoner *au secret* had a prison name; that of Latude was Daury.

MONSIEUR, — In compliance with your wishes I have several times visited the prisoner Daury in the Bastille. Having carefully examined his eyes, and reflected on all he has communicated, I am not surprised that his sight has almost entirely failed. For many years he has been deprived of sun and air; he has been chained hand and foot in a cell for forty months. . . . The winter of 1756–57 was extremely severe; the Seine was frozen over, as in the year preceding. During this period the prisoner was confined in a dungeon with irons on his hands and feet, and no bed but a truss of straw, without covering. In his cell there are two loopholes, five inches wide, and about five feet long, with neither panes of glass nor shutters to close them. Throughout the day and night his face is exposed to the cold and wind, and there is nothing so destructive to the sight as frosty air, — especially during sleep. A continual running at the nose has split his upper lip until the teeth are exposed; the intense cold has decayed them, and the roots of his mustachios have likewise perished. (The walls of the Bastille are from nine to ten feet thick, consequently the chambers are extremely damp.) This prisoner, unable to endure his situation, resolved to commit suicide. With this object he remained one hundred and thirty-three hours without eating or drinking. They forced open his mouth with keys, and compelled him to swallow food by main force. Seeing himself restored to life against his will, he contrived to secrete a piece of broken glass, with which he opened four principal veins. During the night his blood flowed incessantly, and there remained scarcely six ounces in his body. He continued many days in a state of insensibility. . . . He is no longer a young man, and has passed the meridian of life, being forty-two years old, and has gone through very severe trials. For fifteen years he has been a constant prisoner, and during seven of them entirely deprived of fire, light, and sun. . . . I have considered it my duty to be thus minute in my report, as it is useless to waste the public money in paying me for my visits or remedies. Nothing but the termination of his sufferings, with fresh air and exercise, can preserve to the prisoner the feeble remnant of his eyesight. Air will strengthen every part of his frame, and exercise will disperse the humors in his head, which at present bring on the convulsive fits he is subject to, — fits which will ultimately extinguish the powers of vision.

(Signed) DEJEAN.

This heart-rending letter produced no effect. It needed an overflow of the Seine, which put the floor of the dungeon under water, and wet the feet of the turnkeys who brought him food, to procure any alleviation.

The room into which he was next moved had a view of the open sky, and was much less damp and miserable. He was separated, however, from his rats, which he regretted bitterly until he contrived to tame two beautiful white pigeons, which he caught from his loophole with a noose. His delight when the pigeons built their nest, and hatched their brood inside his cell, amounted to ecstasy. All the officers of the Bastille came to look at them. But, alas! the turnkey (one of those who had suffered punishment some years before for his escape) resolved to deprive him of his pets, or to make him pay dear for the privilege of keeping them. He already received one bottle of wine in seven of the prisoner's allowance. He now demanded four; and when this was refused, he pretended an order from the governor to kill the pigeons. Latude's despair drove him to sudden madness. The turnkey made a movement towards the birds. Latude sprang forward, and with his own hands destroyed them. "This was probably," he says, "the most unhappy moment of my whole existence. I never recall the memory of it without the bitterest pangs. I remained several days without taking nourishment. Grief and indignation divided my soul."

Not long after this a change came in his condition. A new governor, the Comte de Jumilhac, came to the Bastille. He was a man of generosity and mercy, and took pity on

Latude, whom he permitted to walk every day two hours on the roof. He also procured him an interview with M. de Sartine, lieutenant of police, who had succeeded M. Berryer. From this time forth for twenty years Latude's existence was one long struggle with De Sartine.

Encouraged by the interest which at first he believed himself to have inspired in the new minister, he made two new plans for the good of the public: one for the better regulation of the currency, subsequently adopted, with little benefit to France, by the National Assembly; the other a plan for the establishment of national granaries, the expenses of which were to be met by a tax on marriage.

This plan was considered so important that De Sartine wished to adopt it as his own, and offered his prisoner an annuity of three hundred dollars to give it up, promising his influence to procure his liberation. "I would not part with my plan for fifty thousand crowns down!" cried Latude, vehemently.

"If I were in your place," said the *aide majeur* of the Bastille, deputed to conduct the negotiation, "I should think myself too happy to receive the proposal."

"No doubt you would — if I were *you!*" replied the prisoner, with a sneer. He thus made himself two powerful enemies; and Father Griffet prophesied the truth when he told him, "Your refusal, and more particularly the manner in which you made it, will incense M. de Sartine against you, and I fear he will give you reason to repent."

The food of the Bastille seems to have been sufficient, though Latude complained bitterly about the cooking. It ought to have been far better than it was, for the king paid from a dollar and a quarter to two dollars a day for the subsistence of each prisoner.

Whilst walking on the roof of the Bastille, Latude heard from a soldier who had served under his father, that the old man was dead. This cut off his supplies of money. From that time his relations took little notice of him, with the exception of his mother, who must have been a second wife, as she speaks of him as her only son, while he tells us that his elder brother, the Comte de Vissac, succeeded to the title of Marquis de Latude.

Here is a letter that the poor mother addressed to the Marquise de Pompadour. She was occasionally permitted to send a letter to her son: —

"My son, madame, has long groaned in the dungeons of the Bastille for having had the misfortune to offend you. My grief surpasses his. Day and night his sad fate torments my imagination. I share all the agony of his sufferings without having participated in his fault. What do I say? Alas! I know not how he has displeased you. He was young, and had been led astray by others. How differently must he reason now! The reflections of a prisoner are very opposite to the vain thoughts of unbridled youth. If he, madame, is unworthy of your pardon, extend your indulgence to me in his stead; feel for my situation; have compassion on an afflicted mother; let your heart be softened by my tears. Death will soon close my eyes. Do not wait till I am in my grave to show compassion to my son. He is my only child, the sole shoot of the stock, the last scion of my family, the only prop of my old age. Restore him to me, madame, you who are so kind-hearted (*si bonne*). Do not refuse me my son, madame; give him up to my affliction; restore him to my entreaties, my sighs, my tears."

Latude's next attempt was to throw a package from the roof of the Bastille to some one who would pick it up and forward it to its destination. Having made himself as obnoxious as possible to the *aide majeur* and two sergeants deputed to watch him in his walk, he was left to himself while they conversed together; and he contrived to establish a correspondence by signs with two young workwomen, whom he observed at an upper window in a neighboring street. After some time he made them understand that he would throw them a package.

This package the arrogant, exasperated, imprudent young man filled with a memorial addressed to a literary man named La Beaumelle, containing a secret history of Madame de Pompadour's early life, abounding in scandals. "I steeped my pen in the gall with which my whole heart and

MME. DE POMPADOUR.

soul were overflowing," he says. He wrote upon a shirt, with a pen which, in anticipation of our pens of the present day, he fashioned out of a copper coin. But ink was wanting. For eight years he had never been allowed fire or candle. He affected toothache, got one of his guards to let him have a whiff or two of his pipe, and having let it go out begged for his tinder-box to light it again. In this way he obtained and secreted a bit of tinder. Next he pretended to be taken with violent pains, and the doctor ordered him some oil. This he put in a pomatum pot with a wick made of threads drawn from his linen. By friction he obtained a spark which set fire to his tinder. It enabled him to light his lamp, and he was in an ecstasy of triumph and happiness. With this lamp and an old plate, he got lamp-black, which he mixed with some syrup prescribed for him by the doctor, and then proceeded to pen his memorial to his own destruction.

Sept. 21, 1763, he flung his package. Mademoiselle Lebrun picked it up as he intended, and he waited the result. Nothing came of it, however, until April 18, 1764, when the sisters held up a placard at their window : "*The Marchioness de Pompadour died yesterday.*" Wild with delight and hope, he wrote on the instant (having in the interval been permitted to receive writing materials) to demand his liberation from M. de Sartine. Every official in the Bastille had been charged not to communicate the news of Madame de Pompadour's death to the prisoners. The lieutenant of police was therefore amazed on the receipt of this letter. He sent for Latude, and told him that his liberation depended upon his divulging the channel through which the news had reached him. Latude broke into violent language, little calculated to advance his interests. In vain he subsequently offered De Sartine the project about the granaries ; the personal enmity of Madame de Pompadour had passed into the body of the minister, and a few months later Latude further exasperated De Sartine by writing him another abusive and indignant letter. In consequence of this, he was removed to Vincennes with especial orders to the governor to keep him safe, and to put him in an *oubliette.* Here he was taken very ill, and the good governor, M. Guyonnet, took pity upon him. He gave him a better chamber and allowed him to walk, attended by three guards, in the garden of the castle. The result of this last indulgence was that Latude made his escape in a dense fog. "Seize him! seize him!" was shouted all over the grounds of the castle. "Seize him!" cried Latude, running ahead of the others, until he reached the sentry at the gate, whom he threw down, and jumped over as the man was gaping with surprise.

Latude took refuge close to the Bastille with the Lebrun sisters. They were daughters of a hair-dresser, and were poor, but very good to him. They had, however, mismanaged his memorial. His scheme had been to place it in safe hands, while he threatened Madame de Pompadour with its circulation. The first thing he did in the Lebrun house was to write a letter of repentance and submission to M. de Sartine.

What effect this appeal may have produced cannot be known. Its answer miscarried; and Latude, more angry than ever at finding no notice taken of what he wrote, threw himself at the feet of the Prince de Conti.

A reward of one thousand crowns was this time offered for his return to prison. All channels of communication with the court appeared to be closed. He, however, contrived in the middle of winter, weary, torn, famished, and looking like a lunatic, to reach Fontainebleau, and there requested an audience with the good Duc de Choiseul, the prime minister. The duke, influenced, as Latude maintains, by M. de Sartine, believed him to be out of his senses, and returned him into the power of the police, who restored him to Vincennes, where he was immured in a more frightful dungeon than any he had yet inhabited. It had four iron-plate doors, each one foot from the other, and no other opening whatever. It was six and one half feet long by five and three quarters wide, just long enough to lie down in. Here, to increase his sufferings, he was informed that Viel-Castel, the sergeant from whom he had escaped, had been hanged. Months after, a compassionate sentinel, moved by his grief at the supposed fate of the poor fellow, assured him that it was a falsehood.

His escape put it out of M. Guyonnet's power to give him any more indulgences. "M. de Sartine," he said to his prisoner, "lays the blame of your escape on me. He is furious at it. Your case is hopeless. From henceforward I can only pity you." Here is a letter from him, however, at this period, found among the records of the Bastille.

To M. de Sartine.

MONSIEUR, — I have this morning visited the prisoner Daury. I found him given up to despair as usual, but always submissive, and entirely disposed to agree with any conditions you may prescribe as the price of his liberty. I am sorry to add that grief has destroyed his appetite, but he still retains his mental faculties. Heaven grant this may continue! I have the honor to be, etc., etc.

About this time three of the police were sent by M. de Sartine to say: "You can by one word obtain your liberty. Give M. de Sartine the name and the address of the person who has possession of your papers. He pledges his word of honor no evil shall be practised towards him." Latude replied: "I entered this dungeon an honest man; I will die rather than leave it a knave and a coward."

After this, in frightful darkness, for in the *oubliette* he could distinguish neither night nor day, his sufferings would have reached their close, had not a compassionate turnkey brought the prison doctor to visit him, who insisted he must be moved at once to a better room. The reply was that M. de Sartine had expressly forbidden it. The doctor, however, insisted, and the removal was accomplished. By degrees his strength returned to him, and he requested pen and ink to write to M. de Sartine. These were judiciously refused him. Probably the officers at Vincennes were afraid lest the lieutenant of police should find out that he was not still in his dungeon.

His next enterprise was to bore a hole with an auger through the wall of the donjon of Vincennes. This he did by means of part of an old sword and an iron hoop from a bucket, which a year before he had picked up and secreted in the garden. This garden he was no longer allowed to walk in, but by a stratagem he succeeded in being double-locked into it for half an hour, and returned to his prison very happy, with the broken sword in the leg of his drawers, and the hoop round his body.

The granite wall was five feet thick. It took Latude twenty-six months, with his imperfect tools, to make his aperture. The hole was long displayed to visitors, and very probably may still be seen. Latude himself showed it to the Prince de Beauvau during the early days of the Revolution. It was made in the shadow of the chimney-piece, and closed by a cork ; a long peg was thrust through it, not quite the length of the hole. If anybody had observed it from without, or sounded it, they would have found it only two inches deep upon the garden side. Latude then fashioned a wooden wand about six feet long. To this he tied a bit of ribbon, and thrusting it through the hole he secured the attention of a prisoner who was walking in the garden. This was a Baron de Venac from Languedoc, confined nineteen years for offering impertinent advice to Madame de Pompadour. There was another prisoner there, arrested on suspicion of having spoken ill of the same infamous woman. There was also an Abbé Prieur, who had conceived the idea of phonetic spelling. He wrote on the subject to Frederick the Great, as one of the patrons of men of literature, "a letter consisting of words of his own composition, and of course they were wholly illegible." According to custom, it was opened at the post-office. Ministers, not being able to comprehend the contents, imagined they beheld hieroglyphics full of treason and danger, and the unfortunate abbé was committed to Vincennes for an offense, adds Latude, "that at most merited a short confinement in a mad-house to teach him to spell." He had been in captivity seven years.

Another prisoner had been arrested at Antwerp on suspicion of being the author of a pamphlet against Madame de

Pompadour, which he had never seen. He had been twe three years in confinement. No evidence had ever been produced against him, nor had he ever been allowed any opportunity of proving his innocence. An old man whose daughter was an inmate of the *Parc aux Cerfs*, was confined on a *lettre de cachet* obtained by that daughter, who dreaded his remonstrances on the infamy of her career.

There were also three other prisoners in close confinement for daring to express the views of honest men upon an infamous monopoly, which towards the end of Louis XV.'s reign almost reduced the kingdom to bankruptcy.

All these prisoners were confined on *lettres de cachet*, which were orders for the arrest and imprisonment of individuals in the king's own handwriting, countersigned by a secretary of state and sealed with the king's seal. Many of these were distributed to important persons, and to heads of noble families, who kept them for their own use, and filled up the space left blank for the prisoner's name with that of some victim of their own selection. No one imprisoned on a *lettre de cachet* could be defended by counsel. *L'ami des hommes*, the father of Mirabeau, is said to have used fifteen of them. When a member of a noble house had done anything to offend its head, or had committed any offense whose exposure would have been painful to other members of his family, he was quietly disposed of by a *lettre de cachet.*

One day in 1774 Latude, in a fit of petulance, declared that he would rather be sent back to his *oubliette*, never to quit it until M. de Sartine sent a lawyer to hear and to advise him, than remain forever disregarded. He was taken at his word, and the next day was removed to the dark and loathsome cell he had once nearly died in. About this time M. de Sartine was made minister of marine, and his place in the police was supplied by his personal friend Lenoir.

Not knowing of this change, and still endeavoring to write to M. de Sartine, Latude on one occasion procured a light by means of several straws tied together, which he thrust out, while his jailer's attention was turned a moment, to a candle that the man had brought into the gallery while handing to the prisoner his daily food. With this Latude instantly lighted a lamp he had prepared in his pomatum pot, and covered it over with a sort of beehive he had constructed with wisps of straw. When it was discovered that he had possessed himself of a light, the turnkeys began to dread him as one who had a familiar demon.

All the pains he took to address M. de Sartine in various strains, vituperative or pathetic, were entirely useless. That minister had long before given orders that no letters from Latude were to be opened, even by his secretary. When the Bastille was destroyed, nearly one hundred of these documents were found with their seals unbroken.

It seems probable that at this period Latude really lost his reason. As he was recovering, having been removed to a better chamber, the door of his cell opened, and the lieutenant of police announced a visit from the prime minister, the good and great M. de Malesherbes. When Latude told him he had been imprisoned twenty-six years, his face expressed the deepest indignation. He told him to take heart, supplied him with money, and took him under his protection. But De Sartine, as Latude always suspected, did all that fear and vengeance could suggest to prevent his liberation. He informed M. de Malesherbes that Latude was a confirmed lunatic, and he was in consequence removed to the hospital for insane prisoners at Charenton.

He went to this place with the new name of Le Danger instead of that of Daury, and with an especial recommendation to the brethren who had charge of the insane to treat him with severity. It was not long, however, before he entered into communication with prisoners in the next chamber. These were not lunatics; they were young men of good family but ungovernable dispositions, confined by their relatives on *lettres de cachet.* They led sufficiently comfortable lives, had good food and good society. The chief among them was a young man named Saint-Luc, who took compassion on Latude, and succeeded in interesting the brethren in his *protégé.* Latude became a favorite even among the madmen.

Among these last at Charenton were some who were subject to periodical fits of frenzy. While these lasted they were chained in subterranean dens, or confined in iron cages. When they recovered they were taken back to the other prisoners. One of these men told Latude that in one of the dreadful cages was D'Alègre, his former comrade. His mind had given way after he was restored to the Bastille. He had become a raving maniac, and for ten years had been confined at Charenton. Latude requested permission to visit him. He found a squalid spectre, who replied to all he said to him with curses. In vain Latude tried to recall himself to his remembrance. This was in 1770. D'Alègre was still living in 1790.

Thanks to the good offices of one of the prisoners, confined under a *lettre de cachet* for drawing his sword upon his elder brother, an order for Latude's liberation (July 7, 1777) at last reached him. He set out on the instant for Paris — like a madman — clad in rags, and without a sou in his pocket.

On arriving, he sought out a man from his own village, who told him that the people of that place believed that after his escape to Holland he had embarked for the West Indies, and had perished on the ocean. This man lent him twenty-five louis. With this money he fitted himself out with clothes, and next day visited, as he had been directed to do, the lieutenant of police, M. Lenoir.

The order for his release had been accompanied by directions to repair at once to his native town of Montagnac, which order Latude was determined to evade, if possible.

Lenoir received him kindly enough, and gave him the address of a person charged by his family to provide him with necessaries. He even allowed him to go to Versailles to see the mother of his prison friend. At Versailles, by some means, he obtained an audience with the king (then Louis XVI.), and told his story. What he said on this occasion probably roused the fears and anger of the king's ministers. He was ordered to leave Paris at once, and found himself under the deepest displeasure of Lenoir.

Alarmed at this, he took passage on a flatboat to Auxerre. Three days later he was arrested on the road, and taken back to Paris. There he was thrust into the Bicêtre, — one of the lowest prisons.

At the Bicêtre he was treated as a miscreant and common malefactor, and was associated with wretches chained, like himself, in stalls along a gallery, "as horses are chained in a stable." Latude was now fifty-three years old, and nearly one half of his life had been passed in prisons. In the Bicêtre all Latude's resources failed him. His friends, misled by the representations of the police, imagined he had been guilty of some ignominious crime, and seem to have abandoned him. He was herded with the lowest of his kind, and descended from his place as a gentleman. In vain he protested his innocence, and implored a trial. From that time (1777) for upwards of six years, his autobiography, now a very scarce book, is a monotony of misery. His heart had even turned against the rats. "Those accursed beasts," he calls, in the Bicêtre, the animals who in the Bastille twenty years before had been his friends. He lost even his name, and was known as Father Jedor. He was covered with scorbutic sores, and sent to a hospital, a place still more loathsome than the prison.

At last he was removed to a more comfortable apartment, an alleviation he soon forfeited by trying to interest a visitor (the Princesse de Beaulieu) in his favor.

About this time M. Necker was called to be the king's prime minister, and Madame Necker made a visit of inspection to the prisons. Her account of what she saw caused an eminent man, the President de Gourgue, to visit the prisoners. These men, dregs of rascality though they were, all seem to have felt compassion for Latude. They directed M. de Gourgue to his cell, and even one of the guards rejoiced to see the visitor shedding tears over its inhabitant.

"The worst part of your case," said De Gourgue, "is that you are confined under a *lettre de cachet*. Send me a memorial of your sufferings, and trust to my good offices."

For nine days Latude sold his pittance of black bread to

procure writing-paper. When his memorial was finished, with his last shirt and a pair of silk stockings, he bribed a prison underling to convey it to his protector. The man was drunk, and dropped it in the street.

Happily for Latude, it was picked up by a woman who became his friend and guardian angel. The envelope was wet and stained. The seal was broken. The signature was, "Masers de Latude, a prisoner during thirty-two years at the Bastille, at Vincennes, and at the Bicêtre, where he is confined on bread and water in a dungeon underground."

Having read the record of his sufferings, this good woman, Madame Legros, resolved to effect the liberation of Latude. She copied the paper before she sent it to its destination. Her husband was a private teacher, and she kept a little thread-and-needle store. They had no personal influence, and their resources were very limited. On M. Legros' delivering the package with his own hands to M. de Gourgue, that gentleman told him that he had been greatly affected by the writer's story, and had taken steps on his behalf, but had been informed that for thirty-two years he had been a confirmed lunatic, whose confinement was necessary for his own and others' safety.

Still M. and Madame Legros would not give up the cause of their *protégé*. Madame Legros sought out the chaplain of the Bicêtre, and obtained from him a certificate of the prisoner's sanity. She also went to the prison, where she saw the prisoners who were not *au secret*, and learned that the object of her interest was known amongst them as Father Jedor.

With three louis, a great sum for her, she bribed one of the turnkeys to deliver to Latude a letter and a louis d'or. This was the first he had heard of his benefactress. He replied by imploring her to give up his cause rather than run any risk on his account.

Both husband and wife, having made several copies of the memorial, approached various influential persons in Latude's behalf. M. Lenoir said that Latude was not in the Bicêtre, but was a confirmed lunatic at Charenton. He added that he was accused of no crime, but his release would be dangerous to society. Afterwards he shifted his ground, and declared that, since Latude was imprisoned by the express orders of the king, he should not be justified in disputing the commands of his Majesty.

This announcement alarmed all those whom Madame Legros had already interested in Latude's favor. She, however, would not relax her efforts, and addressed herself to upwards of two hundred persons with varying success.

Next Madame Legros obtained an interview with Latude. She saw him for a few moments as he was conducted through the courtyard to receive a visit from a former chaplain of the Bicêtre, and she was permitted by the humanity of his guards to exchange a few brief sentences with him.

The first dauphin was born Oct. 22, 1781; and Latude, in common with other political prisoners, hoped for deliverance. He appealed, in presence of the king's commissioners of pardon appointed to examine the prisoners of the Bicêtre, to M. Tristan, the governor, as to his behavior during the four years he had been in his custody. M. Tristan confessed that he had never given him cause of complaint.

The Cardinal de Rohan, who was present, seemed much affected by his story, and spoke to the king upon the subject; but Louis, irritated by the result of his former interference, declined to reopen the matter. Meantime the cardinal was beset by Madame Legros, and at last referred her to M. de Saint-Prest, one of the king's ministers. Saint-Prest described her *protégé* as a common thief and an abandoned criminal; and though she complained of this outrage to the cardinal, the affair of the diamond necklace was approaching a crisis, and that poor gentleman needed all his court influence to keep himself out of the Bastille.

Next Madame Legros applied to a celebrated lawyer, the advocate De la Croix. He was barred from carrying the case before any tribunal by the law forbidding lawyers to defend any prisoner confined by *lettre de cachet*, but he took up the case warmly, and interested a certain Madame D. (could it have been De Staël?), wife and daughter of a minister. This lady became as much interested in Madame Legros as in the prisoner; but taking advantage of her position, she came to the Bicêtre, and there heard from Latude's own lips his miserable story.

Not long after this he had an interview with Lenoir, who could find no better evidence of his madness than that a man must have been mad to have attempted an escape from the Bastille.

Next De la Croix interviewed De Sartine and drove him to exposing the real cause of Latude's detention. "If this man should obtain his liberty, he will take refuge in foreign countries, and write against me."

M. de la Croix suggested that if he were released there were persons willing to be held responsible for his good behavior. This remark, after six more months of delays, deceptions, and disappointments, facilitated the desired end. The result was finally due to the exertions of Madame Necker, who refused to divulge to any one how the order for Latude's release was obtained.

In sending the good news to Madame Legros, Madame Necker wrote as follows: —

"The individual through whose powerful influence I have so long and ardently endeavored to attain the object of our mutual solicitude is in some measure apprehensive of the consequences. We fear lest the future conduct of our *protégé*, excited by the remembrance of his wrongs, should lead him into actions which might cause us to repent. I rely on your prudence and management in a matter which really includes the happiness of my life, for, from reasons exclusively personal, I should suffer cruelly if M. de Latude were to excite any just cause of complaint against him after the steps I have taken in his favor and the responsibility I have incurred. Since you have judged it proper to acquaint him with my name, and he has expressed himself fully sensible of the interest I have evinced, I entreat you to require from him, as the only token of his gratitude I shall ever have occasion to exact, his full and unqualified forgiveness of the many injuries he has sustained, and a profound silence on the subject of his enemies. This is the only course by which he can expect happiness, and it is absolutely essential to my tranquillity that he should adopt it. I leave this important matter entirely in your hands, madame, in the fullest confidence, and relying on the sentiments of esteem and attachment with which you have inspired me."

But the pardon was accompanied with a most distasteful condition: Latude was to be exiled to Montagnac, there to reside under the surveillance of the police. Madame Legros earnestly represented that, if separated from herself and her husband by a distance of two hundred leagues, they could not possibly watch over him as they had pledged themselves to do, "and prevent the ebullitions of temper or the natural dictates of long-suppressed indignation."

At last she obtained the necessary papers permitting Latude to reside in Paris, on condition of never appearing in the coffee-houses, or on the public walks, or in any place of public amusement.

March 22, 1784, Latude quitted his prison. He accompanied his good friends to their humble dwelling, where a chamber had been prepared for him. He gazed around him with the rapture of a child, and the ordinary comforts of life seemed luxuries beyond his imagination.

Soon came the kind anonymous lady who had assisted Madame Necker. On quitting Latude she left him a purse of gold and a letter. The latter was full of kindness and good sense, and reiterated the wise counsels before given him.

By degrees a small income was secured by private subscription to enable Madame Legros and her husband to support themselves and the new member of their household. It amounted to about four hundred and fifty dollars. The Monthyon prize for 1784 (that is, the prize given to the poor French person who in the course of the year has performed the most virtuous action) was unanimously awarded by the Academy to Madame Legros, but her receiving it was opposed by the king's ministers.

At the taking of the Bastille in 1789, Latude was in Paris. He does not seem to have been among the attacking party,

MADAME NECKER.

but the next day he was carried over the castle in triumph, and encouraged to take possession of the relics of his escape and the papers relating to his captivity.

In 1790 he published his autobiography, and in the year following brought suit for damages against the heirs of Madame de Pompadour. He succeeded in obtaining a verdict, but probably did not reap much benefit from his success, as he died a poor man in 1805, at the advanced age of eighty-two, after having gone through tortures and privations enough, one would think, to have prematurely destroyed a frame of iron.

As we know, the Revolution began in May, 1789, with the meeting of the States-General. In this body the Commons, soon becoming supreme, formed what is called in history the Constituent Assembly; that is, an assembly to make a constitution. While these things went on at Versailles, Paris was in a ferment, and the ferment was spreading to provincial towns. On Sunday, July 12, excitement was rising to fever heat. Some of the agitators were arrested and imprisoned, but to imprison one was to raise up others. The Palais Royal, with its gardens and arcades under the very windows of the Duc d'Orléans, rang with inflammatory oratory. "To arms!" was the cry But the populace had no arms. Arms were even wanting to the National Guard. The mob broke open prisons; they broke open the arsenal; they plundered the King's Garde Meuble, — the depository of curious things belonging to the crown. In it they found two little silver-mounted cannon, a present to Louis XIV. from the King of Siam. A rumor rose that arms were concealed at the Invalides, and thither the mob marched on Monday, July 13, at five in the morning. Old M. de Sombreuil, governor of the Invalides, had had twenty men at work all night unscrewing the locks of the muskets in his care, amounting to twenty-eight thousand. But in six hours they had only unscrewed twenty locks, their sympathies being with the populace. The mob broke in and seized the muskets, and then from twenty-eight thousand armed men the cry arose, "To the Bastille!" One rather wonders why the Bastille was the object of attack; no men of obscure birth were commonly imprisoned there. It was garrisoned only by eighty-two old Invalides and thirty-two young Swiss soldiers. However, it had cannon and ammunition; its guns could fire upon Paris, and it was a sort of landmark of the Old Régime. Its destruction would be an object lesson to tyranny.

Old M. de Launay, its governor, had made what preparations he could, but he had only one day's provisions. His walls were nine feet thick; he had a moat and two drawbridges. He had also had missiles of all kinds piled on the battlements, paving-stones, old iron, etc., and cannon in every embrasure. Above all, he had a powder magazine, and professed his intention of blowing up the place, the garrison, and himself rather than surrender. But what were a hundred and thirty-four men against a hundred thousand?

The Invalides fired a cannon, and killed some of the crowd. Then the rage of the assailants rose to fury. The King of Siam's cannon were impotent to reply, but the fire brigade was called out, and attempted to squirt water into the touch-holes of the cannon. The first gun had been fired at 1 P.M.; the garrison fought on till five. The Invalides, shot down whenever they showed themselves, grew disheartened. They reversed their muskets. They pinned some napkins together, and showed a white flag; while the Swiss put out a paper with an offer to surrender, their terms being, — Pardon to all.

Some attempt was made to march the garrison as prisoners to the Hôtel de Ville; but M. de Launay was torn in pieces before he could be got there, and his queue was borne aloft as a trophy, the sole remnant of his massacre. The Gardes Françaises, however, trained soldiers, interfered, and, with a few exceptions, saved the lives of the rest. The Bastille was levelled to the ground. A column to Liberty now stands where it once stood. "Its secrets came to view," says Carlyle, "and many a buried despair at last found voice. Read this fragment of an old letter: 'If for my consolation Monseigneur would grant me, for the sake of God and the most

Blessed Trinity, that I could have news of my dear wife, were it only her name on a card to show that she is alive, it would be the greatest consolation I could receive, and I should ever bless the goodness of Monseigneur.' — Poor prisoner, who namest thyself Quinet-Démay, and hast no other history! It was fifty years before the fall of the Bastille that thine aching heart put these words on paper, to be at length heard and long heard in the hearts of men!"

In the Bastille at the time of its capture there were found seventeen prisoners. The list, obtained by a foreigner who was present, is preserved in the Imperial Library of St. Petersburg.

Twelve of these persons were counterfeiters and forgers, among whom was one officer of rank, Jacques Luc Pillotte de la Barolière.

The remaining five were: —

JACQUES DE LA DOUAI, a spy of M. Lenoir, employed to report on men of letters. He had entered into an agreement with a foreign bookseller to import interdicted books on joint account. An accomplice betrayed him.

HENRIETTE SANDO, arrested under the false name of Comtesse de St. Anselme. A dressmaker, imprisoned for bringing into France a proscribed pamphlet.

ANNE GÉDÉON DE LAFITTE MARQUIS DE PELLEPORT, author of many pamphlets obnoxious to the government. He exerted himself to save the life of M. de Launay after the taking of the Bastille.

JEAN JACQUES RAINVILLE, arrested for being the owner of a package of books entitled, *Au rédacteur du petit Almanach des grands hommes*.

DE WHIT, arrested in 1782. No one ever knew who he was, nor what he was imprisoned for. He had been at first confined at Vincennes with the Marquis de Sada, who was subsequently sent to Charenton. De Whit had lost his reason, and could give no account of himself. Some thought him a Comte de Lorges. He was consigned to Charenton.

The key of the Bastille was forwarded by Lafayette to General Washington. It now hangs in a glass case in the hall at Mount Vernon.

The Bicêtre continued to be a prison until after the massacres of September, 1793. It was then besieged by a ferocious mob. The prisoners were all liberated and fought side by side with their jailers, though they had no arms but iron bars torn from their windows, and their broken fetters. At last they were overpowered by numbers, and then commenced a general massacre. In vain Pétion exerted himself to stop the carnage. When all was over it was said that six thousand dead bodies lay within the precincts of the prison. There were no political prisoners in the Bicêtre at that period, and nothing but a thirst for blood could have prompted the massacre.

Vincennes is still used as a military prison.

CHAPTER II.

A PEASANT'S VIEW OF THE REVOLUTION.[1]

MANY persons have taken upon themselves to write the history of the great Revolution made by the laboring classes and the *bourgeoisie* against the nobles in 1789. These writers have been men of education, men of talent, who looked on things from a point of view that was not that of the people. I am an old peasant myself, and I shall speak only of what concerned the peasantry. A man's chief business is to look after what concerns himself. What a man has seen with his own eyes he knows about. He may as well turn it to others' advantage.

You must know, then, that before the Revolution the lordship and jurisdiction of Phalsbourg in Lorraine, in which I lived, contained five villages. Two of these were free villages; but the inhabitants of the other three — men and women — were serfs, and could not leave the limits of their *seigneurie* without their magistrate's permission.

This magistrate — the *prévôt* — administered justice in Phalsbourg in a sort of public building; he had jurisdiction over all persons and their property; he bore the sword of justice; and he had even the right to hang any man whom he thought proper. The building where our *maire* now has his office, and where the National Guard now has its head-

[1] From Messrs. Erckmann and Chatrian's Mémoires d'un Paysan, which I think has never been translated. The authors took their narratives from the lips of peasants; and their books, though in the form of fiction, may always be relied upon as history. Père Michel, the Paysan, was a native of Lorraine, the most oppressed province in France. As is always the case in rural revolutions, the primary grievances of the peasants were against the landowner, the tax-gatherer, and the money-lender.

quarters, was in my young days the place where they used to put prisoners to the torture when they would not confess their crimes. The *prévôt's* orderly and the executioner used to put them to such horrible pain that we could hear their screams in the market-place; and the next thing that happened was that a scaffold was erected on a market day under the great elms, and the executioner would hang them, holding them down by putting his two feet upon their shoulders.

At Phalsbourg there was what was called the *haut passage;* which meant that every wagon-load of manufactured goods, whether linen, woollen, or anything else, paid a tax at the barrier on entering the jurisdiction. So did every wagon-load of lumber, or wood not in the rough, and every wagon loaded with expensive luxuries, velvets, silks, or fine linen. A pack-horse paid twelve francs; a basket on a pedler's arm paid three francs; a fish-cart, or a cart with farm produce,— butter, eggs, cheese, etc.,—paid its tax; and salt, wheat, barley, iron, all had to pay, too. A cow, an ox, a calf, a pig, or a sheep had to pay, sometimes very heavily; so that the inhabitants of Phalsbourg and its surrounding villages could neither eat, drink, nor clothe themselves without paying a round sum in taxes to the Duke of Lorraine.

Besides this there was the *gabelle*, or salt tax, and a law which obliged all householders, lodging-house keepers, or tavern-keepers to pay to his Highness six pots of wine or beer for every cask of those liquors that they sold. The duke likewise had his right to a percentage upon every sale of landed property; and all grain sold in the market-place paid an additional tax to him.

There were municipal taxes levied upon every booth erected at the three fairs held yearly in Phalsbourg; and his Highness had the right to pasture his sheep and cattle wherever he pleased. He could cut wood in any man's wood-land, and claimed a share in all the gains of the fullers and the weavers.

Of the great tithes, two thirds went to the duke, and one only to the clergy. The tithe on wheat belonged only to the Church; but his Highness contrived mostly to get hold of it, because he cared more for his own pocket than he did for religion.

The town of Phalsbourg in my boyhood was little like what you may see to-day. Not a house in it was painted; all had very small doors and windows set deep in the masonry, so that the rooms where our tailors and weavers carried on their work were always in semi-darkness.

The soldiers of the garrison, with their big cocked hats and their frayed white greatcoats down to their heels, were about the poorest of us all. They were furnished but one meal a day by the government. The innkeepers and keepers of cook-shops who had to supply their other food used to beg scraps from door to door for the poor devils. This continued until within a few years of the Revolution.

Our women were worn and haggard. A gown passed down from grandmother to granddaughter, and men wore the *sabots* of their fathers' fathers.

There were no pavements in the streets of Phalsbourg, no street-lamps in the darkness. The window-panes were very small; many had been stuffed with rags and paper for twenty years.

Through all the poverty in our streets the *prévôt* would stalk in his black cap, and mount the steps up to the *mairie;* young officers (all noble, for no man could be an officer in those days without his quarterings) would lounge about in little three-cornered hats and white uniforms, with their swords at their sides; Capuchin friars would pass through our streets with dirty long beards, serge robes, no shirts, and red noses, going — troops of them — up to their convent, turned into the town schoolhouse at the present day. . . . I see it all in my mind's eye as if it were but yesterday; and I say to myself, "What a blessing for all of us that the Revolution ever took place, — but most of all has it been a blessing to the peasantry!"

For if poverty was great in the city, it was worse than you can imagine in the country. In the first place, all the dues and taxes paid by the burgher were paid by the peasant as well; and the peasants had other exactions to suffer besides.

In every village of Lorraine, either the *seigneur* or the monks owned a farm. All the best land was included in these farms; poor people had nothing to cultivate but indifferent soil. Nor could they even plant on their own land what they pleased. Meadows had to remain meadows; ploughed lands must be ploughed over again. If the peasant had been allowed to put his wheat-field down in grass, the clergy would have lost their tithe of grain; if he had turned his pasture lot into a field of wheat, he would have diminished the *seigneur's* right of pasturage. His land was under the obligation of supporting fruit trees which belonged to the convent or the *seigneur*, who sold the fruit every year. The farmer had no right to cut down these trees, and if they died he was expected to plant others in their stead. The shade they made, the trampling of the crops when the fruit was gathered, the impediments they put in the way of ploughing, were all very hurtful to the small proprietor.

Then, too, the nobles had the right to hunt over the lands of their peasantry, to gallop over the peasant's crops, to ravage his fields; and the peasant who killed one partridge or one hare even, on his own land, was in danger of the galleys.

The *seigneur* and the monastery had also special rights of pasturage; that is to say, their flocks might go out to graze on waste lands an hour earlier than those of the people in the village. The cows and sheep of the peasants, therefore, only got their leavings.

Again, the farm of the *seigneur* or the monastery had the right to maintain pigeons. These pigeons flocked over the fields. The peasant had to sow twice as much seed as he need otherwise have done, if he hoped for any harvest.

Furthermore, every head of a family had to pay his lord every year fifteen measures of oats, ten fowls, and twenty-four eggs. He also owed him three days' labor for himself, three for each of his sons, three for each laborer he hired, and three for each horse or cart. He was bound to mow for him his grounds around the château, to make his hay and carry it to the barn at the first stroke of the great château bell, or else he had to pay three sous fine for each time he failed in doing so. He was bound to haul all stones or wood needed to keep the château in repair. The lord was expected to give him only a meal of bread and garlic each day he worked for him.

This is what is meant by *la corvée*, — a word that has now passed into the French language to express what is intolerable labor.

If I were to go on to tell you how the *seigneur* had his oven, where all bread had to be baked, and his press, where all his peasants had to make their wine, and pay him for the use of them; if I were further to tell you how the executioner had a right to the hide of every beast that died of itself; and were I to describe all the troubles and exactions attendant on the collection of these rights, and the tithes, and so forth and so on, I should never have done. There was a poll tax besides, and a tax on furniture.

After Lorraine was united to France, the king claimed the twelfth part of all produce for the expenses of his government; but he claimed it from the lands of the peasants alone, — the lands of the nobles and the clergy paid no taxes. Then the monopoly of salt and of tobacco was in the hands of "farmers," and the price was made excessive to the people; and there was the *gabelle*, or the salt tax, which was peculiarly oppressive.

All this might have been endured had the *seigneurs* and the *abbés* and the priors spent any of the money they received from us in cutting canals, draining the marshes, improving the roads, building schoolhouses, or doing anything else for the public good. But when we saw such a man as the Cardinal Prince Louis de Rohan, a high dignitary of the Church, leading the life he did at Saverne, making a mock of honest men, allowing his lackeys to beat poor people on the highway to make them get out of the way of his carriage; or when we saw the noble gardens, the vast pleasure-grounds, the statues, and the fountains, created by our nobles at their country seats, in imitation of Versailles, it seemed enough to break our hearts, for all the wealth expended on such luxuries came from our toil, and the whole system was supported by the military service of peasants' sons.

When these men once enlisted in a regiment, they forgot the sorrows of their village. They forgot their own mothers and sisters; they recognized no ties but those that bound them to their officers, — nobles who had bought them, and at whose orders they would have massacred every living soul in their own village, saying that it was for the honor of the flag, — *pour l'honneur du drapeau*. And yet not one of these men could ever rise from the ranks and become an officer! The born serf could never wear an epaulette. When a man lost a limb in the service or was otherwise disabled, all he got was a permit to go and beg through the country. The smart ones would lounge round the tavern doors and do their best to enlist drunken men, and so themselves secure the bounty; the more reckless and adventurous took to highway robbery. Gendarmes had to be sent against them. Sometimes two or three companies were sent. I saw a dozen robbers hung on one day at Phalsbourg; nearly all of them were old soldiers licensed to beg after the Seven Years' War. They had lost the skill to labor, they had not a farthing of pension, and were all arrested and condemned for robbing a roadside tavern near Saverne. So now you understand what was meant by the Old Régime. The nobles and the convents had *all*, and the laboring people had *nothing*.

Things are all altered now, thank Heaven! The peasants have their share of the good things of this world, and of course I too have my little portion. Everybody around here knows Père Michel's farm, his beautiful Swiss cows the color of *café au lait*, and his six yoke of work-oxen.

I have no right to complain. The Revolution has done much for *me*. My grandson Jacques is in Paris, at the École Polytechnique. He is in the first class there. My granddaughters are well married. My namesake, my youngest and favorite grandchild, talks of being a doctor. All this I owe to the Revolution. Had I been a grandfather before 1789, I should have had nothing. I should have labored all my life for the *seigneur* and the monastery. As I sit here in my big armchair, with my old dog at my feet, and glance out at my apple-trees covered with white blossoms, or listen to the cheerful sounds from my own farm-yard, I think of the wretched cabin where my poor father and mother lived, and my brothers and sisters in 1780, with its four bare crumbling walls, its windows stuffed with straw, its thatch rotted by rain and snow, — a kind of black mouldy lair, where we were all stifled in the smoke; where we shivered with cold and hunger. And when I think how my poor parents toiled incessantly just to give us a few beans to keep the life in us; when I remember how ragged we were, how haggard, and how care-worn, — I shudder; and when I am alone tears come into my eyes.

No, indeed! you can't make *me* believe that poor people were happy before the Revolution. I recollect what people call "the good old times," and yet in those days old men talked to us of times a great deal worse, — that time of the Thirty Years' War, when peasants were strung up to the trees like fruit; and after war came pestilence, till you might travel leagues without seeing a single living soul.

Imagine in those days a poor laborer like my father with a wife and six children, without a sou, without a foot of land, without a goat, without a fowl, with nothing but the toil of his hands on which to live. There was no hope anywhere for him, or for his children. No better fate than his was open to his family; it was the natural order of things. Some people came into the world nobles, and had a right to everything; others were born serfs, and must expect to remain in poverty from generation to generation.

Yet, in spite of these things, when the spring came, and the sun shone into our cabin after the long dark months; when it showed us the cobwebs between the beams, the little hearth in the corner, and the ladder to the loft; when we grew warm, and crickets sang without, and all the trees grew green, — we felt it, after all, to be a pleasant thing to be alive. We children lay on our backs upon the grass clasping our bare feet in our little hands; we whistled, we laughed, and looked up in the sky, or tumbled in the dust, and were happy.

But the worst trouble of all was that peasants, almost without exception, were in debt to some money-lender. I recollect, as soon as I can remember anything, hearing my father say when he had sold some of his baskets, or a dozen or two of his brooms: "Here is the money for salt, and here for beans and for rice, but I have not a sou over. *Oh, mon Dieu! mon Dieu!* I had hoped to have a little over to go to Monsieur Robin!"

What my father and mother suffered from this debt cannot be described. They lay awake to worry over it; the thought of it never left them; they grew old under the burden of it. The debt had been contracted to buy a goat. The goat had died. It had been paid for ten times over in interest, but the principal had never been repaid. Their only hope lay in the thought that if one of their sons drew a blank in the conscription, they might sell him for a substitute. People must indeed have been poverty-stricken before they could find hope in the sale of their sons. We boys thought it only natural that our father and mother should sell us. We always considered ourselves as belonging to them, like cattle.

In those days, when I had to run home alone on dark nights after staying too long at my uncle's, where I was employed as a farm boy in his stable, I used to carry with me a lighted torch to scare the wolves; and sometimes, long after I had crept into my bed of leaves in the loft, beside my brothers, I would hear sounds in the distance, by which I knew that wolves were howling round some stable, jumping up eight or ten feet to get in at some opening, and falling back upon the snow. Then there would be some short, sharp yelps, and then the whole pack would rush down the village street, like a whirlwind. They had seized some poor watch-dog, and were carrying him off to the rocks to tear him in pieces.

One afternoon I found my uncle with a basket before him containing roots cut into small pieces. A pedler, who was one of his friends, had brought them to him from beyond the Rhine, saying that they came out of Hanover, that they would produce plants so good to eat and in such great quantities that our people would have plenty of food all the year round. He recommended us to plant them, saying that if they came into use there would be no more famine in the land, and that they would be a veritable blessing to every one.

These were potatoes. There was great opposition to them at first in our country. They came from Hanover; they were heretic roots. It was reported that they produced leprosy; and for one season nobody would buy them or eat them. But, happily for us, before the time for planting them the next year, a gazette reached us which said that a good fellow, one Parmentier, had planted some of these roots in the neighborhood of Paris, that he had sent some to the king, who had eaten of them; and then everybody wanted to plant potatoes, in consequence of which all that my uncle had on hand sold very profitably.[1]

[1] The extract I have given shows the working of the feudal system in the days of its decay. The French Revolution swept it utterly away, not only in France, but all over Europe. We think so much of the horrors and excesses of the Revolution run to riot, cruelty, and madness, that we forget what it seemed to men in its early stages, and what we ourselves would have thought of it had we never known its sequel. — E. W. L.

CHAPTER III.

PARIS IN 1787.[1]

IN the month of May, 1787, three young men of Nancy, then the capital of the province of Lorraine, set out upon a journey. They were to visit Paris, and afterwards descend the Seine to Havre. Their objects were to see the world and to purchase seeds and agricultural implements; for they belonged to the middle class, and had no social pretensions or ambitions. They were frugal, although bent on pleasure; and one of them wrote a journal, in which he recorded their observations and their joint stock of experiences, for the benefit of their respective families. Two years later (although no word in the journal shows that change or trouble was at hand) all France was ablaze with revolution. The record of their journey, having served its purpose, lay forgotten in the drawer of an old writing-desk, until recently a descendant of the writer drew it from its hiding-place. He gave it to the world through the "Literary Supplement of Figaro," as an interesting picture of a Paris very different from the Paris of the Third Republic or the Second Empire. The style of the young man's narrative is clear, straight-forward, and unsensational. Its language differs about as much from the French of modern newspapers and novels as the Paris it describes does from the heaven of the good American, in the appearance of its streets and the every-day ideas which shaped its manners.

Our three young men, Thiry, Jacquinot, and Cognet (their historian) left Nancy by diligence, May 7, 1787. Their fellow-passengers were an Englishman, and a friar of the

[1] Contributed to "Appleton's Journal," December, 1880, by Mrs. E. W. Latimer.

order of St. Francis. The friar they found a bore, while the Englishman was intelligent and amusing. Their first stage was to Ligny, which they reached in a pouring rain. There they supped upon delicate trout, and went to bed for about three hours. Anxious, however, to get as much as possible out of their journey, they got out of bed at 3 A. M. to walk around the town of Ligny, where they found wide streets and handsome houses. We judge that at that time ideas of the seclusion of women regulated domestic architecture, for they note with surprise that one of the principal of these houses "had windows looking on the street." At Bar, Jacquinot paid a visit to the good-looking housekeeper of a certain M. Arnoud, who had a small place under government, but the rule of the establishment seems to have been, "No followers allowed," and the visit was resented as an intrusion by her master.

At St. Didier, the next stage of their journey, they got an excellent dinner for twenty-five sous each. At Vitry they changed horses, and were struck by the free and easy manners of its pretty women, some of whom stood at their windows to watch them as they waited beside the diligence; and one lady, of high consideration, as they heard, actually waved her hand to them, as their carriage rolled away. With Châlons they were not well pleased: their supper was dear and bad; the women were ill dressed, and took no interest in travellers. "They had no notion how to put their clothes on," says our observant traveller. "They wore full-dress *chignons* with morning *déshabillé*."

At Châlons they left the diligence, and hired a cabriolet. The weather was very bad, and they were greatly indebted to their landlady, who laid some old cloths over the frame of their vehicle. At Sézanne they passed the night with an uncle of Jacquinot, who took them to see "The Prodigal Son" performed by ragged actors in a barn, the stage being separated only by coarse curtains from a stable full of horses.

From Sézanne they went forward on foot, hoping for good quarters at a certain abbey on their route, to the prior of which Jacquinot's uncle had given them a letter of recommendation. The prior, however, by no means honored the draft on his hospitality. At Meaux they insisted on supping on mackerel, the first salt sea fish they had ever tasted, but the mackerel having *un léger goût de décomposition*, Jacquinot alone could stomach them.

On the 15th of May, a week after they left Nancy, they found themselves at 8 A. M. before the gates of Paris. They breakfasted in a *guinguette*, or canvas booth, and then sought a fellow-countryman from Lorraine who had engaged three bedrooms for them in the Rue Montmartre, opposite the courtyard of the diligence. Their trunk (they travelled with light luggage) had arrived before them; and having changed their clothes and had their heads dressed, they proceeded to the Palais Royal. "The beauty of the buildings," says Cognet, "the regularity and elegance of the arcades, and the magnificence of the shops hardly impressed us more than the vast number of people who flocked there at midday. It is the rendezvous of strangers, idlers, and the most noted courtesans in the capital, so beautifully dressed that one might have mistaken them for court ladies."

At three o'clock they went to dine with a friend at Hue's restaurant in the Passage des Petits Pères, where they had excellent entertainment for thirty-three sous apiece. The dining-hall was large, and could seat from sixty to eighty persons at small tables. Then they went forth to walk up and down the Rue St. Honoré, and to see for themselves how well its evil reputation was deserved. They were informed that it was not respectable for any woman in Paris to look out of her windows on the street, and wondered how their fair friend at Vitry would have felt could she have known what conclusion would be drawn from her behavior by a Parisian.

Returning to the Palais Royal they went to the Beaujolais, a little theatre much the fashion at that period, where children made gestures on the stage, while others sang behind the scenes. They saw three comic operettas at this place, and at nine o'clock were out again, and enjoying in the arcades of the Palais Royal "the *coup d'œil* offered by the brilliant light, not only from street lamps hung between each arcade, but from the number of lamps and candles in the shops, which illuminated the richness of the goods displayed, in contrast with the dark walks under the chestnut-trees."

The next day, the first thing they saw on going out, at ten A. M., was a great crowd of people in the Rue Neuve des Capucines, waiting with impatience for the drawing of the royal lottery. "That ceremony took place," says Cognet, "with all the pomp and publicity calculated to tranquillize an anxious public. The lieutenant-general of police, whose rank is considered equal to that of a minister, stood on a scaffolding surrounded by a group of officers. On the same scaffolding was the wheel of fortune, standing beside which was a child with a fillet over his eyes. The wheel turned, a little door opened, the child put forth his hand, took up a paper lying in the opening, and gave it to the lieutenant-general of police, who opened it, with his hands held up over his head, before the crowd. The number, then proclaimed aloud, was exhibited on a frame in large figures to the people. When all the numbers were drawn, the noise was very great. The crowd dispersed, most of them cursing their ill luck, but all ready to test it again upon the next occasion."

Thence our young men turned into the Place Vendôme, one side of which was then occupied by the church and convent of the Capuchins. The convent gardens extended at that time to the garden of the Tuileries, from which they were separated by a narrow space, now the Rue de Rivoli. To this place four years later the National Assembly removed when the court was forced to leave Versailles and occupy the Tuileries; but no shadow of such coming events hung over the minds of the young sight-seers as they gazed at the equestrian statue of Louis XIV., then occupying the centre of the square, or stood inside the convent church and wondered at the simplicity of the monument to Madame de Pompadour.

The Boulevard was to Paris in that day what the Bois de

Boulogne and the Champs Élysées are in ours. This Boulevard (for they then spoke of it in the singular) was very different from the Boulevards as we know them, the trees that were their glory then having been nearly all cut down during successive revolutions. "The Boulevard," says our authority, "consists of two grand avenues of four rows of trees each, under which people walk on foot, while in the middle is a wide *chaussée* intended for carriages. In dry weather this road is watered twice a day. On *fête* days, if there is no public *divertissement* to celebrate the occasion, the Boulevard is the rendezvous of all Paris. There are generally four lines of carriages abreast for more than two leagues. The shabby *fiacre* rumbles alongside of the most brilliant equipages. Along this drive are the handsomest houses in Paris, and, besides two theatres, there are shows and curiosities of all kinds shown very cheaply under the trees. There are also three or four *cafés*, beautifully fitted up, where, from 2 P. M. to 11, a band plays without intermission."

The opera-house of that day excited the admiration of our provincials. It had been built in seventy-five days. It was entirely of wood, and its builders had not been willing to guarantee it for more than five years. Those years had passed, and it was still in perfect order. Its façade was on the Boulevard St. Martin. Its curtain was *de toute beauté*. It re-represented Parnassus, Apollo crowning the Arts, and the Graces standing by him. The perfection of the scenery, and the mechanical appliances for moving it, the vastness of the auditorium, and the brilliancy of the ballet, — especially the performance of the celebrated Mademoiselle Guimard, — delighted our young men even more than the singing.

They went next day to see the Halles, and were struck by the general activity that prevailed in them, and by the brutality and vile language of those men and women who so soon after were to become the greatest power for evil in the world.

The garden of the Tuileries (or Thuileries, as they write it) was much as we have known it in our own day, but the palace was unoccupied and dilapidated. "The trees are of prodigious size, and their branches meet together, forming an impenetrable shade. This spot is the resort of respectable *bourgeoises*, and of such ladies of quality as, having no carriages, wish to take the air without being elbowed by disreputable women. They are brought to the gates in sedan chairs, which are left outside with their porters. All this is in excellent taste, and one feels on entering the garden that it is the refuge of virtue. When we quitted the Tuileries, we crossed a desert spot called the Champs Élysées, and soon found ourselves inside the park of the celebrated M. Beaujon."

That day they had a bad dinner for thirty-six sous apiece, and complain that in fashionable places proprietors and waiters show much less regard to guests out of the provinces than to *seigneurs* of the capital. "To get a good dinner at these places, one has either to show a red heel, or to drive up in an equipage that stamps you as one concerned in government finance, the jingling of money being as good as a title to those who preside there."

They were struck by the activity prevailing on the quays on both sides of the Seine. These were crowded with all sorts of merchandise and provisions, and each quay was called after the product to which it was especially devoted.

There was an Italian opera in those days in Paris, but the performers sang in French. The opera-house was situated on a wide open space surrounded by buildings in the course of construction. They admired the skill of the police in keeping order among the fashionable carriages, and they there saw a great many *seigneurs* and *grandes dames*.

The Bois de Boulogne is described as a park nearly a league from Paris, used by the Parisians for picnics upon *fête* days. At that time one of the curiosities of the Bois was a ruined palace called Madrid, built by François I. on his return from captivity. It had as many windows as there were days in the year, and the exterior had been covered with porcelain tiles, but the whole was going to decay. Not so the country house of the Comte d'Artois in the same neighborhood, whose English gardens, winding walks, and falling waters are admirably described as *imitant péniblement la nature.*

The Jardin Mabille of that day was called "Wauxhall," and was attended by our young men with but little edification; the orgy, however, broke up in time to send them to bed by eleven o'clock.

The Cathedral of St. Denis was then in all its glory. "*C'est là*," exclaims our young philosopher, in words less trite before the Revolution than they are to-day, "*le terme de la puissance de nos rois*." The treasure-room contained reliquaries and chalices of inestimable value. There, too, were the crowns used at the coronation of French sovereigns, the sword of Charlemagne and his crown and sceptre. But the most wonderful thing of all was a chalice carved out of a single agate, the work of one man's lifetime, which had been left by will to the cathedral by the Abbé Sugger. There, too, they saw the royal mantle of purple velvet spangled with gold *fleurs de lis*, and lined with ermine. It weighed a hundred and eighty pounds. It was the custom of the place always to keep in the chancel, lying under a magnificent canopy, the coffin that contained the body of the last king during the reign of his successor. Louis XV. died of small-pox, and his body, being unfit to embalm, was buried. A catafalque, however, covered an empty coffin, and lights burned round it night and day. They observed with satisfaction that the body of Turenne "lay honored among those of kings;" they did not know that six years later, when the dead bodies of the kings would be dragged from their resting-place, his alone would be spared that ignominy.

The mania for building and decorating country places was the prevailing folly of that period. Well might Waller's warning to Englishmen a century back have been applied to courtiers bred in the school of Louis XIV. and his successor: —

> "If you have these whims of apartments and gardens
> Of twice fifty acres, you 'll ne'er see five farthings;
> And in you will be seen the true gentleman's fate, —
> Ere you 've finished your house you 'll have spent your estate."

At Neuilly they saw the flower-garden of M. de Saint-James, who had squandered four millions of francs upon his country place. Money had been frittered on cockney absurdities of all kinds. Grottoes had been lined with fish-bones; cascades had been shrouded by glass; and one grotto was brilliantly lighted by reflections thrown upon yellow glass balls recalling the cave with trees of jewelled fruit entered by Aladdin. These marvels, and the really beautiful conservatories and pineries, must have been destroyed during the Revolution.

The friends attended the one hundredth representation of Beaumarchais's "Figaro" at the Français. The performance began at five o'clock, and there was a great struggle to get in at the doors. The theatre had seven tiers of boxes, crowded by a delighted audience, and the pit *had seats*, as they remarked, and was filled by people of fashion. The difficulty of getting out again was great, for before the theatre there was a piece of waste ground full of open drains and numerous excavations.

Notre Dame at that period was the richest cathedral in the kingdom. Over its entrances were life-size statues of twenty-eight kings of France, all afterwards destroyed at the Revolution. The high altar, soon to be desecrated by a *fille de l'opéra* in the guise of the Goddess of Reason, was of porphyry, and the chapels were full of noble statuary and precious marbles.

On the 25th of May Jacquinot came of age, and his companions celebrated the event by a most sumptuous breakfast, costing them two francs and a half apiece. They visited the Church of the Maturins, where they saw an altar-cloth that Cognet describes as "marvellous, the only thing of the kind that exists. *Brocatelle de soie d'or et argent.*"

The Gobelins was just as we have all seen it, no changes in that establishment having been effected by the Revolution. They dined outside the *barrière* for eighteen sous apiece, "as well as we could have done within the walls for twice that sum," and they spent the afternoon in seeing one of the saddest sights that ever disgraced humanity. The

Salpêtrière was a place of confinement for all kinds of unfortunate women. The establishment in 1787 contained seven thousand of them, and was presided over by twelve Sisters of the order of Ste. Claire. Among the women of loose character they saw Madame de la Motte, the infamous heroine of the "Diamond Necklace," who, escaping soon after during the Revolution, is said, under the assumed name of Comtesse Guacher, to have become partner in the evangelization of Russia with Madame de Krudener, the friend of the Emperor Alexander. Although classed with the Magdalens on the register of the establishment, Madame de la Motte had a room to herself, and was not obliged to wear their dress, a robe of coarse woollen, fashioned like a sack. The young men bribed their guide to let them see her. "She has the deportment and manners of a lady of quality," says Cognet. "She seemed very much surprised by our visit; but as it probably was a change to her, she did not resent it, and entered into conversation with us. She was dressed like a lady in *déshabillé*, and was busy fluting something when we entered."

The other women slept five in a bed. The kitchens were neat and commodious. Seven coppers made soup for the seven thousand women, half an ox to each copper, — which seems a miserable allowance. They were all occupied, generally with needlework, and among them were several women who were there by choice. The hospital and nursery departments were likewise visited; but the Sisters with all their care "could not prevent the air of these places from being intolerable. The most dreadful sight we saw, however," says Cognet, "was that of the poor creatures deprived of reason." Some of his details are too shocking for repetition. Those liable to fits of fury were kept chained in kennels, and an iron barrier cut them off from personal communication even with the keepers of the establishment. Their lairs were cleaned out twice a day with rakes, and their food was thrust in to them. Among these wretched creatures was a beautiful young girl, who had loved a young nobleman who had betrayed her. "If it had not been for the fetters round her beautiful bare arms, we could not have believed that she was subject to attacks of violent mania. Her melancholy beseeching looks proved that in lucid intervals she realized the horrors of her situation." She hid herself in her kennel at their approach, but afterwards came out, and made gestures to Thiry. When they came back she was in a paroxysm of despair, and was tearing her flesh and clothes. Many had only an old quilt for a covering.

No traveller could visit Paris without going to Versailles. On Whitsunday our young Lorrainers went thither with a great crowd. Their first sight was the procession of those who wore the grand cordon of St. Louis. All noblemen so decorated left the king's apartment at midday, and went in procession to the chapel, followed by the princes of the blood, the queen, her ladies, and the king himself. The dauphin, whom the queen held by the hand, was not the sufferer of the Temple, but his elder brother, who died two years after this Whitsunday, — June 4, 1789. "Our queen's features are not perfect," remarks Cognet; "but she seems more beautiful than any lady at court because of the nobility of her expression and the splendor of her carriage. Even when dressed in very humble garments, it would be easy to guess that she was born to a throne. Her great dignity does not impair her grace. She has an enchanting smile and a peculiar turn of her head. The king's countenance shows his great kindliness, and his glance, though it is timid (*dépourvu d'audace*), is full of majesty. The dauphin," Cognet also remarks, "is a very pretty boy, but he seems sad and sickly. Though hardly five years old, he behaved admirably at mass, and only once made a little friendly gesture to his cousin, the Duc d'Angoulême, when the grand cordon was conferred on him." The richness of the court costumes amazed the young provincials. The queen and the princesses were literally covered with jewels. The Duchesse de Polignac and the Princesse de Lamballe were pointed out to them as the queen's intimate friends. All present were not required to wear swords, but every one who did so was admitted to the palace on that occasion. "The only fault that we could see in the apartments," adds Cognet, "was perhaps a too lavish profusion of gold."

The grand fountains played, and the young men were interested in the menagerie, particularly in the rhinoceros. One wonders what became of him in the Revolution! "Versailles," says our young writer, — and his observation is as true now as it was then, — "seems still to be pervaded by Louis XIV." The Louvre at that time was in process of reconstruction, and the part finished was full of artists' studios and workshops of all kinds, granted rent free to persons who had influence to secure them.

On the Sunday after Whitsuntide they left Paris for St. Cloud in a flatboat, containing three hundred persons. On reaching their destination, where the fountains did not play till five o'clock, they made their way on foot across country to Versailles, and visited the Trianon.

At the Petit Trianon, "the queen's plaything," they saw her English garden, her farm, her farm buildings, a ruin, a plain, a forest, and a mountain, all artificial, and on a tiny scale. "The queen comes here frequently," says her young subject, "to get rid of the burthen of her greatness. She loves to be alone here for hours at a time. The house is in no sense a palace. The walls are covered with straw-work, alternating with worsted embroidery; the floors are spread with matting imitating *marqueterie*. In the garden there are none but wild flowers. There is no etiquette observed at the Petit Trianon; none of the *distinctions du tabouret* prevail there. As we were leaving the bathing rooms, we were apprised of the arrival of Marie Antoinette; and as we had not time to escape through the gate, our guide hurried us into the dairy. The queen approached, accompanied by one of her court ladies; but she dismissed her presently, and came alone directly toward us. She wore a simple dress of clear white cambric, a *fichu*, and a head-dress of lace; and in this quiet dress she seemed even more queenly than in the court costume in which we had last seen her. Her way of walking is peculiar. She glides forward with inexpressible grace, and her head was thrown back more proudly when she thought herself alone than when she was in the midst of pomp and people. Our queen passed close to the place where we were hid, and we all three had an impulse to step forth and kneel before her. We were divided between the wish that she should see us and the fear that she might do so. As soon as her Majesty had passed, our guide made us leave the garden. As it was four o'clock, we took a carriage which soon brought us to St. Cloud."

At this time the first fire department was being organized in Paris. One of the sights they went to see was *La Samaritaine*, a dilapidated piece of machinery that had been constructed for forcing water from the Seine to the Tuileries in case of fire. They remarked at the time that the recent discovery of fire engines (*pompes à feu*) would supersede this old machine. This prophecy was fulfilled for them as they returned home from St. Cloud. As they came in sight of the Tuileries, they saw part of the Pavillon de Flore on fire; and while interesting themselves in the *pompes*, which were mounted upon boats in the Seine, Jacquinot was pressed into the service, and compelled to work hard for eight or ten hours. The Tuileries seems to have been always thought particularly liable to conflagration.

Thiry had been greatly depressed for more than a week past, and, declining an expedition to Marly, took to his bed. His illness, however, proved to be homesickness. He was pining for his family; and having made up his mind to return to Nancy by the next diligence, he grew perfectly well again. His companions saw him off, and then went to the beautiful country seat of the Prince de Condé (the unfortunate Duc d'Enghien's grandfather) at Chantilly. The place was extraordinarily beautiful, and was everywhere decorated with illustrations of La Fontaine's "Fables" in sculpture. Chantilly they thought as charming as Versailles was dull and magnificent. Among other things, they saw in the armory the swords of Jeanne d'Arc, and of Henri IV.

On the 11th of June they wrote a letter to say that they

should soon be home, sent off their trunk by diligence, engaged their places for the following week, and spent the day in executing commissions. They had some difficulty in getting their trunk through the custom-house, which then examined every article that left Paris, but this being accomplished they prepared for a fresh jaunt to see the ocean.

They started on foot through Marly and St. Germain, and at Poissy took a flatboat —*galiote*— on the Seine. This vessel had no seats, no cabin, and no protection from the weather, so that they suffered terribly from a blazing sun, but it was a cheap mode of travelling; eight hours of it cost them each thirty sous. They hired two rough Norman ponies at Roulle, and rode twenty-one miles on them to Rouen, paying another thirty sous apiece for the animals. They saw the sights of Rouen, the same as in our own day, and continued their journey by flatboats and on hired horses to Honfleur, the harbor of which was then full of vessels from the Baltic, but it was being rapidly filled up by sand. On the 15th they saw Havre and the sea for the first time, and bathed in salt water at once. They ate turbot, lobster, and various shellfish, and went on board a man o' war corvette, and admired the merchant shipping. They went to the theatre as a matter of course, and, in short, made the most of their one day's stay at Havre. They were very much interested in all they saw, but thought Havre a very dear city to live in. They had the good taste to admire the scenery along the banks of the Seine on their journey back to Rouen, and Cognet informs us that at that time the city contained a hundred thousand inhabitants. They visited the market-place where poor Jeanne d'Arc was burned, drank Norman cider, and went to the theatre, where they made two in an audience of ten, the manager having quarrelled with the public. Partly on foot, and partly in a flatboat, they made their return journey from Rouen to Paris. The last stage of their journey, on a wet night, in an intolerable crowd upon the bare deck of the boat, was very uncomfortable. They were interested, however, in an escaped nun they had on board, who made no secret of her adventures.

"She was a girl of no personal charms, who had been put into a convent against her will. She got out by climbing up some trellis-work beside a wall, until she reached the top, when she slipped down into the road. There is little doubt she will continue to *slip* more," adds Cognet, "as she goes further."

They stayed three more days in Paris, and then (June 22) in the society of a Jesuit father, "good company and no bigot," a spur-maker and his son, the Sieur Bouthoux, a bookseller of Nancy, two Englishmen who could not speak French, and a tobacco agent from Lunéville, they started for Nancy. The journey was uneventful, without any accident to the passengers, though the diligence, in going down a steep hill without brakes, at one stage ran over its two postilions, who were left behind under charge of charitable persons, while the Englishmen mounted the horses, and carried the diligence through to the next post-town.

Thiry had come out one stage to meet them. They all breakfasted together at Toul, and there the young men took leave of their fellow-travellers, for the route of the diligence did not lie through Nancy. In a few hours they were safe at home, "enjoying," as Cognet concludes, "each of us on his own part the pleasure that others felt in our safe return, after seven weeks' absence."

CHAPTER IV.

COURT LIFE AT VERSAILLES ON THE EVE OF THE REVOLUTION.

[*From the pen of a nineteenth-century reporter.*[1]]

PERMIT me, good reader, to borrow the services of Asmodeus, and, without being either a philosopher, a humorist, or an historian, to take you into Paris — the Paris of 1789 — in the character of a modern reporter.

The first thing that will strike us is the height of the houses, the narrowness of the streets, and the dimness of the shops. There are fewer gable roofs than I expected, and more vehicles of various kinds than I had supposed. The buildings and monuments that I recognize appear strange to me, because of the great difference in their surroundings; and in the streets is a throng noisily, boisterously, brutally gay, giving to old Paris an air of activity and movement for which I was not prepared. I look steadily at the costumes of the crowd. They are not what I expected. I had imagined I should see in the streets of Paris personages like the actors in comic opera. Not a bit of it! There are very few bright colors worn on the streets, very little velvet, and still less silk. Stout blue, brown, and black cloth is worn by the men. Workingmen wear trousers, and are dressed like the peasants of western France in our own day. Where are the great nobles, all embroidered in gold? A moment ago I caught sight of a man dressed in pink silk, but he was a street singer in the guise of a marquis. Where are the real marquises? Oh, I forgot. They are all at Versailles. We will go to Versailles, then, and begin with the court circle.

When Louis XIV. died, Louis XV., not daring to keep up the same state as his majestic great-grandfather, took up

[1] From the "Supplément Littéraire du Figaro," translated by me and published Feb. 23, 1889, in "Littell's Living Age." — E. W. L.

his quarters in the left wing of the château, which was divided into small suites of apartments; and in these same small apartments lives Louis XVI. His royal spouse prefers the Trianon. But we will begin, in our capacity of invisible reporter, with Louis himself.

He was born at Versailles, Aug. 23, 1754; so that he is now, in 1789, thirty-five years old. He is very stout, but he is also very muscular, and more quick in his movements than his people give him credit for. His forehead recedes, his nose is short, his chin fat, and his complexion slightly florid. His eyes are commonly without much expression, but when excited his glance can be stern and severe, — which is a great contrast to the usual kindly expression of his physiognomy.

The king has the manners of a gentleman, but not those of a prince. His movements are brusque and awkward. Physically and morally, his defect is indecision. Like all weak men, he has occasionally sudden spurts of violent temper. His morals are so pure that his virtues are sneered at by his licentious nobles, while they have failed to attract the good opinion of his people. He adores his queen, and cannot bear to hear her slandered, though sometimes his affection seems to turn to bitterness. He can occasionally be as jealous as a bourgeois, yet he trusts her in everything.

One day he said, "M. Turgot and I are the only two men in France who really love the people." He *does* love his people, beyond doubt; but he distrusts them, though he has as yet no conception of their latent capacity for revolution. At this moment, as we look at him, he is going through a terrible struggle with financial and political difficulties. His relief comes when he can give himself up with his whole soul to his much-talked-of labors in locksmithing and watch-making. Indeed, there is not in all Paris a more skilful workman. His appetite is formidable; we will say more about it by and by. It is only when he works like a journeyman and feeds like Gargantua that he seems gay; his soul is ordinarily heavy within him.

He cannot forget all the cruel little intrigues which have already darkened the splendors of his reign, and are indeed a sort of prelude to the terrible misfortunes about to fall on his family. Such things as the affair of the diamond necklace, the scandal of the "Marriage of Figaro," played at court, the queen taking a principal part herself, in spite of his prohibition, the gossip about Marie Antoinette's having been married seven years before she became a mother, worry and agitate him. He is sad, very sad; and what is now mere anxiety will before long turn to horror.

Marie Antoinette, born Archduchess of Austria, is now thirty-four. Supremely elegant, brought up in the most aristocratic court of Europe, she has all the faults and all the charms of the aristocracy of the eighteenth century. Proud and yet frivolous, jealous of the prerogatives of her station and yet impatient of the restraints of etiquette, she shocks the nobility by her want of dignity and the *bourgeoisie* by the lightness of her behavior.

Is she beautiful? Not precisely. But she belongs to that class of women who, in the language of our own day, are called "captivating." Her profile is aquiline, possibly a little too much so; her eyes are very bright; her mouth charming; her complexion brilliant; her manners easy, free, and sometimes a shade wanting in queenliness.

She is a mark for the most rascally insinuations, particularly on the part of some members of her husband's family. An evil motive is imputed to her most innocent fancies; as, for example, that of dressing like a shepherdess when she lives in her pretty little cottage at the Trianon. Thousands of songs are sung about her in the streets. Some will continue celebrated, and need not be here mentioned; some are obscene, and not to be repeated; but here is one that I have never heard before, — nor probably you, reader, — which I heard a man humming at Versailles, almost within earshot of the Trianon: —

"La bergère de Trianon,
Quand on dit oui, ne dit pas non;
Elle est sensible, mais volage;

LOUIS XVI.

Elle accommode à sa façon
Le bon garçon, le gros garçon,
Qui l'osa prendre en mariage."

"The shepherd maid of Trianon,
If you say *oui*, will not say *non;*
Tender but changeable, 't is said her
Arts can manage (how 's not known)
The good fat fellow on the throne
Who has dared to wed her."

If such things are sung within earshot of the court, what am I likely to hear in the city?

The Comte de Provence, the king's next brother, was born in 1755. He has a high forehead, denoting intelligence; his eyes are bright and piercing, his mouth scornful, his manners easy, but haughty at the same time. Since his elder brother ascended the throne, he bears the title of Monsieur. He dabbles a good deal in politics, and is in open opposition to the influence of the queen and her coterie. He surrounds himself with men of letters, has a caustic wit, and is skilful at mystifications, is fond of quoting Latin, cares little for women, and is a singular mixture of excessive aristocratic exclusiveness and of progressive tendencies. He understands England and admires parliamentary and constitutional government, makes fun of "Gothic" proclivities, and paves the way for the rising power of the *bourgeoisie;* but yet he is prince of the blood, down to his very finger-nails.

What a contrast the Comte d'Artois presents to his two brothers! He is Charles Philippe of France now, but forty-two years later will have been Charles X. and be for the second time an exile at Holyrood. He is a tall young man, slender, elegant, and active, — a handsome fellow, gallant to the verge of libertinism, without much education, but with natural talent. Being an accomplished rider, he has during the last year or two brought racing into fashion, — for there are races in Paris in 1789. He owns a stable and trainers and jockeys, whom he calls *des jaquets.*

See, yonder comes a boy four years old, fair, gentle, ex

quisitely graceful. He is the son of Louis XVI. and of Marie Antoinette, — the poor boy who will endure such sufferings in the Temple. There he will live for months without uttering a word; now he chatters like a little man. Indeed, some of his sayings show the spirit of the eighteenth century. He first made the remark attributed nowadays to many children, "If God sends rain to make the corn grow, why does He let it fall upon the pavement?"

His sister, the future Duchesse d'Angoulême, is playing with him, but without much vivacity. Her disposition is not melancholy yet, but she is dominated by a precocious feeling of dignity.

The king rises at seven, says his prayers, and then proceeds to dress. He then goes to mass, receives his ministers and ambassadors, dines, takes a walk, works at his watch-making, and joins the queen at the Trianon; holds public and private audiences, eats his supper, and goes to bed.

He rarely changes his dress during the day, unless he has to leave the château. To-day he is wearing a coat of gray silk, ornamented with silver. His small-clothes are of the same material, his waistcoat is white satin, embroidered in silk with roses and green leaves, with silver spangles and silver buttons, like those on the coat, but smaller. He wears a three-cornered hat, trimmed with a silver cord, and carries a long cane with a gold knob. His shoe-buckles are silver, and his lace ruffles are *point d'Alençon.*

At one o'clock I see him at his dinner. The steward of the household has shown me the *menu*, and, what is more, he has let me see the prices.

Beef stewed in its own juice.
Rice soup.
Onion and chicken soup.
Pâtés de foie gras.
Chicken pâtés.
Mutton chops.
Stewed rabbit.
Chicken wings and trimmings.
Salmi of red partridges.
Spring chickens à l'Allemande.
Veal kidneys glacés.
Blanquette of chicken, with truffles.
Squabs à la D'Huxelles.
Ham and spinach.
Turkey à la Périgueux.
Three fat pullets; one larded.
Eighteen larks.
One young duck from Rouen.
One chicken from Caux.
Six partridges.
Three woodcocks.

The cost of all this amounts to two hundred and eighty francs. Living seems to have been more abundant and far cheaper then than in our own day. Such a repast served in 1889 by a leading Paris *restaurateur* would not cost less than one thousand francs, without wine.

The court balls are charming; they dance gavottes and minuets, and sometimes even a dance called the *chaconne*, derived from the ballet of the opera, for stately dances are going out of fashion. The queen, being a native of Austria, has introduced the waltz and several Hungarian dances, to the great scandal of old members of the Old Régime. In other respects the court at the château can hardly be said to amuse itself. It is preoccupied with politics. The great social interest is at the Trianon.

The Little Trianon is a sort of earthly paradise in miniature. A great deal of unnecessary fuss has been made about this graceful fancy of the queen's, which, as royal fancies go, is not expensive. It is a vision of Watteau realized by a rich and charming woman. It is *opéra comique* incarnate; it is foolishly and divinely fascinating.

The little palace is the most perfect expression of the eighteenth century. It has a little theatre and a temple to Cupid. A belvedere is on the summit of a hillock in the park, and near it are the farm buildings, the dairy, the school, and the temple to Love. Ah, what a charming spot! Here the queen walks and rests, drinks milk, eats curds, makes cream-cheeses, wears pink or blue *percale*, and a straw hat trimmed with blue-bells or cornflowers. Her dearest friends are there her company. There is the Princesse de Lamballe, and the Princesse de Polignac, and her favorites among the gentlemen, Comte Adhémar, Comte Patastron, and M. de Vaudreuil. All conform, with the best grace in the world, to this elegant caprice of the queen, who, weary of gayety, masked balls, sleighing parties, and other court amusements, has now taken a fancy to play the shepherdess, after the pattern of those in Florian. All her guests wear village costumes; the royal princes and princesses take their share in these elegant and innocent diversions. The king is the village miller. He may be seen carrying on his back heavy sacks of grain and flour. His strength is herculean. The queen is milkmaid, and serves out her milk to the good villagers of the neighborhood.

Monsieur — that is the Comte de Provence — is the schoolmaster, and teaches little boys from the neighboring villages. He is particularly delighted with this travesty; and as he has always had a taste for letters and a dash of the pedagogue in his disposition, he plays his part with wonderful success. One day, a boy, too young to have learned respect for royalty, flung a paper pellet across the room, which hit the prince in the face. His Highness rose, and seized the delinquent by the ears. "Ah, Monseigneur," cried the boy, "you are only *making believe* to teach school, have mercy, and only *make believe* to whip me!"

The evenings at the Trianon are very gay, and are unrestrained by ceremony. They play on the harpsichord, they sing Garat's songs, they talk a little scandal, — not much, however. Sometimes stories are told of gayety or gallantry, but they would have seemed insipidly virtuous to the Queen of Navarre. Madrigals are also written to Queen Marie Antoinette.

"I seek in verse to celebrate the beauty I adore,
I think of it — rethink of it, in vain;
My happy heart with thought of it with joy so runneth o'er
My mind cannot find words to weave the strain."

Sometimes they even presume to write epigrams on cruel ladies. Here is a specimen: —

"You have sworn me love eternal
Often, lady fair;
And the vows you swore, as often
Sailed away on air.
I know it too well, loveliest;
And, if the air were slow,
You 'd agitate your gilded fan
And make them faster go."

Before they separate for the night after these pleasures,

they wind up — let me whisper it, lest it encourage evil tastes in the Paris of 1889 — with onion soup ! [1]

ON THE QUEEN OF FRANCE ASKING FOR VERSES ON HER DEFECTS.
By M. DE BOUFFLERS.

Would you know what Rumor lays
To the charge of Antoinette ?
That she 's often light it says,
Fickle, mad, and a coquette.
And is it so ?
Ah, yes ! but know
So nice the line that fancy draws,
Her very slights
Create delights,
And Cato's self would smile applause.

If for business or for pleasure
The hour by herself be set,
One, 't is said, may wait her leisure ;
'T is a trifle to forget.
And is it so ?
Ah, yes ! but know
That when one next beholds her face,
All wrongs adieu,
Delights renew,
And time flies on with double pace.

That *I* and *me* fill all discourse
And *self* runs on supremely ;
'T is said she finds no other source,
She loves herself supremely.
And is it so ?
Ah, yes ! but know
The case is just, you 'll find ;
What blame to prove
That she should love
What 's loved by all mankind ?

[1] It must have been on one of these occasions that the Marquis de Boufflers addressed some charming lines to Marie Antoinette, who had asked him to tell her of her faults. I have never seen the original of M. de Boufflers' poem. But a translation of it was in an extract book made by my mother in her youth, and she made me learn the verses when I was a little girl. I have an impression that she told me the translation had been made by one of the literary young men in Boston in her day, — Mr. Ticknor, Mr. Prescott, Mr. Tudor, or Mr. Parsons. — E. W. L.

Few people know that it was Pascal of the "Lettres Provinciales" who first conceived the idea of establishing omnibuses in Paris. The scheme was tried, but in 1789 had been given up. Instead, we can find plenty of hackney-coaches. They are heavy, cumbersome, ill built, and have each a pair of horses. The drivers are all in rags, but some wear old dress livery coats in tatters. There is also a sort of cabriolet hung very high upon large wheels like those in Naples, and there are plenty of sedan chairs, some of them very luxurious, and borne by well-dressed stout chairmen. There are a few *coucous*, but as yet these are not in all their glory.

In 1789 the Parisians had no prescience of M. Haussmann, but instinctively their souls longed for him. A distinguished architect, M. Dewailly, is, at the very moment of our visit, about to exhibit, with the king's permission, in the salon of the Louvre, a project for laying out the streets of Paris afresh, almost like that of the future Baron Haussmann.

Alas! in 1789 the Louvre, the Tuileries, and the Palais Royal are surrounded by a network of disreputable streets, the haunt of cut-throats, thieves, and burglars. Near the Hôtel de Ville there are some peasants' cottages, with their dunghills,[1] and pigs wallowing in the mire; while geese splash and cackle in the gutters.

The public drive is along what was then called the Grand Cours, but subsequently was renamed the Avenue des Champs Élysées. The Champs Élysées is a kind of wood, where skittle players and football players make matches with each other. Private equipages drive in that part of the wood which lies back of the gardens of the houses of the Rue St. Honoré. The Cours de la Reine is separated from the Champs Élysées by a ditch where those who play *cochonnet* (an old-fashioned village ball game) come to amuse themselves.

The Pont Neuf may be compared to the heart of the animal system. It is the centre of circulation in Paris in 1789. Police agents take their stand there, and expect to arrest the

[1] See Book IV. Chapter IV. on Robespierre.

men who are "wanted." If they do not find them there, they go to the Palais Royal. The openings to the bridge are a great place for *camelots*, — that is, the Cheap Jacks of that period, — and likewise for recruiting sergeants, who employ all sorts of arts to entrap the unwary, and the statue of Henri Quatre looks down with a complaisant smile on all this fraud and hurly-burly.

But the real centre of Parisian life in 1789 I know to be the Palais Royal. It is nine o'clock in the evening, and in spite of the non-discovery of gas, or of electricity, the Palais Royal is a blaze of light from one end to the other. Under the arcades jewellers display their wares behind the little panes of their narrow windows which glitter like the stars. Here are long chains of jewels, pearls, and precious stones; watches by wholesale, rings of all kinds; diamond or rhine-stone ear-rings, snuff-boxes, gold mounted work-cases, things that constitute our modern bric-à-brac, filigree jewelry, and gold, silver, or enamelled cups of antique shapes with ebony handles. The drapers and mercers have rich stuffs hanging from the ceiling to the floor of their establishments, and those who pass by finger them, — not always with clean hands.

There are restaurants, *cafés*, and eating-stands. Drinking and eating go on at all hours, street musicians are endeav-oring to charm those who are sitting at dinner, and beggars are imploring charity with a nasal whine.

In the gardens and under the arcades lounge a singular and promiscuous crowd. Dandies dressed in silk elbow vagabonds swarming with vermin. An English family all agape with curiosity has encountered a party of Turks, wear-ing enormous turbans, who pretend to take no interest in any-thing around them.

Young men of fashion sit on chairs at their ease in the garden, staring at the women through their glasses, eating ices and reading the gazettes, for the place is as bright as day. The news of the past twenty-four hours is discussed. There are disputes and quarrels and reconciliations. De-bauchery in the Palais Royal takes no pains to hide itself; it is there on its own ground.

Sometimes great people visit the minor theatres as a joke. On one such occasion the queen, smelling the tempting savor of some cabbage soup that was being served on the stage, had a bowl full of it brought up to her box, and shared it with the Princesse de Lamballe.

To turn to the fashions of 1789. We will begin with the ladies' *coiffures*. They are outrageous. The caricatures of the time tell of heads being dressed to resemble frigates. But I dare not vouch for this. It may be caricature.[1]

There are new fashions in caps of all kinds, — caps *à la Gertrude*, which imitate those of peasant women; caps *aux sentiments repliés* (that is, "caps of repressed feelings"), and of "the slave emancipated," etc.

Bonnets are worn only by great ladies and by wealthy *bourgeoises*. They are commonly of straw, tall in the crown, and trimmed with silk, ribbon, and lace. Emerald green intermixed with very bright pink is extremely fashionable. It is proper for ladies in public to carry a fan in one hand and a little velvet mask in the other, which, however, is rarely put on.

Men think it good taste to dress simply in the street, in dark cloth, after the English fashion; soot-color (*suie des cheminées de Londres*) is very fashionable. The hats are tall, tapering, and have a silver buckle in the middle of their ribbon. Small-clothes are of nankeen, or nankeen color, opening at the sides with seven pearl buttons. White stockings it is not good taste to wear on the street; they should be white with blue stripes. Men carry muffs occasionally, as well as the ladies.

It is the correct thing for a man of fashion to carry two watches, and to hold in the hand a bamboo cane with a gold knob, or one of porcelain. Dandies carry the cane up to the shoulder, like a musket.

Besides soot-color, coats are made of apple-green cloth, bottle-green, dead-leaf, and beef-blood. This last *sang de bœuf* is quite the rage. It is worn with a white silk waistcoat,

[1] True, however. Madame d'Oberkirch describes such a *coiffure* on the head of Marie Antoinette.— E. W. L.

and small-clothes made of satin, of an untranslatable color, *tête de nègre.* The shirt bosoms and the cuffs are trimmed with lace. If boots are worn they must be of soft leather; yellow top-boots are the height of the fashion, but only the most advanced dandies can venture to wear them. The hair is commonly powdered, but some men of rank have given up powder, and have their hair simply tied behind with a black ribbon.

Little boys are dressed like sailors, partly because that costume is worn by Monseigneur the Dauphin.

What would you say to me if I left Paris without seeing the Bastille? That mysterious prison, which in a few weeks will be destroyed, is now only guarded by a few old Invalides. One may be permitted in 1789 to visit the dungeons, for there is nobody there. Prisoners pay pretty high for their board and lodging,[1] but apart from the expense they are not badly fed.

There is, properly speaking, no garrison in Paris. The Swiss in their red uniforms are at Versailles, and the brilliant and faithful *gardes du corps* (body-guards) are there too. The Gardes Françaises are intrusted with the maintenance of order in the capital. Their regiment contains 4,878 men. All wear a white uniform with blue trimmings. This regiment is much permeated by the new ideas. The officers are all of the purest blood of the nobility, and the non-commissioned officers are often of the best *bourgeois* families. The soldiers never keep their family name. They exchange it for that of some flower, — Fair Rose, Fine Tulip, Mayflower, etc. They are in the highest order as to dress and equipments, and walk with a brisk step, twirling their mustachios. Very little can be said for their morality, or, in their love-affairs, for their sense of honor.

It is in the Halles (or great market-places of Paris) that the lower class of the Parisians appears in all its glory. Let us take a look at the Halles. There is the Butter Halle,

[1] The king made handsome allowance for their subsistence, but this, for the most part, seems to have gone into the pockets of the governor, M. de Launay. — E. W. L.

the Fish Halle, the Marché des Proubaines, the market for green-stuff, and the potato market under a large shed; and the flower-market, covering in all nearly ten thousand square yards. There is nothing to shelter the provisions from the inclemency of the weather, except immense red umbrellas. The market-women (*dames de la Halle*) have all sorts of privileges. They wait on the queen with their congratulations when she becomes a mother, and on the king when he begins his reign; they figure in many Parisian ceremonies (as they continue to do even in 1889), and probably will to the end of the chapter.

Sometimes they are very pretty, but rarely decently polite. Some boast that they have belonged to the Halles, mother and daughter, since the time of Saint Louis. They have an especial vocabulary called the *dictionnaire poissard*. Their abuse is occasionally sublime. Alliteration plays a great part in their invectives. Let us go up to one of them. There is a great smell of codfish. Housekeepers, grisettes, soldiers, and well-dressed men are swarming round the fish-stalls. A young girl timidly comes up to a stout, red-faced woman.

"Madame, how much do you ask for this eel?"

"One livre for you, my Venus of love."

"No; ten sous."

"Ten sous! Do you suppose I stole it? Get home with you! I wish the boys were out of school! I'd make them run after you, you baggage! . . . Ah, well, my little love, you may have it, after all, for ten sous."

The sound of a violin is heard. A man is singing in the street. What does he sing? You might guess beforehand.

"La boulangère, d'où viens-tu?
J'arrivons de l'Autriche,
Si je n'avions que ma virtu,
Je ne serions pas ben riche, vois-tu,
Je ne serions pas ben riche!"

And, lastly, as to the police. The lieutenant of police is as powerful as a minister of state, indeed, more so. His secret influence is almost boundless. He can hush up any matter he may please. He can put any obnoxious person quietly out of the way. There are about three hundred agents called *mouchards*, who serve under him. It is no longer the custom to beat the watch; but the security of the capital, especially during the hours of darkness, leaves much to be desired. Professional thieves are numerous in proportion to the population. It is not prudent to walk abroad after nine o'clock in the neighborhood of Notre Dame, in the Champs Élysées, or even on the Boulevard.

BOOK III.

THE COLLAPSE OF FRENCH ROYALTY.

I. The Flight to Varennes.
II. Count Axel Fersen.
III. The Tenth of August and the Massacres of September.
IV. The Princesse de Lamballe.
V. Last Hours of the King.
VI. Marie Antoinette and Robespierre.
VII. Closing Scenes in the Life of Marie Antoinette.

CHAPTER I.

THE FLIGHT TO VARENNES.[1]

THE most interesting chapter in Carlyle's prose epic, the "History of the French Revolution," is the one that records the story of the Flight to Varennes. But of late years memoirs, journals, and public documents bearing on the subject have been brought to light, which correct some errors in Mr. Carlyle's narrative. These are especially the memoirs of Madame de Tourzel (1883) and the Diary and Letters of Count Fersen (1877).

The Flight to Varennes was not merely a picturesque and thrilling episode in the French Revolution, it was also a great crisis in European history. Europe at this time was in dread of the approach of Jacobinism. The *émigrés* were beseeching every court, not only to deliver their sovereign from the durance in which he was placed, but to stamp out a fire which endangered their own security. The Comte d'Artois had formed a plan by which France was to be invaded from several sides at once, — from the South by Spain, from the East by Savoy, from the North by the Austrians.

[1] Abridged from an article in the "London Quarterly Review," 1886.

The centre of this combination was the Emperor Leopold II., who had recently succeeded his brother Joseph as sovereign of Austria.

The position of the Emperor Leopold was an exceedingly difficult one. The proposed scheme of invasion depended on the successful escape of the king and his family from Paris, which would have secured the sympathies of all Europe, but there was great danger to Austria, surrounded as she was by enemies, should she act alone.

The king was to go to Montmédy, but he was not to stop there. A camp was to be formed round the old château of Thouelle in the neighborhood. Bouillé's faithful German regiments were to be joined by a number of *émigrés*; but, above all, ten thousand Austrian troops were to be massed upon the frontier a few miles from Thouelle. Once out of Paris, the king would be a free agent. He would dissolve the Assembly, restore the clergy to their possessions, and by thus destroying the basis on which the value of the *assignats* rested (*assignats* were the government's promises to pay out of the sale of the confiscated estates of the nobles and the clergy), he would cause a bankruptcy in France, and deprive his rebellious subjects of their sources of credit. Escape would be the potent engine of a counter-revolution.

The flight of the king from Paris had long been planned and discussed, but it did not assume a definite shape until after April 18, 1791. On May 29, the date of departure was fixed for June 12; but a democratic waiting-maid of the dauphin did not leave her service till the 11th. Sunday evening, June 19, was next agreed upon; but at the last moment another waiting-maid of the dauphin who could not be trusted caused the delay of another day.

The most active agent in preparations for the flight was Count Axel Fersen, commander of the Royal Swedish Regiment in the king's service, and an intimate friend of the king and queen. On the afternoon of Monday, June 20, he paid a last visit to the royal family at the Tuileries. He found them resolved on departure, notwithstanding a prevalent rumor that their plans for flight had been discovered. They were both deeply affected. The king said to the count, in taking leave of him, that he could never forget all he had done for him. The queen wept bitterly. To avoid suspicion, she drove out with her children to the gardens called Tivoli, and told her daughter while there that she must practice discretion, and not be surprised at anything she might see or hear. Fersen then returned to his own house to make his final preparations; he visited the hotel of Mr. Quentin Crauford in the Rue de Clichy, to see whether the new berline, built for the king's journey, had arrived from the coachmaker's. At eight o'clock he went again to the Tuileries with a letter to the queen, informing her of a slight change in the arrangement made for the waiting-maids. As he took the letter to the Tuileries, everything seemed quiet. At a quarter to nine the three body-guards who were to act as outriders for the royal party, came to Fersen for instructions. He then sent off a chaise, which was to convey the two waiting-maids to Claye, gave his last orders to his coachman, Balthasar Sapel, and then mounted the box of the hackney-coach in which he was to drive the royal family to the barrier.

The queen returned from her drive to Tivoli at seven o'clock. She then submitted herself to one of those elaborate feats of hair-dressing which excite our wonder in the portraits of the time. This process lasted more than an hour, and she then had an interview with the three body-guards who were to accompany her in her flight. Passing to her drawing-room, she found the Comte de Provence, who had just taken an affecting leave of his sister Elisabeth. He had come with his wife to supper, as was their custom every evening. The supper was served at nine, and lasted nearly two hours. Monsieur and his wife were to leave Paris that night by different roads. They did not know whether they should join the king at Montmédy, or should ever see him again. The brothers indeed then met for the last time. Monsieur left the Tuileries, never to re-enter it until he did so as Louis XVIII. in 1814. After supper the queen dis-

DUCHESSE D'ANGOULEME AND THE DAUPHIN.

missed her servants as soon as possible. She then went to bed, or appeared to do so, and the attendant shut the door of the passage leading to her room. The dauphin, on returning home from Tivoli, had eaten his supper and had been put to bed at nine o'clock. Madame (his young sister) had given orders to be called at eight o'clock. About eleven at night the queen knocked at the door of her son's chamber. He was fast asleep; but when she told him he was to go to a fortress where he would command his regiment, he threw himself out of bed and cried, "Quick! quick! give me a sword and my boots, and let me be off!" He was dressed like a little girl, in a costume which Madame de Tourzel had already provided. His sister, who had been awakened earlier, wore a cheap dress of muslin which had been bought a few days before for about three quarters of a dollar. A piece of it still exists in Orleans. The two children, with their governess and the two waiting-maids, met in one of the queen's apartments. The queen looked out into the courtyard and saw that everything was quiet. The hackney-coach was standing close by a door in the furthest corner, through which the royal family were to make their escape. Fersen, who had made every preparation with skill and rapidity, sat, dressed like a coachman, on the box. This door led from the apartments of a noble who had emigrated, and was left unguarded. The queen solemnly intrusted her children to Madame de Tourzel, who with her charge passed through dark passages to the unlocked door, and then out into the court. Fersen lifted the children into the coach, handed in Madame de Tourzel, and drove off. A short time afterwards the two waiting-maids were sent down another staircase; a cabriolet was waiting for them on the other side of the Pont Royal, and they drove off to Claye.

Fersen, knowing that the king, queen, and Madame Elisabeth could not arrive immediately, took a turn round the Quais, and then came back by the Rue St. Honoré to the Petit Carrousel. He waited three quarters of an hour, but no one came. Lafayette's carriage, guarded by dragoons, drove by with flashing lights. Lafayette was on his way to the *coucher* of the king, whom he held a long time in conversation, for grave suspicions of flight that night had been aroused. The guards had been doubled; every one was on the alert.

Lafayette at last drove away. The king was seen to bed by the servant who had charge of the rooms. The doors of the great gallery were locked by the porter in attendance, and the keys were placed in his mattress, where they were found the next morning. As soon as the king was left alone, he got up and dressed himself for the flight.

After the hackney-coach had been waiting in the Carrousel three quarters of an hour, a lady was seen approaching it. She was Madame Elisabeth. Her attendant had left her when within sight of the carriage. Not long after came the king. He told Madame de Tourzel he had left the Tuileries by the great gate, and that his shoe-buckle having become loose he had stopped to arrange it with all the coolness in the world. They waited for the queen some little time, and it was probably then that Lafayette's carriage passed a second time, and the king could not repress an insulting exclamation as it flashed by him. He looked upon Lafayette as his jailer. The story of the queen losing herself in the Rue de Bac is apocryphal; but on leaving the palace she found a sentinel posted at the top of the staircase she was about to descend, and had to wait till she could pass him. She afterwards told Fersen, on his visit to Paris in the February following, that, passing through the Great Carrousel, her conductor did not know where to find the Little Carrousel, and, at her suggestion, asked a horse-guard. When she got into the carriage the king embraced her, and cried, "How glad I am to see you here!"

Fersen by a roundabout route then drove to the Barrier of Clichy. The guard-house at the barrier was lighted up. Every one was *en fête*. A marriage was being celebrated with drinking and dancing, and the royal party passed unrecognized. A short distance beyond the gate they found the berline, a large travelling carriage made to hold six persons. It was drawn by four strong Norman horses. Fersen's coachman, Balthasar Sapel, was riding postilion on one of them, and M. de Moustier, a tall body-guard, was on the box. Another body-guard, who had conducted the fugitives through the Carrousel, was on the dicky of the hackney-coach; while M. de Valory, the third, was spurring, on one of Fersen's horses, to Bondy, to order that a relay of horses might be ready when the travellers arrived.

The hackney-coach was driven up close to the berline. The doors of both were opened, and the royal party stepped from one to the other, unobserved. Then the hackney-coach, having served its purpose, was tumbled into a ditch. Fersen mounted the box, and by his side was Moustier. He repeatedly called out to his coachman to be quick, and not to spare the horses. Balthasar said afterwards that, thinking his master might kill his own horses if he pleased, he urged them to such speed that the three leagues, or seven and a half miles, between the barrier and Bondy, were made in half an hour. At any rate, they went at a good pace. The fresh horses ordered by Valory were waiting for them in the road.

Fersen, after begging earnestly to be allowed to accompany the party, took an affectionate farewell. Happy would it have been had the king granted his request, and kept him with them! He leaped upon the horse from which Valory had dismounted, and, travelling by cross-roads, reached Belgium in safety.

It has been erroneously said that the carriage in which the royal family were making their escape was a lumbering coach, conspicuous by its form and splendor. This is quite untrue. It was a sound, well-built carriage. The bill of the coachmaker who made it has been preserved. The body was painted black and green; the running gear, as was usual in those days, was yellow. It attracted no attention in itself; and an older carriage would probably have broken down on the road.

At Claye the waiting maids were overtaken, and the whole party proceeded in full daylight to Meaux. The king was in high spirits. "At last," he said, "I have escaped from that town of Paris where I have drunk so much bitterness;

be assured that, once in the saddle, I shall be very different from what you have seen me up to the present moment."

He read aloud a copy of the memorial he had left behind to be presented to the Assembly. He anticipated the happiness with which he would endow France, the return of his brothers and of his faithful servants, and the possibility of re-establishing the Catholic religion, and repairing the evils of which he had been the unwilling cause.

At about eight in the morning he looked at his watch and remarked, "Lafayette must be in a terrible state of mind now!" It has been said that the king walked up the hills, "enjoying the blessed sunshine" and generally conducting himself imprudently. But in point of fact there was no sunshine. The day was dull and cloudy. The king only left the carriage once during the long journey and then spoke to no one.

The travellers were amply supplied with provisions, which had been placed for them in the carriage. The children walked up one or two of the long hills, but occasioned no delay. Before reaching Châlons the horses fell twice, and broke the harness; this took an hour to repair, and with that, and the delay at Paris, they reached Châlons two hours too late. They had travelled more than seven miles an hour including stoppages, and that, with a heavy carriage and post-horses, was a very good pace.

When the king reached Châlons he believed himself in safety. At the next post, called Pont Sommevesle, he was to find a detachment of soldiers from Bouillé's army, and thence similar detachments were to be posted all along his route till he reached Montmédy. But when they reached the lone post-house of Pont Sommevesle, not a soldier was to be seen. Where was Choiseul? Where were the Lauzun hussars that should have been there waiting? The king felt as if an abyss had opened beneath his feet. The horses were quickly changed, and the berline moved on, but a heavy weight was on the travellers' hearts, — a foreboding of calamity.

It was not the fault of Bouillé that his arrangements miscarried; they had been skilfully and carefully made. But his subordinates were inexperienced and harebrained men. Most of them had not been informed of the importance of the mission with which they were charged, and believed that they were detailed only to escort a treasure. Bouillé indeed was expecting money to pay his troops about this time. Troops had been posted at Pont Sommevesle, at Clermont, at Ste. Menehould, at Varennes, at Stenay, and at Sedan. But all went wrong, owing in the first instance to the snapping of the first link in the chain of communication.

M. de Goguelat, an officer possessing the confidence of the king and queen, had been sent by them to Bouillé to assist him in making the last arrangements. The choice was an unfortunate one, because, of all the blunderers in this affair, none were so bad as Goguelat. He disobeyed the most important orders that were given him, and everything left to his discretion was badly done.

How was it that the king on arriving at the post-house at Pont Sommevesle, where he expected to find his escort, found not a soul to meet him?

The Duc de Choiseul, commander of the royal dragoons, had been sent by Bouillé, from Metz, in order to give the king the last information about the preparations for the escort. Fersen expressed at the time a doubt as to whether he was the best instrument for the purpose. Although devoted to the cause of the king, he was frivolous and hasty, and had not that spirit of calm patience and decision which was needed in the difficult crisis. However, he was very rich, and of high rank, was colonel of a distinguished regiment, and was able to furnish from his own stables relays which would be needed for the royal party at Varennes. It was arranged that Choiseul should leave Paris ten hours before the king. At two in the afternoon the queen sent to him her private hair-dresser Léonard. Choiseul took him with him in his carriage, without telling him where he was going. They slept at Montmirail, left that town at four the next morning, and arrived at the post-house of Pont Sommevesle soon after eleven. Choiseul found his orderly there with two horses. The hussars had not arrived, but they appeared an hour later. M. de Goguelat, who was in command of the party, found Choiseul still dressing, and delivered to him a large packet of orders which he had received two days before from Bouillé. Choiseul picketed his horses, and gave bread and wine to the hussars. The orders brought by Goguelat to Choiseul were very precise. Choiseul was placed in command of all the troops posted along the road, having full liberty to employ force if he thought it best to do so. If he should hear that the king had been arrested at Châlons, he was to attack the town, and to attempt a rescue. In such a case he was to despatch orders all along the line, so that he might be supported. When the king arrived at Pont Sommevesle, it was from him that Choiseul would receive his orders. If the king desired to be recognized, the hussars were to escort him with drawn swords to Ste. Menehould. If the king wished to remain incognito, he was to allow him to pass quietly, and half an hour after was to follow him along the road, and was to post a body of hussars between Ste. Menehould and Clermont, who were to remain there for fifteen hours, and intercept every one who came by, either on horseback or in a carriage, from the direction of Paris. This would effectually prevent the king's being pursued. Further, as soon as he was aware of the king being at hand, he was to send M. de Goguelat to inform the several detachments, or, if this was impossible, he was to carry the news himself. Choiseul did none of the things that were expected of him. By some strange miscalculation it had been said that the berline might be expected to arrive at Pont Sommevesle at half-past two in the afternoon at latest. Supposing that the royal family left Paris punctually at midnight, this would have allowed a pace of eight miles an hour including stoppages, and without any accidents. Choiseul says, in a paper he wrote in his defense, that when three o'clock and four o'clock came, and the courier who was to precede the royal carriage had not arrived, he became very anxious, especially as the inhabitants of a neighboring village, believing that the soldiers had come to make them pay their rents, were assuming a threatening attitude. At four o'clock he sent off Léonard, the hairdresser, in his own post-chaise to inform the detachments posted on the road that the party expected had not arrived, and that the scheme had probably collapsed. He waited with his hussars, he says, till half-past five, or a quarter to six, and then retreated, not by the highway, but by cross-roads to Orbéval. When the king reached Pont Sommevesle at half-past six, he found no one there to give him news of the party of hussars, and no sign of any disturbance among the neighboring peasantry.

Choiseul's neglect to wait for Valory, whether preceding the king or not, was inexcusable. He knew Valory to have orders if the king failed to reach Bondy to ride on and inform the detachments that the enterprise had failed.

When Valory reached Pont Sommevesle and found no soldiers, he asked no questions even of the post-master, but, ordering fresh horses to be ready for the carriage, rode on to Ste. Menehould, the next post town.

At Ste. Menehould all was confusion and uncertainty. Léonard had passed through with news that the treasure would probably not arrive that day; and Captain d'Andoins, the officer in command, in spite of the remonstrances of Lagache, one of his non-commissioned officers, who appears to have been in the secret, ordered his troopers' horses to be unsaddled and his men dispersed. Half an hour after this had been done, Valory galloped up, and twenty minutes later came the berline.

The town by this time was in great excitement. Knots of people had gathered in the streets. Something was on foot, they knew not what; and a formal request was made to the mayor to issue arms to the new National Guard which had been already enrolled.

As the carriage stopped at the post-house it excited much attention. Captain d'Andoins kept in the background, but contrived to whisper to those in the carriage: "Your plans have miscarried. To avoid suspicion I will go away." He also made a sign to Valory to harness quickly; but Valory interpreted this as a wish to speak to him, and their conversation roused the attention of the crowd. Just as the fresh horses were being harnessed, J. B. Drouet, the postmaster, arrived from a field he had been cultivating in the neighborhood. He was a young man of twenty-eight, but he had served in the Condé dragoons, and had seen the queen at Versailles. He now thought he recognized her. At this moment the king put his head out of the window to speak to Valory, and Drouet, by a sudden inspiration, compared the portrait on the *assignat* which Valory had just paid him for the relay with the head of the traveller. He noticed the long aquiline nose, the short-sighted look, the spotted complexion; and when a message from the town council came to ask his opinion, he had no doubt that the berline contained the king and his family. Indeed, the recognition of the king seems to have been made simultaneously by many of the loiterers. Suspicion ran from mouth to mouth. The crowd seemed determined to molest the travellers. Lagache, resolved that one soldier at least should do his duty and follow his sovereign, clutched his reins in his teeth, and with a pistol in each hand broke through the crowd, firing a shot as he passed out of the town. He followed the berline towards Clermont, but, with the fatality which accompanied every incident in the flight, he went astray in a wood, and did not reach Clermont till eleven at night, when the king was already a prisoner at Varennes. After the berline had passed, D'Andoins tried to assemble and mount his dragoons, but was prevented by the populace, who forced the soldiers to surrender to the mayor.

Drouet, accompanied by three other citizens of Ste. Menehould, set off at once to spread their news. As they galloped out of the Châlons gate, the newly armed National Guard, mistaking them for soldiers, fired on them. One was killed, another dangerously wounded. Then a cry arose, "To arms!" The tocsin was sounded. All the town was on the alert.

Meantime the king was passing through a beautiful

MARIE ANTOINETTE.

country along the banks of the river Aire. A narrow bridge, after passing through the town of Varennes, crosses that river; and beyond the bridge was the Hôtel du Grand Monarque, where fresh horses were waiting for the travellers. There was no one to tell them this. It had been at first arranged that horses should be ready for them before entering the town on the road from Clermont; but Goguelat, at the last moment, had altered this arrangement, and neglected to give notice to the travellers.

Varennes was not a post town. Travellers usually took another road to Verdun. Varennes was a peaceful little place; its inhabitants were that day engaged in preparing for a *fête*, when the hair-dresser Léonard rode in with his message to the troops of failure and despair. The horses waiting for the berline at the Hôtel du Grand Monarque were Choiseul's private property. Léonard tried to get them for his carriage, but was refused. He, however, procured others. Had he continued on the road to Montmédy, he would have met Bouillé, and perhaps have induced him to advance and see what was the matter; but, stricken with the common fatality, he took the road to Verdun. Having done all the mischief he could by his journey on the king's route, he now discontinued it at the very moment when he might have been of use.

The travelling carriage stopped at the entrance of the town of Varennes, where they expected to find horses waiting for them. Nothing was to be seen. Every house was in repose. In vain the king knocked at a door; he was angrily told to go away. The three body-guards went off to look for the expected horses. The queen roused up a gentleman, M. de Préfontaine; but he had been ill, and could give her no information.

At this moment two riders, Drouet and a friend, spurred past the carriage, crying out to the postilions: "Don't go on. Unharness your horses. Your passenger is the king!"

Valory, after a fruitless search for the relay of Choiseul's horses, came back to the king, who met him with the words, "We are betrayed!" Their only course was to hurry forward, but the postilions refused to go on; they said that their mistress had charged them to go no further than the entrance to Varennes, because they were wanted for the hay harvest the next day. It is said that this woman never forgave herself for having thus caused the deaths of the king and queen. At last the body-guards, by threatening violence, induced the postilions to remount and take the carriage into Varennes. But thirty-five minutes had been lost. Drouet had the start of them, and it was too late.

Drouet pulled up at the Bras d'Or tavern, where, though the time was nearly eleven, a few young men still lingered. Drouet entered in haste, drew the landlord aside, and told the news, enjoining him at once to rouse all trustworthy people, who must see to it that the king was arrested. The landlord called up his opposite neighbor, the mayor, M. Sauce, while Drouet went to barricade the bridge which united the two parts of the town. All this while two captains of dragoons, Charles Bouillé and Raigecourt, were sitting at the window of their hotel, doing nothing. They heard a little movement in the town, but paid it no attention. Sauce sent his little children to rouse people from their beds. Seven young men armed, prepared to stop the carriage. The postchaise with the two chamber-maids came first. They were asked for their passport, and on their saying it was in the second carriage were suffered to pass on. The occupants of the berline told the party who detained and questioned them, that they were on their way to Frankfort. Sauce held up a lantern, and scrutinized the faces of the travellers. At last the passport was delivered to him. He remarked that it was signed by the king, but not by the President of the National Assembly, and that in consequence of this irregularity he must detain the travellers till the matter could be looked into; and when the postilions attempted to proceed, they were stopped by armed men, who cried, "If you go a step further, we fire!" Nothing was left for the royal family but to get out of their carriage.

M. Sauce offered them the hospitality of his house. On the ground-floor was a grocer's shop, with a strong smell of tallow, particularly disagreeable to the queen. The upper story was reached by a narrow corkscrew staircase, unchanged to the present day. On the upper floor there were two rooms, one looking on the street, the other on the courtyard. In the back room, about fifteen feet by twenty, was collected the majesty of France. The king seated himself in the middle of the room in an armchair; the queen asked for some hot water, wine, and clean sheets, probably for the children. The dauphin and his sister were placed upon a bed and were soon asleep, with Madame de Tourzel seated at their side. The body-guards sat on a bench beneath the window. It is incredible that the king should not have been rescued at this moment. Sixty hussars were in their barracks at a short distance from the bridge, with their horses saddled, ready to start at any moment; that they were useless in this crisis was owing to Goguelat's errors. By some strange infatuation he had sent their own commander, D'Eslon, off to Bouillé, where he could be of no use, and left his men in charge of a young lieutenant of eighteen, Rohrig by name, who lost his head and did nothing. As soon as he found himself in difficulty, he crossed the river by a ford and galloped off to Bouillé. Charles Bouillé and Raigecourt did the same. By this time the whole town of Varennes was on foot. Barricades were built across all the streets leading to the country. Two or three pieces of ordnance, which were rusting in the stables of the old town hall, were dragged forth and placed partly on the bridge and partly on the entrance of the road from Clermont.

Meantime, about one o'clock in the morning, arrived Choiseul with his forty dragoons, — the body who should have waited at Pont Sommevesle. They were halted by a barricade and the two old pieces of cannon; but a few dragoons under Damas reaching the spot at the same moment, they pushed easily through the barricade and entered the town. Choiseul marched straight down the street, not stopping at the house where the royal party were prisoners, till he reached the hussar barracks, which he found deserted, the hussars and their young commander having crossed the ford and galloped off to Bouillé.

Choiseul drew up his soldiers, who were Germans, and told them that the king and queen were prisoners in the town, and they must rescue them. His words were responded to by a shout of "Der König! Die Königin!" He trotted his troops back to Sauce's house, and was there joined by Damas, who had just learned that the fugitive hussars had even carried off Choiseul's horses intended for a relay. At this moment very slight firmness on the soldiers' part or that of their commander would have saved the king; but there was the usual hesitation and delay.

In the house the king had acknowledged himself. Some of those around him were moved to tears, and Sauce was almost ready to give way. Outside, however, was a surging crowd, kept up to their purpose by Drouet. The king assured all those who heard him that he had no intention of leaving France, — he was not going beyond the frontier. A voice cried, "Sire, we don't believe you!" The queen did her best to touch the hearts of Madame Sauce and Sauce's mother, to induce them to persuade Sauce to let the party proceed. Old Madame Sauce, an old woman of eighty, fell down upon her knees bursting into tears, and kissed the hands of the children.

When Goguelat entered the room, Louis said to him, "Well, when shall we set off?" He answered, "Sire, we wait your orders." Damas suggested placing the whole party on seven horses belonging to the hussars, and carrying them off, guarded by the remainder of that body. But Louis feared a stray ball might kill one of them. It would have been far easier to have cleared the road by a charge, and then to have driven off in the berline. But at last the fatal decision was taken of waiting for Bouillé.

Meantime, by four o'clock, ten thousand peasants from the neighboring towns and villages had reached Varennes. The barricades were strengthened, and the hussars before Sauce's house found themselves between two fires. Goguelat at this time was wounded by a pistol-shot in an altercation with a National Guard. This shot might have been the signal for a massacre ; but the hussars, instead of attacking the crowd, fraternized with them. Jars of wine were passed from trooper to trooper; soon the soldiers were half drunk, and calling, "Vive la nation!"

As the sun rose over the lovely valley of the Aire, Sauce asked the king to show himself to the crowd from the window which overlooked the street; Louis saw a dense mass of peasants armed with muskets, scythes, and pitchforks, and some women staggering, half tipsy, among the crowd. As he stood at the window there was a deep silence; and when he told those who could hear him that he was going to Montmédy, but that he would afterwards return to Varennes, there was a thunder of applause, and reiterated cries of "Vive le roi!" "Vive la nation!"

At five in the morning an officer of hussars burst into the room where the royal family was assembled, with a bare sword. It was Captain d'Eslon, who had commanded the one hundred hussars left at Varennes, who had been sent off to Bouillé by the blundering of Goguelat. On hearing news of what had happened from Rohrig, D'Eslon instantly, with seventy of his men, galloped back to Varennes. He was stopped at the bridge, and, having little ammunition with him, he dared not charge, but after a parley was permitted to enter the town on foot, and, presenting himself to the king, asked for orders. The king replied he was a prisoner, and had no orders to give him.

Time was running on. The town officials were deliberating what they should do about the king's departure, when two messengers from the National Assembly arrived. One of them was M. de Romeuf, Lafayette's aide-de-camp, who was intimately known to the king and queen. The latter, when she saw him, cried, "Sir! is that you? I never could have believed it!" It is indeed possible that had Romeuf been alone he might have given the royal family an opportunity to escape; but he handed to the queen a decree of the Assembly which ordered the return of the royal family to Paris. Louis read it over the queen's shoulder and said, "There is no longer a king in France." The queen was less calm. "What insolence!" she cried; and seeing that the paper had fallen on the dauphin's bed, she seized it and threw it on the ground, saying it should not sully the couch of her son.

After this, the only chance for the king was to gain time for Bouillé to arrive. The deputies and the people were eager he should set out instantly for Paris. Louis supplicated for delay. "Could they not wait until eleven o'clock?" A hasty breakfast was served for them. The two children were still asleep, and the king dropped to sleep also. As a last resource, one of the waiting-maids (Madame de Neuville) declared herself to be seized with a violent attack of illness. The king refused to desert her, and a doctor was sent for. But all these stratagems produced only an hour and a half's delay, and Bouillé and his soldiers did not appear. The shouts of the impatient mob surged upward from the street. The carriages had been harnessed and brought up to Sauce's door; the royal family slowly and sadly descended the winding staircase. The king walked first, and was followed by Madame de Tourzel and the two children; Choiseul gave his arm to the queen, Damas to Madame Elisabeth; the body-guards were placed on the box, guarded by two grenadiers with bayonets fixed in their muskets. When the royal family had entered the carriage, Choiseul, who had been the chief cause of their calamity, closed the door.

It was half-past seven in the morning. What had caused the delay of Bouillé? The king had only left Varennes one quarter of an hour when a detachment of the Royal Allemand regiment appeared on the outskirts of the town, commanded by the Marquis de Bouillé in person. The bridge being defended, he tried to cross the river by a ford, but got entangled in a mill-race. The marquis had spent the night on the road between Varennes and Dun, the next town, sleeping by the wayside, with the bridle of his horse over his arm, but before news of the king's capture reached him he had left his post and returned to Stenay. As soon as he heard it, he lost no time in giving his orders, but they were slowly obeyed. Though the horses had been saddled all night, the detachment was not ready to set out till five. With a few stirring words to his soldiers concerning the capture of their king, Bouillé placed himself at their head, distributing among them four hundred louis by way of encouragement. They rode quickly, but when they reached Varennes, the king was well on the road to Clermont. Even then Bouillé would have charged had there been any hope of success, but, convinced that it was impossible to effect a rescue, he turned rein to Stenay and crossed the frontier that night, to die in England nine years after.

For the royal family the heat and the dust on their return journey were terrible. They reached Ste. Menehould at half-past one, and were stopped at the gate, while the mayor delivered a municipal address. The royal family lunched in the town hall. The queen showed herself to the crowd with the dauphin in her arms; and as the king and queen passed through the chapel where the prisoners in the town heard mass, they distributed money to the poor unfortunates whose case was like their own.

In the fields beyond Ste. Menehould, M. de Dampierre, an old gentleman who had shown them some respect, was dragged from his horse and murdered. The assassins returned to the royal carriage bearing his head in their blood-stained hands.

The king and his family would gladly have stayed a day at Châlons, to recover from their fatigue. But the patriots, seeing that the sentiment of the town was in their favor, sent for a large reinforcement from Rheims. These roughs arrived at ten in the morning, and breaking into the palace rushed into the chapel where the royal family was hearing mass, and interrupting the service hurried them into their carriage with such precipitation that a large sum of money was left behind.

Between Châlons and Épernay the queen offered a poor hungry wretch a piece of *bœuf à la mode*, that Fersen had had put into the carriage. A voice cried: "Do not eat it!

Do you not see they wish to poison you?" The queen immediately partook of it herself and gave some to the dauphin.

Between Épernay and Dormans, Pétion, Barnave, and Latour-Maubourg met the royal party as commissioners from the National Assembly. Pétion and Barnave took their places in the berline. Latour-Maubourg preferred to travel with the waiting-maids, telling the king that he could depend on his devotion, but that it was important to gain over the two others. Pétion's conduct was brutal, vulgar, and indecent, but Barnave conducted himself like a gentleman. The queen complained to Fersen of Pétion's conduct when they met in February, 1792.

Saturday, June 25, was the last day of their prolonged torment. It lasted thirteen hours, from six in the morning to seven in the evening. During the whole day the travellers were exposed to the glare of a midsummer sun and to the insults of the mob. At the barrier of Paris they were met by a dense crowd of citizens. No one raised his hat, or spoke a word. They entered the garden of the Tuileries by the swinging bridge, and were protected as they dismounted by the care of Lafayette.

Such is the true story of the flight to Varennes, more touching in its naked simplicity than any device of art could make it. The royal family had many chances in their favor; and they would have escaped if every one of those chances had not turned against them. If Choiseul had waited a short time longer at Pont Sommevesle; if he had retired at a foot-pace along the high-road; if he had passed through Ste. Menehould soon after the berline left it; or had halted at the parting of the ways instead of losing himself precipitately in pathless woods; if Goguelat had remained behind at the post-house, according to orders; if D'Andoins had not unsaddled the horses of his dragoons just before the berline arrived; if Lagache had not lost his way in the woods; if Damas had kept his men ready for action; if Charles Bouillé and Raigecourt had not shut themselves up in their bedroom; if an orderly whom they sent out for news had spoken with the berline when he met it outside Varennes; if Valory had crossed the bridge to the Hôtel du Grand Monarque; if Goguelat had not altered the position of the relays; if the hair-dresser Léonard had taken the road to Stenay instead of losing himself on that to Verdun, — if any one of these things had turned out differently, the royal family might have been saved!

CHAPTER II.

COUNT AXEL FERSEN.

ALL who read the sad story of the Flight to Varennes cannot fail to take a deep, an almost personal, interest in Count Fersen. His fate was as tragic as that of those he planned to save; and as it is not widely known, a brief extract from a recent article in the "Gentleman's Magazine" may find an appropriate place among these narratives.

It is in connection with the flight of Louis XVI. and Marie Antoinette, which, well conceived and boldly executed in its earlier stages, ended in such miserable, disastrous failure at Varennes, that the name of Jean Axel de Fersen is chiefly remembered, — not in virtue of his own stainless and gallant life, or of its most terrible and tragic ending, but of that link, broken only in death, which connected him with a beautiful, heroic, discrowned woman; a queen in whose slow martyrdom, in whose last lonely hours of anguish, men and women of whatever faith, of whatever politics, must always feel a loving sympathy almost as fresh as when in those days of terror all Europe stood aloof and waited for news of her fate. Count Fersen waited with the rest, but he at least had done what he could to save her, in memory of those bright bygone days, when together they had danced in merry company in gay ball-rooms; together had glided in gilded sleighs over the frozen snow; together had wandered through the gardens and the woodlands of the Little Trianon. These two had played together in tragedy and comedy on a mimic stage; and when the other actors vanished, falling away from her, — the inspirer of their pleasures, the life of their sports, — like

COUNT FERSEN.

sapless leaves at the first pinch of frost, it was but natural that this man, who loved her disinterestedly when so many professed devotion and paid a homage which had always some private end in view, should stand by her as long as he could; that he should to the last, when his actual presence would only have been an added danger, cheer her from a distance by his words of courage and counsel.

Of all the European sovereigns, Gustavus III. of Sweden was the stanchest friend that the French royal family possessed, so that Count Fersen could at least feel that in all he strove to do for them as an individual, he had his master's approval. "If I can serve them," he writes to his father, "what pleasure will it not give me to acquit myself of a part at least of the obligations I owe them! What a sweet satisfaction for my heart if I am able to contribute to their happiness!"

Marie Antoinette had kept a few friends — a very few — out of the wreck of her life, and none held a closer place in it than Axel de Fersen. Calumny battened on their friendship and called it an intrigue; but calumny had pursued the queen from the moment when, a girl of fifteen, she set foot in France, and never was able to produce a single proof positive against a virtue that was exposed to every temptation, subject to every contamination.

That Fersen was a man to whom, as a woman, Marie Antoinette's heart might naturally have responded, one can well believe. She found, in his gentle reliability and steadfast truth, a support and companionship she sorely needed; he possessed all the attributes that charm as well. And their friendship, begun in sunshine, starting gayly on the smooth tide of prosperity, outlived the foundering of many others. Long after, when Marie Antoinette's graceful coquetries were washed out in bitter tears, when her heart was dead to all personal hope and joy, and beat only in throbs of anguish for her husband and her children, her letters to Fersen attest how inalienable a place he held in her gratitude and affection. He was perhaps foremost in her mind when in her sad last hours she wrote her farewell letter — one of the noblest and most pathetic letters ever penned by woman — to Madame Elisabeth; a letter never delivered to her to whom it was addressed, but found among the papers of Fouquier-Tinville. "I had friends once; the idea of being separated from them forever, and of their sorrow, is one of the greatest regrets I carry with me in dying. Let them know at least that until my last hour I thought of them."

Jean Axel de Fersen was born in September, 1755. He came of a noble Swedish family distinguished in the annals of their country for military achievements and high personal character. At the age of fifteen he was sent abroad with a tutor to pursue his studies, and three years later he paid his first visit to Paris (1773). Versailles was at its brightest, the court was at its gayest, and M. de Fersen's rank and connections gave him the *entrée* of the highest society. The Swedish ambassador wrote with positive enthusiasm to Gustavus III. in his young fellow-countryman's praise: "It is not possible to behave with greater tact and discretion than he does. With the handsomest of faces and plenty of wit, he could not fail to succeed in society, and he has done so completely. Your Majesty will certainly be pleased with him. But what so especially makes M. de Fersen worthy of your favors is that he is of a singular nobility and elevation of mind."

The autumn of 1778 found him again in Paris, where he was welcomed back by Marie Antoinette, then Queen of France, as an old friend. Marie Antoinette was always especially gracious to foreigners. She felt she could allow herself to be so. When some one pointed out to her the dangers of showing such preference, and the offence it might give to the French nobility, she answered sadly, "They are the only ones who ask nothing from me."

Her intimacy with Fersen and their evident pleasure in each other's society soon attracted the attention of the courtiers. It was whispered that the queen was deeply in love with the young Swedish nobleman, and thence they jumped to the worst conclusions. As soon as Axel de Fersen became aware of these slanders, he hastened to put an end to them, by requesting, as a great favor, to be appointed aide-de-camp to Comte Rochambeau, then on the point of departing for America. A great lady had the effrontery to say to him before he left, "*Comment, monsieur!* you abandon thus your conquest?" "If I had made one," replied Fersen, with quiet dignity, "I should not have abandoned it. I depart free, and unhappily without leaving behind me any regrets."

The Swedish ambassador wrote on this occasion to his master, King Gustavus: "I confess I cannot help believing she has a *penchant* for him. I have seen indications of it too certain to be able to doubt it. The young count has behaved on this occasion with admirable modesty and reserve; above all, in the part he took in leaving for America. The queen's eyes could not quit him in those last days; in looking at him they were full of tears."

Alas, poor queen! If she loved him, or would have loved him under other circumstances; if, in her early loveless life, her warm heart, craving for affection, turned to his, — is it to be wondered at? Is it the subject for a sneer?

So Fersen, the aristocrat, crossed the seas to draw his sword on the side of democratic liberty. As Rochambeau's aide-de-camp he was at the surrender at Yorktown, and he remained in America till peace was concluded in 1783. On his return he received honors from his own sovereign and from Louis XVI., and found himself in command of one of the foreign regiments in the service of France, the Royal Suédois, at the age of eight and twenty.

Axel de Fersen was no narrow-minded aristocrat. He had indeed fewer prejudices than most men of his class, having in his father's house been brought up in an atmosphere of liberal ideas. At first the Revolution, which, on his return from America, he found impending, seemed to him a beginning of better things for oppressed, tax-laden France. To use his own words, it was "A healthy malady, only requiring a good doctor." Then as the months passed, and the fever heat grew higher and higher, the near prospect appalled him, and his hopefulness turned to dismay. Early in 1790 he resigned his command of the Royal

Suédois, and was commissioned by Gustavus III. to reside in Paris and be the agent of his direct communications with the king and queen. In Paris, therefore, he remained, forming one of the ever-dwindling group of friends and counsellors on whom the King and Queen of France could really depend.

In the summer of 1791 he planned and carried out the escape which ended so fatally at Varennes. He did not "disappear into unknown space," as Carlyle says, when he quitted the royal party at Bondy. He hurried across country to Mons, over the frontier, whence he addressed a few triumphant lines to his father, telling him that the royal family were well on their way to Montmédy, and that he himself was about to rejoin them. At midnight the next day, June 23, he wrote to his father again, this time in bitter grief and disappointment. "My dear father, all is lost, and I am in despair. The king has been arrested at Varennes. Judge of my sorrow, and pity me." Perhaps he was most to be pitied when shortly after there reached him a sad little letter from the unhappy queen. "I exist," it begins, "that is all. How anxious I have been for you, and how I compassionate you for all you will suffer in not having news of us! May Heaven grant that this may reach you! We are watched day and night, but that does not matter. Be easy. Nothing will happen to me."

Count Fersen's father was now anxious that he should return to Sweden, but Fersen soon convinced him that he must not desert the king and queen, nor go out of reach of news of them. He fixed his headquarters in Brussels, where he found himself surrounded by French *émigré* nobility, who disgusted him with their levity and selfishness.

By means of cipher and sympathetic ink, he continued to correspond regularly with Marie Antoinette, directing and advising, as well as keeping her constantly informed of all that went on in Europe. They are sad enough reading, those letters, and her answers; a record of hope deferred; of repeated disappointments; of plans of escape that came to nothing; and, saddest of all, pathetic allusions to the time "when we shall meet again in better days." They did see each other once more. On Feb. 11, 1792, Fersen left Brussels, disguised as a courier, having at last obtained the queen's permission to risk a visit to Paris. On the 13th he saw her in a brief interview. On the 21st he spent some hours at the Tuileries with the king and queen, and took tea and supper with them. At midnight they parted. Fersen returned to Brussels, narrowly escaping arrest on the way.

In the following month King Gustavus III. was assassinated; and in him Count Fersen lost an affectionate friend and protector. The French royal family also lost its strongest support. The successor of Gustavus was a very different character, and pursued a different policy. He joined the Allies, and, with the Empress Catherine, planned an invasion of France by way of Normandy. Thenceforth Axel de Fersen's political influence was practically at an end.

Throughout the summer of 1792, Marie Antoinette continued to write to him brief letters, addressed to an imaginary M. Rignon from an imaginary friend in Paris. In July she wrote: "I still exist, but it is by a miracle. . . . Do not distress yourself too much on my account."

After the royal family were imprisoned in the Temple, correspondence became almost impossible; and to Fersen's bitter anxiety was added the trial of enforced ignorance. The public papers brought him news of the September massacres; of the king's trial and execution; of Marie Antoinette's separation from her children; then of her removal to the Conciergerie. From that time, though her friends hoped against hope and struggled with despair, they must have known that her fate was practically sealed; but the months dragged on slowly, one by one, and she still lived.

In Fersen's diary, written at Brussels, Oct. 19, 1793, is a full account of a man named André, who declared himself willing, for the sum of two million francs, to contrive the queen's escape. The next day Fersen learned that there was no longer any need for his plans; on October 16, the queen had been executed.

"Although I was prepared for it," her friend writes, "the certainty overwhelmed me. I had not the strength to feel anything. . . . It was frightful not to have any positive details, to know that she was alone in her last moments, without consolation, without any one to speak to, to whom to give her last wishes. It fills one with horror. Those monsters of hell! No! without vengeance my heart will never be satisfied."

After this, till 1800, Count Fersen was employed on various diplomatic missions. He then returned to Sweden, where the last ten years of his life were spent. He was rich, and had a great position, but death had deprived him in a few years of all those whom he most cared for, — his beloved queen, his father, his mother, his sister, his dearest friend; and private griefs and public anxieties combined to make his life a sad one.

Sweden was passing through troubled times. Gustavus IV. was deserted by his people, and in 1809 was forced to abdicate. Charles XIII. was elected to the throne, and Prince Christian of Schleswig-Holstein was to be his successor. A year later Prince Christian died suddenly, and Count Fersen, now Grand Marshal of Sweden, was suspected by the populace of having contrived his death in the interest of the aristocratic party.

On June 20, the day of the prince's public funeral, the police warned Charles XIII. that an *émeute* was in preparation, and that Count Fersen's life would be in danger if he attended the obsequies. The king, however, took no precautionary measures. The funeral procession, as it entered Stockholm, was headed by a detachment of cavalry, followed by a gilded coach drawn by six horses, in which sat Axel de Fersen, in his gorgeous uniform of grand marshal, covered with sparkling decorations. He had not gone far before a clamorous crowd gathered round his carriage, threatening violence and calling him Prince Christian's murderer.

At last, at the turning of a street, an immense concourse of people made the progress of the procession impossible. They pulled open the carriage doors, and dragged Fersen out, but he managed to take refuge in a house near by. It was only for a moment's breathing space. The general in command of the troops, warned of his peril, sent a handful of soldiers, too few to contend against the infuriated mob. It would not be balked of its prey. Fersen was once more torn from his would-be protectors, dragged through the streets to the Hôtel de Ville, and there in the courtyard brutally, horribly murdered, — he, to whom a soldier's death would have been so welcome, or who would have gladly died on the scaffold with the woman he loved! Did he in his last moments remember her noble forgiveness of her murderers? At least he had time to gather his senses together, and to follow her example. An on-looker told afterwards that just before his death he struggled to his knees, crying aloud, "Oh, my God, who callest me thus to Thee, I implore Thee for these, my murderers, whom I forgive!"

CHAPTER III.

AUGUST THE TENTH AND THE SEPTEMBER MASSACRES.

WE have seen Mr. Griffith's account of the 9th and 10th of August in the streets of Paris, and in the house of Mr. Morris, the American ambassador. He witnessed the attack on the Tuileries from the Quais, but could not see what was passing inside the palace or the gardens. We will take an abridged account of this from Mr. Carlyle.

About dark on the evening of August 9, the drums beat the *générale* in all the streets, to call out the National Guard. Then Paris knew that disorder was on foot. A fearful game was ready for playing in this Paris Pandemonium, or City of all the Devils. Yet the night was warm and clear and calm.

Pétion, the popular mayor of Paris for the moment, had been to see the king, and by a manœuvre was detained in the garden of the Tuileries, so that the Hôtel de Ville was left without a mayor, who until four o'clock in the morning walked the garden under the stars. Then the Legislative Assembly, which had been sitting all night, heard of his plight and sent for him to give an account of Paris, of which, of course, he knew nothing.

That night there was little sleep in the palace. Its apartments were crowded. Seven hundred gentlemen had been summoned to die with or for their king. Among them was old Marshal Maillé, past eighty years of age. Then the alarm rang out from all the steeples, among them that of St. Germain l'Auxerrois, which had rung the signal for the St. Bartholomew two hundred and twenty years (all but fourteen days) before.

At the Hôtel de Ville, meantime, there was a revolution; the municipal authorities were put out, and new men were put in their places, Danton among them being chief.

In this manner waned the slow night, amid threats, anxiety, and the sounding of the tocsin; men's temper rising to the hysterical pitch; but, as yet, nothing was *done*. Few people, one imagines, slept that night in Paris, but the king lay down in his clothes, rubbing the powder out of his hair on the side that his head had pressed the pillow.

Three times the new municipal government at the Hôtel de Ville had sent for Commandant Mandat, who, they heard, had issued orders to the National Guard that, if attacked, they were to fire on the populace. At last he obeyed the summons, and was at once ordered off to prison. He never reached it; for on the steps of the Hôtel de Ville the mob snatched him from the gendarmes and tore him to pieces.

Seventeen persons were taken up as suspicious characters in the Champs Élysées and carried to the guard-house of the Legislative Assembly. Eleven of these promptly made their escape; then two more got away in the confusion. The remaining four were massacred. All this was in the dawn of the 10th of August.

Meantime the National Guards at the Tuileries, having lost Mandat, their commander, were without orders, and, having stood in their ranks all night without food or sleep, they went off to their own homes. The queen was led to a window by Madame Elisabeth, and they stood watching the sun rise gloriously over the Jacobin Church, and the roofs of the southeastern quarter. Before the National Guard dispersed, the king went down into the Carrousel with old Marshal Maillé, to review the troops, still stationed there to defend him. Not a voice cried *Vive le roi!* but there were growls of *Vive la nation!* Then he knew that hope was over.

The tocsin brought the Sections from all quarters of the city. They were led on by the Marseillais. The cannoneers in the Carrousel refused to fire on the mob. Then there remained for the royal family but one chance of personal safety. The king was implored to seek refuge under the roof of the Legislative Assembly. He sat some time in silence, his hands upon his knees, his body bent forwards, and gazed fixedly into space. Then, looking over his shoulder to the queen, who stood behind him, he said, "Let us go."

King Louis, the queen, sister Elisabeth, the two royal children, the Princesse de Lamballe, and their governess then left the Tuileries, to which one only was ever to return. They were attended by officers of the popular party and a double rank of National Guards, the steady Swiss Guards gazing mournfully and reproachfully after them, for no orders had been given them, and they were left deserted.

Oh! ye staunch Swiss! Oh! ye gallant gentlemen in black! for what a cause are ye to spend and to be spent! Look out from the western windows. Ye may see King Louis placidly holding on his way, the poor little Prince Royal sportively kicking the fallen leaves. Frenzied men, crowding behind the guards, are ready to tear them all from their defenders. But a deputation of legislators comes out of the hall, and royalty in safety ascends the staircase, a blue grenadier lifting the poor little Prince in his arms.

All in the Château is now uncertainty and confusion. The courtiers in black disappear, mostly through such side-issues as they can. The poor Swiss know not how to act. One duty only was clear to them, That of standing to their post. They will perform *that*.

The mob arrives, breaks in, and fills the Court of the Carrousel. The black-browed Marseillais are in the van. Suddenly there is a roar from the three Marseillaise cannon. It was eight in the morning.[1]

The Swiss, who had stood to their posts, but peacefully, responded to the cannon-shot by a rolling fire of musketry. Not a few of the Marseillais, after their long, dusty march, have made halt there. The mob, exposed to fire, is driven back.

But they rallied with vengeance in their hearts; and from

[1] At that sound Thomas Griffith awoke, and he saw what happened afterwards.

MADAME ELISABETH.

all patriot artillery, great and small, roared a responsive whirlwind. Then came an order carried by some brave man from the Legislative Hall to the Swiss to cease firing. Alas! it was too late. Terror and fury ruled the hour. The Swiss, pressed in on from without, paralyzed from within, ceased to shoot, but not to be shot. One party of them, attempting to fly by a back street, was utterly destroyed. Another, rushing through fire to the Legislative Assembly, found refuge on its back benches; three hundred darted out in column, and hoped by way of the Champs Élysées to reach the Swiss barracks at Courbevoie, where other Swiss had been stationed to aid in the escape of the king.

Then came firing, and murdering in the streets. House porters who were called *Suisses* in those days were shot down, whether Swiss or Frenchmen. Some Swiss found refuge in private houses, and the Marseillais, so fierce of late, were eager to save some of them. One man, Clémence, a wine merchant, stumbled forward to the bar of the Assembly, holding a rescued Swiss by the hand; telling passionately how he had succored him with pain and peril, how he will henceforth support him, being childless, and then fell in a swoon, embracing the poor Swiss, at which the Assembly applauded. But most of the Swiss were butchered. Fifty, some say fourscore, were marched as prisoners to the Hôtel de Ville, but the ferocious people burst through their guards and massacred all of them.

Surely few things in the history of carnage are more painful than this massacre of the Swiss. Honor to you, brave men! — and pity through all time! *He* was no king of yours, — this Louis! — and he forsook you! Ye were but sold to him for some poor sixpence a day. Yet ye would do work for your wages, and kept your plighted word. Let the traveller as he passes through Lucerne turn aside to look a little at their monumental Lion. Not for Thorwaldsen's sake alone. Hewn out of living rock, the figure rests there by the still calm waters, the granite mountains keeping watch all round.[1]

[1] Cf. Carlyle's "French Revolution."

Meantime patriot onlookers and others gazed on the dreadful scene across the Seine (Thomas Griffith among them). But there was another young man looking on who thought that had the Swiss had any stout man to command them, they might have beaten back the mob after its first repulse. He was a man well qualified to judge; a young lieutenant of artillery, Napoleon Bonaparte, who ever after had the sincerest pity for King Louis and his family, and contempt and detestation for popular mobs.

It is strange to reflect that while these things went on, on the 10th of August in Paris, men and women were carrying on their own affairs: women were busy with their children and their housekeeping, men were breakfasting in *cafés*. Even Mr. Morris, who had invited a party of guests that day to dine with him, records in his journal that he welcomed them with regrets and apologies for the spoiling of his fish, owing to the extreme heat of the weather.

On that day, the 10th of August, 1792, the Revolution was consummated; monarchy, and the Constitution which the Constituent Assembly had been at such pains to put on paper, were both swept away. The government of France fell into the hands of a self-constituted executive body, the Committee of Public Safety.

Real danger from foreign potentates was threatening France. Prussia and Austria had armies in the field; and from fifteen to twenty thousand emigrant gentlemen, all members of the aristocracy of France, with the king's brothers at their head, were on the Rhine at Coblentz, only waiting for the Duke of Brunswick, their commander in chief, to lead them on. Paris had been for some months in a ferment, wild with what it was pleased to call patriotism; La Vendée, faithful to the cause of its king and of its priests, was up in arms.

The populace of Paris when "in a ferment" is simply "off its head;" its one idea is *treason*. Unhappily during the summer of 1792 the king had found it impossible to sign two bills passed by the Legislative Assembly. One was a decree for banishing all priests who would not violate their consecration oaths and renounce obedience to the Pope, by taking the oath required by the Constitution; the other was to authorize the formation of a camp on the outskirts of Paris of twenty-five thousand picked patriot volunteers.

The king used his power of veto, and defeated for a time these two measures. Then rose all over Paris that song of *Ça ira*, one verse of which is as follows: —

> "Madame Veto m'a promis
> De faire égorger tout Paris!
> Dansons la Carmagnole! Dansons la Carmagnole!
> Dansons la Carmagnole!
> Et ça ira!"[1]

The country by a decree of the Assembly had already been pronounced to be in danger. All its chief generals, notably Lafayette, were suspected of being traitors. Each municipal official sat in the middle of his section in a tent erected in some open space, over which waved a flag inscribed, THE COUNTRY IS IN DANGER; and topmost stuck a pike surmounted by a *bonnet rouge*. Before him was a plank table, and on it was an open book, behind which sat a clerk like a recording angel, ready to write down the names of those in the section who were ready to enlist, and save the country.

Excitement rose to fever heat when the celebrated proclamation of Brunswick appeared. It said that all Frenchmen who did not instantly submit and join his forces should be declared traitors. Any National Guard or civilian, found in arms resisting the German forces, should be promptly hanged. And if Paris, before Brunswick reached it, should have offered any further insult to the king, Paris should be blasted asunder with cannon-shot and military execution, while the like ruin should fall on all cities that refused to submit; they should be left smoking ruins.

[1] They even named a frigate the "Ça ira." She came into Boston harbor during the days when the truculent Citizen Genet was ambassador at Washington, hoping to arouse Revolutionary fervor. It is said that her captain nailed to his mainmast a list of Boston aristocrats who should be guillotined. But the large family of Amory proving too long to enumerate, he ended his list of proscription with "Et tous les Amorys."

In the midst of this excitement the Marseillais, eight hundred strong, had arrived in Paris, singing their heart-stirring song. On Sunday, August 5, — five days before the fatal 10th of August, — King Louis held at the Tuileries his last *levée*. Never had a *levée* been so crowded. But sad anxiety sat on every face, and many eyes were filled with tears; while outside the tricolored ribbons, which guarded the approaches to the palace, the legislature was debating, Sections were defiling, and all Paris was astir demanding *déchéance*; that is, the king's deposition. Within the ribbon, however, a proposal was on foot for the hundredth time, that of carrying off his Majesty to Rouen and the old Château Gaillon. The Swiss Guard at Courbevoie was all ready. His Majesty himself was *almost* ready. Nevertheless, for the hundredth time he, when the point for action had been reached, drew back, and wrote, after his faithful servants had waited palpitating, an endless summer day, that "he had reasons to believe the insurrection was not so ripe as they supposed."

All this, if it cannot justify the rising of the 10th of August, at least enables us to give some reasons why popular excitement rose to fury against the king; but there was neither reason nor excuse for the murders perpetrated by municipal connivance at the prisons, twenty-three days later, on Sept. 2 and 3, 1792. For these murders Danton must be held primarily responsible; and the only excuse ever given was that the volunteers about to set forward to the frontier wished to strike a blow which should paralyze with terror all aristocrats in Paris, and sweep away hundreds of those who in the event of a counter-revolution might jeopardize the safety of the wives and children whom they left behind.

It is thought that 1,089 prisoners were massacred in the prisons of the Abbaye and La Force, besides those in the Bicêtre, which was taken by storm. Three men who escaped death in the two former prisons have written accounts of their personal experience, — Jourgniac, a soldier, Maton, a lawyer, and the Abbé Sicard, a distinguished teacher of the deaf and dumb.

Jourgniac says: "Towards seven o'clock on Sunday night of September 2, I, being in prison in the Abbaye, saw two men enter our room. Their hands were all bloody, and they were armed with swords. A turnkey with a torch lighted them. He pointed to the bed of Reding, a wounded Swiss, who was one of us. Reding spoke with a dying voice. One of the men paused, but the other cried, 'Allons donc!' He lifted the unfortunate Swiss from his bed, and carried him out on his back to the street. He was butchered there. We all looked at one another without speaking. We clasped each other's hands. Every man looked down in silence on the prison pavement, on which lay the moonlight checkered by the shadows of the triple stanchions of our window. At three in the morning we heard them breaking in one of the prison doors. Our first thought was, that they were coming to kill us in our room. Then we heard by voices on the staircase that they were attacking a room in which some prisoners had barricaded themselves. They were all butchered there, as we shortly gathered from words and cries.

"At ten o'clock the Abbé Lenfant and the Abbé de Chapt-Rastignac appeared in the pulpit of the chapel (then used as part of our prison). They had entered by a door from the stairs. They told us simply that our end was at hand, that we must compose ourselves and receive their last blessing. As if by an electric shock, — an impulse not to be defined, — we all fell on our knees, and we received the blessing. It was a solemn moment, a scene never to be forgotten, — those two old men with white hair blessing us from the pulpit above us, death hovering over our heads awaiting us and them. Half an hour after, these priests were both murdered, and we heard their cries."

Maton, the lawyer, who was in the prison of La Force, says that "at seven o'clock on Sunday night," the same hour at which Jourgniac in the Abbaye commenced his narrative, "prisoners began to be frequently called out from among us, and they did not reappear. We wondered what this might mean. Each man had his own opinion, but the majority of us were persuaded that the memorial I had drawn up for the National Assembly was having its effect, and that we were about to be liberated. At one in the morning the iron door which led into our corridor was opened anew. Four men in uniform, each with a naked sword and blazing torch, came up the passage preceded by a turnkey. They were in search of the adventurer La Motte, husband of the woman who had planned the swindle of the diamond necklace, but they did not find him. We heard them say, 'Come, let us search among the corpses.' Imagine what terror these words, 'Let us search among the corpses,' threw us into. I saw nothing for it but to resign myself to die. I wrote my last will, concluding it by an earnest petition that the paper should be sent to its address. Scarcely had I laid down the pen when there came in two other men in uniform. One of them, whose arm and sleeve up to the very shoulder were covered with blood, said he 'was as tired as a hodman who had been beating plaster.' An old man was called out. Sixty years of virtuous life could not now save him. They said: 'À l'Abbaye!'—which was, in fact, his death sentence. He passed out of the outer gate, gave a cry of terror at sight of the heaped corpses, covered his eyes with his hands, and died of innumerable wounds. At every fresh opening of the grate I thought I should hear my own name called and see my murderers enter. I flung off my night-clothes; I put on a coarse dirty shirt, a worn coat, no waistcoat, and an old round hat. These things I had sent for a few days before, in fear of what might happen. The rooms on our corridor had been all emptied except ours. We were four together whom they seemed to have forgotten. We all prayed together to be delivered from our peril. Baptiste, our turnkey, came up by himself to see us. I took him by the hands. I conjured him to save us. I promised him a hundred louis if he would take me home. A noise coming from the outside gate made him leave us hastily. The noise was made by a dozen or fifteen men armed to the teeth. We lay flat to escape observation. We had seen them from our window. We heard them cry, 'Upstairs! Let not one escape!' I took out my penknife, and considered where I should stab myself. Then I reflected that the blade was much too short, and also on religion.

"At last on Monday morning, September 3, between seven and eight o'clock, four men came in with sabres and bludgeons. To one of them Gérard, my fellow-townsman, whispered earnestly. The result was that his bribes and promises induced them to spare three of us. Me they would not spare. Four sabres were crossed over my breast, and they led me down. I was brought to their bar before a personage wearing the tricolored scarf, a sign he was in office, who was sitting as judge. He was a lame man, lank and tall. He recognized me seven months after in the street, and spoke to me. I have heard his name was Chepy, and that he was the son of a retired attorney. Crossing the court, I saw Manuel, who was anxious to save some of the prisoners, haranguing in his tricolored scarf."

Maton went through a species of trial which, by favor of Chepy, ended, not in assassination, but in what he calls his "resurrection."

The Abbé Sicard was in the *violon;* that is, a small prison cell near the guard-house. About three o'clock Monday morning the *killers* bethought them of this *violon*, and began knocking at it from the courtyard. "There were three of us," says the Abbé Sicard, "in this little place. My companions thought that they perceived a kind of loft overhead. But the ceiling was very high; only one of us could reach it by mounting on the shoulders of both the others. One of them said to me that my life was more useful than theirs. I resisted. They insisted. They would take no denial. I flung myself on the neck of these two deliverers. Never was scene more touching. I mounted on the shoulders of the first, then on those of the second; finally I was in the loft, whence I addressed to my two comrades the expression of a soul filled with natural emotions."

We are thankful to learn that those two generous companions did not perish. The Abbé Sicard was not found in his hiding-place. Jourgniac was brought before the Tribunal. He had gained over one of his guards by speaking Provençal to him. He saw old Marshal Maillé tried and sentenced. The marshal was eighty years old, the same who three weeks before had gone forth from the Tuileries with the king to address the troops in the Carrousel. The presiding judge, a man in gray, was either more merciful than his associates, or he was weary of his work, or Jourgniac's defence really moved him. When he had ended his cross-examination he took off his hat and said: "I see nothing to suspect in this man. I am for giving him his liberty. Is that your vote?" To which all the judges answered: "*Oui! Oui!* It is just!" Then arose shouts within doors and without. The prisoner was escorted forth by three men with shoutings and embracings. Thus Jourgniac "escaped," as he says himself, "out of trial by jury and the jaws of death."

And all this time, in one of the courtyards of the Abbaye, Billaud-Varennes, a member of the existing government and one of the leading deputies from the Assembly, in his tight puce-colored coat, black wig, and scarf of office, was standing among the corpses haranguing the *killers*, — *les tueurs*, — for that was the name by which they were known. "Brave citizens," he cried, "you are extirpating the enemies of Liberty! You are doing your duty. A grateful Commune and Country would wish to recompense you adequately, but cannot, for you know its want of funds. Whosoever shall have *worked* in a prison shall receive a draft for One louis. Continue your work!"

The pay-roll of those dreadful days of massacre is in existence to this day.

Nor were these massacres of September 2 and 3 the only work done by the killers. Less than a week later, on Sunday, September 9, a body of them went out to Versailles, and there earned more blood-money and the thanks of a grateful Committee of Public Safety. Mr. Griffith has told us how he met them on his way to Versailles returning to Paris, with bloody heads on pikes, and was constrained to applaud their villany.

A number of prisoners had been sent to Orléans to be tried as state criminals; among them was a whole cabinet of the king's late ministers. But the new authorities thought that they should be brought up to the capital, that so the end might be quicker. A wretch, who called himself Fournier the American, because he was born in Martinique, was sent down to Orléans to bring to Paris these fifty-three prisoners. When nearing Paris, he heard of the September massacres, and was advised (or received orders) to stop at Versailles. The prisoners travelled in country carts, their guards, some on horseback and some on foot, marching around them. At the last village the good mayor of Versailles came out to meet them, being anxious for their safety. It was Sunday, September 9, and Versailles was full of murderers, who had done their work in Paris six days before, and had marched out to Versailles in the expectation that more awaited them. As the procession entered the broad Avenue of Versailles, with its four rows of great trees, the prisoners found it swarming with ferocious men, awaiting their arrival. Through this crowd the tumbrils and their guards made their way with difficulty; "the Mayor," says Carlyle, "speaking and gesturing his persuasivest amid the inarticulate growling hum, which growls ever the deeper even by hearing itself growl, not without sharp yelpings here and there."

At last the procession turned into a narrow street, and here the mob had the prisoners at a disadvantage. The murmur and the yelpings became a continuous yell; savage figures sprang on to the shafts of the tumbrils, — the first spray of an endless coming tide! The mayor pleaded and pushed, half desperate. He was thrown down and carried off in men's arms. Amid horrid noise and tumult as of fierce wolves, the prisoners sank massacred, — all but eleven, who escaped into houses and found mercy. The prisons, and what other prisoners they held, were with difficulty saved. The clothes stripped from the dead were burned in bonfires. The corpses lay heaped in the gutters till the next day.

And thus it was when Mr. Griffith and M. de Coulanges drove at nightfall into Versailles.

CHAPTER IV.

THE PRINCESSE DE LAMBALLE.[1]

THE Princesse de Lamballe, Marie Thérèse Louise de Savoie-Carignan, was the daughter of Prince Louis Victor Joseph, of the house of Savoy-Carignan, fourth in descent from Charles Emmanuel I., Duke of Savoy. She was also first cousin on her mother's side of Victor Amadeus III., King of Sardinia. It may be further stated for the relief of those who dislike climbing genealogical trees, that she was the great-grand-aunt of Victor Emmanuel, *Il Re Galantuomo*, first king of United Italy. Born in September, 1749, she received as she grew up a careful education. Before she had completed her seventeenth year, it had been arranged between the courts of Versailles and Turin that she should marry the Prince de Lamballe, a great-grandson of Louis XIV. and Madame de Montespan.

The Duc de Penthièvre, father of the Prince de Lamballe, was the richest subject in France, his yearly income amounting to five millions of francs. He was now a widower with two children, a son and a daughter. His disposition was grave almost to melancholy. The pleasures of the world were distasteful to him; and although holding the office of High Admiral of France, he seldom appeared at court. His time seems to have been spent in attending to his religious duties and assisting the needy on his various estates, which he visited in regular succession. A more confirmed rake than his son, the Prince de Lamballe, was not to be found; it was with a view of steadying him, if possible, that his father persuaded him to marry. The monotony of domestic life, however, soon wearied the Prince de Lamballe, and he re-

[1] From an article in "Temple Bar."

PRINCESSE DE LAMBALLE.

turned to his old habits. The vicious example of his cousin, the Duc de Chartres, encouraged him in this course till death cut short his disreputable career.

After a short time spent in retirement in the Abbaye de St. Antoine, the young widow joined her father-in-law and his daughter at the Château de Rambouillet. Here she threw herself with zest into the simple amusements of country life, gardening with Mademoiselle de Penthièvre, reading with the poet Florian (a member of the household), and seconding the duke in his deeds of benevolence. He used sometimes to call her *Marie la folle*, so exuberant were her spirits in those days.

When Marie Antoinette became dauphine of France, in 1770, she found sympathy and friendship in the Princesse de Lamballe, five years older than herself. It was a welcome surprise to meet this good, sweet-tempered, sprightly companion in a court at once formal and corrupt. On becoming queen she revived, in favor of the princess, the lucrative office of superintendent of the household of the queen, a post which as a piece of state economy had been abolished some years before. This led to animadversion and grumbling in several quarters.

The close friendship between the queen and the princess was for a short time ruffled by the fancy taken up by the former for a far less worthy favorite, Madame de Polignac. This lady till then had been living in needy obscurity. She was by the queen's favor advanced to an important post at court; and her husband, Comte Jules de Polignac, was created a duke and appointed director-general of the posts, a lucrative position.

Madame d'Oberkirch, an Alsatian lady, who travelled in 1782 with the Grand Duke Peter and his charming wife (born Princess Dorothy of Montbelliard), thus writes to the grand duchess, her friend and former school-fellow : —

"The Princesse de Lamballe is very pretty, though her features are not regular. She is lively and playful, but without, I should say, much talent. She avoids discussions, and agrees with you at once rather than embark on an argument. She is a sweet, kind, obliging woman, incapable of an evil thought. The shaft of calumny has always failed to reach her. A widow at nineteen, she has since devoted herself entirely to her father-in-law and the queen. She gives immensely in charity, more than she can afford, often depriving herself of many things that she may the more effectually assist the poor. She is called 'the good angel' by the people on the different estates of the Duc de Penthièvre."

Meantime the Revolution was approaching. The mutterings of the coming storm, long heard in the distance, sounded louder and nearer. The Comte d'Artois and many of the nobles hastened to emigrate. The Polignacs escaped to the frontier under a feigned name.

On the evening of the 21st of June, 1791, the day of the king's flight to Varennes, Madame de Lamballe set out for Aumale, where the Duc de Penthièvre and his daughter, the Duchesse d'Orléans[1] (mother of Louis Philippe), were living. Quickly explaining what had taken place, she urged them to accompany her in her flight to England, whence she hoped to rejoin the queen; but as they were not to be persuaded, she was off again as soon as her horses had been changed. She reached Boulogne the following morning, and, finding an English ship about to sail for Dover, she embarked immediately. At Dover she stayed two days, and then proceeded *via* Ostend to Brussels, where she received news from the Count de Fersen of the capture of the royal party at Varennes. Her first impulse was to go back to France without delay, but those about her who were building

[1] This lady, divorced from her dissolute husband, lived afterwards in great poverty at Genoa. My father in 1810 was asked by the admiral at Gibraltar to carry her a box of valuables without charging freight on it, the perquisite of captains of men-of-war who undertook the responsibility of conveying specie or jewelry. "The poor old lady can't afford to pay," said the admiral. My father gladly undertook the commission, and used to give an amusing account of being invited by the duchess to dinner. The state was great, the viands scanty, and the story always ended with, "Luckily I was dismissed in time to get on board Sir Charles Cotton's ship, and eat a supplementary dinner." — E. W. L.

their hopes on the advance of the Duke of Brunswick and the *émigrés*, persuaded her to remain at a distance watching events. She did not adopt the views of the French *émigré* nobles collected at Coblentz. She shared the distrust which the queen had always felt of the Comte de Provence, who was already aspiring to the dignity of regent of France; and she knew that the intrigues of the *émigrés* only irritated the Revolutionists, and added to the difficulties of the king, now little better than a prisoner in his palace of the Tuileries.

As time went on, the news from Paris became blacker and blacker, and the tone of the queen's letters more hopeless. Her Majesty continued to adjure her friend to remain out of harm's way; yet occasionally a cry escaped her which proved that she yearned for her presence. There is the ring of real despair in the following letter, which the princess received on the 13th of October, 1791: —

"I am heart-broken at what I see passing around me, and can only entreat you not to come back. The present moment is too terrible. Although I have courage enough on my own account, I cannot help feeling uneasy for my friends, more especially for one so precious as you. I do not therefore wish you to expose yourself uselessly to danger. It is already as much as I can do to face circumstances calmly, at the side of the king and my children. Farewell, then, dear heart. Give me your pity, since from the very love I bear you your absence is perhaps a greater trial to me than it is to you."

If Madame de Lamballe had hesitated before, hesitation was at an end on the receipt of this letter. On the 15th, she made her will; on the 16th she set out for France. Four months had elapsed since she and the queen had been parted, and in that brief space what a change had come over Marie Antoinette! She looked ten years older; her bright color had fled; her hair was gray. She had prepared a gift for the princess, which she presented to her on their meeting. It was a ring containing some of her hair with the inscription, *Blanchis par le malheur.*

Madame de Lamballe at once became an object of suspicion to the Jacobin party. Everything she did was watched and misrepresented. Newspaper attacks on her were frequent. The public mind was inflamed against her. She was able to pay only two brief visits to her father-in-law, the Duc de Penthièvre, after her return. The duke was naturally averse to her remaining in Paris, but there she conceived was her proper post, and thither she returned. When she left the duke for the last time, he observed to one of his attendants: "My daughter's devotion to the queen is most praiseworthy; but in going back to her she is making a great sacrifice. *Je tremble qu'elle n'en soit victime.*"

In all the humiliations and dangers to which the king and queen were thenceforth exposed, the Princesse de Lamballe shared. When, on the 20th of June, 1792, a rabble army of men and women carrying pikes, hatchets, and knives, broke into the palace, she was at the queen's side, enduring for two long hours their threats and insults. Through the anxious night of the 9th of August, when an attack on the Tuileries was momentarily expected, she remained with the queen and Madame Elisabeth in the cabinet adjoining the council-chamber. With them she listened as there broke forth from the church towers far and near the sound of the tocsin, — the death-knell of the monarchy. After watching the sun rise in the sky ominously red, she repaired to her own rooms, where her attendants were collected, awaiting events. She stood a moment at a window overlooking the Pont Royal, and gazed at the excited crowds hurrying along the quays. One of her ladies now observed a cloud on the princess's usually cheerful face, and, thinking to encourage her, said: "Let us hope that the day of our deliverance has at last come; the king's adherents are more numerous than you think;" and she pointed to the soldiers guarding the bridge, picked men from the battalion of the Filles St. Thomas, the only loyal section of the National Guard. But the princess's eyes filled with tears as she answered: "No, no; nothing can save us now. I feel that we are lost."

As daylight increased, the beating of drums and rumble of the cannon of the Marseillais announced the approach of the insurgents. About seven, Louis XVI. yielded to the advice of those around him and quitted the palace with his family, to seek the treacherous protection of the Assembly. Madame de Lamballe and Madame de Tourzel were the only ladies permitted to go with them. On entering the Assembly, the king took his seat beside the president. The queen, the children, and the ladies were conducted to the benches reserved for foreign ministers, but, one of the deputies objecting to the presence of the sovereign during a debate, they were removed to the *loge du logographe*, or reporter's box,— a sort of cage, ten feet square, railed off from the hall. Hardly had this change been made, when the roar of cannon and the rattle of musketry proved that the conflict at the palace had begun. The din increased each moment. The walls and roof of the Assembly were struck by bullets; the doors were assailed with violence; there was a panic among the deputies, many of whom sprang from their seats in alarm. Presently cries of victory were heard from without. A messenger burst in to announce that the palace was in the hands of the populace, and that the Swiss Guards were in flight. Thereupon from the hall and from the galleries rose shouts of "Vive la nation! Vive la liberté!"

The heat in the reporter's box on that long summer day was suffocating. The royal family and the two ladies remained there sixteen hours, during which a decree was passed suspending the authority of the king. It was not till one o'clock in the morning of the 11th that they were taken to an adjacent building, where four small rooms had been prepared for them.

Madame de Tourzel was in great anxiety about her daughter Pauline, a girl of seventeen, who had been left in the Tuileries. Happily she was safe, and during this day obtained leave to join her mother.

By nine o'clock the party was back again in the reporter's box. Dr. John Moore, an Englishman, then in Paris, who saw them on this day, thus describes them:[1]—

"From the place where I sat I could not see the king, but I had a full view of the queen. Her beauty is gone. No wonder!

[1] Dr. Moore's account agrees minutely with Mr. Griffith's.

She seemed to listen with an undisturbed air to the speakers. Sometimes she whispered to her sister-in-law or to the Princesse de Lamballe. Once or twice she stood up, and leaning forward surveyed every part of the hall. A person near me remarked that her face indicated rage and the most provoking arrogance. I perceived nothing of that nature, although the turn of the debate, as well as the remarks made by some of the members, must have appeared to her highly insolent. On the whole, her behavior in this most trying situation was full of propriety and dignified composure."

The following day, Sunday, was spent in like manner; on Monday they were removed to the Temple. Pétion, the mayor, and Manuel, the *procureur* of the Commune, accompanied them.

A dense crowd lined the streets. In the Place Vendôme there was a halt that the king and his party might witness the overthrow of the statue of Louis XIV., to be succeeded ten years later by the column to the Victories of France, under Napoleon Bonaparte.

It was dusk when the sad party reached the Temple, which, prison though it was, must have seemed to them a refuge. The queen, on hearing that they were to be removed to the Temple, had implored Madame de Lamballe to leave her and seek an asylum with the Duc de Penthièvre or in England; but the princess, constant in her devotion, refused. She was not suffered long to remain the stay and comforter of her royal friend. A week later, on the 19th of August, municipal officers carried off the princess and Madame de Tourzel, saying they were wanted at the Hôtel de Ville to be examined concerning some secret correspondence. The parting of Marie Antoinette and of Madame Elisabeth from the friends who had shared both their prosperity and adversity was heart-rending. "They clung together," says Hue (a valet of the king, who was present), "with arms intertwined, uttering *des tendres et déchirantes adieux*."

After a brief examination at the Hôtel de Ville, the two ladies and Pauline were taken to the prison of La Force. This prison, traces of which have been long swept away, consisted of two separate buildings in one enclosure, the Grande and the Petite Force. In the latter, where only women were confined, principally thieves and debtors, the three ladies were placed in different cells; but the next day, on Manuel's visiting them, he yielded to their joint entreaties and reunited them in one good-sized room. Here they passed ten days together.

On the 19th of August, news reached Paris that the Prussians had taken Longwy on their march to the capital. The fury of the populace passed all bounds. The gates of Paris were closed, and hundreds of suspected persons were thrown into prison. The Commune (that is, the municipality at the Hôtel de Ville) assumed the government; and the Assembly, completely awed, neither remonstrated nor objected.

When the Duc de Penthièvre, after an interval of terrible suspense, learned that his daughter-in-law had been removed to La Force, he sent a messenger to Manuel offering him any sum he chose to name for her release. Overtures of the like nature in favor of the Tourzels are believed to have been made by members of their family.

At midnight on Saturday, the 1st September, as the prisoners were asleep, the door of their room was opened, and a voice said, "Mademoiselle de Tourzel, get up at once and follow me." It was no time to ask questions; Pauline rose, and, having dressed with all speed, went out. She found a member of the Commune named Hardy awaiting her. He took her to a room below, gave her a peasant's costume, which she slipped over her own clothes, and led her away.

"You can imagine," writes Madame de Tourzel subsequently, in a letter describing these events, "whether I slept again or not after Pauline was gone. When our breakfast was brought we were told that Paris had been in a state of commotion since the previous evening, that massacres were expected, that the prisons were threatened, — indeed, that many had been broken into already. I then felt sure that it was in order to save Pauline that they had removed her, and my only remaining regret was at not knowing whither she had been taken. I saw plainly enough the fate in store for the Princesse de Lamballe and myself. I will not say that I saw it without dread, but I was able to endure the idea at least with resignation. It seemed to me that presence of mind alone would enable me to surmount the dangers before me, and I ceased to think of anything except how to preserve it. This was by no means easy, for the extreme agitation of my unhappy companion, the questions she kept asking me, the terrible conjectures she formed, almost deprived me of what courage I had. I tried to reassure and calm her; but finding this impossible, I proposed that we should cease talking, since we only increased our fears by exchanging them."

Towards evening the two were suddenly summoned and taken down into a courtyard, "where," says Madame de Tourzel, "were many other prisoners, and a multitude of shabbily clad, savage-looking men, most of whom were drunk."

As they stood there bewildered, a man with a more respectable air than the rest approached Madame de Tourzel, and let drop the words, "Your daughter is saved." The speaker was none other than Hardy, who had rescued Pauline the night before. In her brief colloquy with him and other bystanders, Madame de Tourzel had her attention occupied a few moments. When she looked round the princess had disappeared.

The courtyard was getting emptied by degrees. The prisoners, she was told, were being taken one by one to undergo a trial, after which they were either let off or killed by the people stationed outside. At length she was herself called and led before the judges. The knowledge that Pauline was safe, and that her own rescue was intended by Hardy, for so he had informed her, gave her courage. Her interrogation over, Hardy and ten others surrounded her and conducted her into the street, where the ruffians employed to butcher the defenceless prisoners were collected. A cry was raised that an aristocrat was being allowed to escape; but, thanks to the boldness of her escort, Madame de Tourzel was dragged unharmed through the mob, and hurried forward till a *fiacre* was obtained. Into this she was pushed, her deliverers mounting after her, some inside and some out. They were then driven at full speed to the house in which Pauline had taken refuge. On the way there, Madame de Tourzel made eager inquiries as to what had become of the Princesse de Lamballe; but at mention of that name, Hardy shook his head, and was silent, adding after a moment that he would have saved her too, had it been in his power.

By night the prison of La Petite Force was empty. Of those shut up there, many had been slain, some liberated, and a few transferred to La Grande Force to be dealt with later. Among these was the princess, who when Madame de Tourzel lost sight of her in the courtyard was already on her way to her new cell. Her removal from one part of the building to another, just when many of her fellow-captives were set free, shows that the Commune was determined to sacrifice her. That Manuel himself wished to save her seems not unlikely; yet to have pleaded with his ferocious colleagues for the life of this particular prisoner, the friend of Marie Antoinette, branded with the odious name of Bourbon, might have brought suspicion and ruin on himself. He was therefore content with directing some of the hired assassins to assist in her rescue, — if occasion offered.

In this same prison of La Force, on this same Sunday night, was the lawyer Maton, who tells us in his narrative that "one prisoner after another was torn from us to meet his fate. At every opening of the grate I expected to hear them call my name."

About six o'clock on Monday morning (September 3), about the time Maton was led before the tribunal and acquitted, there came a lull. The "killers" had gone to refresh themselves with wine, and to receive payment from the Commune for their night's work.

Worn out with fatigue, and already half dead from excitement and fright, the princess flung herself upon her pallet and possibly yielded to a hope that all was over. But she had not long lain there when the door of her cell was thrown open, and two rough-looking men in the uniform of the National Guard entered. They told her to get up and come with them directly, as it was intended to remove her to the Abbaye. She replied that as all prisons were alike to her, she was as ready to remain in her present one as to go to another; she entreated them therefore to leave her where she was. Upon this they departed, but only to reappear after a short absence and inform her that obey she must, for her life depended on it. At the same moment the noise outside the prison recommenced, and loud cries of "La Lamballe! La Lamballe!" reached her ears.

Leaning on the arm of one of the men, — she was too weak to walk alone, — she descended to the prison hall, where the men acting as judges were seated with the jail register open before them. The hall was filled with armed executioners, whose hands, faces, and clothes were stained with blood; while from the gateway came the yells of the mob, calling for a fresh victim. On entering this scene of horror, the princess fainted away and remained in that state several minutes upheld by her two conductors. She regained her senses presently, but the awful reality to which she awoke made her swoon afresh. At length she seemed to have revived sufficiently to undergo her interrogation. The following, according to particulars obtained from an eye-witness, were the questions asked her and the answers she gave: —

"Your name?"

"Maria Louisa, Princess of Savoy."

"Your condition?"

"Superintendent of the queen's household."

"Were you aware of the conspiracies at court on the 10th of August?"

"If there were any conspiracies on the 10th of August, I had no knowledge of them."

"Then swear to love liberty and equality, and to hate the king, queen, and royalty."

"I will take the first oath, but not the second. It is not in my heart." Here somebody standing by — probably one of Manuel's emissaries — whispered in her ear, "Swear, or you are a dead woman."

The prisoner made no reply, but, raising both her hands, pressed them against her eyes as though to shut out some hateful vision. At the same time one of the judges gave the usual signal of dismission, saying, "Let Madame be set at liberty." This sentence, like "Take her to the Abbaye," meant that she was condemned. The princess no doubt interpreted the words literally, for, on hearing them, she turned and made a step towards the gate. Thereupon two of the murderers caught hold of her by either arm, and led her out between them, with the intention, it may be, of saving her if they could. But on getting outside, among the tigers in human form surging around her, on seeing the ground strewn with corpses, on hearing the savage yells that greeted her appearance, her senses again forsook her, and she fell backwards between the men, who continued to drag her along. Instantly she received on the head a blow from a bludgeon; this was followed by a stroke from a sabre, and then a rain of pike-thrusts brought her to the ground. But her martyrdom was not yet complete. Before death came to her release she had undergone tortures and indignities from which we would willingly avert our eyes, and after death her body was treated with unparalleled barbarity and a brutality too revolting to be here described.

After the removal of the princess and Madame de Tourzel from the Temple, the dauphin had been taught by his mother a little prayer for each, which he repeated daily at her knee. The first question the king and queen always put to Manuel, when he came, as he often did, to visit the Temple, was how it fared with the prisoners at La Force, his answer being usually that they were *en sûreté*, or else *tranquilles*. The latter was his report on the third day of September at eleven o'clock. Probably he had not the heart to tell what had really happened.

The king's personal attendant, Cléry, vividly describes what took place in the Temple that same afternoon: —

"While the king and queen were at dinner, the beating

of drums and the cries of the populace were distinctly heard. The royal family quitted the dining-room in considerable alarm, and assembled in the queen's room, while I went down to dine with Tison and his wife, who were on service in the Temple. We had hardly taken our seats when a head on the point of a pike was held up to the window. Tison's wife gave a loud scream. The barbarians outside evidently thought it was the queen's voice, for we heard them laughing immoderately. Imagining that her Majesty must be still at table, they held their trophy in such a position that had she been in the room she could not have helped seeing it. It was the head of the Princesse de Lamballe. Although marked with blood, it was not disfigured; her fair hair, still in curl, waved round the end of the pike. I rushed at once to the king. Terror had so altered my expression that the queen observed it; but it was important to hide from her the cause. All I wanted was to warn the king or Madame Elisabeth. However, there were two municipal officers in the room. The queen inquired why I was not at dinner. I told her I was not feeling well. Just then another officer of the Commune entered, and began conferring mysteriously with his colleagues. The king begged them to let him know if their lives were in danger.

"'The report has got about,' replied they, 'that you and your family are no longer in the Temple, and the people are calling for you, if you are here, to show yourselves at the window. But this we are not going to allow. Good citizens should display more confidence in their officials.' All this time the uproar without went on increasing, and we could hear a volley of abusive language levelled at the queen. Another officer of the Commune then walked in, followed by four men deputed by the people, to certify to the presence of the prisoners. One of these last, who wore the uniform of a National Guard with epaulettes on his shoulders and a long sabre in his hand, insisted that their Majesties should appear at the window. The other officers, however, still objecting, he brutally addressed the queen: 'They only want to prevent your seeing La Lamballe's head, which has been brought to let you see how the people avenge themselves on their tyrants. I advise you to appear, therefore, unless you wish the people to come up here.'

"On hearing these words, the queen sank down in a fainting-fit. I flew to her assistance, and, with the aid of Madame Elisabeth, placed her in a chair, where her children, bursting into tears, strove to bring her to herself. As the man who had spoken seemed disposed to linger in the room, the king said to him sternly, 'We are prepared for anything, monsieur; but you might have spared the queen the knowledge of this terrible calamity.' The fellow then departed with his comrades; their object in coming was accomplished."

There were other hearts to be wrung at tidings of the fate of the Princesse de Lamballe besides those of the captives in the Temple. News of the crime reached Vernon, where the Duc de Penthièvre was living, at midnight on September 3; but the old man was not told of it. It was broken gently to the Duchesse d'Orléans in the morning; and she, stifling her own anguish as best she could, had to decide how the cruel truth should be conveyed to her father, his state of health being such that it was thought dangerous to cause him too sudden a shock. A plan was at last agreed upon and adopted. It was early, — not seven o'clock, — and the duke still slept. On awaking he found his daughter, his chaplain, his physician, and his secretary, with others of his household, seated in his bedroom. He looked inquiringly from face to face; but no one smiled, no one spoke. There was a deep, significant silence, broken at length by the sobs of the duchess, who had hidden her face in her hands. Then the truth dawned on him. His worst fears had been realized; his cherished daughter-in-law was no more. Raising his clasped hands heavenwards, he exclaimed, "Oh, my God, thou knowest, I think I can have nothing to reproach myself for!"

His first emotion over, he became calm; but from that day he drooped and declined. Six months later he was carried to his grave.

CHAPTER V.

THE KING.

ON the one hundredth anniversary of the execution of King Louis XVI., Jan. 21, 1893, the "Figaro," in its "Supplément Littéraire," published the most complete and authentic account obtainable of his last hours, illustrated by copies of the street placards circulated among the populace in the streets of Paris. This account is here republished in translation.

An overwhelming majority in the National Convention had, on Dec. 26, 1793, pronounced the king guilty of "treason to the nation." Then came the question what should be his punishment. All the deputies, seven hundred and forty-nine in number, were at their posts, except forty who were absent on missions; and it was voted that the session should not close until the question was decided.

Eye-witnesses have told us of the scene of this third voting, and of the votings that grew out of it. The session lasted, with a few brief intervals, from Wednesday to Sunday morning. Long nights wore into days; the paleness of the morning spread over all faces; again and again the wintry shadows sank, and the dim lamps were lit in the Assembly, while member after member mounted the tribune steps to speak his fateful word.

As man after man mounts, the buzz is hushed till he has spoken, "Death," "Banishment," or "Imprisonment till the Peace." Many say, "Death;" many too say, "Banishment." The unhappy Girondists, who would willingly have saved the king, are driven by fear for their own lives to vote

LOUIS SEIZE
ROI DE FRANCE ET DE NAVARRE.
NE A VERSAILLES LE XXIII AOUST M.DCC.LIV.

LOUIS XVI.

for "Death." Manuel[1] voted for "Banishment." Philippe Égalité, late the Duc d'Orléans, the king's cousin, father of young Louis Philippe, — then fighting beyond the frontier under Dumouriez, — voted for "Death;" at which word from his lips, even the Jacobins shuddered; and it is said that the next man who voted cried aloud: "Citizens! I had intended to vote 'Death;' but I vote 'Banishment,' that my vote may not be the same as that of the man who has just voted before me!"

And yet the scene in the Assembly was not all tragedy. The women — *the tricoteuses, Dames de la Halle* — were there in force, applauding every death vote. In the galleries, wine and brandy were drunk as if in a saloon. Betting went on outside, and in some cases inside of the Hall of the Assembly; but within, for the most part, was restlessness, impatience, and the uttermost weariness. On Thursday night, when the last vote was being taken, a sick deputy, wrapped in blankets and carried in a chair, was brought in to vote for mercy.

Alas! the vote was death by a small majority of fifty-three. If we deduct from the death vote and add to the other the twenty-six who said death, but coupled it with some recommendation to mercy, the majority would have been but One.

Then brave old Malesherbes, who had asked leave to be the king's advocate, pleaded with tears for delay, — for an appeal to the people, — but in vain. On Sunday morning, January 20, the final vote was taken: "Death within twenty-four hours!"

On Sunday at three o'clock, three commissioners went reluctantly to announce his fate to the king. Their leader, Garat, who was much moved, read the sentence. Louis, who knew what was coming, drew from his pocket a paper, which contained these words: —

I ask a delay of three days, to enable me to prepare myself to appear in the presence of God.

[1] In 1840, forty-eight years after this, I saw Manuel, a tall, spare, gray-headed man, sitting on the benches of the Mountain, in the Chamber of Deputies. — E. W. L.

I ask permission to see without witnesses the person I shall designate to the Commissioners of the Commune, and I beg that this person may not be subjected to any fear or disquietude by reason of the act of charity he may have shown me.

I ask to be delivered from the perpetual surveillance that the Conseil-Général of the Commune has established over me in the last few days.

I ask, during this interval, to be permitted to see my family when I may ask for them, and without witnesses.

I should earnestly desire that the National Convention would at once take charge of my family, and would allow them to withdraw freely and without indignity to any place they may think proper.

I recommend to the kindness of the nation all the persons who have been attached to my service. Many have put all they owned into the purchase of their appointments, and must now be in great need, as well as those who depended for support upon their pensions. Among those who received pensions from me there are many old men, women, and children who had nothing else to live on.

Done in the Tower of the Temple, Jan. 20, 1793.

LOUIS.

After having given this paper to one of the commissioners, the king gave to another a memorandum in another handwriting than his own. It was the name and address of the priest he had chosen to be with him to the last, — M. Edgeworth de Firmont, who lived 483 in the Rue de Bac.

The Commissioners went back to the Convention, and gave an account of their mission.

The National Convention then decreed that Louis was free to have whatever minister of religion he might choose, and to see his family without witnesses. It also declared that "the nation, always wise and just, would take care of his family."

It paid no attention to what the king had said with reference to his pensioners and retainers; and it declined to give Louis the three days' delay he asked before his execution.

Then it drew up a placard to be posted on all the walls of Paris.

I. The execution of the sentence on Louis Capet will take place to-morrow, Monday, January 21.

II. The place of execution will be the Place de la Révolution, formerly La Place Louis XV., between the *pied d'eftal*, and the Champs Élysées.

III. Louis Capet will leave the Temple at eight o'clock, so that the execution may take place at midday.

IV. Commissioners of the Department of Paris, Commissioners of the Municipality, and two members of the Criminal Tribunal, will be present at the execution; the Secretary of this Tribunal will draw up an account, and the Commissioners and others, as soon as the execution shall be over, will return to the Council, which shall sit until they do so, and give in their report.

THE PROVISIONAL COUNCIL.

(Signed)

ROLAND. CLAVIÈRE. MONGE.
LEBRUN. GARAT. PASCHE.

By Order of the Council GOUVELLE.

The barriers of Paris were ordered to be closed, the Sections to be under arms. All citizens were warned to be upon their guard against any disorder attempted by the enemies of liberty and equality.

Louis, when the officers of the Council had quitted him, remained alone for several hours. At first he stood motionless for some time, as if thinking. Then suddenly he stamped his foot, and began to walk up and down his chamber in much agitation.

Mercereau, a stone-mason, a rude, rough man, who made a point of coming to the Temple as dirty and disorderly as possible, was one of the municipal guards on service at the Temple that day. Louis walked slowly into the room where his guards were stationed, and after a few undecided steps he approached the wall, on which a copy of "The Rights of Man" was posted. He pointed with his finger to Article Eight, which said: —

"The Law is not to inflict penalties unless they are evidently and strictly necessary. No one can be punished except in virtue of a law passed before his crime was committed."

"If that article had been followed, many disorders would have been spared," Louis said to Mercereau.

"True enough," said the man, carelessly.

A few moments after this Louis showed a wish to go to his wife. Mercereau would not allow him. Louis insisted, saying he was authorized. Mercereau would not yield the point, and flatly refused him permission.

Louis was now indeed separated from his family, — his wife, his sister, and his children. From August 13, when they had all been carried to the Temple, they at first lived all together in the Little Tower; but towards the end of September the Commune ordered them to be placed in the Large Tower.

This Large Tower was erected about the year 1200 by Brother Hubert, a Templar who had inherited a fortune. It stands in an enclosure of 120 to 130 *hectares;* this enclosure includes a variety of buildings of all dates, especially the palace of the Grand Prior, erected in 1667. The Comte d'Artois lived in it when he was in Paris, and there he several times received his sister-in-law, Marie Antoinette, after her churchings at Notre Dame.

The Tower was divided into four stories. The basement floor was given up to the municipals; the first floor (*premier*) was for the *corps de garde;* the next was divided into four rooms, — an ante-room, the dining-room, the king's bed-chamber, and a tiny one in which Cléry slept, — his *valet de chambre.* The story above this was occupied by the queen, her children, and the Princess Elisabeth.

The furniture in the king's rooms was very scanty, — a writing-desk, a bureau, four upholstered armchairs, an easy-chair, several common straw chairs, and a table. There was a looking-glass over the fireplace, and a bed with green damask hangings, which had belonged to one of the captains in the suite of the Comte d'Artois. There were four turrets that ran up the sides of the Tower. One of these, adjoining the king's bed-chamber, he used as an oratory; another held his wardrobe. One contained the staircase, another the firewood.

About six in the evening, Garat, the minister of justice, accompanied by Santerre, the commandant of the National Guard, came back to announce to Louis XVI. the resolutions of the Convention. They brought with them in their carriage the priest whom Louis had desired to see.

When Garat's mission was accomplished, he and Santerre withdrew, and Louis was left alone with the priest. The Abbé Edgeworth de Firmont was of Irish origin. He belonged to the diocese of Paris, and indeed was its vicar-general. For some time he had been the spiritual director of Madame Elisabeth, who, foreseeing what might happen to her brother, had recommended him. After the massacre of priests in September, the Abbé Edgeworth had gone into hiding at Choisy-le-Roi, taking the name of Essex. Louis, at the beginning of his trial, sent him word, through M. de Malesherbes, that he might need his services. The Abbé Edgeworth accepted the duty, and changed his lodgings to the Rue de Bac.

The abbé and the king retired to the little chamber in the turret which served as an oratory, and remained there alone together nearly two hours.

About half-past eight, Louis's interview with his family took place. In view of making the order of the Convention (which was that the interview should take place without the presence of witnesses) agree with an order of the Commune that Louis was not to be left out of sight of his guards for one moment, this interview took place in the dining-room, which was divided by a glass door from the ante-chamber.

Marie Antoinette came down first, holding her son by the hand; then Marie Thérèse and Madame Elisabeth. Louis held each long in his embrace. He spoke to them at intervals; the princesses sobbed. At a quarter past ten they went back to their own chambers, having made the king promise that he would see them again in the morning.

Louis went back to the oratory with his confessor. He came out about midnight, and Cléry undressed him. "Cléry, wake me at five o'clock," he said. Then he lay down and went to sleep.

Paris was awakened the next morning by the sound of drums. The *générale* was beaten in all quarters of the city. The National Guards assembled in their Sections. The greatest precautions had been taken. One hundred and fifty thousand men under arms formed a line from the Temple to the place of execution. All persons living along the route were enjoined to keep their windows closed.

The new instrument of execution, adopted at the suggestion of Dr. Guillotin, a member of the Constituent Assembly, had already done work on the Place du Carrousel, and was now erected on the Place de la Révolution (since 1830 the Place de la Concorde). It was put up about fifteen yards from the place where the obelisk of Luxor now stands, and on the spot where had stood the statue of Louis XV., overthrown by the populace on the 10th of August. The bronze of the statue was then presented to Latude, so long a prisoner in the Bastille and at Vincennes.

The guillotine was placed on a platform surrounded by a railing, and was reached by several steps. The head was turned towards the Tuileries.

The crowd was great, though the weather was bad. The night had been cold and rainy, and it was still raining.

A rumor began to be circulated that the night before a member of the Convention, who had voted for the king's death, had been stabbed by a royalist.

A little pamphlet had been circulated, called "The Breviary of Parisian Ladies," to oppose the execution of Louis XVI. It exhorted the ladies of Paris to dress themselves in mean clothes, and to mix in with the terrible Dames de la Halle, who stationed themselves round the guillotine, and raise the cry of "Pardon! Pardon!" on the appearance of the king. But the Dames de la Halle got wind of this intention, and declared that they should stay at home.

Louis was sleeping peacefully when at five o'clock Cléry prepared to light his fire. The noise he made aroused the king, who drew his curtain.

"Has five o'clock struck?" he said.

"Yes, sire, on several of the town clocks, but not yet on

ours." The fire being lighted, Cléry came to the side of the king.

"I have slept well," said Louis; "I needed rest. The events of yesterday tired me greatly."

Then he rose. With Cléry's assistance he put on a clean shirt and gray small-clothes, a white waistcoat, and a purple coat. He took out of its pockets his pocket-book, his eye-glasses, his snuff-box, and several other little objects, which, together with his purse, he laid upon the mantel-piece.

When he was dressed, the Abbé Edgeworth, who had lain sleepless and undressed on Cléry's bed, came to him. The abbé wore a plain black coat. Cléry pushed the bureau into the middle of the chamber, and arranged it as an altar. The necessary things had been brought from the Church of the Capuchins in the Marais the night before.

The mass began at six. Cléry assisted the priest in the service, reading from a prayer-book handed to him by his master.

Kneeling on a little horsehair-covered cushion, Louis followed the service with great earnestness, and received the bread of the communion; then, when the mass was over, he went back alone into his oratory.

At seven o'clock he came out and gave Cléry his seal, his wedding-ring, and a little package of hair. He charged Cléry to give these things to the queen, and to make her his last farewell.

A few minutes after this he asked for a pair of scissors. The municipal officers hesitated. "We must know what you want them for," they said.

"That Cléry may cut my hair," replied Louis.

The municipals deliberated half an hour, and then decided that he could not have the scissors. The king appeared annoyed, and insisted. He turned to one of them, saying, —

"I would not have touched the scissors. I would have let Cléry cut my hair in your presence. Try again, monsieur; see if you cannot have this granted to me."

The municipals, however, persisted in refusing.

It was growing light. The sound of the drums beating the *générale* could be distinctly heard in the Tower.

"I suppose they are calling out the National Guard," said the king to his confessor. And as the noise increased, and the sound of the tramp of horses and of men was heard in the courtyard, together with orders shouted by the officers, he added, "I think that they have come."

The evening before, when he quitted his wife and family, he had promised to see them again; but the abbé had assured him that such an interview would only make them endure a trial more terrible than their first parting, and that he had better, for their sakes, deprive himself of the sad consolation of bidding them a last farewell. The king agreed and submitted.

From seven to eight o'clock there was constant coming and going in the Tower of the Temple. The king was disturbed several times on various pretexts. He was even treated very roughly by some of the municipals on duty. He did not seem much moved by it, and only said to his confessor, "You see how these people treat me; but we must learn to bear everything."

About eight o'clock the door of his room was flung open. Santerre, the commandant of the National Guard, entered with his staff and ten generals. These were accompanied by two Commissioners of the Commune of Paris, men who were ex-priests. Their names were Bernard and Jacques Roux.

Louis came out of his little turret chamber.

"You have come for me?" he said to Santerre.

"Yes."

"Give me one moment."

He went back into the turret, and came out again almost immediately, followed by his confessor. He held a paper in his hand. It was his will, which he had made shortly before, on Christmas Day.

He spoke to Jacques Roux, and said to him, —

"Monsieur, I beg you to give this to the President of the Conseil Général of the Commune."

Jacques Roux answered brutally, —

" We did not come here to do your errands, but to escort you to the scaffold."

"Very true," said Louis, gently.

He then turned to Citizen Baudrais, a commissioner set over the guard at the Temple, and asked him to take charge of the will. Baudrais accepted the trust, and received the paper.

At this moment, perceiving that all present wore their hats, the king asked for his, which Cléry brought him. It was a three-cornered hat, the only serviceable one he had. He put it on, and then, speaking to the persons present, he begged them to show kindness to his family, and added:

"I also commend to the care of the Commune Cléry, my *valet de chambre*, who has always faithfully served me. My wish is that he should pass into the service of the queen — of my wife," he said, correcting himself.

Nobody answered.

Santerre then said, " Monsieur, it is almost time we should be going." Louis withdrew for the last time into his oratory, to collect himself. In a few minutes he came out again. Again pressed by Santerre to set out, he stamped with his right foot on the floor, and said, "Marchons!"

The procession then moved. At the top of the staircase Louis perceived Mathey, the *concierge* of the Tower, and said to him, —

" I was a little too sharp with you the day before yesterday. Forgive me, Mathey."

The man turned his head aside without an answer and slipped away.

Louis walked across the first courtyard, then he turned round, and gave a farewell glance at the Tower of the Temple.

In the outer court a carriage was waiting, — a green carriage, — and two gendarmes held the door open. The carriage belonged to Clavière, the minister of public contributions. It was provided at the last moment, because the Commune was averse to Louis's being taken to the Place de la Révolution in the carriage of the mayor, which had been the order of the Executive Council.

As the king approached, one of the gendarmes jumped into the carriage and seated himself on the front seat. Louis got in next, then the Abbé Edgeworth. Both took the back seats. The other gendarme then took the fourth place. He was Lieutenant Labrasse.

More than ten thousand men under arms were massed around the Temple, forming a double line. The procession, preceded by drums beating, and trumpets sounding, moved on. It was a little past eight.

As the carriage turned out of the Temple gate, a few women's voices cried, "Pardon! *Grâce!*"

The rain had ceased, but a dense, chill fog hung over the city. The procession gained the line of the Boulevards by the Rue du Temple. Cannon, rolling heavily over the slippery streets, went before and behind, escorted by ten thousand men.

It was a melancholy spectacle. Everywhere on the cross streets, and on any open space, were National Guards under arms. The crowd was silent.

Every precaution had been taken.

Nothing positive was known by the authorities, but it was rumored that the royalists would attempt to save the king. The Abbé Edgeworth had been informed of such a project. Possibly Louis still hoped that the devotion of some few of those once faithful to him would save him from impending death upon the scaffold.

And indeed these expectations seemed likely to be realized. The procession had just reached the Boulevard Bonne Nouvelle, when, near the Porte St. Denis, a man forced his way through the crowd, followed by three others, younger than himself. All four brandished their swords, and cried: "*À nous, français! À nous!* All those who wish to save their king!"

There was no echo to this cry. No one in the crowd responded. The friends on whom the rescuers had counted had not reached the rendezvous. The little party, seeing itself deserted, tried to profit by the confusion caused by its rush to escape, but one of the *corps de réserve*, apprised by a vidette, fell upon them. They separated. Two managed to escape. These were the Baron de Batz and his secretary Devaux. The two others, closely pursued, rushed up the Rue de Cléry. They were followed, captured in a house, and cut to pieces.

The drums and trumpets concealed the noise made by this attempt. Those in the carriage with Louis knew nothing of it, and drove on along the Boulevard du Temple, the Boulevard St. Martin, and the Boulevard St. Honoré.

Louis at first tried to talk to the Abbé Edgeworth, but the noise was so great that he could neither hear nor be heard. Then the abbé offered him his breviary, in which he read such psalms as the priest pointed out to him.

The horses went at a walk, and their progress was so slow that it took nearly two hours to traverse the two miles which separated the Temple from the place of execution. It was past ten when the carriage stopped on the Place de la Révolution.

"We have arrived, if I am not mistaken," whispered Louis in his confessor's ear.

The executioners approached the carriage. There were five of them, — Charles Henri Sanson, their chief, his two brothers, Charlemagne and Louis Martin, and their two assistants, Gros and Barré.

Sanson stood ready for his dreadful task. It was his duty, but in his heart he grieved for it.[1] He even hoped that something might occur which would prevent the procession from arriving at the scaffold, or that the victim might be torn from him by a popular rising. He did not know what might happen, and he, his brothers, and the assistants carried concealed weapons. Under their loose jackets they all had daggers and pistols, and their pockets were filled with cartridges.

As time passed and no procession appeared, Sanson

[1] See Balzac's short story founded on fact, "Une Épisode sous la Terreur."

began to hope that he would be spared this execution; but soon a hoarse murmur rose from the Rue de la Révolution (now, as formerly, the Rue Royale), and the carriage containing the victim appeared. There was nothing left for Sanson but to do his terrible duty.

One of his assistants opened the carriage-door. Louis, before he got out, laid his hand on the knee of the Abbé Edgeworth, saying in a firm voice to the two gendarmes who were in the carriage, —

"Gentlemen, I commend this gentleman to your care. See that after my death no insult is offered to him. I charge you to look after him."

They were silent. Louis repeated his words.

"Yes, yes. We will take care of him. Let us manage it," said one of them. Louis then got out of the carriage. It was at that moment exactly twenty minutes past ten.

The scaffold was on a platform which had been erected upon the pedestal of the former statue of Louis XV., and faced the château of the Tuileries. It was surrounded by a railing, and mounted by six very steep steps. A wide space around it had been kept clear, and this space was bordered by cannon.

Inside of the space there were from sixty to one hundred drummers; dragoons on horseback, with close-clipped horse-tails on their helmets, formed a half-circle. On the Place were massed battalions from the Sections of Gravilliers, Arcis, and the Lombards. The Fédérés of Aix and Marseilles were at the entrance of the Champs Élysées. Dugazon, the actor, on horseback like Santerre, whose aide-de-camp he was, was near them. He acted in so pretentious a manner that the crowd fancied he was playing an important part in the king's execution.

Louis, meantime, was standing at the foot of the scaffold. Without speaking he took off his coat, untied the queue that confined his hair, took off his cravat, and opened his shirt, so as to uncover his neck and shoulders. Then he knelt down to receive the final benediction of his confessor.

As he rose the executioners approached him with ropes in their hands.

"What are you going to do?" he said.

"We must bind you," replied one of them, — Martin Sanson.

"Bind me! No! I will never consent to that. Do what is ordered you, but you shall not bind me. You must give that up."

Martin, however, tried to bind him. Charlemagne came to his assistance. It was clear that if opposed they would use force.

A struggle was on the point of taking place, when Sanson gave the Abbé Edgeworth a look. The abbé, greatly moved, then said, —

"Sire, in this new outrage see a last resemblance between your Majesty and that Son of God who Himself will be your reward."

This intervention ended the painful scene. Louis submitted.

"But, indeed," he said to the abbé, "nothing but our Lord's example could have induced me to submit to such an insult." Then he turned to the executioners, saying: "Do what you will. I will drink the cup to the very dregs."

The two assistants tied his hands behind his back and cut his hair.

The steps of the scaffold were hard to mount. The fog and the sleet had made them slippery, and Louis had not the support of his hands, but he leaned on the Abbé Edgeworth as he mounted. It was twenty-two minutes past ten.

As soon as he reached the platform, Louis, whose face was flushed, stepped quickly round the scaffold, and, leaning on the railing on the left side, which faced the Garde Meuble, he cried: "Be silent, drummers! I wish to speak."

The drummers obeyed. The noise ceased. Then, in a voice so strong that it was heard all round the scaffold and even as far as the garden of the Tuileries, Louis cried, —

"I die perfectly innocent of all the imaginary crimes that have been laid to my charge. I forgive all those who are the cause of my misfortunes. I trust that my blood may assure the happiness of France. . . ."

While he was speaking there was perceptible agitation among the National Guards placed near the scaffold; some of them, thinking that the preliminaries of the execution had already lasted too long, were anxious to stop his speech; others insisted that he should be allowed to go on. Even the opinion of the executioners was divided. The moment was critical.

Santerre promptly put an end to it. At the first words spoken by Louis he rode up to the scaffold, and, lifting his sword, cried out, "I brought you here to die, not to harangue!" Then to the executioners, "Do your duty." At the same moment he signed with his sword to the drummers to go on. They obeyed him. Their drumming drowned the words of Louis. No doubt he may have cherished a secret hope that he might move the spectators, for his face expressed great disappointment. A man named Bonvard, an actor in the Théâtre de la République, who was placed near the scaffold with his battalion, said afterwards that when the drums began to beat, the king grew "as yellow as a quince." He said also that Louis, still standing by the railing of the scaffold, seemed for a moment to be waiting till the drums should cease, and that he made some slight resistance when the executioners came up behind to seize him.

Be that as it may, the scene lasted only a few moments. Louis, hopeless of being heard, yielded, and let the executioners do what they would with him. They bound him and placed him on the plank. A loud cry was heard. The knife fell, and the head rolled into the basket.

One of the assistants, — the youngest one, — a man named Gros, seized it by the hair, and, walking twice round the scaffold, showed it to the people. It was twenty-four minutes past ten o'clock.

The crowd responded with cries of "Vive la Nation!" "Vive la République!"

The Abbé Edgeworth de Firmont, who during the king's

last moments had remained upon his knees repeating the prayers for the dying, then rose, descended from the platform, passed through the ranks of the dragoons, which opened to let him through, and as rapidly as possible sought refuge in the house of M. de Malesherbes.

There had been some talk of firing cannon on the Pont Neuf as soon as the head of "Louis le Dernier" should have been severed; but the plan was given up on pretense that the head of a king when it fell ought not to be of more consequence than the head of any other malefactor. Shouts, repeated from one crowd to another, spread the news.

The great mass of the spectators in the Place de la Révolution and its neighborhood showed signs of joy. Men cried: "Vive la Liberté! Vive la République! Vive l'Égalité! Perish all tyrants!" They sang hymns to Liberty; they embraced one another; they shook hands; they danced round the guillotine, and on the square, and on the bridge, once called the Pont Louis Seize (now the Pont de la Concorde). Those nearest to the scaffold pressed under it, or climbed the steps. They dipped their pikes, their bayonets, and sabres in the blood. Others tried to soak it up on their handkerchiefs.

A man got upon the guillotine, pulled up his sleeve, filled his hand with clots of blood, and three times sprinkled the spectators, crying out as he did so: "My brothers, we have been threatened that the blood of Louis Capet would fall upon our own heads. Thus let it fall! Louis Capet has often dipped his hands in our blood. Republicans! the blood of a king brings you good fortune!"

In vain a more sober citizen remonstrated: "My friends, what are we doing? All that is passing here will be reported. Men will depict us in foreign countries as a savage people thirsting for blood."

They answered him: "Yes! thirsting for the blood of despots! Tell it, if you will, to all the world! . . . We should have been far better off this day, if on this spot where a statue was erected to Louis XV. our fathers had erected his scaffold!"

Around the guillotine there was still commotion. The hat and coat of the king were torn in shreds, and men quarrelled over the fragments. One of the executioner's assistants was selling the hair of the victim. A young man who wanted, not a few hairs only, but the ribbon that had tied the king's queue, paid him a louis. Another who looked like a foreigner — an Englishman — gave fifteen francs to a boy, and begged him to dip a very handsome white handkerchief in such blood as remained on the scaffold.

A *sans-culotte* took some on his finger and put it to his lips. "It tastes devilishly salt!" he cried. The Fédérés dipped bits of paper in it, stuck them on their pikes, and went off shouting, "See the blood of a tyrant!"

The dead body of the king was quickly taken away. A long wicker basket had been prepared, and the moment the execution was over the body was flung into it, and a cart carried it to the graveyard of La Madeleine (where the Chapelle Expiatoire was afterwards erected). This graveyard had been given up in 1720, but it was reopened in 1770 for the interment of the poor creatures who had been crushed to death at the *fête* given on that very spot at the marriage of Louis (then dauphin) with Marie Antoinette. A hundred dragoons on horseback escorted the body.

A grave had been dug, twelve feet deep and six feet wide. Two priests were standing by it without surplices and without tapers. They put the body in the grave uncoffined, with two full baskets of quicklime, and filled it up without any further ceremonies.

The cart, as it drove back, let the wicker basket fall. The crowd rushed at it and renewed the scenes around the scaffold. Some rubbed the bottom with rags, others with handkerchiefs, and some with bits of paper. One man dipped two dice in the blood.

Whilst all this was going on, the Conseil Général of the Commune was in permanent session. From the moment that the procession left the Temple, messengers, about every six minutes, arrived to report what was going on and at what place they had left Louis. A few of the members of the Council were much moved. It is said that the savage Hebert shed tears. One of his neighbors was surprised at this. "The tyrant," he said, "was very fond of my dog, and often patted him.[1] I was thinking of that."

The Council was presided over by the *ci-devant* marquis, Duroure. When it received notice that the execution had taken place, Duroure burst out laughing, and flinging up his arms shouted, —

"My friends, the affair is over! the affair is over! Everything went off admirably!"

A few moments afterwards Santerre came in, accompanied by the Commissioners of the Commune; and Jacques Roux gave a *viva voce* account of the events in which he had participated.

The sitting of the Convention took place as usual. It began at eight in the morning, and ended at half-past four. Vergniaud, the Girondist leader, that day presided.

Whether it was that the members of the Assembly felt repugnance to speak of the execution then going on as the result of their own votes, or whether they were under the influence of apprehension as to its personal consequences on themselves, they spoke of nothing but the murder of one of their own number, Lepelletier Saint-Fargeau, which had taken place the day before. He had voted for the king's death, and had been stabbed by a royalist in a *café*. A deputy related the particulars of his death, dwelling emphatically on what he considered a significant meaning in his last words: *J'ai froid.*

Other deputies mounted the tribune and declared that their lives had also been threatened by assassins. They did not say who had threatened them, but they were evidently impressed with the necessity of taking exceptional precautions. Barrère proposed that domiciliary visits should be made, to seek out and arrest any royalists who might be hiding themselves in Paris. The Assembly contented

[1] If this was so, it was probably during the long hours of the king's trial; or Hébert and his dog may have visited the Temple. — E. W. L.

itself, however, with decreeing six years' imprisonment in chains for any one who did not denounce an *émigré* living under his roof.

The Assembly then received a touching request from an old servant of Louis XVI.'s father. The Abbé Leduc asked permission to carry to Sens and there lay in the tomb of his own family the mortal remains of his old master's son. The Convention refused to accede to his request.

As for Robespierre, he remained at home all day. The evening before he had requested Duplay, the cabinet-maker, in whose house he occupied a little room, to close carefully the door that opened on the Rue St. Honoré. This was done accordingly on the morning of January 21. Eléonore, Duplay's daughter, supposed to be engaged to Robespierre, was surprised at this and asked the reason.

"Your father is right," replied the deputy; "something will pass which you ought not to see."

On Sunday, the night before the king's death, Marie Antoinette, in deep grief after her last interview with her husband, went up to her chamber, on the highest story of the Tower of the Temple. She flung herself, dressed, upon her bed. She passed all night shivering with cold and trembling with apprehension. Madame Elisabeth and Marie Thérèse occasionally dozed. The little dauphin slept.

At six o'clock the next morning, the three women rose. The king had promised to see them again before he left the Temple, and they were expecting the summons.

At a quarter past six their door opened. They thought the summons had come. But, no, — it was a prayer-book that was wanted for the mass about to be said in the king's chamber. They gave the book, and waited. The book belonged to the wife of Tison.

The windows of the Tower had been boarded up, so that they could see only the sky. They could perceive nothing of what passed outside.

At seven o'clock Marie Antoinette asked leave to go down into her husband's chamber. The municipals, much embarrassed, eluded her request, saying that the king was much occupied. She insisted again. Then one of them went to inquire if Louis XVI. would see his wife; but he did not come back with any answer.

About this time the dauphin, who was now up and dressed, understood the terrible situation. He sprang from his mother's arms and rushed to the guards, clasping their knees and crying, —

"Let me go, messieurs! Let me go!"

"Where do you want to go?"

"To speak to the people, — to beg them not to kill my papa — the king. . . . In the name of God, messieurs, let me go!"

The guards pushed the boy aside. He went slowly away, but kept on crying, "Oh, papa! papa!" Marie Antoinette pressed him in her arms, — him and his sister. She begged them to imitate their father's courage and never to think of avenging his death. She wanted them to eat some breakfast, but they refused.

Then they heard the noise of drums and horses in the courtyard, but did not know what it might mean. Marie Antoinette, however, seemed to guess.

"It is all over," she said, weeping. "We shall never see him again."

The morning was passed by all in the greatest anxiety. Suddenly they heard cries and yells, mingled with the noise of fire-arms.

"Oh, the monsters! they are glad!" whispered Madame Elisabeth, lifting her eyes to heaven.

The little prince burst into tears. Marie Thérèse screamed aloud; Marie Antoinette was choked with sorrow.

About one o'clock dinner was brought in. Marie Antoinette could not touch food. A terrible anxiety oppressed her. She wanted to know how her husband in the death-hour had borne himself, — how he had died. She begged for the details. She asked leave for Cléry to come to her. This favor was refused. And the day ended for her and hers, as it had begun, in uncertainty and sorrow.

All that morning Paris had worn an air of mourning. The

murder of Lepelletier de Saint-Fargeau two days before had made the Revolutionists apprehend a royalist rising. Rumors of the domiciliary visits which had been projected called to mind those which had preceded the massacres of September, and made others dread new dangers.

But about midday, when it was found that the execution had taken place without hindrance, and that the measures taken by the authorities were limited to strengthening the armed posts and patrolling the streets, the city resumed by degrees its usual aspect.

The rich shops, the booths on the Boulevards, and workmen's places of work were, however, only half open, as on days of half-holiday (*petite fête*). The population seemed to be divided into two very distinct parties. All who grieved over the tragical event and who dreaded its consequences stayed in their houses. The women in general were very sad. Those on the contrary who were under the influence of political passion applauded the execution and gave way to demonstrations of joy. The *cafés* were crowded with *sans-culottes*, who drank, harangued, and danced and sang.

Men were crying pies and cakes on the very spot where the tragedy had taken place. Citizens conversed together about the events of the day. Some regretted Santerre had caused the drums to stifle Louis's last words. Others approved what he had done — and then they fell to arguing.

Before nightfall rumors began to circulate. It was said that Philippe Égalité had witnessed the execution of his cousin; that he had been seen at the moment when the executioner held up the bloody head, but then had ridden off in haste on a horse that was held for him.

A soldier who had been decorated with the cross of St. Louis died of grief on hearing of the execution of his king; a bookseller named Vente, a man formerly attached to the King's Menus Plaisirs, became crazy; a wig-maker in the Rue Culture Ste. Catherine, a known royalist, was seized with such despair that he cut his throat with a razor.

Some people remarked that the number 21 had played a great part in the life of Louis. It was on the 21st day of one month that he was married by proxy; on the 21st day of another that the crowd, at an exhibition of fireworks to celebrate his nuptials, trampled each other to death on the Place where he was executed. The dauphin was born on January 21; the flight to Varennes was on June 21; September 21, the Assembly abolished royalty; and several other times the number 21 had been connected with his misfortunes.

False rumors of course soon began to spread. It was asserted that the young princess, Marie Thérèse, on hearing of her father's death, had died of grief, and that Marie Antoinette had been taken from the Temple and carried to another prison.

On the evening of January 21 hardly any one but *sans-culottes* were to be seen in the streets of Paris, and these, excited by a day of drinking and shouting, fraternized more demonstratively than ever with each other.

"Other kings of Europe would," they said, "have made war upon us, at any rate; now we shall all be more eager to beat them. The same impure blood flows in the veins of all kings; we must purge the earth of it and them."

The clubs were all open that night, but the most interesting sitting was in that of the Jacobins. After the example of the deputies in the Assembly they seemed only anxious to avoid mention of the king's death, and to discuss the murder of Lepelletier de Saint-Fargeau. Citizen Saint-André made an emphatic eulogium on the deceased. A brother of Lepelletier then rose, and, by degrees, they made out a sort of legend concerning him and his death. It was remembered that he had said four months before, "Happy are the founders of the Republic, even if they pay for it with their own blood." And an historic expression was substituted for his commonplace last words, "I am cold." Then the club voted that its members, in a body, should attend his funeral. Not one word was said about the execution of the king.

The theatres that night were open as usual, but the attendance, except in the pit, was very small.

The newspapers said little, and that little was much the

same in all of them. One paragraph on the subject was, however, emphatic. It was in the "Journal de la République," edited by Marat.

"The head of the tyrant has fallen beneath the sword of justice. The same stroke has severed the very roots of monarchy amongst us. I now have hopes for the Republic! How vain were the fears with which the supporters of the dethroned despot endeavored to inspire us as to the consequences of his death, in hopes of snatching him from the scaffold! . . . The remainder of the day has been perfectly quiet. For the first time since the Federation the people seemed animated by a serene joy. One might have thought our citizens had taken part in a religious festival. Delivered from the weight of an oppression which has so long crushed the nation, and penetrated by a feeling of fraternity, all hearts have yielded to the prospect of a happier future."

It has been frequently related that the last words of the Abbé Edgeworth to the king were, "Son of Saint Louis, ascend to heaven!" But one who was near the scaffold has said, "These words were circulated from mouth to mouth, but I did not hear them." And the Abbé Edgeworth himself declared that he had no recollection of having uttered them.

All members of the diplomatic corps quitted Paris after the king's death, except the minister of the United States, Mr. Gouverneur Morris. He had not given up his post, but retired to his country house about thirty miles from Paris.

The day when the news reached London consternation was great. The Theatre Royal, in which two pieces were to have been played that night, commanded by George III. and Queen Charlotte, was closed; and the Marquis de Chauvelin, ambassador of France (now become Citizen Chauvelin), was ordered to quit England immediately. He left London the next morning for Paris.

The reigning King of Sardinia, Victor Amadeus III., had married the Princess Marie Adelaide Clotilde, sister of Louis XVI. (she was called Gros Madame); while his two sisters, Maria Josefa and Maria Theresa, were the wives of the Comte de Provence and the Comte d'Artois. As soon as he heard of the death of Louis, he showed marks of the greatest sorrow. Then he raised his hands to heaven and exclaimed that if his people wished to adopt French fashions he was ready to step down from his throne. Indeed, in his first moments of despondency he abdicated. His people were touched by his grief, and refused to part with him. They begged him to let them take a new oath of fidelity. He consented, and was carried back to his palace in triumph.

The Emperor of Germany was visiting the Prince de Coloredo when the Duc de Richelieu informed him of the death of his brother-in-law. "Sire," he said, pointing to the crape upon his arm, "the cup of crime is full, and I have received the sad commission of informing you."

"Monsters!" cried the emperor. "Has everything ceased to be sacred in their eyes?" And he burst into tears.

At the courts of Madrid, Berlin, and St. Petersburg, sorrow and indignation were intense. Again the Duc de Richelieu was the messenger who carried the sad tidings to the Empress Catherine.

At Rome the news increased public indignation, though it could not increase the hostility of the government, which a few days before (January 13) had allowed the populace to murder, in open day, Citizen Bassville, secretary of the French legation, because he had displayed the tricolor of the French Republic.

The Comte de Provence, the king's brother (subsequently Louis XVIII.), was at Hamm in Westphalia. The news reached him on the 28th of January. He at once assumed the title of Regent of the Kingdom, and addressed a proclamation to Frenchmen who were exiles in foreign lands.

The Prince de Condé on January 30 had a funeral service in the Black Forest for Louis XVI. An anonymous author composed this epitaph.

> "Here lies King Louis. His own subjects slew him,
> In spite of all the good he tried to do them,
> Who by a courage never told in story
> Changed his dread scaffold to a Throne of Glory."

Thus perished Louis XVI., King of France and of Navarre, aged thirty-eight years and five months lacking two days, after having reigned eighteen years and been in prison five months and eight days.

When the king was dead, his ring and other remembrances, which he had wished his family to keep for his sake, were withheld from them; and the only personal remembrance which his sister, who was tenderly attached to him, was able to secure, was a battered old hat, which by some accident had been left in the Tower. This hat she treasured as a most valuable relic. It did not, however, long escape the prying eyes of the municipal officers, who took it away, saying that its preservation was a suspicious circumstance!

CHAPTER VI.

MARIE ANTOINETTE AND ROBESPIERRE.[1]

A BOOK appeared in France in 1880, called the "Memoirs of Klindworth." Klindworth was a diplomatist who took an active part in public life during the early half of the present century. He was on terms of personal intimacy (at least he says he was) with Talleyrand, Metternich, the Duke of Wellington, Lord Palmerston, and M. Guizot; his book consequently abounds in new facts, such as underlie the graver pages of pure history. One of these is a detailed narrative, given to him by a certain M. Grandidier, charged by Robespierre with a secret mission to Vienna, in July, 1793. The object of this mission was to detach Austria from the coalition against France. In this extract from the pages of Klindworth, Grandidier speaks for himself.

"Baron Thugut, prime minister and minister for foreign affairs in Austria at that period, received me very amicably on my return to Vienna; and when I informed him in a preliminary brief interview that I had brought with me fresh instructions to continue negotiations on the basis he himself had proposed, he testified his satisfaction, and invited me to dinner the next day. I went to his official residence, therefore, at the time appointed. We dined *tête à tête*, and the dinner was a very good one. Our conversation turned on France, and on the general situation of affairs. After dinner the minister, having left me for a moment, returned with a lady who was at that time known as Madame Charles de

[1] From the "Supplément Littéraire du Figaro." Translated by me and published in "Littell's Living Age," Dec. 18, 1880. — E. W. L.

Poutet, but subsequently she got leave to emblazon on her carriage and her scutcheon a countess's coronet. She was an exquisitely beautiful woman; her limbs were as finely formed as those of a model, and she had the most perfect carriage of the head I ever saw. I was dazzled by the vision. The minister introduced us. She spoke French fluently with no German accent, and had, in a remarkable degree, that gift of conversation which is so rarely met with, out of France.

"As she took leave she said, 'Come and see me to-morrow at one o'clock. I want to talk to you.' Punctual to the appointment, I was shown next day into a spacious apartment in the Imperial Palace. The lady did not keep me waiting, but received me cordially, and invited me to take a seat beside her.

"'Before I begin to speak of other things,' she said, 'I had better tell you that presently a lady will appear and pass through this room. I beg you do not rise or take any notice of her.'

"This happened very shortly. 'It is the empress,' said Madame de Poutet. 'Her curiosity to see you has brought her here. Ah! you have no idea,' she added in a tone of irony, 'how very narrow-minded you will find us in this place. We cross ourselves when any mention is made of France, and really and truly most people imagine that each French republican carries a private guillotine in his pocket. But a truce to this nonsense: let us talk of your affairs. I know your mission, but you will never succeed so long as Queen Marie Antoinette and her daughter are not set at liberty and sent back to their family. Blood relationship, public decency, and family honor absolutely require this condition before there can be any question of understanding between Austria and France. Let me ask you a few questions. I quite understand how Monsieur de Robespierre may not have thought of this in the busy situation in which he finds himself, but how does it happen that this obvious view of the matter has not presented itself to you? The situation of the queen cannot but be a barrier to all *entente* between us, till it is changed.'

"I tried to speak, but she begged me to let her finish on this subject all she wished to say.

"'You must not imagine,' she continued, 'that any personal feeling of sympathy makes me speak as I am doing. I have very little sympathy either for the queen or for her late husband. One who has been born a king should know how to mount his horse and to defend his royalty; and the queen of a great country, especially in a time of trial and misfortune, should not lead a life of pleasant dissipation. *Les peuples* resemble monkeys; they like to imitate one another. If Charles I. of England had never been beheaded, you would not have put to death Louis XVI. But the queen is alone now, without her husband; what harm can she do you? To put women to death is as atrocious as it is stupid; and, indeed, have you any right to bring the queen to trial, since on the death of her husband she resumed her position as Archduchess of Austria? She belongs to us.'

"Madame de Poutet here paused. She seemed waiting with impatience for my answer.

"'After what you have done me the honor to say, madame,' I replied, 'I regret exceedingly that our minister did not speak to me on this subject before I left France. When our interview closes there will be one of two things for me to do: either I must go back to Paris and ask for fresh instructions, or I must ask for them in writing and await them here.'

"'Very good,' she said in a decided tone, 'stay here and *write*.'

"After a moment's pause she added, 'After all, it does but add one brief clause to our treaty. What are your own views upon the subject?'

"'I have no opinions about it,' I replied. 'The liberation of the queen is no small matter, in the state of ferment existing in the minds of men in France. On the other hand, M. de Robespierre well understands the art of government, and I know him well enough to feel that he would not hesitate to brave public opinion, if firmly resolved, as I think he is, to make peace with Austria.'

"'*Qui veut la fin veut les moyens*' (he who desires the end accepts the means), she said. '*Write.*'

"My answer speedily arrived from Paris. It was short and precise: 'Granted. Come back to Paris as soon as possible, with the draft of the treaty finally drawn up, and accompanied by a commissioner with full powers, in writing, to carry out the extradition.'

"I did not lose a moment in informing M. Thugut of this important news. He told me to communicate it at once to Madame de Poutet. She received me most cordially and graciously.

"'I see,' she said, 'that all will now go right between us. The queen will be restored to us with the young princess. Remember what I said to you from the beginning. *That* is the indispensable condition of our *entente*, and I will immediately set to work with Thugut to arrange everything. And now that we no longer need any concealments, I will tell you plainly that the cession of the Low Countries to France really costs us nothing. We are willing to get rid of that horrid nest of clericalism and rebellion. The Low Countries have been for two centuries a millstone round the neck of Austria, without doing her any good in return.'

"All being as I have told you," continued M. Grandidier, "the treaty was completed without difficulty. After I had had a second conversation with the minister, we both signed the draft of it July 12, 1793."

"When the old man," continues Klindworth, "reached this portion of his narrative, he drew out of a bundle of papers one containing a rough copy of the proposed treaty between France and Austria, and allowed me to read it attentively. After I got home I tried to remember it exactly, and wrote it down. This is the substance of the paper:

ARTICLE I.

From this day forward, and forever, there shall be firm peace, friendship, and an inviolable good understanding between the French Republic and the Emperor of Germany, King of Hungary and Bohemia. Both parties, henceforward, will carefully avoid anything calculated to disturb the reciprocal harmony of their relations.

ARTICLE II.

The former provinces of the Low Countries are ceded by his Majesty the Emperor, forever, to the French Republic; and shall be possessed by that Republic in all sovereignty and proprietary, with all the territories that belong to them.

ARTICLE III.

The Emperor renounces, for himself and his successors, all rights and titles that he has or may yet have on the countries situated on the left bank of the Rhine, from the frontier of Switzerland below Basle, to the confluence with the Nethe above Andernach; comprising the *tête de pont* at Manheim, and the town and citadel of Mayence. The Emperor also promises to employ his good offices with the Empire, that it may consent to the cession of the said territories to the French Republic.

ARTICLE IV.

The French Republic consents that the Emperor shall annex to his dominions the countries situated between the Tyrol and the Danube, the Lech and the Salza; and formally promises him all assistance he may need in arms, if any third power should dispute the aforesaid acquisition, or interfere with the tranquil possession thereof.

ADDITIONAL AND SECRET CLAUSE.

Marie Antoinette, *ci-devant* Queen of France, shall be, together with her daughter, escorted to the French frontier, thence to be returned to Austria, her native country."

"I was anxious," continued M. Grandidier, "to return to Paris with all speed, together with the commissioner fixed on by Baron Thugut to receive the queen's person in the name of the government of the emperor. He was a canon from the Cathedral Church of Waitsen; a man of about forty, with a kind and engaging expression. His name was Soos. He knew German, spoke Latin after the fashion of his countrymen, and French indifferently. M. de Thugut treated me with the utmost cordiality, and told me he hoped soon to see me return with the treaty ratified. I then went to take leave of Madame de Poutet. 'You are a dreadful republican, I know,' she said gayly; 'but, alas! I am greatly in your debt. Salute me farewell, and *bon voyage*.'

"The commissioner and I reached Paris about five o'clock in the morning. An hour later I went to see Robespierre. Mademoiselle Cornelia,[1] always austere and always busy, was drying clothes, and received me in the courtyard. She congratulated me on my return, and told me that *le patron* was closeted with his brother about something very important, and that she had been told to let nobody go up to them. I waited half an hour. After that the door opened, and I went in.

"I was received with civility, and made my report, which was very circumstantial. I then handed to Robespierre a copy of the treaty that had the signature of the prime minister of Austria, announced the arrival of the emperor's commissioner, and gave in an account of my expenses on the journey. Everything was well received. After having read the text of the treaty carefully, and approved it formally, Robespierre expressed in a few words his satisfaction, and, while I was answering him, he wrote a few lines upon a piece of paper.

"'This is an order for you,' he said, 'to be admitted to the Temple to-morrow morning at seven o'clock, with Thugut's envoy.'

"'Must I present him to you first?' I said.

"'There is no need that I should see him,' he replied. 'You can give me an account of the interview. This treaty,' he continued, 'gives me a new map of France, by which I will confound and subdue all traitors, without and within.'

"Then he made me a sign with his hand, as his custom was, and so dismissed me.

"The next morning, at the appointed hour, the canon and I presented ourselves at the Temple. He had put on

[1] The name given to Eléonore Duplay.

a black coat and a white cravat for the occasion, and was furnished with two sealed autograph letters from the emperor and empress to the queen. Two municipal guards and a member of the Council of the Commune were waiting for us. By their orders the jailer opened the doors, and soon we stood in the presence of the queen.

"She was seated on a low stool, busy mending a petticoat of coarse black serge. Her back was half turned towards us, and she paid at first no attention to our presence. Her clothes were in rags. Over her breast was pinned a coarse white kerchief, and her shoes were very much worn. She stooped, like an old woman. She was deathly pale, and we could see distinctly that under her little cap her hair was as white as snow. I made a few steps towards her, and bowing respectfully I presented the messenger of the emperor.

"Then glancing at me for the first time, she cast upon me a look that all the days of my life I shall never cease to remember. Her face, once so gay and brilliant, wore an indescribable expression. It was one of almost stolid idiocy. The canon approached her in his turn, made a low bow and presented his letters. After having read them rapidly, and with apparent indifference, she gave them back to their bearer, and in a hoarse sepulchral voice said in French:

"'You will thank the emperor and empress for their thought of me. You will tell them from me that I desire to die in France, like my husband; and that I am waiting impatiently for the moment that will reunite me to him forever.'[1]

"I wanted to say more, but she made me a sign to be silent, and as she did so rose and went away. My travelling companion was deeply grieved. He wept bitterly. I left him at once to make my report to Robespierre. Robespierre heard me in silence, and I must say without any sign of sym-

[1] It would seem as if Marie Antoinette was prepared to expect some cruel stratagem — a *guet-apens*. And indeed, for she was still stunned by her barbarous separation from her son, how could she have turned her back on Paris, and left him behind? — E. W. L.

pathy or compassion. Then he said: 'It is annoying, but she is right in the main. What part has this woman now among the living?' Then, after a little pause, he resumed, 'You will go back to Vienna immediately with the commissioner, and you will come to me to-morrow morning at five o'clock, to get your orders.'

"When I got back to Vienna, Baron Thugut received me as an old friend. I perceived at once by his manner that the affair of the Temple had not changed his views regarding the policy of the French alliance. Besides which he knew the queen too well, having been on an embassy to Versailles in 1777, to feel great sympathy for her, and I could read plainly in his face that the resolution of the widow of Louis XVI. not to return to her friends in Austria was a matter of perfect indifference to him.

"When I showed him the ratification of the treaty signed by Robespierre, he expressed his satisfaction; but when I asked for that of the emperor in exchange, he said: 'You must feel that that for the present is impossible. The queen must perish, since she wills it so. We must wait until after her execution. Then I will seize the right moment to complete our work, for which I am as anxious as M. de Robespierre.'

"I next called upon Madame de Poutet. Her reception was very different from that of the minister. I never visited her again.

"When I got back to France it was under melancholy auspices. It was during the first two weeks of August, 1793. The country was in a state of great excitement. The Convention had ordered a *levée en masse*, which gave a fresh impulse to the war, greatly to the annoyance of Robespierre, — though of course *secretly*. Then came the capture of Toulon by the English, surrendered to them with our fleet of seventeen sail of the line and five frigates, by the Legitimist traitor Imbert, who in a pamphlet published in 1814 dared to boast of his infamy.

"All this renewed the European crusade against France, and was the cause of fresh alliances against her. New treaties and new subsidies cemented the coalition between England, Prussia, Austria, and Spain. The secret treaty between Thugut and the French Republic, which Robespierre had thought would give his country a new map of France, was buried beneath English gold and European ruin."

CHAPTER VII.

CLOSING SCENES IN THE LIFE OF MARIE ANTOINETTE.

A BRIEF account of the life of the unhappy family in the Temple must preface this account of the last days of Marie Antoinette.[1]

[1] An admirable account of life in the Temple may be found in Lamartine's "Histoire des Girondins;" I have not, however, drawn on it, but in this chapter, and a subsequent one upon the dauphin, I have taken my narrative from a much briefer account, founded on the memoirs of Cléry the valet, and the Duchesse d'Angoulême. I have given the story, however, almost in the words of Mrs. Markham. I was brought up on Mrs. Markham's Histories of France and England. I vividly recall the delight with which, when a child of eight, I devoured surreptitiously (as I supposed) some of the conversations in the History of England. The account here given of the life of the royal family in the Temple seems burnt into my memory. I have read many since, but this one holds a place to which no other can attain in my mind. I have picked out the narrative from the "conversation" that contains it, — each chapter of history being supplemented by a conversation on points of interest. During a residence of fifty years in the United States I have seen only one copy of Mrs. Markham's Histories, and that, to my indignation and surprise, had the conversations left out. I knew Mrs. Markham in my early life. She was wife to the Rev. Mr. Penrose, rector of a parish, I think, in Leicestershire; Markham was a *nom de plume*. I am sorry to think she had no children. She was a daughter of Major Cartwright, who in the first quarter of this century was considered a dangerous Radical; his daughter's Histories are, however, strictly conservative. I must allow myself a little anecdote in connection with Mrs. Markham. In 1846 my father was very active in Admiral Sir Charles Napier's canvass for the borough of Mary-le-bone, and the day the election was decided he asked me to lend Sir Charles Mrs. Markham's History of England. "For," said he, "Sir Charles tells me that he never read a History of England in his life, and now that he is to legislate for his country he thinks he ought to look into one!" — E. W. L.

MARIE ANTOINETTE.

(Leaving the Tribunal.)

The Duchesse d'Angoulême — Marie Thérèse, daughter of Louis XVI. and Marie Antoinette — was about fourteen years of age when she entered the Temple. She had great difficulty in writing her journal; for having been deprived of pens and ink, she had to write with a pencil on such scraps of paper as she could secrete from the municipal guards. These scraps were afterwards collected together and published.

When the royal family was first placed in the Little Tower of the Temple, they had the comfort of being together. There was a good collection of old books there, to which the king was allowed access, and these books and the instruction of the dauphin furnished him with occupation. The princess tells us: —

"My father rose at seven, and was employed at his devotions till eight; afterwards he dressed himself and my brother, and at nine came to breakfast with my mother. After breakfast my father taught my brother his lessons till eleven. The child then played till twelve, at which hour the whole family was obliged to walk in the garden, whatever the weather might be, because the guards who were relieved at that hour wished to see that all the prisoners were safe. The walk lasted till dinner, which was at two o'clock. After dinner my father and mother played at trictrac or piquet; or, to speak more truly, they pretended to play, that they might have an opportunity of saying a few words to one another."

They were, to be sure, allowed to speak, but only in a voice loud enough for those who were incessantly employed in keeping guard to hear what they said. They had observed that when they were playing cards they were not quite so closely watched, and made use of the opportunity of saying a few words to each other unheard.

"At six," continues the princess, "my brother went again to my father to say his lessons, and to play till supper-time. After supper my mother undressed him quickly and put him to bed. My aunt and I then went up to our own apartment The king did not go to bed till eleven. My mother worked a great deal of tapestry; she directed my studies, and often made me read aloud. My aunt was frequently at prayer, and every morning read the appointed service for the day; she read a good many religious books, and sometimes, at the queen's request, would read aloud."

Marie Antoinette was deprived of all her women, but the king was permitted to retain M. Cléry, his valet. At first they were allowed to have a woman to clean out their rooms, light their fires, and do all the harder work; but this woman, who was a low, vulgar creature and a furious Jacobin, proved a great torment to them. At last she lost her intellect, and for a time they had the great trouble and anxiety of attending upon her in the unhappy state to which she was reduced. When she was gone, the two princesses had to make the beds and clean the rooms. The young princess says that she and her aunt were very awkward at this work at first, and that it used to fatigue them exceedingly; but they preferred anything to being pestered with another female Jacobin.

Everything seems to have been done that could have been thought of for the purpose of tormenting the unhappy family. There was scarcely a moment in which they were not exposed to some fresh insult or vexation. They were frequently searched to see that they had no treasonable papers; that is, what the municipal officers chose to call such. They were deprived of almost all their personal comforts. Their needlework was examined, and at last their tapestry was taken away, under pretence that it might afford them some secret method of writing, or of communicating intelligence to each other by hidden signs or devices. While the queen was giving her daughter lessons, a municipal officer was continually looking over their shoulders to see that they were not employed in plots or conspiracies. The wretches even carried their insults so far as to accuse Madame Elisabeth of stealing a china cup which by some accident was missing.

The saddest part of this history of the captivity in the Temple is that which took place on July 3, 1793, only a few days before the queen in her despair was seen by

M. Grandidier. The boy was taken from his mother and delivered over to Simon.

"Then," says the princess, "my poor mother would sit whole hours in silent despair; and her only consolation was to go to the leads of the Tower because my brother went often on the leads of the Tower on the other side. The only pleasure my mother enjoyed was seeing him through a chink as he passed at a distance. She would watch at this chink for hours together, to see the child as he passed; it was her only hope, her only thought. But this mournful satisfaction she was soon deprived of. About a month after the poor boy had been taken away, she was roused from her bed at two o'clock one morning by some Commissioners of the Commune, who ordered her to rise, telling her they were come to take her to the Conciergerie. She was forced to rise and dress herself before these men, who searched her pockets and took everything out of them. They, however, allowed her, as a great favor, to retain her pocket-handkerchief and smelling-bottle, lest she should be faint on the way."

She was scarcely suffered to take a hurried leave of Madame Elisabeth and her daughter. It was on passing through a low doorway that day that she struck her head, and on one of the men asking her if she was hurt she replied, "Nothing can hurt me now."

When Marie Antoinette first reached the Conciergerie, General Custine, the soldier-martyr of the Revolution (who had begun his military career in the United States under Washington and Rochambeau), was turned out of his cell to make room for *l'Autrichienne;* and the position of this cell near the wicket where the non-political prisoners saw their friends was peculiarly disagreeable, since it was mostly surrounded by a noisy crowd, whose filthy language offended the ear by day and night. It must be remembered that in the Conciergerie were confined the lowest class of criminals, as well as political prisoners.

[1] The remainder of this chapter is an extract from an article in the "London Quarterly Review," published in April, 1895.

It is now impossible to identify the exact position of this cell. We only know it was one of the worst in the Conciergerie and in the worst part of the prison.

The removal of the poor queen to somewhat better quarters was probably due to the humanity of the *concierge*. After the *affaire de l'œillet* (a plot to effect the escape of the queen, set on foot by the Chevalier de Rougeville, and which but for an accident might have succeeded), Richard the *concierge* was temporarily deposed, and Bault, a man more disposed to show kindness to the queen, was put in his place.

Those now permitted to visit the cell to which Marie Antoinette was removed cannot fail to feel that it is yet haunted by the tall figure of the queen, wearing her mourning dress of black *caraco*, and under her white cap bearing the proud suffering face that Delaroche has painted. Dumb, yet speaking, it bears witness to the unmanly indignities inflicted on this solitary and most unhappy woman. At the end is a heavily barred window placed high in the wall, which would look out — if it were possible to look through it — upon the courtyard. Marie Antoinette was placed in solitary confinement, and did not mix with the other prisoners, among whom she would have found many a friend, though some of the *sans-culotte dètenus* addressed insults to her window. The wretched place — it is especially damp and cold — is full of memories of the discrowned yet most regal woman who had to bear her woes alone, without the solace of human companionship or sympathy. On the right of the dismal dungeon looking towards the window was an ordinary small prison bed of *sangle* (chaff). An attendant slept in the cell, and behind a *paravent*, or folding screen, were placed two gendarmes. There is now no furniture in the room, but there is the crucifix which she used before leaving for the scaffold; and there is an altar which was erected by Louis XVIII. to the memory of the murdered queen. In entering the cell it is necessary to stoop, and tradition says that this door was made lower in order to compel her Majesty to bow her head before the power of the Revolution. The altar bears an inscription in Latin, which describes the words she wrote in the last hours of her life to Madame Elisabeth, as an "eternal monument of courage, piety, and every virtue." It adds, "All you who come within this place adore, admire, pray."

Two large paintings have been also placed in the cell which have no particular merit, and give the spectator the feeling of their having intruded there. One represents the trial of the queen; the other her removal from the Temple to the Conciergerie.

What weary nights must Marie Antoinette have passed in this bare cell, with the prospect of a terrible death always before her imagination! She suffered especially from two dreads: one that she would be murdered in her cell, the other that she would be torn to pieces by the mob on her way to execution. It needed almost superhuman courage to bear up against such ghastly apprehensions. Then, too, she was distracted by thoughts of her children, and she knew into what hands the dauphin had fallen. She spent seventy-five days in the Conciergerie, coming there on the night of the 2d of August, 1793, and leaving it for her execution on the morning of October 16 of the same year.

She was in no way dangerous to the Revolution, and even the leaders of the Jacobins hesitated for some time to take her life. The king was dead. The dauphin was being debased and slowly killed. They had nearly all they could want, and they had destroyed the direct line of their monarchs. The king's brothers were out of reach, and the widowed Marie Antoinette might safely have been allowed to retreat to Austria,[1] but Robespierre could refuse nothing

[1] We have seen in the preceding pages that this was contemplated by Robespierre; but when the war fever in August, 1793, broke forth afresh, when Toulon was surrendered, and a *levée en masse* was proclaimed, there was no longer any hope of calming the people of France or of propitiating Austria. Then Marie Antoinette's fate was sealed; she could be no longer serviceable in furthering Robespierre's schemes, whether of patriotism or ambition. — E. W. L.

that might please the Jacobins. The *people* of France did not desire her death, but as Riouffe said: "The real France was then dumb and deaf; dumb before the acts of a government only known to her people by its dark deeds and its terrible power; . . . human nature was more degraded in France in one year (the year II. of the Republic) than it had ever been in Turkey in one hundred years."

The incarceration of the queen was attended with all the cruelty which belonged to that godless and inhuman time. She suffered severely from cold and had to use her meagre pillow to warm her feet. Madame Bault, touched by the courteous dignity and suffering of the captive, applied to Fouquier-Tinville for more coverings for the queen's bed, or rather for the bed of the *Veuve Capet.* But the heartless wretch replied: "How dare you ask for such a thing? You yourself deserve to be sent to the guillotine for doing so." The clothes of the unfortunate lady, who in life had been accustomed to splendor, were miserable, worn, and insufficient. No looking-glass was allowed her, but in her pity a girl named Rosalie Lamorilière — the hearts of all the women in attendance on the queen were more or less softened towards her — procured a little common mirror, bought on the Quai for twenty-five *sols d'assignats*, and gave it to the Queen of France, who used it up to and upon the day of her death.

When Marie Antoinette reached her last prison she looked thin, weak, and worn; her hair had grown gray at the temples, and her sight was impaired. One eye, indeed, was of little use to her. She suffered much from hemorrhoids, but there is no record of any attempt having been made to procure her medical assistance. Her jewels had been taken from her, and even the watch she had brought with her from Vienna. The loss of this watch, especially dear as it was through association with her youth, cost the poor queen many silent tears. But she suffered no word of complaint at this or any other insult to pass her lips. After she was dethroned, Marie Antoinette became most truly queenly. All the levities of her days of glory and temptation had been purged and burnt away, and sorrow and suffering rendered her in every respect more noble. She was thirty-eight when she was executed. It would seem that from her entry to her prison to the day of her death, she was never allowed to leave her cell. She was alone with sorrow.

Her personal attendants were one Larivière, a woman of eighty ("*une espèce de poissarde, dont elle se plaignait fort,*" says Gaulot), a young woman named Harel, and Rosalie Lamorilière, who became profoundly attached to her. The Baults had, to please their employers, to hide any pity or sympathy beneath a show of external roughness. There was no chimney in the queen's cold cell, which had to contain herself, her female attendants, and two gendarmes. The Revolutionary soldiers *never* left the chamber. The screen was perforated with holes, to facilitate observation. The bed the queen had used was afterwards assigned to Égalité d'Orléans, who had voted the death of his cousin; and when he had been guillotined, it was given to the Chevalier de Bastion.

The queen appeared for the first time before the Revolutionary Tribunal on Oct. 12, 1793, at 6 P. M. The room in which the Tribunal sat in the Palais de Justice, which formed part of the Conciergerie, is now the *première chambre civile,* and she ascended to it by a staircase now called *l'escalier de la reine.* The place was lit by only two candles. The queen's chief care was to compromise no one by her answers. Her clear, calm replies wanted nothing in dignity, courage, or self-possession.

The second examination, or trial, took place October 14. Hermann was the president of the court, Fouquier-Tinville the *accuseur publique* (or prosecuting attorney), Fabricius the *greffier* (or secretary). The jury (it is as well to hand their names down to infamy) was composed of Gannay, a wig-maker; Martin Nicholas, a printer; Châtelet, a painter; Grenier Crey, a tailor; Antonelle, an ex-deputy; Souberbidle, a surgeon; Trinchard, a cabinet-maker; Jourdeuil, an ex-constable; Gemon, Daver, and Suard. They were all paid hirelings, furious Jacobins, and mortally afraid of Fouquier-

Tinville. The accusation, or indictment, was merely a violent statement of loose, floating prejudices. But Hermann called the queen "*cette moderne Médicis*." She said with lofty eloquence: "I was a queen; you have dethroned me. I was a wife; you have slain my husband. I was a mother; you have torn from me my children. Nothing is left me but my life's blood; slake your thirst in it, but do not make me suffer longer."[1] In spite of the nervous strain of such a trial, the queen maintained her quiet, dignified attitude. She made no appeal to justice or to mercy; she evinced no weakness; she showed almost no visible emotion except when she repelled, with noble indignation, the foul aspersions thrown upon her as a mother. As a matter of course the jury found her guilty on all counts, and she received sentence of death.

It is not hard to imagine that impressive trial scene. We know the room and can easily restore the fatal chamber to its state in October, 1793. Members of the Revolutionary Tribunal, five judges, officials in heavily plumed hats and tricolor sashes, Fouquier-Tinville, Herman, the squalid jury, the gendarmes, the prisoner, — we see them all by the dim candlelight, in that long night, sitting on benches, while, as a background, Jacobin spectators, men and women, crowd round, involuntarily half-awed by the courage of the woman who met her fate so calmly.

Robespierre, until the last days of his tyranny, always affected an appearance of legality; and this even when the only law was his own will. For form's sake the queen was allowed counsel. She had two lawyers assigned her, Chauveau-Lagarde, and Tronçon-Ducoudray. They, well knowing that the case was decided in advance, put forward such pleas as they dared to urge. On leaving the Tribunal to return to her cell, Marie Antoinette was conducted by a lieutenant of gendarmes, De Busne by name. She said, "I

[1] Her exact words were: "J'étais reine, et vous m'avez détrônée. J'étais épouse, et vous avez fait périr mon mari. J'étais mère, et vous m'avez arraché mes enfants. Il ne me reste que mon sang; abreuvez-vous en; mais ne me faites pas souffrir plus longtemps."

can hardly see where I am going." In her cell she was allowed pen and paper, and wrote that long farewell letter to Madame Elisabeth which was given to Fouquier-Tinville, and by him to Couthon, among whose papers it was found.

At five o'clock on the morning of Oct. 16, 1793, the *rappel* was beaten in all the Sections, and by seven o'clock the armed force designed to guard the streets between the prison and the scaffold was ready.

At eight o'clock, Rosalie assisting, the queen changed her linen for the last time. A soldier approached and looked on. "In the name of decency let me change my underclothes without witnesses," cried the outraged lady. "My orders are not to lose sight of you," replied the brutal Jacobin. And she had to manage as she could, crouching down upon her bed, and screened as far as possible by Rosalie. The honest girl tells us that the Committee had ordered that she should have no kind of food on the morning of the execution, but it is pleasant to know that a cup of chocolate *et un petit pain mignonette* (a little tiny roll) were supplied by the charity of Rosalie and Madame Bault. The Jacobins had no doubt issued their chivalrous order in the hope that the poor fainting woman might show weakness in the death-cart or on the scaffold, and so disgrace *l'Autrichienne*, but their base intent was frustrated.

At ten o'clock the turnkey Larivière was sent by the *concierge* into the cell; and to him we owe some knowledge of what passed there. The queen said to him sadly: "Larivière, you know I am about to die. Tell your respectable mother [1] that I thank her for her services to me, and beg her to pray God for me."

Three judges, accompanied by the *greffier* Fabricius, entered the cell. The queen was kneeling in prayer beside her little bed, but she rose to receive them. They told her to attend, as her sentence was to be read to her. She replied in a firm voice: "Such a reading is useless; I know the sentence only too well." They insisted, however, and the clerk read the document. At that moment Henri Sanson

[1] The *poissarde* of whom at first she had had reason to complain.

appeared, a young man of gigantic stature. He said roughly to the poor woman, "Hold out your hands." Her Majesty retreated a step, and pleaded that the king had not been bound. "Do your duty," cried the judges to Sanson. "Oh! *mon Dieu!*" cried the wretched queen; she thought that she was then and there to be assassinated. Sanson roughly seized the shrinking hands, and tied them with cruel force too tight behind her back. She looked up to heaven and tried to restrain her tears. Her hair, when cut off, Sanson thrust into his pocket, and it was burnt in the vestibule. So far we have the evidence of Larivière.

Marie Antoinette was dressed in a white *peignoir*, which usually served her for a morning gown, and wore a *fichu de mousseline* crossed over her breast. On her head was a little plain white linen cap. On that morning, when about to rejoin her husband, she would wear no mourning. A Constitutional priest, M. Girard, curé of St. Landry, was appointed to attend her, but she refused his ministrations. All was ready, and she looked round her cell for the last time. As she passed along the corridors on her way to the cart, she saw several of the other prisoners in the Conciergerie, and took a farewell of them. She asked for a drink of water; and one prisoner, Madame Caron, brought it to her, in a cup which is now preserved as a precious relic in the family of the Comte de Roiset. She drew near the grim office where the business of the prison was transacted, on her way to the portal, at which a tumbril, drawn by a white horse, awaited her. "This is the moment in which to show courage," said M. Girard. Her proud reply still echoes through the history of the Conciergerie. "Du courage? Il y a si longtemps que j'en fais l'apprentissage! Croyez-vous qu'il m'en manquera aujourd'hui?"[1]

She was once more in the open air, and mounted the cart with difficulty, owing to her bound hands. She appeared calm and indifferent to the cruel cries of the mob. Near St. Roch she was foully insulted; but at the angle of

[1] "Courage? I have so long been learning it as an apprentice; do you think it will fail me on this day?"

the Rue Royale, the Abbé Puget, attired as a layman, but recognizable by her, managed, to her infinite comfort, to make her a sign which assured her of absolution *in articulo mortis*. The scaffold was not erected exactly where that of Louis XVI. had stood. It was placed about thirty mètres from the pedestal on which the guillotine for the king had stood, on which now had been erected a statue to Liberty. By accident she trod on Sanson's foot, and in spite of the terrors of the moment the instinct of a lady impelled her to apologize to the executioner. When mounting the steps of the scaffold she lost a shoe, which was picked up and sold for a louis. So long as it was possible, her eyes were raised to heaven. The plank dropped; the knife fell; and the executioner held up the head to show it to the populace.

BOOK IV.

THE REIGN OF TERROR.

I. Marat.
II. Danton.
III. The Feast of the Supreme Being.
IV. The Fall of Robespierre.
V. A Chapter of Episodes.
Robespierre as a Poet. — Robespierre's Private Life at the Duplays'. — The Revolutionary Calendar. — Dogs in the Revolution. — "Which?" by François Coppée.

CHAPTER I.

MARAT.

WE are in the habit of speaking of Marat, Danton, and Robespierre, the three leaders of the Revolution during the Reign of Terror, as if they had acted together in some official capacity, — formed, in short, a triumvirate like that of Octavius, Lepidus, and Antony. This is not correct. What the government of France was during the Reign of Terror it is very hard to define. Power was wielded by each of these three men, but they were rarely colleagues. When the king was deposed after the 10th of August, the will of the Convention was the only recognized government.

Danton was then a deputy, — a young penniless lawyer of Arcis-sur-Aube, with the face of a lion, the voice of a trumpet, and the figure of a Hercules. He had taken a leading part in the deposition of the king and the proclamation of a republic. Marat, after exciting the people by incendiary articles in his newspaper, "L'Ami du Peuple" (subsequently the "Journal de la République"), had pulled the bell of St. Germain l'Auxerrois, which sounded the tocsin

MARAT.

on the 10th of August. Robespierre was not seen during those days, till he quietly reappeared, when calm was re-established, as a member of the Council of the Commune. Those members were apparently self appointed, after the old municipal authorities had been driven away; and Marat was called to preside over his colleagues.

The Convention, not being able to superintend all business as a body, selected a Committee of Surveillance, which soon became the Committee of Public Safety. Its members seem to have acted as ministers. Danton was made minister of justice, and assumed the right of making military appointments, while Carnot regulated the movements of the thirteen armies of France. Danton had risen to importance in the Convention through his prominence in promoting the deposition of the king and the establishment of a republic. His rough-and-ready eloquence also gave him great importance, especially as a leader of the Sections. He has been called the Sans-culotte Mirabeau; he might also have been called the "noble savage of the eighteenth century,"—for much in him was noble, and all was savage. His was a noble presence when he stood up in the Convention, calm among his colleagues, who were terrified by the threatened advance of the Prussians, and by the clangor of the bells that called to arms, and shouted: "Legislators! it is not the alarm cannon that you hear; it is the *pas de charge* against our enemies. To conquer them, to hurl them back, what do we require? *Il nous faut de l'audace, et encore de l'audace, et toujours de l'audace!*" (To dare, and again to dare, and without end to dare!)

Danton was prominent in the affair of the 10th of August, and may be said to have captured the municipal authority at the Hôtel de Ville upon that day. There had been sixty-two districts in Paris, the most revolutionary of which was that of the Cordeliers; in this Danton, who lived within its bounds, had been prominent from the time of his arrival in Paris. The Districts subsequently became forty-eight Sections, that of the Cordeliers retaining its name.

These Sections were at the beck and call of the municipal

government of the Commune at the Hôtel de Ville. The Sections and the municipality formed the Commune; and though Marat was decreed especial honors by this body, the heart and soul of its actions for a time was Danton. Early in 1792, two clubs had broken off from the Jacobins, one going to the right under Lafayette, — this was the Feuillants; the other going to the left under Danton, — this was the Cordeliers. Robespierre retained his connection with that of the Jacobins to the last.

Danton has always been accused of instigating and organizing the massacres of September in the prisons. His name does not appear on official documents in connection with those massacres. Marat and nine others signed a paper applauding what had been done in Paris, and exhorting the municipalities of other cities to do likewise. Marat demanded two hundred and sixty thousand heads of aristocrats (some say two hundred and seventy thousand) to purge the country.

Danton's guilt in connection with the September massacres seems, however, to have been determined by history. At the same date he was calling out all Frenchmen to resist invasion, and it was not inconsistent with his theories that he endeavored, by the terrorism of massacre and punishment, to break the spirit of the royalists remaining in the capital, while French soldiers were marching to meet *émigrés* and Prussians on the frontier.

The prominent part assumed by Danton at this crisis drew on him the jealousy and hatred of the more backward Robespierre. They seem rarely after this to have acted together except when both disapproved the sacrilegious festival of Reason, with its goddess and its orgy; and Danton united with Robespierre to bring Hébert, the instigator of that sacrilegious *fête*, to the scaffold.

Robespierre was a man of theories, — what the French would call a *doctrinaire* revolutionist; he showed the same tendency in domestic life in relation to matters of expense and minor things. Danton was an opportunist, ready to take advantage of anything that might promote his views.

Marat, on the contrary, was hardly what might be called a republican. He was a socialist and an anarchist of the most advanced type, and it was as an enemy of republicanism that he met his death at the hands of Charlotte Corday. Real republicans were ashamed of him. He was the idol of the dregs of the Parisian populace. He had been more than once in hiding, and several times on the verge of denunciation and arrest. He was not a speaker who had great influence in the clubs or in the Convention; he was not a member of the Committee of Public Safety; he was not a ruler who, for good or for evil, could sway the Sections through the Commune; but as *L'Ami du Peuple* he could rouse them through his daily sheet to frenzy. His doctrine was that which we now call Nihilism, — simple destruction of all that is, which others must take the task of building up again, — their work to be also destroyed in the future. Marat was the first to meet his death of these three leaders of the Revolution.

The Revolution, like Saturn, devoured its own children. Those who set up the guillotine perished by the guillotine. These few words seemed necessary before recording the last days of Marat, Danton, and Robespierre. The Girondists and their party had been politically extinguished by the events of May 30 and June 2, 1794; on the first of these days a mob demanded their expulsion from the Assembly, but without result. Three days later, a second mob succeeded.

The greater part of the leading Girondists, after their expulsion and proscription, went into hiding in Paris; [1] the rest fled to the provinces. Eighteen of these last, among them Barbaroux, Buzot, Gorgas, and Pétion, had taken refuge at Caen in Normandy.

This city had become a centre of agitation. It was republican, but it was opposed to extreme measures, and had resolved to set itself in opposition to the tyranny of the Convention. A committee, sitting in the Hôtel de Ville,

[1] From the "Supplément Littéraire du Figaro" of July 15, 1893, — July 13, 1793, being the date of the death of Marat. — E. W. L.

had assembled a small body of troops under command of Generals Wimpffen and Puisaye. The Girondists therefore looked on Caen as a place prepared to make resistance. But events turned out differently from what they anticipated. Instead of the men whom they relied upon, their cause was taken up by a woman.

There lived at Caen in those days a girl of the age of twenty-four, who concealed under an exterior of almost angelic gentleness an active imagination and a mind full of enthusiasm.

She had up to this time lived unknown and in obscurity, though her family had an illustrious origin. She was granddaughter of the great dramatist, Corneille, and she cherished in her heart the same feelings and ideas as those which animated the heroines in her grandfather's tragedies. But bolder than Emilia in his tragedy of "Cinna," she not only conceived her plan but carried it out.

Her person was handsome. One of her contemporaries has given us her portrait.

"Mademoiselle Corday," he says, "was not tall, but she was strongly built. Her face was oval, her features handsome, but on rather a large scale. Her eyes were blue and keen, her nose well shaped, her mouth and teeth were excellent. Her hair was a rich light brown; her arms and hands might have served as models for a sculptor. Her gait and her deportment were full of grace and self-respect."

Marie Anne Charlotte de Corday d'Armont was born in 1768 at St. Saturnin on the Orne. Her father lived on a small property in the neighborhood. Although his birth connected him with the nobility, he was an earnest partisan of the new doctrines. Possibly his poverty inclined him to accept them. He was, indeed, very much straitened in his circumstances, and his wife had died of the strain, after having given him five children, — two sons and three daughters.

As his children grew older and needed education, which to give them was beyond his means, he was forced to part from them, and he was glad to place Charlotte in a convent at Caen, the Abbaye aux Dames.

The mother superior, Madame de Belzunce, and her coadjutrix, Madame Doulcet de Pontécoulant, took a great deal of notice of Charlotte and admitted her to intimacy. It was through this intimacy that Charlotte came to know M. de Belzunce, a young colonel of cavalry, and Gustave Doulcet de Pontécoulant, both relatives of these ladies.

But the Revolutionary hurricane destroyed the peaceful refuge in which Charlotte passed her early girlhood. Convents were suppressed; and the young girl, who could not return to her father, who was now more than ever unable to support her, went to live with an old aunt, Madame de Bretteville. This old lady inhabited an ancient, dismal-looking house called the Grand Manoir. It had nothing grand about it but its name, having only two stories and three windows looking on the street, from which it was separated by a little paved courtyard. An arched door, low and narrow, served for its entrance. A dark passage and a spiral staircase led to the living-rooms on the upper floor.

Charlotte's bedroom was at one end of the house. With its brick floor and its high French ceiling and its immense fireplace, it looked bare and comfortless. Its furniture was scanty, and it was badly lighted, — though it had two windows, one with small diamond-shaped panes, which looked out on the courtyard, while the other overlooked the yard of a neighbor.

But Charlotte little cared for this. She lived with her own thoughts, and her thoughts flew far from her little dark chamber. She gave some help indeed in the household, which had the services of only one old servant; but the rest of her time was passed in reading and dreaming.

Having entire liberty to read what she liked, she devoured all books that fell into her hands. "The Adventures of Faublas," and the "Nouvelle Héloïse," for example; books of philosophy and romances. The authors she preferred were, Jean Jacques Rousseau, Plutarch, and the Abbé Raynal, whose "Histoire philosophique des Établissements et du Commerce des Deux Indes" especially excited her admiration.

The words "Republic" and "Liberty" filled her with enthusiasm. She took the deepest interest in political events. She contrived to see all the pamphlets that appeared at that period. She is said to have read over five hundred of them. She also subscribed to five newspapers, one of which, the "Courier des Départements," was edited by the Girondist Gorsas, and another, "La Patriote Française," by Brissot and Girey-Dupré.

Lonely as she was, all this reading made on her mind and heart a deep impression. Plutarch, when he told her the lives of great men, inspired her first with admiration, then with the desire to emulate them.

Her excited imagination — she having no one with whom she could exchange ideas — made her live, as it were, in company with these heroes. She identified herself with their exalted thoughts, their noble or generous actions, and she began to cherish the idea that she too might be capable of doing something great. Her ardor was intensified by the very air she breathed. Circumstances were propitious to great deeds; men's minds were excited. No one listened with indifference to such words as "the new order of things," "our country," "liberty," and so forth, which were stirring up Old France, and seemed to predict for her a glorious and happy future.

Charlotte, like the ancient heroes she admired, was an ardent republican. She had heartily embraced the republican cause; but she desired a republic as pure as it would be great, and she thought the Girondist party alone likely to realize her ideal.

She was waiting, she was hoping all things from this party, when suddenly things changed. Those whom she politically loved and believed in were overthrown, vanquished, marked out for destruction! Their place was usurped by men of blood, — men who sullied the fair image she had made to herself of the government that should be.

Must all that she had hoped, all she had planned for, go down in this shipwreck? Never!

She thought of her heroes who had died to save their country. She wished to do as they had done, — to be their equal. There was one man who by his writings and his speeches had drawn all eyes upon him. He had asked for heads; he invoked executions, — and against such things Charlotte Corday had set her face. Marat inspired more horror seen from a distance than when he was seen near; not only horror, but fear. It was Marat, the monster, who must be stricken down.

If no one else dared to attempt the task, she would accept it. She would shed his blood, and give her own in exchange. What matter? She would have achieved true glory. Glory and the gratitude of the thousands she would have saved would be hers.

Having come to this resolution, she set about its execution. She wanted neither confidant nor accomplice. The work should be all her own.

Her contemporaries, who could not comprehend her motives, at the time accounted for her action by saying that love and vengeance must have nerved her arm. But there is not a particle of evidence for these vulgar conjectures.

Fouquier-Tinville was the first to make the insinuation. He said, "This female assassin was in love with De Belzunce, a colonel killed at Caen during an insurrection, and from the time of his death she conceived implacable hatred against Marat." The truth is that she hardly knew De Belzunce, who was killed on the 12th of August, 1792; and the first number of Marat's infamous paper, "L'Ami du Peuple," did not appear till the following 12th of September.

As for Barbaroux, she saw him only three times at Caen, and Barbaroux was then living with a woman named Zelia, who never quitted him.

A M. de Franquelin has also been named as Charlotte's lover, and a M. Boisjugan de Mingré. It is not even known that she ever saw either of them.

Later another man was mentioned, a M. Bougon-Longrais, *procureur syndic* of Calvados. This much is true, that he had an affection for Charlotte which may have amounted to love; but it is equally certain that there exists not the smallest indication that she returned his affection. She expressed much friendship for him; he was young and amiable. She appreciated his merits, and they had many opinions and ideas in common; but in the mention she made of him in the letter she wrote to Barbaroux in her last hours, it would be hard to find anything but sympathy and esteem.

The fugitive Girondists had taken up their quarters in the Hôtel de l'Intendance. Charlotte did not know them, but she formed a plan to go and see them, and to enter into relations with them.

She needed a pretext for her visit, and found it in her interest in Madame de Forbin, an old friend whom she had made in the convent, who had lost her pension as a canoness, because she had emigrated six months before. She thought she might influence the proscribed deputies in her friend's favor.

With this design she went, on the 20th of June, to the Hôtel de l'Intendance. She saw Barbaroux, and made her request to him. The Girondin deputy assured her that anything he might say would be worse than useless. But she had her own ideas, and persisted. Then Barbaroux, taking up a pen, wrote to his colleague in the Assembly, Louis Duperret, who had remained in Paris, begging him to do what he could for Madame Forbin.

Barbaroux received no answer, for the letter never reached its destination. Charlotte was far from regretting this. It assisted her in her true design. She resolved to go to Paris and, as she said, attend to the affair herself; she would call on the minister of the interior.

The project soon took shape, and Charlotte prepared for her journey. She was to start early in July. Before leaving home she was present at a review held by General Wimpffen. Under the very eyes of the populace an appeal was to be made for volunteers to form a picked band to march to Paris and put down the Convention. But only seventeen volunteers stepped out of the ranks. Charlotte admired their courage, and, far from being disheartened by the smallness of their number, she felt her own purpose fired by their example.

She asked Barbaroux for a letter of introduction to Louis Duperret. Barbaroux, who suspected nothing, gave her the letter. It contained these passages: —

"I wrote you by way of Rouen to ask your good offices in an affair which concerns a lady who is our fellow-citizen. All that you need do is to get from the minister of the interior certain papers in the case, which you will forward to Caen. . . . All goes well here: we shall soon be under the walls of Paris."

Charlotte continued to conceal her design. Before setting out she paid a visit to the abbess of the convent where she had passed her childhood, but gave not the smallest indication, either in word or manner, of the real purpose of her journey.

Once only she let fall a few words which, had any one who heard them entertained any suspicion, might have given a clue to the real reason of her journey. When Pétion was complimenting *la belle aristocrate*, who was willing to visit republicans, she said: "You judge of me without knowing me, Citizen Pétion. The time will come when you will know better what I am."

The morning that she started on her journey she thus wrote to her father: —

I owe you obedience, dear papa, but nevertheless I am going without asking your leave. I go too without seeing you; it would give me too much pain. I am going to England because I do not think it possible to live happily in France for a long time to come. As I leave I shall put this letter for you in the post, and when you receive it I shall be no longer in this land. Heaven has withheld from us the happiness of living together, as well as many other good things. Perhaps it may show more favor to our country.

Adieu, my dear papa; kiss my sister for me, and never forget me.

(Signed) CORDAY.

At two o'clock in the morning of Tuesday, July 9, she left Caen, taking the diligence for Paris.

The journey lasted two days. On Thursday, the 11th, she reached Paris, and went to the house of Madame Grollier, Hôtel de la Providence, 19 Rue des Vieux Augustins, a street now partly destroyed. That same day she went to see Duperret, who lived in the Rue St. Thomas du Louvre. She did not find him at home; he was at the Convention.

She called again in the evening, and told him the ostensible purpose of her visit, and he promised to go with her the next day to see the minister of the interior.

After she left, Duperret said to his daughters: —

"That seems an odd adventure! The woman seems to me to be intriguing about something. I saw something in her face and in her manner which struck me as singular. To-morrow I shall know what it all means!"

The next day, July 12, he called for Charlotte, and took her to see the minister. Their visit was not received, and they were told to come back in the evening. By this time Duperret had altered his first impression of Charlotte. "I perceived nothing in what she said but what indicated a good *citoyenne*."

At this moment a thing happened which overthrew their plans. Duperret, who was already suspected of holding communications with his proscribed colleagues, was put under surveillance. His house was searched, and seals put upon his papers.

He was not yet arrested, and he went to warn Charlotte, telling her that his recommendation was now useless and might compromise her.

Charlotte thanked him, and said that she should do no more about it. The pretext had served her purpose, and she was not going to carry the matter further.

Duperret questioned her as to what she intended to do, and asked if she would soon go back to Normandy. She answered that she did not know exactly, but that he would hear from her, and he had better not come and see her again.

As they were about to separate, Charlotte seems to have become conscious of her imprudence. She began to feel that she had probably terribly compromised this innocent man, who had so kindly tried to serve her.

"May I give you a piece of advice?" she said. "Leave the Convention. You can do no further good in it. Go down at once to Caen and rejoin your colleagues, — your brothers."

"My place is in Paris. I must not leave my post."

"You are acting foolishly. . . . Again I say escape. Leave before to-morrow evening."

He persisted in his brave resolve. She had already said too much. She stood silent. He was amazed, but went away, not having understood her meaning, and never guessing how these three brief interviews would tell against him.

Meantime Charlotte made inquiries concerning Marat. She learned that he was ill, and not going to the Convention. She had to give up her first design of killing him in his seat on the summit of the Mountain. She determined to go and kill him in his own home.

She spent Friday evening drawing up an address, "*Aux français, amis des Lois et de la Paix*."

"How long, O unhappy Frenchmen, will you take delight in disputes and in divisions? . . . O France! thy repose depends on the execution of thy laws; I do not violate them by the killing of Marat; condemned by the whole universe, he is an outlaw. . . . What court will condemn me? If I am guilty, Hercules was guilty when he destroyed monsters. But were the monsters that he slew as hateful to mankind as Marat? . . . O my country! thy misfortunes rend my heart. I can only offer thee my life, and I thank Heaven for giving me the right so to dispose of it. . . ."

Then came some lines which the grand-daughter of Corneille took from Voltaire's "Mort de César": —

> "Whether the world, astonished, loads my name
> And deed with horror, admiration, blame,
> I do not care, — nor care to live in story.
> I act, indifferent to reproach or glory.

A free, untrammelled patriot am I.
Duty accomplished, let the rest go by!
Think only, friends, how you may break your chains." . . .[1]

She then ends her paper with these brief words: —

"My friends and relations should not be molested: no one whatever knows what I intend to do."

On Saturday, July 13, 1793, Charlotte rose early, and by six o'clock she was at the Palais Royal. Boys and men were crying through the streets the morning news, telling how nine citizens of Orleans had been condemned to death the night before, ostensibly for the murder of Léonard Bourdon, who was perfectly uninjured. Charlotte bought a paper, then she went into a cutler's shop, and paid forty sous for a knife with an ebony handle in a shagreen sheath. She then went back to her hotel. At half-past eleven she came downstairs, took a *fiacre* on the Place des Victoires, and was driven to the residence of Marat, Rue des Cordeliers (subsequently Rue de l'École de Médecine), Number 20. But it was not an easy matter to get admitted to the presence of *L'Ami du Peuple*. The portress, named Pain, the cook Jeannette Maréchal, Simone Evrard, the woman who lived with him, and her sister kept strict watch. Charlotte was told that Marat was sick, it was doubtful when he could receive her; and they refused to hear the entreaties of a woman they did not know.

Charlotte went back to her hotel and wrote a letter to Marat which she sent by *la petite poste*.

"CITIZEN, — I have just come from Caen; your love for our country makes me think you would be glad to know something of the unfortunate events in that part of the Republic. I will come to your house about one o'clock. Have the kindness to

[1] "Qu'à l'univers, surpris, cette grande action
Soit un objet d'horreur, ou d'admiration,
Mon esprit, peu jaloux de vivre en la mémoire,
Ne considère point la reproche, ou la gloire.
Toujours indépendent, et toujours citoyen,
Mon devoir me suffit — tout le reste m'est rien.
Allez! ne songez plus qu'à sortir de l'esclavage!" . . .

receive me, and to grant me a few minutes' interview. I will put you in the way to render a great service to the Republic."

That done, she put off the execution of her project till the evening.

Now as to Marat. He was a man undersized and badly built, with a sallow complexion. He dressed with a carelessness almost amounting to filthiness, and went about always muffled in an old green cloak trimmed with fur. He wore a sort of handkerchief upon his head, and "looked," said one of his fellow-deputies, "like a needy hackney-coachman." As rude in speech as he was careless in dress, he called everybody *cochon*, *bête*, and *animal*,[1] and treated every one accordingly.

As to his principles and disposition, he was a sanguinary madman. He dreamed of nothing but death and annihilation. His policy consisted only in extermination. All honest men were attacked in his paper; he was purveyor for the guillotine, the most shameful blot upon the Revolution.

It was thus that Charlotte Corday looked on the man she was about to sacrifice. It was the general opinion of him, the opinion Marat himself wished people to entertain, and nothing since has come to light to modify it.

But this portrait, although like him in the last years of his life, differs greatly from any portrait that could have been drawn of him when he was younger.

He had been a man of literature and science; these things in 1793 had disappeared; he was simply a ferocious partisan. He had been a young man of elegance and distinction; he had sunk into a squalid, dirty *sans-culotte*.

He was born May 24, 1743, at Boudry, in Switzerland; his father had come from Cagliari in Sardinia. He received a good education, which he completed in literature at Geneva.

After that he travelled much in Europe,[2] learned most of

[1] No terms of reproach in French are more insulting.

[2] Dumas says ill-treatment in Russia soured his whole nature and unsettled his mind.—E. W. L.

the European languages, and called himself, in the language of that day, "a student of humanity."

While in England he got his diploma as a doctor, and about 1777, on his return to France, he was made doctor to the body-guard of the Comte d'Artois. He had at that time so high a reputation for skill in his profession that people paid him *thirty-six livres* a visit.

One remarkably successful cure increased his reputation, his good fortune, and the jealousy of a large number of his fellow-doctors.

The Marquise de Laubespine, niece of one of the most illustrious of the king's ministers, was very ill, and Bouvart, a very celebrated physician of that day, pronounced her case hopeless. Marat was sent for, promised to effect a perfect cure, and kept his word.

The poor woman, full of gratitude, was willing to testify it in every possible way: and Marat became her lover. Then, to please her, he affected the dress and manners of a man of fashion, even carrying his care for the refinements of the toilette to an extreme.

Much occupied as he was with the duties of his profession, they did not cause him to give up his taste for scientific research. He was interested in heat, light, and electricity. He published several works upon these subjects which gave him a considerable reputation as a *savant.*

He flung himself at once into the Revolutionary movement; but his views of the Revolution differed from those that most other people interested in it at its beginning entertained. He thought the disputes between the Three Orders in the States-General absurd. The abolition of the privileges of rank by the nobility seemed to him a ridiculous concession. He did not divide the world into nobles and non-nobles, but into rich and poor; and he saw no sense in giving political liberty to men perishing of hunger.

He became the champion of the needy and the famine-stricken. He called himself, and made others call him The People's Friend, — *L'Ami du Peuple.* The class to whom he gave his sympathy gave him in return its affection and support; and he thus attained immense popularity and power.

By degrees the excitement of the struggle and the fashion of exaggerating patriotism made him lose his head. All obstacles irritated him, resistance exasperated him, and persecution had the result of turning his humanitarianism into ferocious hatred. A skin disease which kept him in a continual state of bodily irritation completed his transformation.

Yet even thus something of his former attractiveness lingered about him. Fabre d'Églantine has described him, and his portrait is worth being retained: —

"Marat was a very small man, hardly five feet high; but he was strongly built, neither too fat nor too lean. . . . He used his arms gracefully, and with much gesticulation. His neck was short, his face broad and bony. His nose was aquiline, but it looked as if it had been flattened. His mouth had a contraction at one corner. His forehead was wide, his eyes light hazel, full of spirit, life, and keenness; their natural expression was gentle and kindly. His eyebrows were scanty, his complexion sallow, his beard dark, his hair brown and disorderly. He walked rapidly, with his head thrown back. His favorite attitude was to cross his arms over his chest. He gesticulated a great deal when he talked in company, and would stamp his foot to emphasize his words; sometimes he would rise on tiptoe when he became vehement. His voice was sonorous, but he had a defect in his tongue which made it hard for him to pronounce clearly *c* and *s*. Yet, when accustomed to his voice, the earnestness of his thoughts, the plenitude of his expressions, the simplicity of his eloquence, and the brevity of his words made his hearers forget the slight defect in his enunciation."[1]

In the time of his greatest straits and difficulties, about the year 1790, Marat found in the attachment of a woman the support and the pecuniary aid he so much needed. This

[1] This has been slightly abridged. Fabre d'Églantine did not cultivate brevity of speech. — E. W. L.

woman, Simone Evrard, devoted herself to him and became his inseparable companion. She watched over him with jealous care.

For eighteen months before July, 1793, Marat had lived with her in a little *appartement* on the first floor of a house in the Rue des Cordeliers.

A large arched passage led to the staircase. Near the door hung an iron chain, to which a bell was fastened. The visitor first entered a rather dingy ante-chamber; then on the right hand was the dining-room, separated by another room from the little closet in which Marat was accustomed to take his bath.

About half-past seven in the evening of the fatal day, Charlotte Corday, with another letter in her hand addressed to Marat in case he should not have received the first, again went to his house in the Rue des Cordeliers.

As before, a close watch guarded all approach to *L'Ami du Peuple*. She met with another refusal. She persisted, and a discussion ensued, the noise of which reached the ears of Marat. He called Simone Evrard, and asked who wanted to see him; and, as he had received Charlotte's first letter written that morning, he was curious to hear what she might have to tell him respecting the situation at Caen. He therefore gave orders that she should be admitted.

Marat was in his bath-tub, of the form of a slipper. He was wrapped in a sheet, which left his arms and shoulders bare. He was writing on a little plank placed before him. He asked his visitor to sit down at his left hand. They thus found themselves on a line; both had their backs turned to the little window which looked on the courtyard. They were alone.

Marat began to question Charlotte on the troubles at Caen. She answered that eighteen deputies from the Convention, in conjunction with the authorities of the Department, reigned supreme there, and that all the men were getting themselves enrolled in order to march on Paris and deliver it over to lawlessness. They were commanded, she said, by the four deputies of the Department.

He asked the names of those deputies, and of their principal supporters.

She named Gorsas, Larivière, Buzot, Barbaroux, Louvet, Bergoeing, Pétion, and others; she mentioned also four more, called administrators.

While she spoke he was writing. When she ended, "I 'll have them all guillotined in Paris before long," he said.

At this, as if she had only waited for some fresh proof of Marat's thirst for blood, she rose, grasped the knife she had concealed in her dress, and with one thrust plunged it into his breast.

"*À moi!*" (Help!) he called to Simone Evrard.

A man named Laurent Bas was in the house, — a folder of Marat's newspaper. He heard the cry and rushed in; he met Charlotte Corday in the next room, knocked her down, and held her tight, bruising her cruelly.

The noise brought Simone Evrard to the spot. She sprang over the body of Charlotte and rushed to Marat. Blood was flowing in great drops from his wound. She tried to stop it with her hand, but in vain; the water in the bath-tub grew rapidly red.

At this moment came in a dentist who lodged in the house. He had his office there, and through his window, which commanded a view of Marat's bathroom, he had witnessed the bloody spectacle. He put a compress on the wound at once. Marat was lifted from his bath and placed upon his bed. Soon it became evident that his pulse had ceased to beat. *L'Ami du Peuple* was dead.

Meantime men from the guard-house of the Théâtre Français (now the Odéon) rushed to the spot, for the news spread rapidly. They rescued Charlotte from Laurent Bas and the women of Marat's household, bound her hands, and stood guard over her.

The commissioner of police soon arrived and questioned her. She answered clearly and simply, with perfect *sang-froid.* She told her motive for the crime. "She had seen," she said, "civil war about to break out in France; and believing that Marat was the chief cause of such a disaster, she had sacrificed her own life and his to save her country."

Had she premeditated the murder? She answered, "I should not have left Caen had I not intended to do it."

They asked her if she had not tried to escape through the window.

"No," she replied. "Had I escaped, it would have been by the door. But I was stopped before I reached it."

The commissioner had her searched. In her pockets they found twenty-five silver crowns, a silver thimble, several assignats, a passport, a gold watch, a trunk-key, and a ball of fine thread.

The sheath of the knife she had used was still in her dress. Other police commissioners came in; one of them saw a paper in her bosom, — the undelivered letter to Marat. He put out his hand to seize it; and she, dreading some insolence, drew back so forcibly that the lacing of her dress burst, and she found her bosom uncovered. Then she begged piteously that they would untie her hands a moment, and allow her to readjust her *corsage*. An assistant did her this service.

She showed her wrists, cut and chafed by the cords, and begged that they would let her pull down her sleeves and put on gloves to hide the wounds made on her wrists by binding them. These requests were granted, and she recovered her habitual serenity.

The whole evening had been taken up by these formalities, but the most terrible was to come. She was to be confronted with the corpse of the man she had murdered. About midnight she was taken to where his body lay upon his bed.

"Yes," she said; "yes! I killed him." Her voice trembled with emotion.

Late as it was, an angry crowd surrounded the house. Charlotte had to be got out of it and taken to prison. It had been decided that that prison should be the Abbaye. As soon as she appeared, cries, shouts of rage, and threats of vengeance rose on all sides. She came near being torn in

CHARLOTTE CORDAY.

pieces. . . . Overcome by all she had gone through during the day, she fainted.

But she came to herself speedily, astonished and disappointed to find herself still living.

"I have accomplished my work," she said as she revived; "others must do the rest."

When she was safe within the walls of the Abbaye, they searched her room at the hotel, and, finding the name and address of Citizen Duperret on a piece of paper, he was at once arrested.

The news of the murder flew rapidly through Paris, causing great astonishment and much excited feeling. Every leading "patriot" thought himself in danger. "The deed may have been done by a woman," they said, "but her party inspired it."

The next day a mob swarmed into the Convention. Several of the Sections presented addresses, and the orator of one of them cried, "Where art thou, David, — thou who hast handed down to posterity the portrait of Lepelletier de Saint-Fargeau dying for his country? — Now another scene has been prepared for thee!"

"I will paint it!" exclaimed David.

In the Council of the Commune Hébert proposed an apotheosis of Marat. The next day the Convention passed a decree that its members in a body should attend his obsequies. The day was fixed for Tuesday, July 16, 1793.

The body was embalmed, but with some difficulty, and a magnificent funeral was prepared. The tomb alone cost two thousand dollars, and the whole expense of the celebration amounted to rather over fifty-six hundred.

He was buried in the garden of the Cordeliers, beneath some trees. Patriotic addresses were pronounced over him, and the lower classes, who really believed him to be *L'Ami du Peuple*, mourned for him. On his tomb it was recorded that he had been murdered by the people's enemies.

Charlotte at the Abbaye was placed in the cell once occupied by Madame Roland, and afterwards by Brissot. Two gendarmes were placed also in the cell with orders not to lose sight of her by day or night. She asked at once for pen, ink, and paper, and wrote the following letter: —

To Citizens composing the Committee of Public Safety: —

Since I have still a brief time to live, may I hope, citizens, that you will permit me to have my portrait painted. I should like to leave this mark of my remembrance to my friends. Besides which, even as men cherish the memory of good citizens, so curiosity sometimes makes them seek memorials of great criminals, which serves to perpetuate horror for their crimes. If you deign to pay attention to my request, I beg you will send me to-morrow some painter of miniatures. I again implore you to let me be alone while I sleep. In which case believe I pray you, in all my gratitude.

MARIE CORDAY.

That same day Charlotte began a long letter to Barbaroux. She had promised to send him news of her journey, and most certainly he never expected the news he would receive.

The letter itself will show better than anything else the state of mind of Charlotte Corday. Her ideas of morality were those of a heathen. She believed herself to have acted like Brutus, and to deserve the same recognition.

"From my cell in the prison of the Abbaye, the same once occupied by Brissot; the second day of preparation for peace.

"You wished, citizen, to receive some account of my journey. I shall not spare you the smallest details. I travelled with some rough fellows, men of the Mountain, whom I suffered to talk without interruption, and what they said being as absurd as they themselves were disagreeable, I dropped off to sleep. I only really awoke when we reached Paris. One of our travellers, who apparently had a fancy for girls who were asleep, took me to be the daughter of one of his friends, attributed to me a fortune that I have not, and called me by a name I had never heard. He ended by offering me his fortune and his hand. When I got tired of his wooing, I said: 'You have entirely mistaken me. We are acting a play, and it's a pity there are no spectators. I will wake up our travelling companions and let them share the fun.' This made him very cross. At night he sang me love-songs, which helped to send me to sleep. I parted from him at last at Paris, refusing to give him my address or that of my father, which he asked of me. He left me much annoyed. I knew that people here might interrogate my fellow-travellers, and I did not wish to know any of them enough to make things in that case disagreeable for them. I followed the advice of uncle Raynal, who says that truth is not due to tyrants. It was through another woman who travelled with me that the police here have found out that I know you, and then they discovered I had spoken to Duperret. You know Duperret's constancy; he told them the exact truth. My deposition confirmed his. They have nothing against him, but his firmness is a crime. I feared, I own, that they might discover I had seen him. I was sorry I had done so, but it was too late. I wanted to repair my error by begging him to go at once to join you; but he would not, being decided to remain in Paris. Sure of his innocence and of that of everybody else, I set about to execute my project. Would you believe it? Fauchet is in prison as my accomplice; he had never even heard of me. But they are not satisfied with only a woman of no importance to sacrifice to the manes of their great man.

"Pardon me, partakers of human nature! — to call *him* a man dishonors your species. He was a wild beast, about to destroy France utterly by kindling civil war. Now may Frenchmen live in peace. Thank Heaven, he was not born in France!

"Four members of the Committee were at my first examination. Chabot looked like a madman, Legendre wished to pretend he had seen me in the morning at his house, — me! who never even dreamed of seeing the man; it was not my mission to punish every one of them. All those who saw me for the first time wanted to make out that they had long known me. I think what they call Marat's last words have been printed; I do not think he said any, but these are the last he spoke to me. After having written down your name and those of the *administrateurs* of Calvados, who are at Evreux, he said, for my satisfaction, I suppose, that in a few days he would have you all guillotined in Paris. These words decided his fate. If the Department puts his portrait opposite to that of St. Fargeau, they had better inscribe these words under it in letters of gold.

"I will give you no account of the great event. The newspapers will tell you all about it. I own that what finally decided me to do the deed was the sight of the courage with which our volunteers came forward on Sunday, the 7th of July. You will remember how they delighted me, and I resolved to make Pétion repent of the doubt he then seemed to entertain as to my feelings. 'Would you be sorry if they did not march?' he said. And then I reflected that so many men marching to get the head of one man might very probably miss him, and at any rate the lives of many good citizens would be sacrificed in the attempt. When I left Caen it was my intention to sacrifice him as he sat on the summit of the Mountain; but he was not attending the Convention. I wish I had kept your letter, it would have clearly shown that I had no accomplices. However, that will be proved in due time. We are such good republicans here in Paris that no one can conceive how one useless woman, whose longer life might have been little good, should have deliberately been willing to sacrifice herself to save her country. I thought they would have killed me on the spot. But some brave men — men really worthy of all praise — preserved me from the fury — a fury certainly excusable — of those whom I had bereaved and made unhappy. Though I had plenty of courage, the screams of those women made me suffer. But when one hopes to save one's country, one must not count what it costs. May peace be established soon, according to my hopes! What I have done is its preliminary. It would never have come while he lived.

"I have deliciously enjoyed complete peace the last two days. The happiness of my country makes my happiness. There is no act of self-sacrifice that does not produce more satisfaction than it costs suffering to decide upon it. I cannot doubt that they will in some way persecute my father, who will have sorrow enough in losing me. If my letters are found, they will be full of pictures of you. If you find any little jokes made about you, forgive me for them. I could not help being a little merry; it is my character. In my last letter to my father I made him think that, dreading the horrors of war, I was going to England. My idea at that time was to keep my incognito, to kill Marat in public, to be killed on the spot, and to leave the Parisians to discover my name, — which they could not have done. I beg you, citizen, you and your colleagues, to do your best to defend my friends and relations if they are molested. I say nothing to my dear friends who are aristocrats; I hold their remembrance in my heart. I have never hated any human being save one. I have proved how much I hated him; but there are a thousand whom I love more than he was hated. An active imagination and a feeling heart would probably have made my life a stormy one. I beg those who may regret me to remember this, and they will be glad to think of my repose in the Elysian Fields, with Brutus and other ancient heroes. Among the moderns there are few real patriots; few who are really ready to die for their country. Care for self prevails. What sad material for the formation of a republic! But first we must secure peace, and good government will come afterwards, provided the Mountain does not get the upper hand. At least, I think so. I am very comfortable in my prison. My jailers are kind men; they have given me some gendarmes to keep me company. I like that well enough during the day, but not at night. I complained of it as indecent, but the Committee has not thought proper to pay any attention to my complaint. That is the doing of Chabot. None but an ex-Capuchin could have thought of such a thing. I pass my time writing songs. I have given the last verse of that one of Valady's to some one who wanted it. I tell all the Parisians that we only take up arms against Anarchy. Which is the exact truth." . . .

Here the letter breaks off. The trial of Charlotte was pushed on rapidly, and on the morning of July 16 an order from the Revolutionary Tribunal transferred her from the Abbaye to the Conciergerie. The decree was at once executed. The President of the Tribunal proceeded to examine her. The great wish of her judges was to prove she had accomplices, to unearth a plot. To this end a series of questions was put to her, all of which she answered simply and clearly, with invariable frankness.

When they asked her why she had come to Paris, she answered, —

"I only came to kill Marat."

"What motives made you determine on so horrible an action?"

"His crimes."

"What crimes do you accuse him of?"

"The desolation of France and the civil war he was about to ignite in all parts of the country."

"On what do you found such an imputation?"

"His crimes in the past were the indication of his crimes in the future. He instigated the massacres in last September; he kept up the fires of civil war, that he might be named dictator; he assailed the authority of the people by causing deputies to the Convention to be arrested on the 31st of May last —"

"When you struck him did you mean to kill him?"

"I certainly did."

"So atrocious an action could not have been committed by a woman of your age unless it had been suggested by some one."

"I told no one what I thought of doing. I did not feel I was going to kill a man, but a wild beast who was devouring Frenchmen."

The president, Montané, then questioned her as to her relations with Barbaroux, Duperret, and others. He told her that no one would believe she could have committed such a crime unless some one had instigated it.

"You must know little of the human heart," she said. "It is easier to execute such a project prompted by one's own hatred than by that of others."

Finally, the president asked her if she had counsel.

She said she would call on Citizen Doulcet de Pontécoulant, a deputy from Caen, to defend her.

She was then taken to the Conciergerie. She was to be re-examined the next day. She spent her time in finishing her letter to Barbaroux.

"I have been transferred to the Conciergerie, and the gentlemen of the grand jury have promised to forward you this letter, so I go on with it. I have undergone a long examination; pray get it if it is published. I had written an address, which was found upon me on my arrest, to 'The Friends of Peace.' I cannot send it you. I shall beg them to publish it, but probably I shall ask in vain. Last night I had a fancy to present my portrait to the Department of Calvados; but the Committee of Public Safety, from whom I asked permission to have it painted, has given me no answer. Now it is too late. I beg you, citizen, to show this letter to Citizen Bougon, procureur general syndic of the Department. I do not write to him for several reasons. First, because I am not sure he is now at Evreux; secondly, because, being tender-hearted, he may be made sorry by my death. I think, however, that, being a good citizen, the hope of peace in France will bring him consolation. I know how much he desires it, and in doing my best to bring it to pass I have fulfilled his wishes. If any of my friends ask to see this letter, refuse it to no one.

"I must have a lawyer for my counsel; it is the custom. I have chosen mine from the Mountain; I chose Gustave Doulcet. I fancy he will refuse the honor; it would not, however, entail much labor. I had thought of asking for Robespierre or Chabot. I shall ask leave to dispose of the remainder of my money, and I should like it to be given to the wives and children of those brave men of Caen who have started for the relief of Paris.

"I was surprised that the populace let them take me from the Abbaye to the Conciergerie. It is a fresh proof of the moderation of the people. Tell this to our good fellow-townsmen at Caen; they sometimes break out into little insurrections which are not so easily controlled.

"To-morrow at eight o'clock my final trial takes place; probably by midday I 'shall have lived,' as the Romans said. The inhabitants of Calvados ought to be thought highly of if their women show that they are capable of courage. But I do not know how it will be at the last; and it is the end that entitles work to a crown. I have no occasion to affect indifference to my fate, for up to this moment I have not felt the smallest fear of death; I only value life for its power to be useful. I hope to-morrow Duperret and Fauchet will be set at liberty. It is said that the latter took me to the Convention, to the reserved seats in the gallery. What business would he have had to take a woman there? As a deputy he had no business to be in the reserved seats, and as a bishop he ought not to have been escorting women, — so this is a little punishment for him; but Duperret has nothing to reproach himself with.

"Marat is not to be buried in the Pantheon, though he well deserved it. I beg you to make a collection of all documents appropriate to compose his funeral oration. I hope you will not give up the cause of Madame Forbin. Here is her address, if you wish to write to her: Alexandrine Forbin, at Mendresie, near Zurich, Switzerland. Pray tell her that I loved her with all my heart. I will now write a few lines to papa. I send nothing to my other friends: they had better forget me; any sorrow for my death would dishonor my memory. Tell General Wimpffen that I think I have helped him to gain more than a battle would have done, by facilitating peace. Adieu, citizen. May all who love peace think of me.

"The prisoners in the Conciergerie, far from insulting me, like the people in the streets, seemed to pity me; misfortune makes the heart more compassionate. This is my last reflection.

"July 16, 8 P.M. CORDAY.

"*To Citizen Barbaroux, deputy to the National Convention, a refugee at Caen, Rue des Carmes, Hôtel de l'Intendance.*"

She then wrote to her father, M. de Corday d'Armont, Rue de Bêgle, Argenton.

Forgive me, dear papa, for having disposed of my own life without your permission. I have avenged many innocent victims; I have prevented many evils; the people, when they see things in their true light, will some day rejoice that they were delivered from a tyrant. When I tried to persuade you I was going to England, I hoped to keep my incognito; but I found it impossible. I hope you will not be molested; should you be so, however, I know you will find defenders at Caen. I have chosen Gustave Doulcet for my counsel, but such a deed has no defense; I take a lawyer only for form's sake. Adieu, dear papa. I beg you to forget me, or rather to rejoice at my fate; the cause in which I suffer is noble. I send kisses to my sister, whom I love with all my heart, as I do all my relations. Do not forget this line from Corneille: —

"Le crime fait la honte, et non pas l'échafaud."

My trial is to-morrow at eight o'clock.

July 16. CORDAY.

The next day, Wednesday, July 17, at eight o'clock in the morning, Charlotte was taken before the Revolutionary Tribunal. Montané presided, assisted by three other judges. Fouquier-Tinville, prosecuting attorney, was in his place.

The twelve jurymen took their places facing the prisoner. Their names are obscure, except that of Leroy, ex-Marquis of Montflabert, who changed his royalist name for the appellation of Dix-Août (10th of August).

After the usual questions the judge asked if she had counsel.

"I chose a friend," she said, "but I have seen nothing of him. Apparently he had not the courage to undertake my defense."

The truth was Gustave Doulcet had not received Charlotte's note, and did not know of her request till some days later.

The judge then named for her counsel Chauveau-Lagarde, with Genier for his junior.

Witnesses were called. The grief of Simone Evrard affected Charlotte. "I killed him," she cried, hoping by this confession to put an end to a painful scene.

She denied nothing. She stoutly affirmed that she alone had planned the crime; that she was a republican, and had been driven to the deed by her love for France and the Republic. She was asked if she thought she had killed all the Marats. "No," she answered; "but the rest will be filled with fear."

While she steadily answered all questions, she was quite alive to what went on around her. She observed that a spectator was sketching her; and having failed to receive any favorable reply from the Committee of Public Safety as to her portrait, she turned her head so that he could get a good view of her.

They showed her the knife with which she stabbed her victim. She turned away her eyes and said hurriedly, "I recognize it; I know it." Fouquier-Tinville then spoke: "You must be very familiar with crime." She gave a sharp cry and said, "Oh, the monster! Does he take me for a common murderess?"

Her letter to Barbaroux was read, and its reading seemed to gratify her. Her allusion to Chabot, the ex-Capuchin, made her laugh. Fouquier-Tinville's speech was more moderate than his wont. The facts spoke for themselves; there was really nothing to be said either by the defense or the prosecution.

Her counsel Chauveau-Lagarde described in after days the emotion with which all the proceedings of that day had filled him. He made what defense he could, appealing to the jury on the ground that the murder was an act of political fanaticism. "As I spoke," he said afterwards, "a look of satisfaction illuminated her face."

When the verdict was given and sentence of death pronounced, she turned to Chauveau-Lagarde and said: "Monsieur, I thank you for the courage with which you have defended me in a manner worthy of me and of yourself. My money has been confiscated by these gentlemen, but I wish to give you a still greater testimony of my gratitude. I beg you to pay for me what I owe in the prison, and I count on your generosity."

Chauveau-Lagarde accepted this singular legacy, and paid the debt, which amounted to thirty-six francs.

"I had hoped that we should have breakfasted together," said Charlotte to Richard, the *concierge* of the Conciergerie, and his wife, "but the judges kept me so long yonder I had to break my promise."

She refused the religious services offered her by Abbé Lothringer, a Constitutional priest.

"Thank those," she said, "who sent you, for their attention; I am much obliged to them, but I do not need your ministry."

The last hours of her life were employed by her in what she had more at heart. The young painter Huer, who had begun to take her picture during the trial, was admitted to finish it in the prison. The picture is now in the Gallery at Versailles.

In general, there was little interval between sentence and execution, but this time the latter was retarded by a dispute between the chief judge and Fouquier-Tinville about certain words in the indictment, which so excited the public prosecutor that he forgot to sign the order for the execution, and it was not till some hours after, when he found Sanson standing at his office-door waiting for it, that he remembered the omission.

"*Quoi! Déjà?*" said Charlotte, as the executioner entered. She tore a fly-leaf from a book, and wrote a few lines expressing her resentment and contempt for the man who she (unjustly) thought had declined to be her counsel.

She herself cut off two locks of her beautiful hair. One she gave to the painter, the other to Richard, for his wife. Then she gave herself into the hands of the executioner.

She was clothed in the red smock always given to murderers. The cart waited before the door of the Conciergerie; a fierce crowd surrounded it. When Charlotte appeared there was a loud volley of shouts and execrations, whilst a thunder-storm burst over the city, and thunder and lightning filled the air.

The rain, the flashes of lightning, and the claps of thun-

18

der had no effect on the curiosity of the crowd. So great was the mob that the cart could only move very slowly. Charlotte stood up, though Sanson offered her a chair. She wished calmly to look on at the explosion of hatred which was bursting all around her.

At the same time there were not wanting marks of sympathy, — nay, even, of admiration. Some people had forgotten her crime and thought only of her rare courage and serenity. Among these unknown friends was one man in particular. He was a young deputy from Mayenne, Adam Lux by name, whom the Revolution had excited to enthusiasm, and the Convention had welcomed into its body.

Adam Lux drew close to the cart and testified his passionate admiration for the victim with unparalleled warmth and demonstration. He proclaimed her to be "more noble than Brutus," and he wished he were about to die with her. He did, indeed, die subsequently as she had died, — by the guillotine.

Three other spectators wished to gaze on the young heroine, but they stood at a window in the Rue St. Honoré. They were Robespierre, Danton, and Camille Desmoulins. What reflections would have crowded on their minds as they looked down upon her in the cart, could the veil that hid their own fate been withdrawn!

Slowly the tumbril made its way onward. It was two hours since it had quitted the Conciergerie.

"You must find the time long," said Sanson to his prisoner.

"Bah!" she answered, "we are sure to get there at last."

When they turned on to the Place de la Révolution Sanson tried to place himself so that she would not see the guillotine, but she stooped and leaned forward. "I have a right," she said, "to be curious. It is the first time I have ever seen one."

Still, notwithstanding her courage, the sight made her grow pale. She recovered herself, however, almost immediately. She stepped down from the cart and mounted the scaffold. Then she bowed to the crowd, and some thought she was about to address them with a few words. She was drawn back, however. One of the executioners pulled off the white *fichu* which covered her neck and breast. A faint blush colored her cheeks. Then she lay down on the plank; the knife fell; her head dropped into the basket. One of Sanson's assistants, Legros, seized it, held it up to the people, and slapped the face. Tradition says her cheeks blushed at the outrage.

With thunder and lightning, and occasional gleams of a summer sun breaking through the clouds, the execution took place. The body was at once removed to the graveyard of the Madeleine, and buried without further ceremony. In 1804 a cross was placed over her grave, but in 1815 her remains were finally interred in the cemetery of Montparnasse.

Never did any citizen receive such honors after death as did Marat. We say nothing of his funeral orations, in which the terms in which he was praised were blasphemous. His heart was placed in a vase of agate, found among the treasures of the Garde Meuble. A monument was erected to him on what is now the Place du Carrousel, and it was inaugurated a month after his death.

David fulfilled his promise, and painted Marat in his bath-tub. His bust — that of *L'Ami du Peuple* — was paraded through the Sections.[1] More than thirty cities or villages asked the honor of taking his name; chief among these was Havre, which became Havre-Marat. Children were called Marat as their "given name." His picture was hung up in the schools, and rings, brooches, watches, and cravat pins had his portrait. Various dramas were put upon the stage concerning his death and his apotheosis, — for example, "Marat dans l'Olympe," a comedy with songs; "L'Arrivée de Marat aux Champs Élysées," etc. Verses and ballads concerning him were sold in all the streets.

On Nov. 19, 1793, the Convention decreed Marat the honors of the Pantheon. This was a month after the exe-

[1] As we have seen in Mr. Griffith's reminiscences. — E. W. L.

cution of the queen. On Sept. 21, 1794, the ceremony took place with extraordinary splendor.

But even then the popular devotion to *L'Ami du Peuple* was on the decline. A few months later the Convention, though it did not dare to reverse its vote, decreed that the honors of the Pantheon should be given to no citizen till he had been dead ten years (Feb. 8, 1795).

This was the prelude to the unpantheonization of Marat. In January they had begun to pull down his monument. On February 26, his remains were turned out of the Pantheon and placed in a neighboring graveyard.

Ever since that time his name has been a mark for execration, and his own blood shed by Charlotte Corday has not effaced the stain upon his memory made by the torrents of blood which he shed.

CHAPTER II.

DANTON.

HÉBERT and his fellow-atheists, who said in their hearts there was no God, and yet inconsistently took pleasure in provoking Him to anger and insulting Him, were sent to the guillotine on March 7, 1794. The Hébertists were the *new* Cordeliers. The *old* Cordeliers were followers of Danton. There was great confusion both in the club of the Cordeliers, and in that of the Jacobins. The condemnation of Hébert led to clamors against Pitt. If the Revolution had been instigated to excesses which compromised it in the eyes of other nations, who could have been the instigator of such excesses but Pitt? The Jacobins suspected some of their own members of being concerned in a conspiracy to bring the Revolution into disrepute, and determined to purge themselves. Camille Desmoulins had given them offense, and there rose murmurs against Danton himself, "though he bellowed them down, and Robespierre embraced him in the Tribune." In those days too there was unearthed a financial scandal, in which Philippeaux, a representative, Fabre d'Eglantine, Chabot, and Bazire were implicated. Philippeaux's real offense was that on his return to Paris after a mission to La Vendée, he brought back an ill report of General Rossignol, who was a stanch adherent of Robespierre. He made a similar charge against Westermann, who had led the Marseillais to Paris, and who had also been sent into La Vendée.

Danton had grown weary of turmoil and confusion. He had gone down with his young wife to Arcis-sur-Aube, his birthplace, the scene of his boyhood. After the proscription of the Girondists he had been urged to escape, to hide himself, to seek an asylum in some foreign land. He replied, "If free France casts me out, there are only dungeons for me elsewhere. Does a man carry away his country on the soles of his shoes?"

On the purgation of the Jacobin Club each member was asked by Saint-Just: "What deed have you done for which, in case of a counter-revolution, you would be guillotined?" Camille Desmoulins had assuredly done many such deeds; had given many pledges of good faith to the Revolution. He was, however, cast out by the Jacobins, and soon after sent to prison by the Committee of Public Safety. Danton had ceased to be a member of that committee. Three months after its establishment he had proposed that all power should be given to it, and a sum of fifty millions of money. The power it assumed; the money was not voted; and Danton from that day forth would have nothing to do with the committee, though it repeatedly solicited him to return. It was a body in which the members held brief terms of office, but they re-elected themselves when those terms expired. The Committee of General Security was to it a sort of sub-committee.

After the arrest of Camille Desmoulins, things became so threatening that Danton's friends urged him vehemently to leave Arcis and return to Paris. Dreading the result of the impending struggle between Danton and Robespierre, some friends of the former brought about a meeting between the rivals, but this meeting did but inflame the hatred and jealousy they were so anxious to appease. "It is right," said Danton to Robespierre, "to repress Royalists; but we should not strike except where it is useful to the Republic; we should not confound the innocent with the guilty."

"And who says," cried Robespierre, "that even one person who was innocent has perished?"

On hearing of the result of this interview, Danton's friends again urged him to escape, and so avoid his probable arrest.

"They dare not arrest me!" cried Danton, proudly, and would take no measures to insure his safety.

DANTON.

But on the morrow news spread over Paris that Danton, Camille Desmoulins, Philippeaux, and Lacroix were prisoners.

On the 13 Germinal, An II. (April 2, 1794), the trial of Danton for conspiracy against the Republic, and that of his accomplices (so called), took place.[1] Excitement ran high in Paris, and crowds surrounded the Palais de Justice. The accused were Jacques Paul Danton, Camille Desmoulins, Hérault de Séchelles, Philippeaux, and Lacroix, — all members of the Convention, all leaders in the Revolution. Their accusers were their colleagues, Robespierre, Saint-Just, and Couthon, — the same who a few months before had brought the Girondists to trial.

Every precaution had been taken to secure conviction. Herman, the judge who presided, could be relied on to interrupt and impede the defense of the accused, or, if necessary, to suppress it entirely. Four other judges sat with him on the bench, all creatures of Robespierre. Fouquier-Tinville was the public prosecutor, and the jury was composed of what in the language of the times were called *des hommes solides;* that is, men whose opinion could be relied upon beforehand.

As a further precaution, Danton's case was united to that of men arraigned for a financial scandal in connection with the Compagnie des Indes, several of whom there is no reason to doubt were dishonest stock-jobbers. It made Danton indignant to be placed in the dock beside men of this character, of whom there were eight, all being accused as his accomplices, and he as theirs.

Danton, Camille, Philippeaux, and Lacroix had been arrested in the last night of March, 1794, and carried to the Luxembourg. Danton, when warned of what was coming, had replied with supreme disdain, "A man who sleeps at home every night with his wife is never a conspirator."

The vigorous action of the two committees took him by

[1] From an article in the "Supplément Littéraire du Figaro," April 7, 1894.

surprise. "He seemed," said one who witnessed his arrest, "rather ashamed of having been duped by Robespierre."

His arrival at the Luxembourg made a great sensation among the prisoners.

"On this very day of the month," he said, "I proposed the establishment of the Revolutionary Tribunal; now for that act I ask pardon of God and of my fellow-men. I never meant that it should be the scourge of humanity; I intended that by legal process it should prevent such massacres as took place in September."

Then, turning to the prisoners, who all gazed at him with astonishment, amazed to find him one of themselves, he said, "Gentlemen, it was my hope that I might soon effect your deliverance; but, unfortunately, here I am a prisoner among you. I do not know what will be the end."

He was confined in a dungeon next to that of Lacroix, with whom he conversed in a loud voice, being glad to let the other prisoners hear his opinions and reflections, which through some of them might be transmitted to posterity.

Some of his remarks have been thus preserved: —

"I leave everything in France in deplorable confusion. There is not a man among her rulers who knows anything of statecraft."

"What proves the Sieur de Robespierre to be a Nero is, that he never spoke with more affection to Camille Desmoulins than just before his arrest." [1]

"In times of revolution, authority falls into the hands of rascals."

Once he said, "If I could give my manliness to Robespierre and my legs to Couthon, the Committee of Public Safety might yet last for a while."

Then, thinking of his little house at Arcis-sur-Aube, where his young wife was awaiting his return, he began to speak of its rural beauty, of its trees, of its repose. "Better," he cried, "to be a poor fisherman than a man who tries to govern men."

[1] Robespierre had been best man, not long before, at Camille Desmoulins's marriage.

That evening the prisoners, after examination, were sent to the Conciergerie. The next day, the 13th Germinal (April 2), came the trial.

At two in the morning the accused were brought before the Revolutionary Tribunal. The first place, that of the criminal of most importance, was not accorded to Danton, but to the ex-Capuchin and swindler Chabot; then came Bazire, and then Fabre d'Églantine.[1] The design was to dishonor Danton by trying him in the company of men accused of dishonorable ways of making money. But though he entered fifth among the prisoners, all eyes were fixed on him. There he stood, the man of the Tenth of August, of the massacres of September, the founder of the Revolutionary Tribunal before which he was now arraigned. Of Herculean strength and of colossal frame, "he sat on the *banc des accusés*," as an eye-witness expressed it, "as the gentleman of *sans-culotterie*." His face was deeply pitted by the small-pox, his nose was snub, his nostrils in the air, his lips prominent, and his small eyes darted around him keen glances of scrutiny and of disdain. He believed himself about to crush the accusation by his vehement oratory, as he had so often crushed his enemies in the Convention.

Two men, one of them the handsome Hérault de Séchelles, separated him from Camille Desmoulins. The jury were then sworn. Camille Desmoulins objected to one of them, with whom he had once had a personal quarrel; but this objection was set aside.

Danton was asked the usual questions. He answered, —

"My residence? I shall soon be nothing; afterwards I shall be in the Pantheon of history. Whichever it may be, I little care."

[1] Fabre d'Églantine, who is known to posterity by a name "which," says one of his admirers, "is a poem in itself," was really Philippe Fabre (*Anglice*, Philip Smith, or Philip a worker in metals). The d'Églantine was assumed because he had gained the Églantine prize in a literary competition in Provence, — one of those societies which Macaulay says "turned those who might have been thriving attorneys and useful apothecaries into small wits and bad poets."

The trial (not of Danton and his friends, but of the rest) proceeded. The next day Westermann was brought in and placed among the prisoners; he was the personal friend of Danton, and that outweighed all his services in the cause of the Revolution.

The report of Saint-Just to the Convention, accusing Danton, was then read; he was denounced as "a partisan of royalty." At length Danton was called upon for his defence.

"Danton," said the presiding officer of the Tribunal, "the Convention accuses you of having favored Dumouriez: of not having made known what manner of man he was; of having taken part in his projects of liberticide —"

Then Danton broke forth with indignation and vehemence. The judge interrupted him. "Danton," he said, "such audacity is the accompaniment of crime; the innocent are calm. No doubt you have the right to speak in your own defense, but you must restrict what you say within the bounds of moderation."

"No!" answered Danton, "audacity in self-defense may be wrong, but audacity on behalf of the nation, of which I have shown many proofs, is right and lawful." And in the same strain of indignant eloquence he continued his defense, protesting that all men knew that he had been the true friend of the people, the most ardent defender of liberty. "As I look over this list of lies," he cried, "this list of horrid accusations brought against me, I shudder through all my bodily frame!"

Here Herman again interrupted him, saying that he was wanting in proper respect to the Convention, the Tribunal, and the Sovereign People. "Marat," he added, "was accused like you, and was acquitted. He defended himself with respectful words. I cannot point out to you a better example."

At this Danton lost command over himself. He flamed with anger. "I! — Do you say that I sold myself to Mirabeau, to Orleans, to Dumouriez? That I was the partisan of royalists and royalty? Bring proofs. Bring hither those who accuse me, and I will trample them into dust. Vile impostors, stand forth; let me pluck away the mask which hides you from public vengeance!"

Again he was interrupted by the court, and went on more calmly, "I have things to reveal; I demand to be heard in silence. The safety of the country may depend on what I say."

This was too much. Herman had no intention of letting him proceed on this line of defense. He rang his bell violently. "A man speaking to defend his life cares nothing for your ringing," cried Danton, and continued.

The jury then proceeded to interrupt him by all kinds of questions. To speak with his accustomed eloquence was impossible. While Danton was thus being harassed by the jury, Herman and Fouquier were exchanging scraps of paper. These scraps were afterwards found among the documents of the trial.

"In half an hour I shall put a stop to Danton's speaking," wrote Herman to the prosecutor.

"I have some questions to ask the court concerning affairs in Belgium!" cried the accused.

"They are not now in order," was the reply. "We must get on faster."

And get on they did. Here is the newspaper report of the proceedings. "Danton spoke for some time with the energy and vehemence he has so often displayed in the Convention. . . . As he reviewed the accusations personal to himself, he had great difficulty in suppressing his passion. His voice grew hoarse. It was evident that he needed rest. Seeing this, his judges proposed to him to suspend his review of the accusations brought against him, that he might answer them with more calmness and effect. Danton accepted the suggestion."

Danton being thus silenced, the trial of his friends proceeded.

Hérault de Séchelles defended himself with energy, Camille Desmoulins with less spirit. Lacroix, when interrupted by Herman, cried, "Is this trial only a farce, that I am not allowed liberty of speech?"

Fouquier here interposed, "It is time to put an end to all this. I shall write to the Convention and ask for orders. They will be followed exactly."

Philippeaux, who was about to enter on his defense, here said, "You may condemn me to death, — I submit. But I forbid you to insult me."

The next day another prisoner, Lhuillier, ex-*procureur général*, was arrested and brought in.

Westermann, when his turn came, said, "I have received seven wounds, all of them in front. The only one I ever had in the back is this *acte d'accusation*."

The men tried for dishonorable money dealings were not interrupted in their defense, which could not injure men in power.

Danton and his friends eagerly demanded that the court should hear their witnesses. Herman, who had no intention that they should be heard, was anxiously expecting an order to that effect from the Convention. At last, at four o'clock, he was called out. He found two members of the Committee of General Safety awaiting him. "Here is what you asked for," said one of them, presenting a paper. "Now you can go on quite at your ease," said the other. "I can tell you we had need of this," answered Herman, with a laugh. He returned to the court, and with an air of great satisfaction read a decree, by which "any one accused of conspiracy who shall resist or insult judges appointed by the nation, shall be at once stopped and shall not be allowed to speak further."

On the reading of this document a great tumult ensued, and in the midst of the confusion the court was adjourned.

The next day, the 16th Germinal, Herman refused to allow Danton and his friends to bring forward their witnesses. Danton and Lacroix protested. The judge answered that it was useless, for he had more numerous witnesses at hand who could contradict their testimony; he had not summoned them, he said, because he wished strictly to obey the orders of the Convention; and when Danton and Lacroix insisted, he pointed out that a decree of the convention permitted a jury after three days to cut short a trial, if they declared themselves satisfied.

The trial being thus stopped, and the accused taken back to prison, Herman and Fouquier went into the jury-room and told the jury that they must now end the trial by declaring themselves satisfied. The jury obeyed.

They returned to the court-room. Each juror was asked the usual question, only on this occasion the question assumed the form of an announcement, as thus: —

"There has existed a conspiracy intended to restore monarchy in France, to destroy the national representation and the republican form of government. Citizen-juror, is Lacroix guilty of having taken part in this conspiracy?" And so on for Danton, Camille Desmoulins, Philippeaux, Hérault de Séchelles, and Westermann.

For the others the formula was different: "There has existed a conspiracy tending to defame and dishonor the national representation, and to destroy republican government by corruption."

All were pronounced guilty, except Lhuillier.

Public interest was now concentrated on Danton and his friends. Hérault de Séchelles, who had said, when their defense was stopped, "These proceedings do not surprise me. They are worthy of those who are thirsting for our blood," received his sentence with the words, "What I expected!"

Poor Camille Desmoulins, who had been employing his solitary hours in prison by writing a long and piteous letter to his wife, could not receive sentence of death with equal calmness. "Oh, the monsters! the villains!" he cried, "and to think that I should have been the dupe of Robespierre!"

"My friend," said Hérault, "let us show them how to die."

Philippeaux had one moment of weakness, but he soon recovered himself. Lacroix and Westermann were calm and said nothing. As to Danton, he did not bemoan himself like Camille Desmoulins, but he could not restrain his feelings. He foamed with rage. He uttered the most dreadful curses against his murderers. His words came so fast that they were hardly intelligible. A few were afterwards remembered by those who heard them: —

"I have at least the consolation of believing that the man who dies as chief of the *faction des indulgents* will be pardoned by posterity."

"What matters my death? I have gloried in the Revolution; I have spent much; I have had many a revel in my day. Now we 'll go to sleep."

The carts were waiting in the courtyard of the Conciergerie. The condemned were at once placed in them. Danton had recovered his self-possession, and even his gayety. He tried to console Philippeaux, who was utterly cast down at the thought of his poor wife and child. He joked Fabre d'Églantine, who seemed wrapped in sadness, and he expressed great pity for poor Camille, who tried to cry out to the crowd as the cart passed them: "People! oh, people! you are deceived by those who govern you!"

Danton endeavored to silence him, saying, "Be quiet! Have nothing to say to that vile *canaille!*"

Then he asked the executioner if he might be allowed to sing. Sanson replied that singing was not forbidden.

"Then try to remember some lines I have just been making," Danton said, and he sang, —

"Nous sommes menés au trépas
Par quantité de scélérats;
C'est ce qui nous désole.
Mais bientôt le moment viendra
Où chacun d'eux y passera;
C'est ce qui nous console."

When they reached the Place de la Révolution the carts stopped. Hérault de Séchelles got down first; before mounting the steps of the scaffold he wanted to embrace Danton, but the executioner's men prevented this and dragged him away.

"Wretches!" cried Danton, "would you like to prevent our lips from meeting in the *panier?*"

Camille Desmoulins continued his laments till death had silenced them.

Danton, too, though he showed no lack of courage, had a moment of tender recollection. "Oh, my poor wife," he cried, "my beloved wife! shall I never see you again?"

Then recovering himself, he murmured quickly, "Come, Danton, no weakness!"

He mounted the steps of the scaffold, and turning to the executioner said: "Thou must show my head to the people. It is a sight worth seeing."

The execution was soon over, and various were the impressions it made on the spectators. Amidst a confusion of shouts and cries, many asked each other and themselves if this execution of men who had been republican leaders from the beginning was just — or even necessary. Already might be seen the first germs of the tendency to that reaction which in less than four months was to sweep Robespierre and his accomplices to the same scaffold. As Danton had said, he dragged them all down with him in his fall.

Certain lines which were secretly circulated in Paris reflected this opinion.

> "Camille Desmoulins, D'Églantine, and Danton
> Together reached the stream of Phlegethon.
> They paid their passage to the other side
> To Charon, honest ferryman, who cried,
> 'You 've given me too much; 't is double pay.
> Here, take your change!' — 'Nay,' answered Danton, 'nay;
> We 've paid for six; three more will soon appear:
> Couthon, Saint-Just, and — hark ye! — Robespierre.'"

It had been the fashion to speak of Danton as a man steeped in debauchery, and in truth some of his last words, spoken under the excitement of his sentence, tend to support that conclusion. The truth seems to be that there were two men in Danton. In that age, when all was contradiction, this was not uncommon. One Danton was the man who loved his wife with passion; the other the Danton, who breaking away from his home could throw off all restraints in the Palais Royal, and "*se faire bien caresser des filles.*"

When Danton first came to Paris in the early days of the Revolution, he met his first wife, the daughter of a lemonade-seller on the Pont Neuf. She was very beautiful, a tender, loving woman of the domestic type, and an earnest Christian. She it was who in the early days of their marriage worked to support the household. She was the mother of two children. Danton had no success in Paris as a lawyer; he pleaded but one cause, that of the nation. But those were happy days. Husband and wife were all in all to each other. Madame Danton was grave and gentle, Danton as vehement in his gayety as he was in his passions. She was so full of piety and grace that it seemed as if some rays from her heart lit up the atheism professed by her husband.

When Danton left the tribune he came back to love and piety at home; Marat and Robespierre found nothing in that asylum to call off their thoughts from their enemies. They carried their work of politics to their hearths, to their beds, nay, even, into their very bath-tubs. But the loving, pious nature of Madame Danton could not long stand the terrible strain of the Revolution. She sickened and died of fear and horror. After the days of September she felt that the ship was running on a reef and must soon go to pieces. Her own hopes were anchored in heaven. Perhaps she thought that when she reached it she might plead for Danton.

As she grew ill her husband was in despair. He quitted her bedside only to do his duty in the Convention. It was the year '93. His impatience under sorrow added to his vehemence in the tribune, and perhaps to his pitilessness against those he held to be his country's enemies.

Ere she died, the wise and loving woman, knowing the nature of her husband, spoke to him of the necessity of a second marriage. She even pointed out to him the young girl who she desired might be a mother to her children. But Danton vehemently rejected the idea. "Must my children be motherless, then?" said the dying woman. Danton watched beside her corpse till she was buried.

"We shall meet — shall we not — in heaven?" were almost her last words. "Oh, yes, we shall meet," replied Danton, with a smile, but he had no belief in any hereafter.

A week after his wife was buried he, in a savage burst of grief, went to her grave, and endeavored to dig her up, that he might once more embrace her. He fulfilled her wish about a second marriage. But this wife also died within the year, heart-stricken by so many horrors.

Then he married a third time, though his heart was in the grave with his first wife, — his first love. It was with this newly married wife that he retired to Arcis-sur-Aube, whence he was summoned to Paris to meet his doom. It was of this poor woman he was thinking in his last moments, when he "strengthened up his courage to his fate" with the words, "Danton! no weakness," and mounted the steps of the scaffold.

CHAPTER III.

THE FEAST OF THE SUPREME BEING.

THIS account of the *Fête de l'Être Suprême* is by Adolphe Adam, the well-known French musician and composer.[1] He tells the tale as it was told to him by Sarrette, the musical director of the period, the founder of the Paris Conservatoire.

The various misfortunes endured by France in 1793 were surpassed by her experiences in the early months of 1794. The massacres of Lyons and of Nantes were not more horrible than those of Toulon, Orange, and Marseilles. At Orange (a place of small importance) and its neighborhood no less than fifteen thousand persons were put to death in two months. Cries of horror and remonstrance rose on all sides, and reached the ears of the Committee of Public Safety, which answered them by declaring itself satisfied with the conduct of Maignet, the commissioner who had ordered these horrible butcheries; and the Convention indorsed the approval of the Committee.

The name of Lyons was suppressed by a decree; thenceforward it was to be called *La Commune Affranchie*. But Marseilles fared worse: a decree of the Convention declared her to be a rebellious city, which should bear *no name;* a month later, however, another decree permitted her to give up the anonymous and be Marseilles once more. The atrocious folly of such decrees was only equalled by their multiplicity. One day the Convention recorded its approval of an order of a commissioner in the Department of Var, commanding all the masons in his district to form a corps for

[1] Translated by me, and published in "Littell's Living Age," Aug. 23, 1879.—E. W. L.

the total demolition of Toulon; the next day it approved another instance of the energetic government of Maignet, who had burned a village a few leagues from Carpentras because a tree of liberty had been cut down during the night. The villagers all perished in the conflagration, except a few who were shot down by a volunteer company stationed to see that none escaped. Another decree forbade French soldiers to give quarter to any Englishman or Hanoverian. It is needless to add that the various French armies gave no heed to this order.

Those who read of such atrocities very probably imagine that Paris was a sad and silent city in those days. On the contrary, if despair and consternation were in every heart, men took great pains to conceal their feelings. Never had the theatres, the gambling-houses, the drinking-shops, etc., been better patronized. Sometimes all Paris looked like an enormous *guinguette*. From three to five o'clock, on *fête* days, tables stood spread before the houses, to which each family or lodger brought his contribution. A coarse, fierce, dirty patriot was the guest most welcomed at these tables; for every citizen who had any property left was anxious to give no offense to any man who might denounce him in his district, since a reward was paid to all informers at that period, and an especial decree declared the property of any man *detained in prison* to belong of right to the indigent patriots of his own Section.

There were plenty of Revolutionary *fêtes* to take the place of the old Catholic Church holidays, which had been solemnly abolished by a decree of the Convention, Nov. 10, 1793. The goddess of Reason had been enthroned, and the Cathedral of Notre Dame had been assigned to her; whilst the other churches in Paris were devoted to various allegorical and metaphorical divinities, — as Liberty, Conjugal Affection, etc. On the day of the installation of the goddess at Notre Dame, a dancing-girl from the Opéra was elevated on the high altar as her representative. Beside her stood Laharpe, the ex-Academician, the well-known author of the "Cours de Littérature." Holding his cap of liberty, he opened his address by denying the existence of a God; and then, blaspheming our divine Saviour, he dared Him to avenge the insult offered to Him in His temple. As no miracle took place in answer to this impious challenge, the crowd burst into loud laughter and shouts of joy. The nave of the church was then turned into a ball-room. The celebrated organist Séjan was forced to play on the great organ base dance-music of the period, while whirling wretches danced the *carmagnole*, and howled the air of "Ça ira;" after which they broke the statues, tore the eyes out of the pictures of the saints, and burned everything that had ever borne a part in the worship of the Almighty.

On the 21st of January, 1794, there was a splendid *fête* in the Place de la Révolution. It was the anniversary of the day on which fell the last of the kings. Singing and dancing round the guillotine celebrated the occasion, until at last, during a pause in the general mirth, four victims, who stood waiting for the signal, mounted the scaffold, and four heads fell under the fatal axe amidst the shouts of a populace which has always put forth a claim to be called "the people." The guillotine in those days was the favorite symbol. The costume in vogue was a jacket called a *carmagnole*, trousers of coarse cloth, the neck bare or tied with a red handkerchief, and a felt cap, with a long queue. Dandies wore little liberty-caps in their button-holes, little gold guillotines for earrings or for breastpins (if they had any shirts to put them in), and carried stout cudgels in their hands. At dinner-parties little mahogany guillotines were used as table ornaments, mahogany being at that time fashionable and rare. Women wore little gold guillotines in their ears, or as finger-rings, or as clasps to their girdles; whilst all the time the great real red guillotine continued its daily labors, no longer picking out its victims, but sweeping them in almost without inquiry. At first wealth and high birth had been men's title to proscription; but after a while all kinds of offenses against civism had to be invented, to make the number of the executed greater day by day. Those guilty of Girondism and conservatism were not enough. Success in business soon became a crime, devotion to science was a ground for condemnation. Malesherbes perished for pleading the cause of his late master; and when Lavoisier requested two weeks' reprieve, that he might finish the solution of certain problems that would be of use to science and humanity, Coffinhal, the President of the Revolutionary Tribunal, answered, "The Republic has no need of science or of chemistry."

Still the guillotine was not satisfied; all the blood it had shed was, so to speak, of the same color. Robespierre found means to satisfy its new caprice; those who had fed it hitherto became its victims. Rousin, Hébert, the originator of the *Père Duchêne*, Anacharsis Clootz, Chaumette, Vincent, Danton, Chabot, Bazire, Lacroix, Camille Desmoulins, and others soon followed in the steps of Malesherbes; Louis XVI.'s advocate preceded only by a few days his client's judges.

Terror was at its height. Those who still managed to escape the Revolutionary Tribunal, each of whose arrests was but a prelude to the scaffold, had hard work to keep themselves from want, owing to the vexatious police arrangements of this "age of liberty." No man could buy bread, meat, wood, candles, or soap without a permit from the authorities of his Section; and then the articles could not be delivered to him for twenty-four hours, during which time the authorities were verifying his reputation for good citizenship and ascertaining that no denunciations had been lodged against him. Such universal wretchedness may in part account for the mad way in which men gave themselves up to pleasure in days when no one knew whether he should be alive upon the morrow.

Nor was luxury nor a taste for speculation arrested by a sense of danger. New buildings went up in all quarters of the city, and were pushed on with an energy that showed how little time their owners felt that they might have to live in them. Costly furniture was purchased for these new abodes; for the danger of being rich did not seem to affect the desire for riches.

At last, indeed, Paris seemed to grow weary of blood-shedding, and Robespierre began to perceive that he had better apply himself to calm the passions of the populace, and to organize some reaction to the agitations and emotions in which Paris had lived for upwards of a year. By degrees he had got rid of the extremists of his own party, endeavoring to throw on them the odium of acts which they had only helped him to accomplish; and in order to inaugurate a new era of moderation and of brotherhood, which might do him honor, he began by proposing to the Convention a sort of return to a system of worship; but the religion which he favored was of a new kind.

On his motion the Assembly decreed "that the French people recognizes the existence of a Supreme Being and the immortality of the soul." The inscription of this recognition on the dead walls of Paris did not seem an act of solemnity proportioned to its importance. It was resolved that a great festival should be held in honor of the Supreme Being. The Committee of Public Safety was thereupon ordered to organize the festival. History must not forget that upon that committee there were men who occupied themselves solely with their own especial duties; Carnot, for example, who superintended the wars of the Republic, directing fourteen armies from his cabinet, sending plans to his various generals, and planning the combination of their forces; while Lindet only concerned himself with the quartermaster's department, Prieur with the ordnance, and Barrère undertook matters relating to the fine arts.

Barrère sent at once for those who generally undertook the arrangement of the *fêtes* of the Republic. The leader of them all was David the painter, the friend and the creature of Robespierre, — he who the night before his patron's fall exclaimed, "If you drink poison I shall drink it too, and die another Socrates." Happily only one Socrates perished on this occasion, and David survived his first patron, as he was to survive his next, — Napoleon, whose coronation and second marriage live for us in his work as vividly as if we had seen them.

Barrère had a personal fancy for the poet Joseph Chénier, whose moderate opinions seemed to point him out as the proper poet to be intrusted with the composition of a semi-religious hymn, which was to be a feature in the solemnity. Gossec, who was of advanced Revolutionary opinions, was chosen to compose the music. Gossec was then sixty-one years old, and was less celebrated for his operas than for his symphonies, which had paved the way for those of Haydn. Among his religious works was the celebrated Mass for the Dead, which was considered his finest composition.

The *fête* was fixed for the 20th Prairial (June 8), and all the preparations were accomplished. The costumes had been designed and finished, the hymn was written, the music for it composed; everything was ready. The only difficulty was that Sarrette, who always had had the direction of the music in the festivals of the Republic, was in prison. He had been there for two months, and nothing could be done without him. Before telling the reader how this misfortune befell Sarrette, — though, indeed, such misfortunes happened for no reason at all in those days, — we may as well explain by what concatenation of circumstances he had been brought to take so active a part in the Republic's festive celebrations. To do so we must go back a few years.

Before the Revolution the musical organization of France was entirely religious. There were no singing-schools but those attached to the chapter in every cathedral. There young boys were brought up for the Church, but generally, if they proved to have good voices, they deserted to the theatre. There was no musical instruction open to female pupils, except that of the opera-house, where a very few were received. Singing had not yet become an art to be cultivated. All that was necessary to please the public was a loud voice with considerable compass. A full-voiced singer was sure to succeed.

At the small school attached to the Italian opera-house in those days there was some good instruction, but the masters were all Italians, and the school was not open to the public. Orchestras picked up recruits wherever they could find them.

There was tolerable violin instruction to be had in France, but the wind instruments were all played by Germans. The Maréchal de Biron, however, had established in Paris what was called the Dépôt of the Gardes Françaises, to train musicians for the various military bands in the country; so that thenceforward the theatres drew their performers from two sources, their singers from the church, and their orchestras from the army.

When the Gardes Françaises were suppressed in 1789, M. Sarrette, then captain on the staff of the National Guard of his Section, obtained an order to continue the musical school for the benefit of the National Guard. After a while the National Guard was suppressed, and then Sarrette, fearing lest all the musical ability of France would be forced to abandon the country, persuaded the Commune to open a free school for music, the members of which, whether pupils or instructors, were obliged to lend their services at all national festivals.

This school was placed under the charge of Gossec and Sarrette, and started in the Rue St. Joseph. It took the title of Musical Corps of the National Guard, — though that guard had been abolished. It was the source from which all the fourteen armies of the Republic drew their bands.

This school was the germ of the present Paris Conservatory. Its musicians formed the orchestra of the Republic. They took part in all national festivities, and some of them played daily before the legislature. Indeed, music was frequently called upon to make a sort of interlude in the sittings of the Convention. Sarrette, by his co-operation in all the national *fêtes* of the Republic, flattered himself that his civism would be above suspicion, and lived in happy security till he was one day suddenly arrested on the denunciation of a humble inhabitant of the Quartier Montmartre.

This good man, wishing to get rid of the inconvenient practicing of a band of wind instruments in his neighborhood, bethought him of declaring to the authorities that he had heard the proscribed air "Vive Henri IV." played by one of the clarionets. By the ingenious device of denouncing the director he hoped to break up the school. Really and truly his shaft ought to have struck Gossec, but its victim was his co-director.

For nearly three months poor Sarrette remained an inmate of the prison of Ste. Pélagie, expecting every day to be called before the Revolutionary Tribunal, which of course meant sentence and execution. At last the governor of the prison sent for him. "Citizen Sarrette," he said, "the Republic needs thee. Thou art to leave this place, but a soldier will not lose sight of thee till thou hast fulfilled the duty that the country has assigned thee. I do not say farewell, therefore, but *au revoir*."

Sarrette would have preferred a more definite dismissal; but he had to accept things as he found them, and in company with his guard, who stuck to him like his shadow, he went back to his old school-room.

It was with considerable emotion that he saw the place once more, — the school he had created, — for whose future he had dreamed what seemed now impossible things. The cry of joy with which his *concierge* greeted him hardly raised his spirits. The *concierge* had been an old sergeant in the Swiss guard; he had escaped the massacre, and Sarrette had protected him and provided for him. Fortunately this old soldier found an acquaintance in the sentry who accompanied his benefactor. He easily persuaded him that he would pass his time more pleasantly drinking a few glasses in his *loge* than going upstairs with his prisoner to his chamber, especially as he could assure him that the only possible way that any one could get out of the house was to pass by the place where they would be both sitting.

Sarrette, on entering his own rooms, found Gossec and Chénier already in possession. They told him they had got him out of prison in order that he should superintend the production of a hymn they had composed together; that this would bring him into communication with the authorities, and, that being the case, they thought it might lead to his complete liberation.

A little hope was beginning to dawn on the unfortunate

prisoner when his sentry came up to say that he was wanted by the Committee of Public Safety. No one could think without fear of that terrible tribunal, and Sarrette's reception, when he appeared before it, was by no means reassuring.

"Citizen," said Robespierre, who was in the chair, "in three days there will be a *fête* in the garden of the Tuileries and in the Champ de Mars, at which will be produced a hymn in honor of the Supreme Being, now solemnly recognized by the French Republic. Have you prepared anything suitable for such a *fête?*"

"Citizen," replied Sarrette, "here is a hymn, both words and music composed expressly for this occasion." So saying, he handed the chairman a manuscript that he held in his hand.

Robespierre cast a careless glance upon the poetry, but when he got to the last verse and saw the name of its author, his sinister eyes gave a sudden glare.

"What do you mean by this?" he cried, striking his fist on the table before him. "This man is a Girondin — a Bressotin — a friend of Condorcet, — Chénier himself! Has *he* been chosen to celebrate one of the great acts of the Republic? What aristocrat has dared to intrust this work to him?"

And with these words he glanced round the group before him. Carnot was writing. Lindet and Prieur were looking over some marginal notes upon their papers. Couthon, Saint-Just, Billaud-Varennes, and Collot d'Herbois looked as angry as their leader. Barrère, having anticipated a storm, had slipped out of a side door as soon as he saw Sarrette put the paper into the hand of Robespierre.

"Citizen," said Sarrette, quietly, pointing to the soldier at his side, "you may see by the company I am forced to keep that I have not been my own master for some time. I have had no chance to choose or to employ anybody. When I reached my own rooms this morning I found this poetry and this music waiting for me. All I have done is to bring them here for your approval."

"Where do you come from?" asked Robespierre.

"From Ste. Pélagie. I have been there three months."

"What are you accused of?"

"I am not accused of anything. The accusation is against the air 'Vive Henri IV.' It had the bad taste to let itself be played by somebody, I never knew by whom, in the municipal musical school-room. That is the reason I have been in prison three months."

Robespierre shrugged his shoulders and thought a moment, then he said, —

"See here, you say you did not choose the author of these verses. I am willing to believe you, but you have got to choose me another author. You must bring me a new hymn for my approval, and the third day from now it must be publicly performed."

"But, citizen, how can I in two days get the words written and the music composed, and the whole copied? I shall hardly have time to get my choirs together."

"Your choirs? What do I want with a choir? I don't want a lot of you paid bawlers at twelve francs a head, which is what you have been hitherto charging the Republic at all her ceremonies. I don't want any choir, — understand? Singers, indeed! Aristocrats, artists, appendages to ancient royalty, fellows who sing for money, and for whoever will give it to them! It's the people — the whole people — who shall sing this hymn, and sing it for nothing. There shall be sixty thousand voices — a hundred thousand voices — two hundred thousand in the choir this time. That's my notion of music. And that's what I expect of you, citizen!"

Sarrette looked utterly confounded.

"Well!" said Robespierre, "what are you standing here for? Make haste, and get everything ready; and remember one thing: you are let out of prison that a hymn to the Supreme Being may be sung; and you will go back to where you came from, if the hymn is not sung according to my idea of it. Now go."

There was no option. Sarrette now perceived that he

would be pardoned if the piece could be written, learned, and executed in rather more than forty-eight hours. But the thing was impossible. Another thing too troubled him; he had been hourly expecting his own death for three months, but he now saw that there was no escape for Chénier. In vain he turned over in his own mind how he could save him.

As he entered his own house his good *concierge* stopped him on the stairs.

"Monsieur," he said (he dared whisper "Monsieur" when nobody was by), "here is a paper some one has left for you; he said it was something very important."

"Who brought it?"

"A little humpbacked man, who would not tell me his name. He said he would call to-morrow for an answer."

Sarrette took the paper, but felt no interest in it, and did not open it. Sadly and slowly he mounted to his chamber.

"Chénier," he said on entering, "you are done for, my poor friend. Robespierre will have nothing to do with your hymn, for no other reason than because you wrote it and because he hates your principles. You must try to make your escape; your death is certainly resolved on."

"Escape! escape?" cried Chénier. "How can I?"

"There is one chance for you," said Sarrette, eagerly; "hide yourself here. No one saw you come in but the *concierge*, and, as you well know, he may be trusted. Our pupils never come into this part of the building. No one will suspect you of seeking refuge in a place belonging to the government. So I must trust, my good fellow, you may be luckier than I, and avoid making acquaintance with Ste. Pélagie. I am going back there."

"Going back!" cried Gossec and Chénier together.

"Yes, indeed," replied Sarrette, sadly. "I was only to be set free if the Hymn to the Supreme Being was duly sung; and you know as well as I do that to get it rewritten, recomposed, and rehearsed in two days is simply impossible."

So saying, Sarrette flung himself into a chair, and the paper he was holding dropped from his fingers. Gossec picked it up.

"What 's this?" he said to Sarrette.

"I don't know. Open it; it is probably something about the school."

All of a sudden Gossec's face became radiant. He sprang from his seat with a cry of joy. "Oh, friends!" he shouted eagerly, "we are saved! we are saved!"

"How saved?"

"My music! you, Sarrette! you, Chénier! The *Être Suprême!* the Republic! everybody! See here!" He waved the paper in the air and read the following letter:

"CITIZEN, — I hear there is to be a great *fête* given in recognition of the Supreme Being, and I send you some verses I have made for the occasion. I should be delighted to think that they were thought worthy of adoption. I will call to-morrow to learn their fate.

"And by an especial providence, by the favor of the Supreme Being himself, the poem is in the same metre as Chénier's, and the stanzas are the same length; he has used some of the very same words. It can be set to the same music without an alteration. Come, my good fellows! Cheer up, Sarrette!" went on Gossec. "Get your choirs together, give out the parts, begin to make the arrangements; we 'll get it sung."

"Choirs!" cried Sarrette. "There are not to be any choirs. The whole population of Paris is to sing."

"The people?" cried Gossec, in despair. "Why, the people can't learn parts."

"There are not to be any parts."

"What? Are they all to sing together?"

"That 's the idea."

"It is not my idea. I won't have my music sung in that way; I 'd rather tear it up than hear it murdered."

"All right, then," said Sarrette, "if you 'd rather see me guillotined. I thought you might be willing to sacrifice your music to save the life of an old friend."

Though Gossec was sixty-one, he was as impetuous as a lad of eighteen. He saw at once the absurdity of his enthusiasm for his own composition. He flung his arms round Sarrette.

"Ah, my good friend!" he cried, "I 'll let them sing it all together; they may sing it in every key at once, and as out of tune as they will. I forgot your life hung on the performance of my music. Let us see; what must be first done?"

"We must get together every musician we know," said Sarrette, "and set them to work. I 'll explain what they have to do when you get them here."

Gossec set out at all speed. An hour after he came back, and with him Méhul, Grétry, Cherubini, and a dozen others, the musicians and composers of the period. All welcomed Sarrette and fell into his views with enthusiasm. He explained in a few words what must be done immediately. All the Sections were to be convoked, and before each was to appear a musician, either playing on some instrument himself or with a pupil to play for him, to teach the people the hymn to be sung by the united voices of all Paris on the day after the morrow. Each promised to do his best for the Hymn to the Supreme Being. Sarrette himself set off for the committee, which was still in session. The words were approved with enthusiasm, and the Sections brought together by sound of drum. That evening and all the next day Paris became a singing-school. Cherubini stood on a balcony overlooking an open square, the Carréfour Gaillon: a pupil, armed with a clarionet, played Gossec's melody. Cherubini sang the words in his vile Italian accent, and then, gesticulating and grimacing like a man possessed, shaking his fists and menacing his pupils when they sang false notes, he proceeded to instruct the crowd before him. Méhul took another quarter, and accompanied himself on a violin. Four other composers of the same stamp conducted similar classes. Plantade and Richer, being singers by profession, gave their instruction with less trouble to themselves, and theirs were the most popular classes. By the next evening the "Father of Nature" might be heard sung, growled, howled, or hummed all over Paris, in every quarter, every street, and every dwelling.

In the course of the same day Sarrette was informed that the citizen Desorgues wished to speak to him. He was so overwhelmed with public business that he was on the point of declining to receive any visitor; but this one entreated so earnestly for admission that he was let in. He was a small, shabby, deformed man, timid and insinuating in manner.

"Citizen," he said, "you cannot guess the reason of my coming."

"Pardon me," said Sarrette, "I think I can. You left a manuscript for me last evening. You have come to ask what decision I have arrived at respecting your poem."

"No," replied the little man, "quite the contrary."

"I don't understand you."

"I have come to ask you to give me back my manuscript and to forget it was ever sent you."

"But why?" asked Sarrette, completely puzzled.

Timidly the old man proceeded to explain.

"I am," he said, "or rather I was once, the Chevalier Desorgues. Notwithstanding some former successes in society," here a grin of self-complacency accompanied his words, "notwithstanding my illustrious name and noble family, I have, for the last four years, been only too happy to live forgotten and unknown. All my friends and associates who did not emigrate in the beginning have, one by one, been suspected, arrested, and guillotined. I am the last remnant of the little colony we formed before the year '92, in the Rue St. Florentin. I am the only one who remains to be summoned before that monster of bloodthirstiness, that terrible tiger — Ah! pardon me; perhaps you are a friend of M. Robespierre? — "

"Not in the least," said Sarrette, with a smile.

"Well, then," continued his visitor, "I live in fear of drawing his notice on myself. I dare not even change my lodgings. Being the last noble, the last aristocrat living in our street, all eyes would be upon me. It occurred to me, however, that some brilliant act of civism might place me above suspicion. But the only acceptable acts of civism nowadays appear to be the denunciation of other people.

Yesterday it struck me that if I could write the Hymn to the Supreme Being, which I could do without violating the principles I have always professed, I might acquire such a reputation as a good republican that I might move in safety from the Rue St. Florentin. But last night I remembered that, on the contrary, I might only draw suspicion on myself, inquiries might be made into my past history; and I have come to you to ask you to give me back my hymn and the letter I wrote you yesterday."

"I am sorry, my dear chevalier, but I carried your hymn yesterday to the Committee of Public Safety, and M. Robespierre, as you call him, was delighted with it."

"What! did the monster think my verses good?"

"Excellent, sublime; and he intends they shall be sung to-morrow — the 20th Prairial — by the whole population of Paris. Why, how happens it that you have not heard your own words sung everywhere since last evening?"

"Monsieur, for months past I have scarcely ever been out of my own doors —"

"Let me advise you to change your mind. Go to the *fête*. Let Robespierre see you and know you. His countenance may be your protection, should you incur any danger."

"Then you do not think he aims at my destruction?"

"On the contrary, I do not believe that he has ever given you a thought, and he will be quite disposed to patronize the bard of the Supreme Being, whose high pontiff he has constituted himself."

By six in the morning an immense crowd took possession of the garden of the Tuileries, which had been closed for some days in order that David might complete his preparations. An immense scaffolding, with ascending rows of seats, was set up against the principal pavilion of the palace, where the Convention then held its sittings. All the deputies were seated on these benches. Before them was an altar or antique tripod, like those used in incantation scenes at the Opera. Two stuffed figures, draped after the Greek fashion, one called Atheism, the other Fanaticism, lay at its foot. Behind the altar was an immense chair, very much after the pattern of a throne, intended for the high priest on the occasion. That high priest was none other than Robespierre; but his friend David could not succeed in persuading him to adopt a costume in harmony with the ancient Greek character which he gave to the rest of his preparations.

Robespierre wore his hair powdered. His white muslin cravat was very carefully adjusted; his shirt and his marseilles waistcoat were of irreproachable whiteness; a bright blue coat, knee breeches, white silk stockings, and shoes with large gold buckles completed his costume, which had no connection with mythology. He stepped to the front of the platform, and, after a few airs, played by the Orchestra of the Republic, to which was assigned a place behind the members of the Convention, he delivered a long metaphysical discourse, which nobody understood, but every one applauded.[1] Then, whilst a hundred thousand voices sang the Hymn to the Supreme Being, he gave a signal with a large bouquet he held in his hand. The two stuffed figures were set on fire. When they were consumed, their ashes were scattered to the winds, after which an immense antique chariot, laden with allegorical personages, clad in Greek costumes, headed a procession which directed its course toward the Champ de Mars, where the same ceremonies were to be repeated. The altar was carried in the procession by ballet girls from the opera, dressed in white tunics like those of the priests of Jupiter. Bundles of rods and ensigns were borne before the altar which needed only the letters S. P. Q. R. to be complete imitations of Roman standards. The grand pontiff and the members of the Convention joined in the march, followed by the orchestra

[1] Carlyle says of Robespierre's orations at the Jacobins: "What spirit of Patriotism dwelt in men in those times, this one fact it seems to us will evince: that fifteen hundred human creatures, not bound to it, sat quietly under the oratory of Robespierre; nay, listened to it nightly hour after hour applausive; and gaped as for the word of life."

20

and the populace. The same proceedings were gone through with on the Champ de Mars, and Sarrette, at the head of his musicians, was just making ready to go home after all was over, when an uproar in the crowd attracted his attention.

He saw Gossec, who had just been recognized by the mob, borne in triumph on men's shoulders. Gossec, not liking the absurdity of being alone in his glory in so elevated a position, had pointed out to his admirers his fellow-laborer, the humpbacked chevalier, whom he perceived in the throng. Instantly a thousand stout, rough men pressed forward and raised the poet to the side of the composer. Their absurd appearance in this triumphal procession, their anxious faces, as they looked at each other with disquiet and astonishment, were beyond description.

They were set at liberty at last, after having been borne round the Champ de Mars, and the *fête* terminated by the mob's singing and dancing the *carmagnole* round the Altar of Reason.

Robespierre was enchanted. Everything had gone off to his entire satisfaction. Sarrette obtained full pardon, and was delivered from the company of his sentry, who, but for his fraternization with an old comrade in the porter's lodge, would have been intolerable. But though delivered from personal anxiety he continued to be very apprehensive as to the fate of Chénier.

A poet is a poet wherever fate may place him. In the tedium of his captivity in the rooms of Sarrette, Chénier wrote the "Chant du Départ," one of the noblest odes in the French language. Méhul, who knew his friend's hiding-place, came often to visit him, full of enthusiasm for those noble lines which Chénier read to him. He completed the work by setting them to music worthy of the words.

Charmed with this noble work conceived and executed almost under his own eyes, Sarrette resolved on the first suitable occasion to bring it before the public. That opportunity soon arrived; the double victory won by the French at Fleurus was to be made the occasion of a national festivity.

Sarrette ventured to present Chénier's military poem to the Committee of Public Safety as the work of a poet who desired to remain unknown. "Ah!" exclaimed Robespierre, "this poem is worthy of the Republic. It is worth all the verses ever written by that vile Girondin Chénier!"

He ordered that the piece should be sent at once to the fourteen armies of the Republic, and that it should be called "Le Chant du Départ." He did better still: this time he let Sarrette engage a choir, which cost more than a population which sang for nothing; however, the choir sang the best, and gave the song in parts, which was much more satisfactory to the composer than the popular method.

The anonymous words and Méhul's music had immense success. But the dangerous mystification of which the Committee of Public Safety had been the victim might any day be brought to light, and this possibility gave Sarrette many anxieties. Happily, not long after, his fears were put an end to by the Ninth Thermidor; and Chénier, after the death of Robespierre, put his name to the poem.

The Feast of the Supreme Being was never again celebrated. A year later, on the recommendation of Lajuinais, public worship was again permitted. The "Chant du Départ" long continued to share with the "Marseillaise" the privilege of exciting the ardor of the French armies; and if it never attained the popularity of the hymn of Rouget de Lisle, it has at least the advantage of never having served as a rallying cry for hordes of ferocious insurrectionists.

Chénier not long after had the pleasure of gratifying Sarrette by getting the legislature of the period, of which he had become a member, to vote for the organization of the Conservatory of Paris, on the basis of a report which his friend had furnished him.

Sarrette survived all other actors in these scenes. He witnessed the prosperity of the Conservatory which he had established, and he beheld the restoration of a French republic in 1848. It may be that he found music less encouraged under the republic of Lamartine than under the republic of Robespierre.

CHAPTER IV.

THE FALL OF ROBESPIERRE.

ROBESPIERRE, when his two chief competitors for popularity and power, Jean Paul Marat and Jacques Danton, had been removed out of his way (Marat on July 13, 1793, Danton on April 5, 1794), began to feel the necessity for applying the brakes to the on-rushing course of the Revolution. We have seen how he planned to make peace with Austria, and to enlarge the borders of French territory by the acquisition of the Low Countries and the frontier of the Rhine. He also firmly rebuked the insolent attitude taken by Citizen Genêt, the Girondist ambassador, toward the Government of the United States; and we have witnessed his semi-comic appearance before all Paris as high pontiff of a revived worship of the Supreme Being.

He was a man of theories, and when he held a theory he was ready at all sacrifices and at all risks to carry it out to the bitter end. His theory of government was that France under a republic must be great, happy, and glorious, and that *he* was the only man who had the will, if he could only obtain the power, to make her so; granted that France would be the better if all her inhabitants were good patriots, — then, exterminate all who were not good patriots and good republicans!

Such had been his view of affairs. But the responsibilities of power had inspired him with disgust and aversion for the most part of his colleagues. A man of pure morals himself, he grew shocked at the wickedness, the greed, and the frenzied folly of his coadjutors. One by one he was bent on their destruction; France should be great and happy when, by and by, he should rule alone.

ROBESPIERRE.

During the year 1793 the mania for change extended to everything, — to times and seasons, weights and measures, and geographical divisions. The four weeks from July 19 to August 17, inclusive, became Thermidor, and 1794 the year II. of the Republic. We have seen how Mr. Gouverneur Morris, the American ambassador, and Mr. Thomas W. Griffith dated their letters according to the Revolutionary calendar. It might have cost any man his head to write July or January.

In Thermidor, therefore, of the year II. of the Republic, the destinies of France seemed all in the hands of Maximilien Robespierre. He had been a man of mark only two or three years; before that time no one would have dreamed of predicting for him an important place in history.

In Thermidor of the year II.[1] Robespierre was thirty-five years of age. He was rather short; his face was sallow and bilious; the English Carlyle calls him, in allusion to his complexion and his honesty, "the Sea-green Incorruptible." His eyes were without sparkle, almost without expression. His voice was sharp and thin. But though he was certainly not handsome, he took pains to be well dressed, and was the only one of the Revolutionary leaders who could have been called neat, or even clean.

He was proud and ambitious. Believing in the subtle power of oratory, he was determined to become a great speaker. But with all his indefatigable perseverance, he never became an eloquent man. Nor was he a man of action; personal bravery was not in his line.

He lived very modestly. In July, 1791, he left the lodgings in the Rue de Saintonge in the Marais, where he had lived with his sister, and accepted the hospitality of Duplay, an upholsterer, in the Rue St. Honoré.

Duplay was not a journeyman, but a master-workman, who owned about fifteen thousand francs in the funds. Robespierre had a little bedroom in his house, with a win-

[1] From the "Supplément Littéraire du Figaro," July 28, 1894, the anniversary of Robespierre's death.

dow looking down on the workshops, or sheds, in which a good many workmen were employed.

He was engaged to be married to Duplay's eldest daughter, Eléonore, a tall woman with marked features. But their love-making was very calm, and they waited patiently for quiet days in which they might begin their married life together.

Robespierre's only passion was for power, and he had showed much skill in getting rid of a multitude of those who stood in the way of his attaining it, — Girondists, Hébertists, and Dantonists. In Thermidor of the year II. (July, 1794) he seemed to have realized his dreams. The Convention obeyed him through fear; the Commune supported him from conviction. But in the Convention he had enemies. That great crowd of deputies, then sitting in the Tuileries, contained a group of Montagnards (Men of the Mountain) who were growing impatient of the yoke of Robespierre. Their leaders were Billaud-Varennes, Collot d'Herbois, Barras, Fouché, Tallien, Fréron, Lecointre, and others. They felt themselves in danger from Robespierre, whom they called "the tyrant," and made ready for a coming struggle.

Robespierre was not averse to it; he hoped to rid himself by a supreme effort from these last opponents. He trusted to the Commune (the city government at the Hôtel de Ville), which could be acted on by Lescot-Fleuriot, Mayor of Paris, and Payan, the National Commissioner; and to the Revolutionary Tribunal, whose President and Vice-President, Damas and Coffinhal, were his warm adherents.

As to the Convention, he doubted not he could checkmate it, thanks to his friends Saint-Just, Couthon, and Lebas, aided by his own eloquence. The chances of a struggle between the Convention and the Commune seemed to him all in his favor. He judged the time propitious for the fight, and he prepared to crush all attempts to revolt against his authority.

On the 8th Thermidor the Convention, presided over by Collot d'Herbois, was in session. Robespierre, who had not attended its sittings for some time, mounted the tribune and prepared to speak.

He read a long speech, according to his custom, the manuscript of which, full of erasures and interlineations, was found among his papers. It was evidently a paper that had been carefully prepared, defending his own virtue, patriotism, and devotion to the public good; and he threatened his opponents in advance, depicting them as enemies to their country and the Revolution. It was the same course that he had pursued successfully several times before.

He complained that he was calumniated. "They call me 'a tyrant,'" he cried. "If I were a tyrant, they would be crawling at my feet." He declaimed against the Committee of Public Safety and against other committees, especially that of finance. He complained of the superabundance of interest felt by the public in military matters, and he cried, "Unless you keep a tight grasp on the reins of the Revolution, you may soon see a military despotism establish itself, and some leader of the factions overthrow your representative assembly!"

He ended by denouncing fresh conspiracies against public liberty, and cried that the Committee of Public Safety ought to be purged, and be then set to work to exterminate traitors.

All this shows plainly what was his object. Indeed, one of his creatures, a member of the Revolutionary Tribunal, had said a day or two before in the hearing of the Convention, though he was in the next chamber, "The Revolutionary Tribunal is awaiting some twenty deputies; the bomb is ready to explode."

Yet Robespierre's authority was still so great that his speech was loudly applauded. Lecointre demanded that it should be printed. Another deputy objected that the Assembly was moving too fast, and proposed to submit the speech to the decision of the two committees. Barrère, not certain how the affair might terminate, approved the printing of the speech, but very vaguely.

The debate continued long. It involved the death or life of many of the speakers. When at 5 P.M. the session closed, the question whether Robespierre's speech should be printed at the public expense was still undecided. Yet in one point of view the session had been of supreme importance; for Robespierre for the first time had met with opposition. He left the Assembly astonished and furiously angry. The wish of effacing the check he had received led him to attend the Jacobin Club in the evening. There he was sure to be supreme, secure of being applauded. He re-read his speech, which his hearers received with acclamations. In order to excite greater enthusiasm for himself personally, he affected to consider himself a victim. "This speech that you have heard," he said, "is my last will and testament. I have seen my fate to-day; the league formed by the wicked is so strong that I cannot hope to escape. I fall without regret. I leave you my memory; let it be dear to you; may you defend it!"

He said something about "drinking hemlock." David, the painter, exclaimed, "I will drink it with you!" Couthon then proposed the expulsion of all deputies from the club who had opposed the printing of Robespierre's speech. This proposal was carried by acclamation. Billaud-Varennes and Collot d'Herbois, who were present, were hustled out of the Jacobin Hall with hootings and even violence.

Leaving Robespierre at the club to enjoy his triumph, Billaud and Collot went at once to the Committee of Public Safety, which then met under the same roof as the Convention, at the Tuileries. There, sitting at the great oval table covered with green cloth, they found Carnot and Saint-Just, both busy with their papers. Saint-Just passed each sheet, when he had written it, to his secretary.

Billaud and Collot, excited by the scene at the Jacobins', at once set on Saint-Just, as the friend of Robespierre, and reproached him with the conduct of his party.

"You are writing denunciations against us at this very moment!" they cried, endeavoring to get possession of his papers.

"Of course I am," said Saint-Just, with an air of mockery. Then, turning to Carnot, he said, "Possibly I am making out yours, too."

Carnot looked up quietly. "If that is so," he said, "what we shall have to do is to shoulder our muskets." With that he went on writing.

Billaud and Collot were not so calm. They became violent. They even declared that they would lock up Saint-Just, and keep guard over him till morning. Saint-Just to appease them had to promise that he would submit his report to the Committee of Public Safety before he gave it in to the Convention. It was a promise he did not intend to keep. He was nowhere to be found the next morning, and up to eleven o'clock the Committee waited for him in vain.

Meantime the deputies in the Convention who had attacked Robespierre were making preparations for the next day's struggle. They needed the support of the more moderate members of the Assembly, whom Robespierre had, to a certain extent, protected; but they won them over to their support.

Robespierre had set spies for some time past over the doings of certain deputies whom he believed to be his enemies, but he was, nevertheless, in complete ignorance of these proceedings. He took a walk in the Champs Élysées with Eléonore Duplay, to whom he was engaged to be married, accompanied by his great Danish dog Brount.

Eléonore was depressed and uneasy, and kept nervously caressing the dog. Robespierre pointed out to her the setting sun, which was going down into the purple west.

"Ah! it will be fine weather to-morrow!" she cried, and the omen seemed to reassure her.

They returned to the Rue St. Honoré, and sat down to supper. The walk had probably calmed the first emotions of painful surprise felt by Robespierre in the Convention, for he was now serene.

"I expect nothing from the Men of the Mountain," he said, "they want to get rid of me, and they say I am a tyrant, but the great body of the Assembly will support me."

He slept that night confident of success, and the next morning, — the 9th Thermidor, — when he left the hospitable house of the Duplays, his last words were: "The majority in the Assembly is pure. Be easy. I have nothing to fear."

Thus began the celebrated 9th Thermidor, — July 27, 1794. The weather was oppressively hot. The Convention had met early. All felt it was a decisive day. Both parties counted on the support of the moderate men in the Assembly. Saint-Just, a friend of Robespierre, spoke first, but his speech was vague and hesitating. He was interrupted before he had gone far by Tallien, and by Billaud-Varennes; both of them were men stained with the worst crimes of the Revolution, but they were now enemies to Robespierre, whom Billaud-Varennes attacked violently, accusing him of not having been willing to prosecute men who had been denounced as enemies of the Republic to the Committee!

Robespierre tried to answer him, but was silenced by howls of "Down with the tyrant!"

"I have seen the formation of the army of a new Cromwell," cried Tallien, "and here is the dagger with which I intend to pierce his heart, if the Convention should support him! I demand that the Convention shall decree his arrest. I demand that it shall remain in session till the steel blade of the law shall have assured the Revolution, and we shall have got rid of him and of his creatures!"

These two propositions were adopted amid great applause; Billaud-Varennes then demanded the arrest of Damas, President of the Revolutionary Tribunal. It was at once decreed, and Damas was dragged from his bench to prison.

Robespierre endeavored to speak. "Down with the tyrant!" cried the Assembly. Barrère and Verdier tried to draw off the attention of the Convention to other topics, but Tallien brought back the Assembly to the point in question. There was great confusion among the deputies. The accusation against Robespierre was, not that he had guillotined innocent moderates or royalists, but that he had caused the arrest of advanced revolutionists. One man cried out: "The blood of Danton suffocates him!" At these words

Robespierre grew pale. "It is then Danton whom you are seeking to avenge?" he said.

As the decree of arrest was pronounced, Robespierre's brother sprang to his feet, crying: "I am as much guilty as my brother. I share his virtues. I ask for a decree of arrest for myself—"

But in the general confusion little notice was taken of this courageous act of fraternal devotion.

In vain Robespierre tried to speak. He uttered only disjointed reproaches and abuse of those attacking him. He had no skill in self-defence. They accused him of having blamed the Revolutionary government for its destruction of the churches, and their desecration. At this there was a cry of "Let him be arrested at once!"

The decree of arrest was passed amid shouts of: "Vive la Liberté! Vive la République!"

"The Republic?" cried Robespierre. "The Republic is lost, for brigands triumph!" No attention was paid to him. The decree of arrest joined with him his brother, Saint-Just, and Couthon. Lebas cried out that such a decree was an outrage, and demanded that his own name should be included. This was done accordingly. Fréron, one of the most sanguinary and infamous of the Revolutionists, led the attack, and declared that Robespierre, Saint-Just, and Couthon had plotted to form a triumvirate. "Couthon," he cried, "has aspired to mount a throne!" "Oh! of course," said Couthon, ironically, pointing to his disabled legs, useless from paralysis, on which he was unable to stand alone.

It was five o'clock; the session closed, and gendarmes carried off the accused to prison.

The Commune, the municipal government of Paris, sitting at the Hôtel de Ville, was faithful to Robespierre. The mayor ordered the tocsin to sound to rouse the Sections; he had the barriers of the city closed, and proclaimed Paris in revolt against the scoundrels of the Convention. But his measures were paralyzed by the fact that Henriot was in command of the troops,—Henriot, the lowest, meanest of all the Jacobins, a man who had denounced his own mother to the Revolutionary Tribunal, that he might rid himself of the care of her. He was drunk that day, as he usually was. On receiving orders from the Commune to call out the Sections, he rushed through the streets, pistol in hand, yelling to the people to take up arms. Some of those who heard him were alarmed, most were disgusted. As he passed a restaurant where a deputy was dining about six o'clock, the deputy saw him through a window, and shouted: "Arrest that man! His arrest has been decreed by the Assembly!" Instantly six gendarmes who were in the street seized Henriot by the collar. The deputy (Robin by name) had him carried off a prisoner to the Committee of General Security, thence to the Committee of Public Safety. Billaud-Varennes and Barrère were there, but they were afraid of compromising themselves too far should Robespierre and his party prove victorious. Robin was indignant with their pusillanimity, and began to be anxious to get rid of his prisoner.

Some officers of the Commune at that moment came up and rescued Henriot without resistance, he being all the time too drunk to know what was being done with him.

The struggle was now between the Commune at the Hôtel de Ville and the Convention at the Tuileries.

Robespierre and the deputies arrested with him were sent to different prisons, — Robespierre to the Luxembourg, his brother to St. Lazare; Couthon, Lebas, and Saint-Just to other places of captivity. But the Commune had sent orders that no prison should receive them; and Saint-Just, Lebas, and the younger Robespierre regained their liberty, but not Robespierre, though he was eagerly expected every moment by the Committee of the Commune sitting in their council-chamber at the Hôtel de Ville. At the gate of the Luxembourg he was met by a municipal officer, who ordered his liberation, and took him and his captors to the Prefecture of Police, where the actors changed places. The captors became prisoners, and Robespierre was free.

The Council of the Commune sent him earnest entreaties — even orders — to join them, but Robespierre seems to have lost courage. All he would do was to send advice to the Hôtel de Ville. The Commune, however, insisted on his presence, and sent a deputation, which at last brought him. His arrival gave courage to his friends. Crowds in the street filed past the Hôtel de Ville swearing fidelity to the Commune.

Couthon was the only one of the arrested deputies not present. Robespierre, his brother, and Saint-Just signed an order to him to join them.

At about 1 A.M. on the 10th Thermidor Couthon arrived, and they all began to deliberate on what should be next done. "Draw up a proclamation to the armies," said Couthon.

"In whose name?" said Robespierre, whose audacity seemed to have forsaken him.

A terrible rain was falling, which greatly damped the ardor of the crowd in the streets. A proclamation was drawn up addressed to one of the Sections called the Section of Pikes, calling upon it to rise in arms. Three members of the Council of the Commune had signed it, and Robespierre had just taken the pen and written the first two letters of his name, when soldiers sent by the Convention burst in. The Convention, having learned what was taking place, had acted at once. The tipsy Henriot had been able to take no military precautions to protect the Hôtel de Ville and the municipality.

The Convention, when it learned of the escape of Robespierre, Henriot, and the other prisoners, was at first in mortal fear. Deputies talked of dying at their posts, and so on. But danger gives courage. Some one proposed that Barras should be their leader, — the Barras who was subsequently the patron of Napoleon. Attended by twelve deputies girt with their scarfs of office, Barras assembled a considerable body of soldiers, and marched on the Hôtel de Ville. At sight of the soldiers the crowd, already disheartened, drenched by rain, and conscious of the lateness of the hour, dispersed at once. Henriot, arriving before the Hôtel de Ville, found his own soldiers of the Sections in command of deputies from the Convention. He rushed up the staircase, crying, "All is lost!" The pen dropped from the hand of Robespierre.

The Commune was at the mercy of its assailants; only, the assailants did not seem to assail. They were bewildered by their own success; they were astonished that they had met no opposition. Many were afraid that preparations had been made to blow up the building. A gendarme, however, named Méda, braver than the rest, entered the Hôtel de Ville, and made his way to the council-chamber. Robespierre was sitting at a table. Méda threatened him with a pistol, and cried, "Yield, traitor!"

Robespierre raised his head. "It is you who are the traitor," he said, "and I will have you shot." As he spoke, Méda raised a pistol in his left hand, fired, and broke his jaw.

Robespierre, thus wounded, fell forward on the table, his blood staining the paper on which he had been about to sign his name.

Méda, after his shot, turned and fled, carrying back his news to those commanding the armed men outside, who at once entered the Hôtel de Ville. As they did so they heard a second shot. Lebas had killed himself.

These shots, the cries and yells that rose, led to a general panic among Robespierre's party. The younger Robespierre, excited and terrified, tried to escape through a window. He walked a few steps outside on the cornice, then lost his balance, fell on the pavement, and broke his legs.

Couthon, most of whose body was paralyzed, had been wounded in the head. He dragged himself into a corner, where he lay motionless, counterfeiting death. Saint-Just did not move. He quietly awaited his doom. Henriot, who, by his drunkenness, weakness, and stupidity, had been the ruin of his friends, thought only of saving his own life. He tried to flee by a back-staircase, but one of Robespierre's friends, furious against him, flung him out of a window. He fell on a dung-hill,[1] which broke his fall. Scrambling

[1] See page 151.

out of this, he took refuge in a drain, whence he was dislodged, and placed with his accomplices. Coffinhal, the man who had flung him from the window, alone escaped, and took refuge in the "Ile des Cygnes," where he was so nearly starved that two days later he surrendered himself a prisoner.

It was two in the morning. The Commune was vanquished. The reign of Robespierre was at an end.

They brought stretchers on which they placed Robespierre, his brother, Couthon, and the body of Lebas. Saint-Just and the others followed as prisoners. The party marched to the Convention, and the doors of the Hôtel de Ville were closed.

At three o'clock Barras and his twelve deputies reappeared in the Convention, and announced solemnly that the palace of the municipality of Paris was in their hands; and, as in those days no one stuck at any accusation, however absurd, against a defeated enemy, they asserted that they had found a seal engraved with *fleurs de lis*, which proved that Robespierre was engaged in a royalist conspiracy.

Then it was announced that the stretcher, on which lay the wounded Robespierre, was at the door. The Convention refused to let it enter.

It was not necessary to send Robespierre and the rest before the Revolutionary Tribunal. They had already been pronounced outlaws. They were taken to the council-room of the Committee of Public Safety. An eye-witness tells us: —

"Robespierre was carried by the same men who had done so from the beginning. He hid his wounded face with his right arm. The party stopped for a moment at the foot of the great staircase of the Tuileries. Many people came round him from curiosity. Some of them lifted his arm to see his face. One said, 'He is not dead. He is still warm.' Another, 'He looks like a fine king! does n't he?' And so on. The bearers were unwilling that any one should meddle with him, and those who were at the foot of the stretcher told those at the head to keep their end well up so as to preserve the little life there was in him. They mounted at last into the great room used by the Committee. They laid him on a long table opposite a window, and placed his head on a box containing some remains of black bread, — soldiers' rations. He did not stir, but he breathed heavily. He placed his right hand on his face; evidently wishing to conceal it. Among those who had brought him were a fireman and a cannoneer, who kept on talking to him, making cruel jests, mocking and reproaching him. /He wore his sky-blue coat and his nankeen breeches as he had done on the day of the Feast of the Supreme Being, seven weeks before; but his clothes were in disorder, and his shirt was bloody. He had no hat and no cravat, and his white stockings had slipped down to his heels. About four o'clock it was noticed that he was holding a kid bag in his hand; it was marked: *Au Grand Monarque, Lecourt, fournisseur du Roi et de ses troupes, Rue St. Honoré, Paris.* He was using this bag to stanch the blood that came from his mouth. About six in the morning Élie Lacoste came into the room with a surgeon, whom he told to dress the wound, "that the prisoner might be in a condition for what might follow."

There is no need to relate how the wound was dressed, men standing round all the time and uttering words of cruel insult, "which he must have heard," says the eye-witness, "for he had still some strength, and often opened his eyes."

Suddenly he rose to a sitting posture, pulled up his stockings, slid to the other end of the table, and reached a chair. As soon as he was seated, he made a sign that he wanted water and a clean handkerchief. He looked steadily at the men around him, and sometimes cast his eyes up to the ceiling. His complexion, which had always been sallow, was now livid. From time to time he made a convulsive movement, but in general he seemed passive.

Saint-Just, who had been brought into the room shortly after Robespierre, was perfectly silent. His clothes were not disordered. Even his cravat was unrumpled. He wore a coat, chamois color, a waistcoat with a white ground, and breeches of pale gray. But, notwithstanding his self-control, his face showed his depression, his sense of humiliation, and his eyes were full of grief.

Around him stood Damas, Payan, and a few others. Robespierre's faithful dog, Brount, had not quitted his master.

About nine on the morning of the 10th Thermidor (July 28), 1794, the prisoners were taken to the Conciergerie. Saint-Just as he entered the hall, where was hung a great picture of "The Declaration of the Rights of Man before the Convention," remarked, "And *I* made *that!*" Those were the only words that passed his lips during those long hours. As for Robespierre, not only was he assailed with all kinds of insulting words, but it is said that one or more men spat in his face and pricked him with their pen-knives.

He asked a turnkey by a sign to bring him pen and ink, but the man answered: "What the devil do you want with pen and ink? Do you think you can write to your Supreme Being?"

The task of the Revolutionary Tribunal was very simple. The accused were all outlaws. It had only to order their execution. It did so, to take effect that day on the Place de la Révolution.

It was not until towards evening, however, that the execution took place. Some time was needed to remove the guillotine from the Place du Trône Renversé to the Place de la Révolution.

The twenty-two prisoners were placed on three carts. Henriot, still half drunk, was placed next to the brother of Robespierre. Couthon lay in the third cart. The procession moved slowly. When in the Rue St. Honoré it stopped before Duplay's house, and a group of women danced round the cart that held the man who had had his home there.

No outrage was spared Robespierre. Carrier, the wretch, made infamous by his *noyades* and cruelties at Nantes, followed the cart, crying, "Down with the tyrant!" The crowd was immense, all hooting, cheering, and cursing. The condemned men seemed imperturbable, and continued silent. The crowd bawled out that they were cowards!

It was past seven in the evening when the procession reached the Place de la Révolution. Couthon was first executed, then the younger Robespierre. Saint-Just quietly mounted the scaffold. When twenty heads had fallen, came the turn of Robespierre. The executioner roughly snatched at the linen which bound his broken jaw, and his cry of pain was heard all over the Place de la Révolution. He was speedily laid on the plank. The blade fell, and the executioner held up the head to the populace. Cries of: "Vive la Convention! Vive la République!" responded to the sight. Joy seemed to manifest itself among the spectators.

Shortly afterwards Tallien congratulated the Convention, inviting it to share in the general rejoicing, "for the death day of a tyrant should be a festival for fraternity."

This revolution known as the 9th Thermidor has never deserved the place it occupies in the history of the Revolution. To us it is memorable chiefly for having opened the prison-doors to many in whom all generations take an interest; but the men who made this revolution were on the whole worse than those who fell in it. It was simply a struggle for power between two sets of Jacobins. The power of Robespierre fell because it had no foundation. Everything that happened was a surprise to all concerned; cowardice and meanness were everywhere conspicuous. Two or three men only showed any energy or decision. Everything was hap-hazard.

Robespierre's sole aim was personal. He wanted to attain supreme power. The enemies he destroyed or opposed were his personal enemies. He makes but a sorry figure among historical personages; his aim was without elevation; even his vices were not *great*. The only act which individualizes him in history is his invention of the worship of the Supreme Being. He had none of the better qualities of those earlier leaders of the Revolution who became his victims.

He was austere in his morals, and incorruptible in honesty. He despoiled no man of his money, — only of his dearest relatives or of his own life. His cruelty was calm, impassive, and had always some personal end in view. But his work on earth was a work of death. Some one thus wrote his epitaph after his execution.

> "Stranger, whoe'er thou art,
> Weep not for me.
> Had I lived, it would have been
> *Death*, friend, for *thee!*"

CHAPTER V.

A CHAPTER OF EPISODES.

Episode First. — Robespierre as a Poet.

WE all imagine that we know everything that can be known about Robespierre, and we know something about Lazare Carnot, grandfather of the late President of the Third French Republic; but few persons suspect that in 1783 they, together with all the young aristocrats of Arras, sang songs in praise of wine and love and beauty, and, crowned with roses, recited in public ballads and madrigals of the Middle Ages.

Both Robespierre and Carnot were active members of the Society of the Rosati, founded in Arras in 1778. The meetings of this society took place on the banks of the Scarpe, in a bower of roses planted for that purpose. The meetings of the Society were held only at the season when roses were in bloom, and the candidate for admission was required to pluck a rose, to inhale its fragrance three times, and to place it in his button-hole, after which, taking a full glass of rosy wine, he drank it at one draught to the health and prosperity of all Rosati, receiving at the hands of the President a diploma in verse, which was to be responded to in like manner.

Here are the verses that Robespierre offered to the Society on his admission, —

THE ROSE.[1]

I SEE in the nosegay you offer
  A sharp thorn, side by side with the rose.
Your poetic words shame the poor proffer
  Of thanks, gentle sirs, in poor prose.

[1] This poem was translated by me from the "Supplément Littéraire du Figaro," and the translation was published in "Harper's Magazine," April, 1889. — E. W. L.

The things you so charmingly said
  Have confused me and rendered me dumb;
The rose is the compliment paid,
  The thorn the poor answer to come.

Ah, yes, in this beautiful *fête*
  Where good fellowship reigneth alone,
What bud with the rosebud can mate?
  What verses can equal your own?
I bewail the sad fate that is ours, —
  The fate that misplaces — alas! — us;
For what the rose is among flowers,
  Your poems would be on Parnassus.

When I ponder your gift I confess
  'T is less generous, sirs, than I thought it,
And my sense of your kindness grows less
  With my knowledge of whence you have brought it.
Your sacrifice, sirs, may be found
  Not so great as the world would suppose;
Since your gardens with laurels abound,
  You can spare me the gift of a rose!

Episode Second.— Robespierre's Private Life with the Family of Duplay.[1]

It is said that M. Sardou, the dramatist, is about to write a history of Robespierre's career; this paper is taken from a conversation in which he freely communicated many particulars he had gathered in his researches.

Some writers have told the public that the house of the cabinet-maker Duplay, in which Robespierre lodged during the months when he held power in France, has been utterly destroyed. This is not so. It is standing intact, and is now inhabited by a M. Vaury. Its number is now 398 Rue St. Honoré. On each side of the *porte cochère* leading to the house, which stands back in a yard, was a small shop in Robespierre's day. One shop was occupied by a jeweller; the other was a restaurant. Two doors away was another for the sale of working materials and embroidery, kept

[1] From an article in the "Supplément Littéraire du Figaro," August 11, 1894.

by Madame Condorcet, wife of a proscribed Girondist deputy. This lady also took portraits, and thus gained her livelihood.

"I have been in the bed-chamber," said M. Sardou, "in which the dictator may be said to have barricaded himself from the intrusion of the world. It was no easy matter to approach him in private. He kept himself well out of reach of troublesome solicitations." The room that he inhabited was completely surrounded by the bed-chambers of the family; and the workmen who carried on their carpentry and upholstery in the back yard were at all times within his sight and call. The chamber of Eléonore Duplay, the *fiancée* of Robespierre (called in her own family Cornélie), was in a different part of the house.

Robespierre had had no acquaintance with the Duplay family before July 19, 1791, when a riot took place after a great reunion of revolutionists upon the Champ de Mars. Robespierre was present at the Jacobin Club that day, where a few of those who called themselves the "friends of liberty" had been assembled. "The courtyard of our Club," said a Jacobin eye-witness of what took place, "was suddenly filled with artillery-men and *chasseurs à barrières,* blind instruments of the fury of Lafayette and his partisans. Robespierre was alarmed at the idea of passing through the courtyard in order to reach his home, when the sitting should be ended. He heard the soldiers uttering curses and threats against the Jacobins, and he knew himself to be a prominent member of the club. He trembled so much that he had to lean on the arm of Lecointre of Versailles, who was wearing the uniform of a major in the National Guard, and on that of Lapoype, afterwards a general of division, but at that time one of the Jacobins.

"Robespierre did not dare to go back to his lodgings, then No. 20 in the Rue Saintonge, where he was living with a man named Pierre Villiers, employed by him at that time as his secretary. He asked Lecointre if he did not know of some place near the Tuileries where a good patriot would shelter him in safety for that night? Lecointre proposed to him to go to Duplay's house, and took him there. From that day forth Robespierre took up his abode with the Duplays."

The house belonging to Maurice Duplay was then 366, but is now 398, in the Rue St. Honoré. It consisted of a hall on the ground-floor and a dining-room opening on the yard; from the dining-room a staircase led up to the rooms above. Duplay and his wife had a large chamber on the story above the ground-floor (*au premier*). Their four daughters had rooms at the back of it. The bed-chamber of Maximilien Robespierre looked to the west; the nephew of Duplay, Simon by name, who acted as secretary to the dictator, and Duplay's young son, who bore his father's name, slept in the next chamber.

The father, Maurice Duplay, was a little more than fifty when he made the acquaintance of the dictator. He was born in 1738, at St. Didier-en-Velay. His parents were Jacques Duplay and his wife, Marie Bontemps. The pair had had ten children. Mathieu, the eldest son, and Maurice, one of the younger ones, became cabinet-makers. Maurice was very young when he left his native village to make his journeyman's tour through France. After long wanderings he settled in Paris, where, in consequence of some fortunate speculations, he soon amassed an enviable little fortune.

After a while he became the owner of three houses, — one in the Rue l'Arcade, one in the Rue du Luxembourg, and one in the Rue d'Angoulême. He himself lived in the house on the Rue St. Honoré, for which he was to pay in instalments eighteen hundred francs, and two hundred francs a year besides as rent to the Sisters of the Conception, who owned the property.

Maurice Duplay had retired from business when the Revolution broke out, and he does not seem to have taken a prominent part in Revolutionary matters.

According to Lebas, as he was a property-holder, he was forced to become a juryman on the criminal court of his Section; and in consequence of holding this position, it was impossible for him to refuse to serve on the jury of the

Revolutionary Tribunal, notwithstanding his repugnance to take part in its affairs.

He was not on the jury that tried the queen or Madame Elisabeth, though some writers have said so, and he exercised his terrible functions as seldom as possible. Sometimes he pleaded the necessity of attending to certain buildings with which he had been intrusted by the government, and thus escaped attending the Tribunal. Most of the trials to which his name is appended took place without him. When, after the fall of Robespierre, Fouquier-Tinville and all the jurymen of his Tribunal were arraigned in the very court where they had exercised their judicial functions, Duplay was the only one who was acquitted. In point of fact he was a thoroughly good man. In forty years of hard work he had acquired about fifteen thousand francs' worth of real estate. But the disorders of the country soon depreciated his property and impaired the prosperity he had laboriously and quietly achieved.

His wealth was in houses. The houses would not let, and Duplay found himself obliged to resume his business. This account is taken from part of a letter from Madame Duplay to her daughter Madame Auzat, found in Duplay's house after the 10th Thermidor.

Madame Duplay was the daughter of a carpenter of Choisy. She was arrested and imprisoned at Ste. Pélagie during the night of the 9th Thermidor, together with her husband and her young son; and she died in the prison, strangled by the women who shared her captivity.

She had had four daughters: Sophie, who married a lawyer named Auzat; Victoire, who never married; Elisabeth, born in 1773, who married on August 20, 1793, the deputy Lebas, who perished with Robespierre; and Eléonore, who was a year older. Eléonore was called Cornelia by her family, from some allusion to the mother of the Gracchi, and she lived until after the Restoration.

The only son of Maurice and his wife was the boy Maurice. He was employed when he grew to manhood as a clerk in the Bureau of the *Administration Centrale* of the

Seine; later, in 1814, he was made superintendent of the hospitals and asylums of Paris, — a post which he held almost till his death, which took place in 1846. Simon Duplay, his cousin, who had been employed by Robespierre as his secretary, had enlisted in the army and lost a leg at Valmy. He then was kindly received by his uncle into his family, where Robespierre made him a kind of humble assistant. We need hardly say that he was not paid much, for Robespierre considered that he did him a great honor by choosing him to write under his dictation. After Thermidor poor Simon was thrown into prison, and all his papers were seized. He married subsequently, and his son became a doctor. Another member of the family, Dr. Simon Duplay, is still living (1894). He is a member of the *Académie de Médecine*, a clinical professor in the School of Surgery, etc.

Robespierre's private life, while he lived with the Duplay family, seems to have been a regular and quiet one. Only thrice did he sleep out of the house, and then he went to visit his sister at Arras. The only recreation he allowed himself was occasionally a walk in the Champs Élysées along the edge of the Jardin Marbœuf, which was the fashionable promenade at that day. More frequently he on his return from the Convention preferred to work quietly at home.

His chamber was very simply furnished. He had a walnut bedstead with flowered blue damask curtains made out of an old gown of Madame Duplay's. There were some straw chairs and a common chest of drawers, and some pine shelves hanging from the wall which held his little library. This consisted principally of the works of Corneille, Racine, Voltaire, and Rousseau. The room had only one window, which looked down upon the sheds where the carpenters did their work, so that all day long Robespierre read and wrote to the sound of saws and hammers.

He got up very early, and the first thing he always did was to go down into the shop and wish M. and Madame Duplay good-morning.

Then he settled himself to work for some hours, taking

no refreshment but a glass of water. Nobody at that time dared to disturb him. Daily, however, he had his hair dressed, and this operation took place on a little open gallery which overlooked the courtyard. At this time persons who wished to look at him could do so. Crowds came in the days of his popularity, but he took little notice of them; generally he read the paper, and calmly ate his breakfast, — a little wine and bread and fruit. When he was not reading he looked straight before him with his eyes fixed upon the ground and his head upon his hand, as if he were engaged in very serious and important thoughts.

After breakfast he went back to his work, until the time came for him to appear at his place in the Committee of Public Safety, or the Convention. He never received anybody in the morning, unless the visitor was willing to avail himself of the time when his hair was being dressed. He dined with the family, and *it is recorded that he always said grace.*

On one occasion he was highly displeased because Madame Duplay made some remark about her table being probably not as good as he ought to have. On principle he never paid more when prices advanced than he had engaged to do at first, because he said it might encourage bad habits on the part of his entertainers, and even during the famine he added nothing to the housekeeping, that they might be forced to make no difference on his account. If he accepted an invitation to dinner he never told them, on the presumption that nothing especial would be prepared for him, so it could make no difference. But, on the other hand, as he was unwilling that these good people should derive no advantages from his position, he did many good offices for their children. The son, who was also a cabinet-maker, he promised to establish in business, or at least to assist in his establishment, and he promised the daughters handsome wedding presents, provided they married citizens who had borne arms for their country.

At table he ate whatever was provided for the family, and drank their sour wine. After the meal was over he had coffee served for him and stayed for an hour in the house ready for visitors; then he generally went out. After he became head of the government he engaged a secretary; but before that his writing was done, as we have said, by the orphan nephew of Duplay, who also did his errands.

He generally came home late, for he would often work in the Committee of Public Safety up to midnight. But even if he was not at the Committee, he never came home before twelve o'clock. Where was he up to that time? No one ever knew. If any one wanted him in the evening he was told to put off seeing him till the next day.

These particulars have been gleaned from the unpublished reminiscences of a contemporary, who speaks also of his extreme temperance, which the world knew already. During the last months of his life he drank nothing but water, being apprehensive that a free use of wine or liquor might make him say something he had better have kept unsaid. The only indulgence he allowed himself was in oranges, a number of which he ate at every meal. A perfect pyramid of them was always placed before him at dessert, and he ate them at all seasons with avidity. It is possible that he may have thought they counteracted his bilious tendency.

In 1785, before the Revolution, Robespierre has been described as a short man, "with insignificant features, much pitted with the small-pox. His forehead was arched and white, his glance dark and uncertain; he looked like a man whose prominent traits of character were hatred and envy."

Another contemporary says that, although his head had none of the leonine character so imposing in Mirabeau and Danton, in spite of their ugliness, there was something in his "persuasive expression" that at once impressed the beholder. "He had long light brown hair, which he wore turned back, a broad forehead, bare on the temples, somewhat arched, and prominent above the eyebrows; his eyes were keen and clear, full of thought, but concealed unfortunately by spectacles, which short-sight rendered indispensable to him; his nose turned up a little; his chin was firm, with a slight dimple. Such was his appearance."

This portrait is wonderfully flattering if we may believe others drawn by his contemporaries, who speak especially of the uncertainty of his glance and the near-sightedness of his vision. Sometimes he wore green spectacles.

As for his clothes, they were always well made, well chosen, and carefully put on; and he alone of the members of the Convention continued to wear ruffled shirt-fronts and lace at his wrists. A painter of the period has described him with his hair well powdered, in a white embroidered waistcoat turned back with some soft color, and in all other respects dressed with the fastidiousness of a dandy of 1789.

What was it in the personality of Robespierre that could have won the affections of Eléonore Duplay? He cared little about her sex. He was too much occupied by dreams of ambition to let himself fall under the influence of a woman. "He cared neither for women nor for money, and took no interest whatever in his own private affairs."

He seems to have accepted the attentions of Eléonore Duplay rather than to have been in love with her. Her face was somewhat masculine, — not a face with which most men would fall readily in love.

She was pale, with thin lips and expressionless eyes. There is a portrait of her in pastel in the Musée de la Révolution. She looks cold and stern, without any charm of gayety or tenderness.

There have been two theories concerning Eléonore Duplay, — one that she was Robespierre's mistress, the other that she was his *fiancée*. Charlotte Robespierre, the dictator's sister, thought that Madame Duplay, being anxious for the honor of having such a son-in-law as Robespierre, did all in her power to make the match; while Eléonore, who was ambitious on her own account, did all she could to captivate the heart of Maximilien. But Robespierre, according to his sister, was not to be captivated. The attentions bestowed on him annoyed and disgusted him. But this view was probably prompted by prejudice and jealousy.

Robespierre found himself the object of warm affection in the Duplay family; and he could not but be sensible of their kindness. They positively adored him; and when he could spare any time from public life, he seemed to revive in this atmosphere of devotion and kindliness. It was especially when dinner was over and they all passed into the *salon* "furnished with heavy mahogany, covered with stamped woollen crimson plush" (*velours d'Utrecht*) that Robespierre enjoyed the society of the family. While the girls occupied themselves with needlework or embroidery, Maximilien would read aloud from Voltaire's works or Rousseau's; from Corneille or Racine. He read well, with much interest in what he read, and enjoyed at the same time the pleasure he was giving.

On Thursdays these meetings lost their family character. Other guests joined the circle. During the time of the Constituent Assembly the brothers Lameth were often there. Afterwards, in the days of the Legislative Assembly, Merlin (de Thionville) came, Collot d'Herbois, Panis, and Camille Desmoulins, whom Robespierre, after serving as best man at his wedding, sent to the scaffold. Artists came also, Gérard the painter, Prudhon, and Buonarotti, an authentic descendant of Michael Angelo, who played the piano. Then there was Lebas, who was a passionate admirer of Italian music and a good performer. So that sometimes for hours politics were laid aside in these reunions.

Lebas was faithful to Robespierre to the last. When arrested with his friend and leader, he blew out his brains. His wife, Elizabeth Duplay, was confined afterwards in prison, where Philippe Lebas, her son, was born. It was this Philippe Lebas who was subsequently chosen by Queen Hortense to be tutor to her son, the future Emperor Napoleon III.

In 1854 Philippe Lebas lived near Paris, at Fontenay-aux-Roses. Every Saturday he went to see his mother, a most respectable old lady, well known throughout her neighborhood for her piety and charity. A little anecdote told by Doctor Latour, who frequently visited her, may fitly close this paper.

When the doctor first knew her his attention was attracted

by a large and handsome parrot, which Madame Lebas seemed to hold in great consideration, and on which she lavished every kind of care and caress.

"The bird was often an interruption to our conversation," said the doctor, "breaking in with bits of the 'Marseillaise,' or the chorus of the 'Ça ira.'

'Ça ira, Ça ira!
Les aristocrates à la lanterne;'

or the other well-known lines from the same song, —

'Madame Véto avait promis
De faire égorger tout Paris.'"

"Hush! hush! my little pet," Madame Lebas would say to him. But the bird seldom paid her much attention when he was in the humor to troll out his demagogic songs.

One day the doctor ventured to say, "Your bird seems very much of a Revolutionist."

"Of course he is," she answered, in a low voice; "he was the parrot of our saint, Maximilien Robespierre." And as she said this, the good lady made the sign of the cross.

"Yes," she continued, "this parrot was bequeathed to me when our family was broken up. We Duplays were devoted to our saint" (here she again made the sign of the cross) "until his martyrdom . . ."

So here was this most respectable old lady, a pious Christian, and a fervent Catholic, whose intellect and whose morals were above suspicion, giving to Robespierre the honor due to a martyr and a saint, and declaring him the victim of the wickedness and perversity of mankind!

She had taught the parrot several sentences above and beyond his original *répertoire*.

One day she said to her visitor, "Come here. Go up to the bird and say Robespierre."

"Hat off! Hat off!" cried the parrot, fluttering his wings.

"Say Maximilien," prompted Madame Lebas.

"Maximilien!" repeated the doctor.

"Martyr! Martyr!" screamed the bird.

"Now say Ninth Thermidor!"

"Ninth Thermidor!"

"Fatal day!" replied the parrot.

"Go on, and ask him where saint Maximilien is now!"

When this question was put the bird answered, —

"In heaven!"

Madame Lebas died at Fontenay-aux-Roses, about 1840. Her son Philippe died in 1860. But what has become of the parrot?

Perhaps he is alive still. Parrots, they say, can live more than one hundred years.

Be that as it may, the story of Robespierre's parrot seems a very touching one, and may well be added to the stories already in circulation regarding the pigeons and the canaries of the same master.

Episode Third. — The Revolutionary Calendar.[1]

One of the things which made the French Revolution memorable was, in the language of the period, that it represented "the triumph of ideas." But the "ideas" of the Revolution were not new; and for the most part they sprang from purely English sources. Even unbelief, which counted for so much in the general overturn of France in the eighteenth century, was no new thing. The fool had said in his heart there is no God, and had become corrupt and abominable before the days of Père Duchêne. Nay, even the Encyclopedists had been anticipated in England by Hobbes, Toland, Tindal, Shaftesbury, and Woolston. The simple solution of the whole matter is, that while ideas had been steadily growing and maturing in English minds, the French mind had lain comparatively fallow. Then, having suddenly awakened to certain ideas, the French philosophers of the eighteenth century imagined they had a monopoly of wisdom, and boldly undertook to instruct the world in those "principles of '89" which they were unaware they had borrowed from England.

[1] Abridged from an article signed Francis Hitchman in the "National Review," 1889.

Amongst the "ideas" of the Revolutionary period none took a firmer root or exercised a wider influence than the reform of the existing standards of weights, measures, and time. As to the weights and measures, some national standard was sorely needed. Arthur Young in his travels, shortly before the Revolution, says, "The infinite perplexity of the measures exceeds all comprehension. They differ not only in every province and every district, but almost in every town." That some reform was necessary in measures and in weights was evident, even to this travelling Englishman, who concerned himself with facts, and not "ideas," and the decimal system introduced into France at that period has proved of both value and convenience, though long after small shopkeepers in by-streets of Paris, or in the country, charged their customers in sous, and sold their goods by the kilo, the aune, and the demi-litre, while the class above them still talks of louis and écus, as their grandfathers did.

All these things were to be swept away in the Revolution of '89. They were marks of feudality, traces of what Victor Hugo has called *le pied de Charlemagne.* The Constitution of '89 had guaranteed "liberty of worship;" the Republic denounced worship of any kind; and the Terror mercilessly guillotined those who were such bad citizens as to seek for moral support in religion. Having got rid of Christianity, having in its own phrase "abolished God" and enthroned a Goddess of Reason on the high altar of Notre Dame, it seemed only natural to abolish the calendar, which, by its nomenclature and divisions of time, recalled its ecclesiastical origin. Helen Maria Williams [1] tells us in her reminiscences of her residence in France, that the desire was openly acknowledged, "by a different nomenclature of the months, weeks, and days, to banish all the commemorations of Christianity and prepare the way for abolishing religion itself."

[1] The life of Helen Maria Williams was certainly not *sans reproche*, although she carefully educated the orphan children of her sister, one of whom lived to be M. Coquerel, the celebrated Protestant pastor in Paris, and she was the author of that beautiful hymn, "When Thee I seek, Protecting Power." — E. W. L.

In the Convention the change was explained and supported by familiar phrases. The calendar in use was condemned as being "anomalous," because there was no reason for beginning the year on the 1st of January, "except the pleasure of Numa Pompilius, who wished to propitiate the god Janus;" because the division of the year into periods of seven days was "unscientific," since a week of seven days does not represent one of the phases of the moon; because it is absurd that the sun should rule the day of twenty-four hours, while the moon regulates the years, and so forth. The order of nature, in short, was out of harmony with the science and philosophy of 1792–93. All that could be done in view of the perversity of nature was, therefore, to make the best of the situation and subdue the recalcitrant months and weeks as completely as possible. The matter was therefore referred to the Committee of Public Instruction, of which Romme was the chairman.

Romme was a singular specimen of the man of science turned politician. His fellow-provincials in Auvergne sent him as their representative to the National Convention, where he at once took his place on the Mountain and devoted himself to the task of remodelling society on democratically philosophic principles. Under the Terror he prospered; but in the reaction which followed the death of Robespierre he was arrested and brought to trial, — "not for what he had done, but for what he was,"— and dramatically ended his life by stabbing himself at the bar of the military tribunal which had condemned him (17th of June, 1795).

His report was adopted by the Convention Oct. 5, 1793; and five days later one of those extraordinary national *fêtes* which fill us with amazement and amusement took place in honor of the event at Arras, a little town best known to fame as the birthplace of Robespierre. These performances excited great enthusiasm in republican bosoms at that time, and there are still some persons who profess to consider them "sublime and affecting."

It is said that twenty thousand people walked in procession at Arras in honor of the new division of time. They were divided into groups according to their ages, and represented the months. Following the twelve months came a little "sacred group," representing the supplementary days which made up the republican year, and last of all came the representative of leap year, — a venerable centenarian, who, after the march past was over, planted a tree of liberty. There were bevies of virgins in white, and parties of artisans who "consecrated their tools by touching the tree of liberty with them." The elders grouped themselves around it and ate and drank, while the youths and maidens waited upon them.

The new calendar succeeded in producing the most admired disorder under the pretext of simplicity and regularity. To begin with, the year was divided into twelve months, each of thirty days, and completed by five days superadded (*jours complémentaires*), with an additional day in leap year. The old week — old as the time of the Babylonians — was suppressed; each month was divided into three decades of ten days each. The day was to be divided into ten parts, each of which was to be divided into ten others, so as to complete the decimal division of time. But the Convention, notwithstanding its enthusiasm for scientific symmetry, hesitated to take a step which would at one stroke have rendered useless every watch and clock in France. Happily, the latter portion of Romme's scheme was set aside and never heard of again. It is said, however, that some dials were actually made on the new system.

The Convention had previously decreed that the new era should begin on Sept. 22, 1792. This was the first day of the year I. of the Republic, and year II. was to begin Jan. 1, 1793. Thus the year I. consisted of only three months and nine days. Romme's system, however, altered this arrangement, and all dates between January and September, 1793, which had been year II. of the Republic, were thenceforward to be considered as belonging to year I.

Romme had named his months I., II., III., etc.; but the Convention called in a poet to supplement his work by giving them fanciful and significant names. The result of the labors of Fabre d'Eglantine, the poet chosen, was as follows: —

	AUTUMN.	
Vendémiaire . .	Vintage month . . .	September 22 to October 21.
Brumaire	Foggy month	October 22 to November 20.
Frimaire	Hoar-frost month . .	November 21 to December 20.
	WINTER.	
Nivose	Snowy month	December 21 to January 19.
Pluviose	Rainy month	January 20 to February 18.
Ventose	Windy month	February 19 to March 20.
	SPRING.	
Germinal	Budding month . . .	March 21 to April 19.
Floréal	Flowery month . . .	April 20 to May 19.
Prairial	Pasture month	May 20 to June 18.
	SUMMER.	
Messidor	Harvest month . . .	June 19 to July 18.
Thermidor . . .	Hot month	July 19 to August 17.
Fructidor	Fruit month	August 18 to September 16.

To complete the year, five supplemental days were added between September 16 and September 22. These days were officially called *Sansculottides*, and were respectively devoted to national festivals: I., in honor of genius; II., of labor; III., noble actions; IV., rewards; and V., opinions. The sixth Sansculottide, which was the extra day in leap year, was to be the Grand Festival of the Revolution, when every one should renew his oath to be free or die.

The days of the decade were to be Primidi, Duodi, Tridi, and so forth till they reached the tenth, Décadi. Lest the people should regret the absence of the names of saints, martyrs, and confessors to which each day had been dedicated in the Gregorian calendar, a list was drawn up of domestic products, implements of agriculture, and domestic animals, to take the place of the lost saints and their festivals. Every Quintidi was dedicated to some animal, every Décadi to some agricultural implement; the rest were devoted to familiar fruits, flowers, and vegetables. For example, take the first decade in Vendémiaire: —

I.	Primidi . .	Grapes.	VI.	Sextidi . .	Balsam.
II.	Duodi . . .	Buckwheat.	VII.	Septidi . .	Carrots.
III.	Tridi . . .	Chestnuts.	VIII.	Octidi . . .	Amaranth.
IV.	Quartidi . .	Colchicum.	IX.	Nonidi . .	Parsley.
V.	Quintidi . .	The horse.	X.	Décadi . .	The tub.

Modern republican historians, apparently ashamed of this fantastic folly, pass it over with slight mention; as a matter of fact, it lasted but a very short time, — long enough, however, for many republican enthusiasts, when the mania for turning Jacques and Pierres into Timoleons, Catos, Brutuses, and the like was dying out, called their children after the herbs and animals dedicated to the day on which they were born. Thus, General Doppet was Pervenche (Periwinkle) Doppet; General Peyron, Myrte (Myrtle) Peyron; General Lamier, Peuplier (Poplar) Lamier, and so on. But the most ardent Jacobin would surely have drawn the line at the names of Parsley, Pumpkin, Carrot, Turnip, Onion, Asparagus, and Dandelion, which in French slang have all an offensive significance.

The new calendar was, however, never acceptable to the French nation, partly because whatever latent piety there was in France — and it is now known that there was far more than is currently believed — was offended by the ostentatious repudiation in it of every trace of religion, but there was an even stronger reason for the unpopularity of the new arrangement. From time immemorial Sunday had been a holiday in France. The claims of religion having been acknowledged by attendance at mass in the early part of the day, the hours remaining had been given up to festivity. The new distribution of time gave only three holidays instead of four in every month, — holidays that were to be devoted to the "contemplation and commemoration of abstract ideas."

In the early days of the Revolution Mirabeau had warned his colleagues that if they attempted to abolish Christianity they would inevitably prepare the way for the annihilation of their work and themselves. The event proved the correctness of this anticipation. The work of completely de-Christianizing the Republic had hardly begun when Robespierre and his fellows were sent to the guillotine.

When fairly in working order, the new calendar, scientifically perfect though it was supposed to be, was found full of inconveniences by the public; for instance, there was the necessity of dating many things twice over, — once to comply with the law of the Republic, and again to be intelligible to the outside world. Of course, it might be highly gratifying to some to date a legal document "10 Messidor, An II.," but in practice it was rather inconvenient to ransack one's memory or one's arithmetic, or refer to an almanac, to find out that the rest of the world knew the date only as June 28, 1794.

Napoleon, who was certainly not wanting in common sense, speedily made this discovery, and had not been long consul before he resolved on a reform. When, in April, 1801, freedom of worship was restored, and it ceased to be a crime to say one's prayers in public[1] the first step was taken by the revival of Sunday. The Décadi was not abolished, but on Sundays the public offices were closed whether they agreed with the Décadi or not, — an arrangement which commonly led to the observance of both days. The change was universally popular. The churches were thronged on Sunday mornings, and the old merry-making of the afternoon and evening, never wholly suppressed, was renewed with more vigor than ever. When the Empire was firmly established on the 15 Fructidor, An XIII. (Sept. 2, 1805), the Senate restored the calendar as it existed before the law of October, 1793. The calendar of the Revolution had nominally lasted fourteen years, but, as it was not brought into operation until Oct. 12, 1793, its actual life was barely twelve years. During that limited space of time, however, it created a perfectly unequalled amount of trouble and inconvenience. It may be doubted whether any human invention has ever given a thousandth part of the annoyance to inoffensive people that has been caused by the scientific

[1] Mr. Griffith says (see page 63) that when he returned to France, in April, 1795, after the fall of Robespierre, he found the churches in Northern France open and thronged.

idea of Romme and his coadjutor Fabre, the poetaster and stock-jobber.

Episode Fourth. — "Which?"

One of François Coppée's charming little poems commemorates an action not without many parallels in those terrible days when men and women waited in prison for death. I translated it, and it was published in "Lippincott's Magazine," August, 1884. It is in my Scrapbook, and I insert in here: —

Which?

Scene. — The Conciergerie. Time. — Thermidor.
Two hundred prisoners lay there, waiting for
Judicial butchery. As, in the hall, their feet
Paced up and down, Death's huge flail seemed to beat
On the last ears of harvest. Big with fate,
Clouds lowered over Paris. The *coupe-tête*
Sweated and toiled; and yet two hundred lay
Ready, expectant, innocent. — Each day
A coarse, fierce, cruel, brutal man appeared
Smoking a pipe, removed it, stroked his beard,
And, spelling over the day's list, called out
Name after name, pronounced half wrong, no doubt.
These were the victims named for that day's cart.
Each rose at once, calm, ready to depart,
Without a shudder — without groan or tear.
Each one embraced his friends, and answered, "Here!"
What use to tremble at a daily call?
Death stood so near — was so well known to all!
Men of low birth and men of lineage high
Walked with an equal fortitude — to die.
All brave alike — noble or Girondist.

It chanced the jailer with the fatal list,
Reading it out to the sad crowd one day,
Called out one name distinctly, "Charles Leguay!"
Two men at once stepped forward side by side.
"Present!" two voices to his call replied.
He burst out laughing.
"I can pick and choose!"

One was a *bourgeois*, old, in square-toed shoes,
Cold and respectable, with powdered wig;
Of some provincial law-court the last twig;

Ex-deputy of the Third Estate, perchance.
The other, with calm brow and fiery glance,
Was a young, handsome officer, — still dressed
In his torn uniform.
"Ha! Ha! I'm blest
But this is funny," roared the man who read
The daily death-list. Then he stopped and said:

"Have both got the same name, — the two of you?"

"We are both ready."
"No; that will not do,"
Replied the jailer. "One's enough for me.
Explain yourselves. I'll settle it. Let's see."

But both were Charles; both bore the name Leguay;
Each had been sentenced the preceding day.

The jailer rolled his eyes and scratched his head.
"The devil take me if I know," he said,
"Which of the two of you I'd better pick.
Here, citizens, you settle it; but be quick,
For Sanson don't like waiting for his cart."

The young man drew the elder man apart.
Few words sufficed. Two questions, and no more.
"Married?"
"Ah! yes."
"How many children?"
"Four."
"Well! — are you ready? Speak, — which is to die?"
"*Marchons!*" the officer replied, — "'t is I!"

Episode Fifth. — Dogs in the Revolution.

We have seen how poor Brount, the Danish dog of Robespierre, followed his master's stretcher, when, wounded, he was carried into the great Hall of the Tuileries, then appropriated to the Committee of Public Safety, and when men gloried in his sufferings, insulted him, pricked him with knives, and spat on him, the dog stayed faithful. Probably he was separated from his master at the door of the Conciergerie. One would like to know what became of him. Did he find his way home to the Rue St. Honoré? and did the same hands that fed, tended, and caressed Robespierre's parrot extend the same kindness to his dog?

One hundred years after this period[1] M. Lozé, a deputy in the French Chamber, whom Parisians call *le canicide*, revived against the dogs of Paris the same barbarous ordinances directed against them in 1792 by the Commander-in-Chief of the National Guard, the celebrated brewer, Santerre, who declared war, a merciless war, against all dogs and cats in "the departments of Paris."

Shortly before, one of the petty states of Germany, that of the Prince of Œttingen, had embarked on a similar crusade. The Chevalier de Lang tells us in his memoirs that the Council of State in that tiny principality seriously discussed the advisability of destroying all the dogs in Œttingen. As a preliminary, officials were to take a census of all dogs, stating each dog's name, his appearance, his age, his breed, and what use was made of him. History, however, further informs us that the prince's scheme fell through.

In Paris, General Santerre was not more fortunate. It is true that the dread of hydrophobia was not then invented. Newspapers had not terrified whole neighborhoods by accounts of horrible experiences, infernal sufferings, and touching cases of inoculation by Pasteur. Santerre had other charges to bring against dogs, and even "harmless necessary cats." France was menaced by all Europe at that moment; Paris might be considered in a state of siege. The troubles arising out of the Revolution and the advance of the allied armies might cut off supplies. A vision of frightful famine rose before Santerre; and he, being a patriot of forethought, calculated how many dogs there were in Paris, and how many cats, all superfluous consumers, and he argued that it would be right to get rid of them, that they might not devour food that could be eaten by citizens.

He stated to the Commune that the food consumed by cats and dogs would probably sustain fifteen hundred persons; it was equal to the loss of ten sacks of flour a day. The dogs and cats were useless mouths, and therefore the Commune should destroy them.

Santerre was a general: he drew up accordingly a plan of

[1] "Supplément Littéraire du Figaro," Nov 12, 1892.

campaign against the foes whom he denounced. Dogs and cats were to be hunted down, arrested, or killed in the streets; but it would be proper also to make sure that the proscribed animals did not take refuge in houses, where many old maids might try to protect with all the energy of despair, the dear companions of their loneliness, their beloved, their cherished, their adored poodles and pussy cats. It would be necessary for the Convention to decree domiciliary visits to hunt for cats and dogs. The National Guard ought to be called out to assist in the work of their destruction.

Santerre had unfortunately not foreseen that an almost unanimous public opinion would condemn his plan of campaign as soon as he announced it to the Convention. The press protested against it, just as, a hundred years later, it protested against the cruel proposals of M. Lozé.

"Dogs and cats," wrote a journalist of the period, "will contrive to make good their escape from General Santerre, and find refuge in places where he cannot get at them. Added to which, these creatures, — born republicans, — who sleep with one eye open, and if possible near an unclosed door, will at the slightest noise make for the roofs and the gutters, and what National Guard is so active as to be able to follow them and catch them there? No, — pardon us for saying it, — but animals know better how to preserve their freedom than men."

By degrees public opinion became greatly excited. The measures proposed by Santerre were said to smack of the Bastille and the Inquisition; the pets of the people were to be excommunicated. Santerre's plan was reactionary, worthy of the days of despotism and of dense superstition. Prud'homme, in his "Révolutions de Paris," thus vigorously denounced it.

"Alas for such dogs and cats," he cried, "as may dare to protest in their own language against the decrees of Santerre! for why should they be refused the right to make their humble petition against the cruel injustice and gratuitous barbarity which he proposes to exercise against them. They will say: 'Brave general, has not your famous expedition into

La Vendée covered you sufficiently with glory?[1] Why must you try to make yourself more famous at the expense of dogs and cats, who have never conspired against any creatures save the citizen's domestic enemies? But gentlemen of the Council of the Twelve, of whom you are the right arm, tell us that "this *canaille* consumes each day ten sacks of flour." Never was so much noise made about ten sacks of flour, even when the mill was grinding it! Has the great Chabot forgotten the services that cats rendered to him when he was shut up in his cell as a Capuchin? Did they not free him from the rats who wanted to share that cell with him? But for the cats they might have followed him into the Committee of Public Safety. Let Chabot give the order, — cats will fight rats still. They say that a beard is a sign of wisdom. Ah, M. Chabot, why did you shave off yours?'"

Good reasons for not interfering with dogs and cats rained down on the authorities. "If you exterminate the cats, mice and rats will replace them as consumers. They will destroy incalculably more grain in the corn market and in the bakeries. That loss will be more than General Santerre's ten sacks of flour a day."

Never was it demonstrated with deeper feeling that dogs are the friends of man. It was asked if dogs had not rendered great services in besieged cities. "Instead of being useless consumers of food," pleaded some of the most practical journalists, "dogs often increase the food supply in a besieged city. In case of extremity may not man turn even his brave friends to advantage by sending them to the slaughter-house? As to cats, more than one patriot must have known by experience that they make sundry succulent dishes."

Some economists took pains to prove that for food purposes dogs and cats were worth more to Paris than the ten sacks of flour a day that Santerre protested they consumed.

"Every Sunday," said the "Révolutions de Paris," "there is at least one *pain bénit*" (one loaf of blessed bread) "in every parish in the city. This *pain bénit*, made formerly of

[1] Santerre failed ignominiously in his campaign against the Chouans.

the finest wheat flour, and almost like cake, is now, it is true, nothing more than common bread, but it is *bread*, and each loaf weighs about four pounds. Now at this moment there are at least fifty thousand municipalities in France; if each has two parishes, — and that calculation is under the mark, — it would make one hundred thousand loaves a week of four pounds each: one million pounds of bread each month snatched from general consumption, lost to the community. . . . To do away with such 'blessed loaves,' and so save thirty millions of pounds of bread, would be a meritorious work, worthy of good citizens."

What answer could be made to such triumphant arguments and calculations? The suppression of *pains bénits* would be certainly an economy that would fully compensate for the loss of the ten sacks of flour bemoaned by the patriotic general.

Another patriot, an enemy of luxurious habits, suggested a better way of saving flour. "Let men and women give up," he cried, "the practice of loading their heads with hair-powder. Let us not waste what may hereafter be to us of prime necessity; and let us deserve the benefits of nature by the use that we make of them. Let *citoyens* and *citoyennes* deny themselves hair-powder and keep their cats and dogs. Women will not look the less charming, and men will seem more manly."

So many arguments, protestations, calculations, remonstrances, and suggested sacrifices could not but outweigh the zeal of Santerre. Before long no more was heard of the slaughter of domestic animals.

Thus while cannon thundered on the frontier, and republican France put forth all her energies to defend her soil; whilst the prisons that had become antechambers to the scaffold were crowded with men and women, and the pavements of the capital were still wet with innocent blood, Paris — Great Paris, even in 1792 — had one soft spot in its heart, and succeeded in saving from slaughter, denunciation, and proscription its amorous tomcats and its curly poodles!

BOOK V.

THE CLERGY OF FRANCE DURING THE REVOLUTION.

I. Exiles for Conscience' Sake.
II. A Conventional Bishop.
III. A Protestant Pastor.

CHAPTER I.

EXILES FOR CONSCIENCE' SAKE.[1]

BY a decree of the Convention, on the 2d of November, 1789, church property was confiscated for the benefit of the State. Bishops and parish priests were to be paid by salaries from the government (as is the case in France at the present day). In many instances this gave a better stipend to the working clergy than they had enjoyed under the old system, while the vast wealth of the higher clergy and of the religious houses was treated as public property, and fell into the hands of the State. During the discussion of this measure it was proposed to go further, and remodel the whole constitution and legal status of the clergy of France. This was accordingly done, and the measures enacted formed what was called *La Constitution Civile.*

The main articles of this "civil constitution" may be briefly stated: "The number of bishoprics was to be reduced, and each diocese was to be conterminous with the newly designated department in which it was situated. Bishops and clergy were also to be elected in accordance with certain democratic forms which were enumerated. But

[1] Taken chiefly from an article published in the "National Review" and reprinted in "Littell's Living Age," Dec. 8, 1888.

these changes troubled the consciences of men who held themselves bound by their vows of consecration and ordination to oppose all change. A bishop could not canonically abandon his see or any part of it, nor intrude his jurisdiction into any part of the see of his neighbor. The only power which could solve this difficulty was that of the Pope, whose sanction was also needed to enable a priest to accept with a clear conscience many other changes included in the *constitution civile*, one clause of which forbade a bishop to apply in person to the Pope for consecration, though he was permitted to write to him, not as his spiritual superior, but only in testimony of the unity of faith and the communion he was bound to maintain with him." The eager reformers in the Constituent Assembly could not, however, wait till this matter should be submitted to the Pope, nor did they, indeed, desire his intervention. The oath required of all bishops and clergy who desired to retain their sees or cures, and to receive salaries from government for their support, was brief, but extraordinarily comprehensive: "I swear to be faithful to the nation and to the laws."

To take such an oath, as it were, on the spur of the moment and at the bidding of the leaders of the Revolutionary party, was an act very impulsive and very daring. The constitution of the Church might indeed be settled by the adoption of the *constitution civile;* but what man who took the oath could know to what he might be binding himself while the laws of the country remained unsettled, and the new constitution for France, to make which the Constituent Assembly had been summoned, was yet unborn? Most men have an objection to taking oaths when they are uncertain to what they commit themselves. At any moment an unfavorable answer might arrive from the Holy Pontiff, and the clergy who had taken the oath would then find themselves placed in a difficult position. Thousands refused it, and threw up their means of livelihood. The bishops almost unanimously declined to accept the constitution, and the Pope repudiated it. Then began the proscription and persecution, not only of the priests *non-assermentés*, but of all who refused to accept the offices of religion from those forsworn ecclesiastics, whom they looked upon as instruments of the devil.

The horrors of 1793 drew on apace. Under the Legislative Assembly France called itself a republic, but had practically no settled form of government. Priests were in those days the especial objects of the fury of the population of Paris, who called themselves "the people," and fear filled the hearts of all those who, in calmer times, would at once have put mob rule down. Priests were hunted to death in the streets and massacred in prisons; almost all who could get away escaped from France through perils of every description.

Not long after came an open declaration of atheism on the part of the new French Republic. To make any open profession of belief in God was *lèse civisme.* As one of the exiled clergy writes, —

"The cathedrals and parish churches were stripped of their ornaments, and taken possession of by the rabble. . . . The statues of our Blessed Lord and of His Mother were thrown down and trampled underfoot, while busts of the most repulsive and blaspheming Revolutionists were elevated and honored in their stead."

One Revolutionist ostentatiously asserted that though he had lived the victim of superstition, he would no longer remain its slave. "I know," he exclaimed, "no other worship than that of Liberty; no other religion than that of Humanity and Country." Jean Baptiste Gobel, the apostate Bishop of Paris, declared, "I submit to the omnipotent will of the People. There ought to be no national worship at all, except that of Liberty and sacred Equality, as the sovereign people wish it to be. From henceforth therefore I renounce and repudiate the Christian Religion."

As a direct consequence of such blasphemy and national impiety, Sunday was abolished; the church bells were silenced; children remained unbaptized; marriage, as a sacrament, or as a Christian rite, was abolished; the sick received no sacred consolation, the dead no religious rites. The clergy were everywhere abused, seized, imprisoned, put to death. Much that was then done to insult and to put down religion finds no place in books of history. Private letters from eye-witnesses have described what then took place. No words, however, can truly depict the horrors of that awful Reign of Terror. One direct consequence was that during the course of six years, beginning in the autumn of 1792, no less than eight thousand of the French clergy — some at one period, and others later, including archbishops, bishops, dignitaries, parish priests, and ecclesiastical students — escaped to England, impoverished, ruined, starving. George III. gave up to them the old Royal Palace at Winchester (since burned to the ground), where nine hundred of these exiled ecclesiastics were housed, and provided with food, clothing, and the common necessaries of life. On Michaelmas Day (September 29), 1792, a "Committee of Relief" was formed in London for the whole country. Among the noblemen and gentlemen who gave it their assistance were William Wilberforce, the Marquis of Buckingham, the Bishops of London and Durham, Henry Thornton of Clapham, and many others, — all men of influence and position, whose names are known even beyond their own country.

The appeals of the committee were widely circulated, and monetary assistance came in at once, for the exiles, in hundreds of cases, owned nothing whatsoever but the clothes in which they stood, a breviary, a pair of spectacles, a skull-cap, a snuff-box, a little money in their purses, and a cloak or a wrapper. Before Christmas, however, temporary relief and food had been provided for nearly four thousand more of the exiled clergy, who landed in ports of England on the British Channel. In many places the country gentry and clergy of the Established Church at once enlisted their neighbors in aid of the strangers, and with no delay sent liberal benevolences in money for their assistance. Several country houses in different localities were offered to the committee in order to provide immediate shelter for those in need.

Nothing could exceed the zeal and charity of all the members of the committee, whose affairs were largely conducted by Dr. Dampier, a gentleman of French extraction, afterwards Bishop of Rochester and Ely. Wilberforce and Thornton, leaders of the evangelical party, were very active; so were Dr. Walter King, afterwards Bishop of Rochester, Dr. Beilby Porteus, Bishop of London, and the Bishop of Durham. The Archbishop of Canterbury was thought somewhat tardy in his actions, but afterwards gave good reasons for delay.

For some months the exiles were provided for by private munificence; but on Sunday, April 19, 1793, a solemn service for the occasion was appointed, sermons were preached, and alms gathered in every church and chapel throughout England and Wales by direct command of his Majesty. This would have taken place earlier had not the Archbishop of Canterbury held it to be more discreet for the prelates of the Established Church to follow in this matter, rather than seek to lead. Everywhere the subscriptions and gifts were large in number, and, considering the poverty then prevailing in the country, they were considerable in amount.

Mrs. Hannah More, then in the height of her popularity, addressed a letter, touching in its simplicity and truth, to "The Ladies of England," which did much good. Oxford and Cambridge, the chapters of some of the cathedrals, and the London College of Physicians, contributed very considerable sums.

Later on a grant from government, personally suggested by the king and recommended by Mr. Pitt, was made, in order to house, clothe, and feed the French exiles. It has been calculated that from 1793 to 1795 £120,000 was expended on this work from the public exchequer.

At the close of 1793, there were 4,068 priests receiving from the English government £7,830 a month, and this in addition to funds raised in churches or by private benevolence. The government likewise made itself responsible for the support of 375 lay persons at the same period, expending for this object £560 a month.

The exiles, scattered through the Southern, Eastern, and Midland counties of England, were received with kindness and favor by the country gentry, and in many houses they were welcome guests. "I cannot forget," wrote the Rev. Thomas Bowdler, "that these clergymen are men who have given up everything which they possessed, and everything to which they looked forward for their support in this world, rather than abandon their duty to God, by taking an oath which they conceived would be perjury."

Meantime the conduct of these exiles showed, according to the same authority, "that they were truly sensible of the unparalleled kindness they received in England, for which they could make no return but by their prayers and good conduct." Many nuns during the year 1795, who had escaped from France to Holland, came over to England, where they were welcomed and supported.

Once or twice the strong Protestant feeling in England was the occasion of trifling difficulties, one of which led to an investigation by the Committee, who commissioned a prebendary of Winchester, Dr. Henry Sturges, to inquire into the controversy. He did so, and on March 23, 1796, reported as follows concerning the nine hundred priests lodged in the King's House: "I confess I have considered their general conduct as exemplary in the highest degree. I have upon all occasions, and to all persons, given this testimony, that during their continuance here, which is now I think above three years, I have never known any of them to be accused of any behavior unbecoming, and have heard all of them with whom I am well acquainted express in the strongest terms their gratitude for the protection, the relief, and the humanity they have experienced from us." During the five or six years that the exiles remained in England many of them died. Their silent and patiently endured sufferings, anxieties, fears, and sorrows bore them down.

In country churchyards in England may be found many of their graves, recording their constancy and their virtues; for instance, here is an inscription in a cathedral church in Oxfordshire, erected by the warden of New College, to the memory of the Archdeacon of Dol: —

"To the memory of the Rev. Michael Thoumin Desvalpon, aged 62, D.D. and C. L., Archdeacon & Vicar General of Dol in Britany; a Man conspicuous for his Deep Knowledge, and his Moral Virtues. Exiled since 1792 for his Religion and his King; favourably received by the English Nation. Deceased at Obery, March 2, 1798, greatly indebted to the family of Mrs. Davey, & interred in this Church at the request & expense of the Rev. Dr. Gauntlett, Warden of New College, Oxford. R. I. P."

A letter dated Oct. 13, 1798, says: "Before those who returned home left the town of Dorchester in Oxfordshire, they publicly thanked God in the prayers of the Church of England on a day set apart, for His mercies and blessings to them, and acknowledged the hospitalities of the English people. The Vicar preached on the occasion, and a beautiful and touching sermon it was. The French priests revered him greatly. He had buried some of their number in the churchyard, when the services were very solemnly done; and they left him memorials of their affection and respect, both as a friend and as the clergyman of the Parish."

The presence of these men in various parts of England, their high bearing, sound principles, and religious demeanor, tended largely to soften British prejudice against the faith of their forefathers. The strong language of the Edwardian "Homilies," the Armada, Guy Fawkes's conspiracy, and the policy of James II., all, more or less, began to be looked upon from a somewhat different point of view, "when," as Sir Walter Scott most acutely remarked, "so many of the British people beheld the blameless lives and dignified patience of these exiled clergy."

CHAPTER II.

A CONVENTIONAL BISHOP.[1]

THE best-known men of the Revolution are unsatisfactory for several reasons. The Girondists were unpractical pedants, unfit to lead at a time when men of action were imperatively called for, and they received the reward of their pedantry in the almost complete annihilation of their party. Danton, the giant, — according to Carlyle, the statesman after the manner of Comte, — was found wanting in the critical moment, and perished before the narrower, but sterner and more constant, fanaticism of Robespierre. Even the "Incorruptible" himself fell from an originally high ideal, and allowed the guillotine to flow with the blood of men whose chief crime in his eyes was that they were dangerous rivals.

Among all these fanatical, weak, vacillating, or deliberately criminal men, there was one who showed a consistent moral purpose; and who, whether right or wrong, seems to have believed what he said, and to have acted up to his belief, — Henri Grégoire, Bishop of Blois. His earliest biographer has said of him, "that revolutions left him as they found him, — a priest and a republican." We first hear of him as a public man some years before the meeting of the States-General, and he died in the year 1831, just after the Revolution of July which overthrew the restored monarchy. He was an author who published several hundred works on various subjects, as well as a priest and a statesman. The word *vandalism* was invented by him *à propos* of the destruction of works of art by revolutionary fanatics, and his

[1] Abridged from an article in the "Nineteenth Century." Reprinted in "Littell's Living Age," Sept. 23, 1893.

innocent creation was solemnly discussed in Germany by learned patriots, who tried to elucidate the question how far the new word was a true description of the Vandals.

When we first hear of Grégoire he was neither stirring up provinces to enthusiasm for universal reform, nor exerting his powers of oratory in the Palais Royal; he was simply trying to

> "Do the good that 's nearest
> Tho' it 's dull at whiles,
> Helping, when he meets them,
> Lame dogs over stiles."

He was collecting books for his parishioners, trying to raise them from that degrading depth of ignorance to which they had been reduced, and which was to bear terrible fruit not long after.

Grégoire had always been a republican. He tells us himself that while a *curé* in Lorraine, before the Revolution, he was a member of a society the object of which was to bring about the annexation of that province to Switzerland, and so to give it the benefit of the institutions of that little republic. He also warmly espoused the cause of the Jews, oppressed by laws whose barbarity was equalled only by their shortsightedness. He wrote a pamphlet in their favor, and appealed to the enlightenment and common sense of the rulers of Europe. Besides this, he was connected with the *Société des Amis des Noirs*, founded to influence public opinion on the wretched condition of slaves in the colonies, and was subsequently the first man in any country who proposed and carried a law abolishing negro slavery.

Grégoire was sent up to the States-General as a deputy from the clergy of his province. He co-operated with the leaders of the Tiers État, though he did not identify himself with them. For instance, he could not understand a Declaration of Rights unaccompanied by a declaration of duties; and he early saw that the more hot-headed members of the liberal party were proceeding in a way which was likely to overthrow society itself.

GREGOIRE, BISHOP OF BLOIS.

Then came the confiscation of church property, which was to assist in paying the enormous debt that was crushing France. This measure was supported by Grégoire. Then came the proposal to remodel the whole constitution of the clergy in France.

We have already seen that the bishops almost unanimously refused the oath to the *Constitution Civile*, and that the Pope repudiated it. Before this, however, Grégoire in his place as a deputy had pronounced in favor of it. He seems to have seen in it the remedy for crying evils, a means for averting the overthrow of religious institutions; to have thought that the Holy Father would not fail to give it his sanction, and under the circumstances he accepted the Constitution.

"I swear," he said solemnly, speaking from the tribune, "to be faithful to the nation and the laws." ("Whatever laws you may make" being implied.)

Most of the sees being abandoned, new bishops had to be appointed, and Grégoire was offered the bishopric of Blois. He refused at first, but was finally persuaded to accept it, to avoid the bad impression that might result from the refusal of one who had voted for the new constitutional system. His new position involved him in many difficulties, for it made it his duty, as bishop under the Constitution, to force on his diocese as far as possible *prêtres assermentés*, contrary to the wishes and the consciences of those over whom they were appointed to serve. A great number of these clergy were men for whom their bishop could have neither sympathy nor respect. They were unscrupulous time-serving men, and many of them married. As a republican, Grégoire must have felt the system of episcopal tyranny to which he was committed revolting to him.

After the flight to Varennes, Grégoire objected to restoring the king, on condition of his accepting the Constitution. "He will swear, but will not keep his oath," he said. And his prediction was fulfilled a year later.

It was Grégoire who, after the events of the 10th of August, demanded the abolition of royalty. He approved the trial of Louis, but as a preliminary proposed the abolition of the punishment of death, hoping that the ex-king might have the benefit of the law. He was not present when the vote was taken as to the king's death, but with four others he signed a paper approving his condemnation, though, before signing it, he scratched out the words *à mort*. All his life after he defended himself from the charge of having been a regicide, insisting that he had never voted for the death of any man.

Grégoire took no share in the works and ways of the Committee of Public Safety, but he was a member of the Committee of Public Instruction, which among other things created the Conservatoire des Arts et Métiers, the Bureau des Longitudes, and the École Polytechnique. By it also the study of music was organized; the deaf and blind received instruction; a school of medicine was founded; and uniformity of weights and measures was decreed. The absurd new calendar was also its work, but not with the consent of Grégoire, who opposed Romme's substitution of Décadi for Sunday.

While this practical work was being carried on in Grégoire's committee, and while another committee was building up the great code of law which still influences the legal system of half the countries of Europe, under the misleading name of the Code Napoleon, the Convention was engaged in all the wicked, wild, and wayward acts which we associate with what we call the Reign of Terror. It had also to contend with the Commune; that is, the City Government at the Hôtel de Ville, which had control over a gigantic organization of the secret societies and sections, and was a formidable rival to the Convention and the Committee of Public Safety. From the establishment of the Republic to the death of Hébert, the Commune was a continual threat to the existing government. It overthrew the Girondins when they were masters of a majority in the Assembly, and Robespierre himself was only able to crush it by a temporary alliance with Danton. The history of Grégoire is mainly allied with one aspect of this struggle. Hébert and Chaumette, the leaders of the Commune, were avowed atheists. The Convention was inclined to religious toleration, but the leaders of the

Commune were fanatical in their hatred of all religion. For a time they got the upper hand; and the churches in Paris and in some of the provinces were profaned by the disgraceful and puerile scenes known as Feasts of Reason. Many constitutional priests and Protestant ministers were carried away by the movement, and renounced their faith. A mummery, which would be laughable, if it were not so painful, was gone through in the Convention, where Gobel, the Archbishop of Paris, and his chaplains publicly divested themselves of their robes of office, and apologized for their errors against the pure light of "Reason."

Shortly after this Grégoire came into the Chamber. He was greeted with loud cries and told to go to the tribune. "What for?" he asked. "To renounce your religious charlatanism." "Miserable blasphemers! I was never a charlatan. Attached to my religion, I have preached its truths, and I will always be faithful to them."

With these words he ascended the tribune.

"I am here," he said, "having a very vague notion of what has happened in my absence. People speak to me of sacrifices for my country. I am accustomed to make them. Is it a question of attachment to the cause of liberty? I have already given proof of it. Is it a question of the revenue joined to my office of bishop? I abandon it to you without regret. Is it a question of religion? This matter is outside your jurisdiction, and you have no right to approach it. I hear some one speak of fanaticism or superstition. . . . I have always opposed them. . . . As for me, Catholic by conviction, priest by choice, I have been called by the people to be a bishop; I have tried to do some good in my diocese, acting on the sacred principles which are dear to me, and which I defy you to take from me. I remain a bishop to do some more good. I appeal to the principle of liberty of worship."

Grégoire's firmness on this occasion drew down on him the filthy abuse of the atheistical party. His attitude entirely destroyed the effect of the apostasy of the weak and timid Gobel and his friends, who sank into insignificance before the noble resolution of the Bishop of Blois.[1] In the worst of times, when even conventional priests hardly dared to appear in the streets in lay dress, Grégoire continued publicly to wear the clerical habit, and he even presided over the Convention, when it came to be his turn, in episcopal costume. Heaven and earth were moved to get him to abjure, but he stood firm. He was flattered, he was threatened; but he was unmoved.

No class of people heaped more abuse on him than the priests who, for conscience' sake, had been unable to take the oath that he had taken. He returned good for evil, and boldly advocated the cause of religious liberty. By his personal efforts, at a time when men were willing to suspect him on the least opportunity, he obtained the freedom of some non-juring priests, who were herded together in confinement at Rochefort, and were becoming decimated by disease brought on by the unhealthy conditions of their prison. Grégoire got no thanks for this; he did not ask for them. He had done his duty, and that was enough.

The Revolution drew to a close. The Directory was no doubt an attempt at a republican dictatorship, but the idea which it represented was for the moment out of place. The nation only waited for the coming of a master, and it had not to wait long.

Under the Directory Grégoire withdrew to his diocese. He busied himself in its administration and in literary work, and did not re-enter public life until the Consulate was established, when he became a senator under the new *régime*. In this position he constantly opposed every advance of Napoleon. Sometimes he was supported by other republicans; sometimes he stood alone. On the question of giving Napoleon the hereditary title of emperor, Grégoire voted in opposition, with only four others, and his was the one black ball that opposed the establishment of the new nobility.

He disapproved the Concordat signed by the Pope and Napoleon; but when it was signed he submitted to it. He refused, however, to make the declaration imposed on constitutional bishops as a condition of their retaining their sees.

[1] See page 64.

He resigned his bishopric of Blois, and wrote a farewell letter to the faithful in his diocese, exhorting them to obey in all things their new ecclesiastical superior.

He was a consistent opponent of Napoleon's government, but was left unmolested in his retirement, though pursued by calumny from the most opposite quarters. Under the Bourbons his case was worse. The returned *émigrés* called him an "apostate," and men who had been republicans while republicanism was the order of the day hated a man whose life was a continual protest against their own inconsistency.

Grégoire became old and feeble, but he lived until his heart was once more gladdened for a moment by the revolution of 1830. He warned his fellow-countrymen, however, against the re-establishment of monarchy. This was the last public act of his life.

On his death-bed he sent for his parish priest. The priest communicated with the archbishop, who wrote to Grégoire exhorting him to make a retraction, and told the priest to exact it before giving him the last sacraments. Grégoire refused, on the ground that he had nothing which his conscience compelled him to retract. The priest left him; and he was finally driven to seek the assistance of a priest who had always been opposed to him, but in whose Christian charity he felt he could confide. He made his confession, received the last offices of the Church, and prepared to meet his Creator. He died on the 28th of May, 1831, at the age of eighty-one. In his will it was found that he had left four thousand francs to found an annual mass for his calumniators and enemies, dead or living.

He died as he had lived, a Catholic and a republican. He had his faults. Some of his speeches breathe a tone of fanatical republicanism, unsuited to our more mature and scientific point of view. But in this he was the child of his period. If sometimes he was carried away by the swift stream of revolutionary opinion, there were moments when he rose to an almost superhuman height, as when he stood alone in the tribune of the National Convention and fearlessly confessed Almighty God.

CHAPTER III.

A PROTESTANT PASTOR.[1]

JEAN PAUL RABAUT, called Saint-Étienne, was born in 1743, the eldest son of the "Desert Pastor," Paul Rabaut, almost the last survivor of the heroic age of Huguenotism. The "Desert" was the wild region of Languedoc and the Cevennes, where Huguenotism lingered after it had been crushed out of the towns. Every pastor adopted for safety a *nom de Désert*; an *alias*, by which he was known among the faithful. Paul Rabaut had at least a dozen "desert names" of his own, and had given to his three sons in their childhood those of Saint-Étienne, Pommier, and Dupuis. To call them by their father's name would have been to expose them as a prey to the pious kidnappers, to whom the law afforded every facility for taking a child out of the control of Huguenot parents. In 1743, it was more than a half a century since Louis XIV. had turned his "booted apostles" loose upon the Huguenots; but the persecution, though not in its first heat, was still far from being over. Paul Rabaut was a fugitive, hiding in caves and thickets; attempts were made to seize his wife as a hostage, and during a hasty flight her child was born in a barn or stable. Throughout his childhood Jean Paul never knew till supper-time where he would sleep; his father regulated the march, and the children were lodged with the faithful in turn. At the age of eleven he was awaked one morning by a troop of grenadiers demanding entrance to a house where his mother had taken refuge. The next year we find him safe in Geneva, boarding with a refugee pastor, and later on transferred to the Lausanne College which

[1] "Gentleman's Magazine," 1890.

JEAN PAUL RABAUT.

Antoine Court, the "Restorer of the Huguenot Church," had founded for training Desert pastors. Jean Paul's inclination seems to have been towards the bar, but as the professions in France were closed to Huguenots, he resigned himself to entering the ministry. At the age of nineteen he returned to France as a *proposant;* that is, a probationary minister. On crossing the border he was met by the news of the capture and hanging of the pastor Rochette, 1762, and with a request that he would preach his funeral sermon.

"If we knew Rabaut Saint-Étienne's early life," says his friend Boissy d'Anglas, "we should find it as full of perils and heroism as that of any Catholic priest under the Terror;" the records that have come down to us are of more peaceful days. For even then the tide was turning. The "affaire Calas" (only a month later than that of Rochette) enlisted Voltaire's advocacy;[1] and Voltaire ruled the public mind in France. By steps too many to relate, the Protestants of France, like the Roman Catholics of England, reached the stage of tacit toleration. Their wrongs, as represented in a play acted in 1767 before the king, drew tears from a court audience. Their meetings for worship in the stone quarries at Nîmes, where they sat under sunshades and on camp-stools, were winked at by the military authorities, their petitions to provincial governors and parliaments were actually read, and men in high places intimated that it was time to act on them.

Meantime Rabaut Saint-Étienne, rejoicing in the new turn things were taking in 1768, made a love-match, and developed into a preacher of local fame, whose sermons on the marriage and coronation of Louis XVI. were commended even by Catholics, and whom the Duke of Gloucester, brother of George III., when passing through Languedoc, came in state to hear. Rabaut about this time drew up a petition for the Huguenot galley-slaves, and subsequently

[1] For a history of the "affaire Calas," the dreadful prosecution of a respectable Protestant tradesman and his family for an imaginary crime, see an article, republished in "Littell's Living Age," Vol. 59.

published a sort of autobiographical novel in London, on the trials of a pastor in the Cevennes.

Next Rabaut wrote a pamphlet called "Homage to the Memory of the late Bishop of Nîmes," saying in its introduction that "it is lawful to praise those when dead whom we would not have praised when living."

The tolerance and moderation of a Huguenot of that age (of which Rabaut furnished twenty examples) are the more to be admired when we consider what was still his legal position, — illegitimated, excluded from the professions, and in strict law liable to death on the gallows.

Such was the state of things in France when Lafayette, fresh from America, and with his head full of liberty and equal justice, visited Nîmes, and introduced himself to the Rabaut household. "The hero of two worlds pressed in his arms the venerable Desert pastor," and urged the pastor's eldest son to come to Paris, and plead the Protestant cause with the king's new ministers. Rabaut Saint-Etienne responded eagerly; his flock subscribed to pay for his journey, — not without qualms as to the dangers of *lettres de cachet* and kidnappers on the road, — but the Paris world gave a warm reception to the *protégé* of its hero. Counts and marquises were amazed to find in this "child of the Desert" a civilized man, with powdered hair and a starched neckcloth, a classical scholar, a philosopher, well read in the works of the Encyclopedists, and of Gibbon and Bacon, and even an elegant poet, who turned odes easily, and had on hand, it was whispered, an epic poem on Charles Martel. The cause he advocated was enthusiastically adopted. Ministers, academicians, and even a bishop showed themselves well-disposed to the Protestants, and in the autumn of 1787 an edict was passed, granting to "non-Catholics" the right to live in France, and there exercise a profession or trade, to contract civil marriages, and register their births and burials. The king proposed the measure, and after some opposition the Parliament of Paris registered it. "You will easily judge," wrote Lafayette to Washington, "with what pleasure I presented last Sunday at a ministerial table the first Protestant ecclesiastic who has been seen at Versailles since the Revocation of 1685."

The Protestants, with joyful and grateful hearts, flocked to insure their legal status; in some cases old men came to register the births of three generations, — father, child, and grandchild. These boons were granted to Protestants under the old *régime*, and there is no knowing, say some, what further reforms the king might have made if his subjects would have left him free to make them.

Rabaut adorned his room with a portrait of Lafayette, inscribed in large gold letters, "My Hero," and returned to Languedoc (March, 1788) to preach a sermon on "Render unto Cæsar, etc.," which was remembered by hearers who were living in 1850. He was now the greatest man in Nîmes, and that not only with his own flock. He had made a name among the *savants*; his new book, on primitive Greek history, had been commended by the learned Bailly, and he had also added one to the twenty-five hundred and odd pamphlets in circulation, concerning the coming States-General. The Tiers Etat of Nîmes elected him first of its eight deputies to that Assembly; from that day his clerical life was over, and his political life began.

Rabaut took part in drawing up the Declaration of Rights, — so soon to be set at nought in every particular. Mainly by his influence liberty of worship was made an especial clause in the Declaration. Only civil rights had been granted to non-Catholics before. The Protestants of Paris, who had hitherto met in a wine-merchant's parlor,[1] now removed to the church of St. Louis of the Louvre, and all the town marvelled to see heretics walk unmolested to their *prêche*, at a time when priests who had not taken the oath (*papistes* they were called in the language of the day) could not appear in the streets without danger and insult.

In March, 1790, Rabaut was chosen President of the Assembly for one fortnight, as was the custom. "How this

[1] See "The Dean of Killerine," a novel by the Abbé Prévost (1735), translated by me, and republished in "Littell's Living Age," 1894. — E. W. L.

would astonish Louis XIV.!" he said, when acknowledging the honor; and to his father he wrote: "The President of the National Assembly is at your feet."

We pass over events already touched upon in 1790, 1791, and early in 1792. In the closing months of that year all lesser matters were swallowed up in the great question whether the king should or should not be brought to trial before the Convention; and against this, Rabaut set himself far too strongly for prudence. His most celebrated speech — and that which ruined him — was made in a vain endeavor to avert the trial, or at least to have it conducted with legal forms and before a properly appointed tribunal. He spoke thus on the subject in the Assembly: —

"You say that it is no new thing for you to pronounce judgment. I reply that that is just what I complain of. I, for one, am sick of my share of despotism. I am fatigued, harassed, tormented by the despotism in which I take part; and I sigh for the moment when a national tribunal shall relieve me of the form and countenance of a tyrant. [*Murmurs.*] . . . History blames the English, not that they judged their king, but that the Commons, secretly pushed forward by *Cromwell* [*Redoubled murmurs, for every one knew that the Cromwell pointed at was Robespierre.*] had usurped the right of judging; that they set at nought the legal forms; that they declared themselves exponents of the will of a people whom they had never consulted. And this very people — the people of London — who were said to have so pressed for the death of the king were the first to curse his judges and to bow before his successor. The City of London feasted the restored Charles II.; the people displayed riotous joy and crowded round the scaffolds of these very judges sacrificed by Charles to the shade of his father. People of Paris, Parliament of France, have you understood me? . . .

"Louis dead will be more dangerous than Louis living," he urged for the last time, after giving his vote for the mild sentence of: "Detention during the war, and banishment afterwards." "I would fain see my countrymen not savage tigers, but disdainful lions!" He had tried to enlist his friends on the side of mercy, but it would appear with small success, since he could not persuade his own brother to anything more decided than: "Death with respite," — a miserable subterfuge. Out of seven Protestant pastors in the Assembly four were regicides, and but one voted with Rabaut.

Rabaut's fortunes were now past mending. His efforts to save the king had cost him his place on the "Moniteur," and that paper was anxious to disclaim all connection with one who, as Camille Desmoulins asserted, had been "charged to poison public opinion."

The tragedy of the Girondins was now beginning, and Rabaut had to play his part as one of the fated victims. It was remembered that he had been the *protégé* of Lafayette, — Lafayette, who was now outlawed and a fugitive, — that he was friendly to the equally abhorred Bailly, that he had been "a creature of Roland," and (even this is gravely noted in Robespierre's papers) that in old days at Nîmes, he had got up a subscription for a book by one Rousin, who had lately come out with a drama of Fayettist tendencies. Jacobin orators, once so ready to play off Protestant against Catholic, now contemptuously hinted that one kind of priest was as bad as another. But the crowning sin charged upon poor Rabaut was that of making faces, with set purpose to put Robespierre out of countenance during one of his best speeches.

Rabaut's fall dates actually from May 18, 1793, the beginning of a week of riot and confusion in the Assembly. Rabaut was chairman of a Committee of Twelve charged to make up a report on the situation. This report he presented on the last day of May, but as it was understood that it would demand the expulsion of certain deputies in the Assembly, and recommend, in short, a *purgation pridienne* — that is, Pride's Purge — of the Assembly, he was never suffered to read it. Rabaut, with five of his colleagues, had spent the previous night, two in a bed, in a house in an obscure faubourg, with doors barred and pistols and swords in readiness, in case of attack. At three in the morning they were roused by the tocsin calling out the Sections. We should like to believe the story that Rabaut, once more acting in his old capacity as pastor, knelt and prayed aloud for France and for the party of law and order, and by his Christian confidence kept up the hearts of his more skeptical companions; but for want of contemporary evidence, we fear we must set down the story as one of Lamartine's little embellishments.

After persistent but vain efforts to read his report the next day to the Assembly, Rabaut shouted: "You refuse to hear it, because you know it would accuse you." At this there arose "an indescribable tumult," in the midst of which a kindly doorkeeper helped Rabaut to slip out, and the rest of the Girondins seem to have followed his example.

On June 2, Rabaut and twenty of his Girondin colleagues were dining with the deputy Meillan, who went to and fro, keeping them informed of what was taking place in Paris, when Rabaut's brother, Pommier, rushed in, crying: "*Sauve qui peut! Sauve qui peut!*" The danger was imminent; the Girondins embraced each other, and did as he advised.

Rabaut, having secured his papers, sought refuge in the house of Miss Helen Maria Williams, and there gave himself up to despair, less for the almost certain loss of his own life than for that of his country's liberty. His name appeared on the list of deputies "who could not be placed under arrest as not being in their domicile." And he was denounced as "that tartuffe Rabaut."

From the house of Miss Williams, Rabaut went to that of a Nîmes Protestant at Versailles. Thence he contrived to send his rejected report to Nîmes, where it was printed, to the intense indignation of the Assembly which it accused. A southern "Federation of seventy-three respectable cities" was formed in the south of France to oppose the domination of the capital, and an enthusiastic reception was given to Rabaut; but the next day the Sectional Assembly at Nîmes retracted all its measures, and declared itself "no longer in a state of resistance to oppression."

Rabaut's supporters fled to Switzerland, and he himself got

back to Paris; there a Catholic from Nîmes, M. Étienne Peyssac, or De Peyssac, a clerk in the government service, remembering old obligations to Rabaut *père*, received into his house the persecuted man and his brother. Here the two walled off with their own hands the end of their host's bedroom for a secret chamber, employing a skilled carpenter to make the door, which was concealed by a book-case placed against it, and here they lay concealed over four months, letting their beards grow, and employing themselves in writing historical letters in continuation of their "Pièces de la Révolution."

Meantime the trial of the Girondins took place. The accused were, of course, all found guilty, and the twenty-one who were actually in the hands of the Revolutionary Tribunal were duly sent to the guillotine.

All through November, 1793, while the guillotine was hard at work shearing off heads (Philippe Égalité's and Madame Roland's amongst others), it was the fashion for apostate Catholic priests publicly to embrace apostate Protestant pastors, and Protestant chalices lay heaped with Catholic pyxes and monstrances before the altar of the Goddess of Reason, ready for the melting pot. Many thought that had Rabaut been at large during those days of grotesque horror, while he lay safe in his hiding-place, Bishop Grégoire would not have stood alone in his courageous protest against apostasy.

The tide of godless fanaticism was just beginning to turn, and Robespierre, through jealousy of Hébert, was appearing almost as the champion of a religious revival, when the end to Rabaut came. On Dec. 4, 1793, Amar, who had acted as public accuser in the trial of the Girondins, announced to the Assembly the capture of the two Protestant brothers.

Who betrayed their hiding-place? It was never surely known. Some said a maidservant; some said the carpenter who had made their door, either through inadvertence or through fear. One story says that, having had a job given him by De Peyssac in the Chamber of the Committee of Public Safety, he overheard such threats against the proscribed and those who concealed them, that for his own safety's sake he gave information. Another account says that Fabre d'Églantine, "powerful, but trembling," thought it might be well to have a secret chamber ready for himself in case of a reverse of fortune, and sounded the carpenter, the best of his trade in Paris. The man understood at once what he wanted. "Oh, yes, citizen! I made a place like that at the Citizen Peyssac's, that I defy any one to find out." Fabre, says the story, went straight and gave information to the Committee of Public Safety.

Another version tells us that the capture was due to Amar himself. He had been an old friend of Rabaut's, and meeting Madame Rabaut in the street, pressed her to urge her husband to take refuge in his house. The Rabauts were glad to relieve Peyssac and his family of charge and danger; an hour of the night was appointed for the removal; Amar entered the house of Peyssac at the head of a party of guards, and the brothers were arrested.

Rabaut was an outlaw *hors la loi*, and no trial was needed. There was, of course, no mercy for a man who had incurred the personal hatred of Robespierre; but one of the few who lived to tell what Fouquier-Tinville's tribunal was like, has told us something of his last moments.

"I was much impressed," says this eye-witness, "with Rabaut de Saint-Étienne. He was condemned the same day that I was interrogated. My hands were bound as a sign of condemnation, and I was led out to wait for the cart. Rabaut came next. He exclaimed, 'I know it now, this tribunal of blood, these judges, these hangmen, who stain with blood the Republic.' 'Hold thy tongue!' cried a gendarme, 'do as this young man does who is condemned like thee, and takes it quietly.' I was about to protest, but Rabaut forestalled me. '*Eh, mon ami!*' he said, 'soon they will not trouble to hear the accused. We are in the hands of murderers.' I was dragged to the wicket. They were about to cut my hair for the guillotine. Rabaut joined his voice to mine, to plead that I was not yet condemned. A turnkey confirmed the fact, and I was removed. Rabaut kissed me.

I see yet his eyes gleam with horror at this new kind of crime, and he forgot that which was being committed against himself, in his interest for me."

Rabaut asked leave to bid farewell to his brother, but learning that this would involve sending to Fouquier-Tinville for an order, he declined to keep the cart waiting, saying, "After all, it would but give needless pain to my brother Let us set out."

In his pastoral days Rabaut was noted for being very comforting to the dying. We trust that he was now able to comfort Kersaint, his fellow-sufferer. Both victims died firmly, though in their case, as in that of many others, to the bitterness of death was added the bitterness of public hate and ridicule. Some laughed at Rabaut's unshaven beard, and the mirth had not ended when the knife fell. Death to such a man must have been hard to bear, — harder than for a royalist, who might glory in it as martyrdom. But a Girondin had so loved the Republic!

Peyssac and his wife were guillotined for having sheltered one who was *hors la loi.* Madame Rabaut at Nîmes learned of her husband's death through a news-seller in the street, and, maddened by grief, she shot herself, sitting on the edge of a well, so that drowning completed the work of the pistol.

Old Paul Rabaut, who had wandered thirty years with a price upon his head, and had never been taken, was now pounced upon, partly as being the father of an *émigré*, and partly as being, if not a priest, next door to one. Too infirm to walk, he was set upon an ass, and led through a shouting crowd to the citadel at Nîmes, built by Louis XIV. to overawe the Protestants. Without hope of life, and without desire to live, he applied himself to console his fellow-captives. The fall of Robespierre released him, but he died in three months, and was buried in his own cellar, Christian burial being still prohibited.

Rabaut-Pommier lay long months in the Conciergerie, a prey to all the ailments brought on by damp. He was at last recalled to the Convention with the surviving Girondins, but finally subsided into a pastor of the Reformed Church at

Paris, and died peacefully in 1820. Two of his printed sermons are preserved. One is entitled "Napoleon the Deliverer;" the other is in praise of the "Restoration of the Bourbons." Rabaut-Dupuis, the youngest of the three brothers, met his death in 1808, when snatching a child from the hoofs of a runaway horse. The child lived to be made *Chef de division* of the prefecture of the Gard in 1853, and bore testimony in a local newspaper to Rabaut-Dupuis's heroism and self-devotion.

BOOK VI.

LAFAYETTE AND HIS FAMILY.

I. Lafayette's Career.
II. Deaths of the Ladies of Madame de Lafayette's Family.

CHAPTER I.

LAFAYETTE'S CAREER.[1]

GILBERT MOTIER, Marquis de Lafayette, was descended from one of the noblest and wealthiest families of France. He was born at Chavaniac, Sept. 6, 1757. He was a principal actor in four great revolutions which changed the political face of the world. In his boyhood he was one of Marie Antoinette's court pages; at fifteen he was an officer in the king's Mousquetaires. At sixteen he married the young granddaughter of the Maréchal Duc de Noailles. All the ladies of this family who could be seized upon by the Committee of Public Safety in 1793, were guillotined for their connection with Lafayette, whose unpopularity was excessive throughout France at that period. The touching narrative of their last moments will be found in the succeeding chapter. It had evidently been communicated some years before its publication to Mr. Lever, the Irish novelist, who incorporated it into his delightful narrative of Maurice Tiernay.

Republicanism was in the air that Lafayette breathed at the period of his marriage. He was an enthusiast for "liberty."

[1] Much of this chapter is taken from an account given to me by Mr. George Ticknor, of Boston, who also published it in an article in the "North American Review." It was given to him by Colonel Huger (pronounced *Ujee*), and by Lafayette in 1825, so that it is entirely authentic as to the abortive attempt of evasion at Olmutz.

He heard of the troubles in America, and rich, aristocratic, and but newly married, he resolved to forsake everything to assist the cause of freedom. The American agents in Paris being too poor to send him to America, he fitted out a vessel at his own expense, and landed not far from Charleston, at one of the darkest moments of our Revolutionary struggle.

He disarmed the prejudice of Congress against foreigners by requesting permission to serve at his own expense, and as a volunteer. Congress, however, gave him rank as a major-general.

He became the aide-de-camp, intimate friend, and disciple of General Washington. "Heart and soul he threw himself into the struggle; seven years of his life were devoted to the service of America, bravely fighting her battles as a soldier, and working for her unceasingly as a diplomatist, to secure her recognition by the courts of Europe. Twice during those seven years he revisited France, to plead the cause of liberty with King Louis; and his sovereign yielded to his prayers, and gave the republicans in revolt six thousand troops, and large supplies of clothing, arms, and munitions of war, with which to help in the great struggle."

That struggle over, Lafayette returned to Paris, and became the hero of the day. "His bust, presented by the State of Virginia, was enshrined, with honors, in the Hôtel de Ville. He was crowned with wreaths, cheered by the multitude, and petted by the court. The people regarded him as the champion of liberty, the king as the upholder of the glory of the arms, and of the influence of France."

For some years after his return to his own country Lafayette busied himself in promoting reforms. He advocated the recognition of the civil rights of Jews and Protestants, and emancipation of the blacks in the colonies.

When the Assembly of the Notables met in 1788, Lafayette made the first motion. "I demand," he said, "the suppression of *lettres de cachet*, universal toleration, and the convocation of the States-General." By orders of electors assembled at the Hôtel de Ville, "he organized the National Guard (an organization rarely on the side of law and

LAFAYETTE.

order), and was made its commander-in-chief. He also, when the Revolutionary party assumed the colors of the city of Paris, added the royal white to red and blue, and prophesied that the tri-color should travel round the world."

How he saved the royal family from utter destruction, — after, however, having exposed them at Versailles to attack, — is a well known matter of history. As the Revolution advanced his popularity declined. Deeply mortified at the failure of his cherished hopes, he resigned his offices and went back to a private station.

When war with Austria and Prussia was declared, however, he came forward to defend the sacred soil of his country. He visited Paris while in high military command to make protest against the rising horrors under the Revolutionary government. He offered Louis XVI. protection as a constitutional king, if he would escape to his army. But the king, mistrusting Lafayette, shilly-shallied, and at last declined. When the royal family was arrested on its way to the frontier to join the more royalist division of the French army commanded by Bouillé, public indignation against Lafayette rose to its height, for he was supposed to have connived at the escape of the king. Commissioners were sent to his camp to inquire into the conduct of the general. He arrested them, and then, since to have faced wild beasts would have been madness, he, attended by a small band of friends, left the camp on horseback. Towards night they came on the advanced guard of the Austrian army. Without declaring their names, they asked permission, as deserters from the French army, to pass through the lines into Holland. Unfortunately, on the frontier of the Grand Duchy of Luxembourg, Lafayette was recognized by one of the *émigré* nobles. The whole party were instantly arrested.

They were consigned to the custody of Prussia, and disgracefully and barbarously she treated them. Loaded with chains they were conveyed in a cart to Magdeburg, lodged, on their way there, in common jails, and insulted by the peasantry. At Magdeburg they were confined for a year in subterranean dungeons; then Lafayette and two others were moved to Moravia, part of the Austrian dominions. Finally, they were placed in separate cells at Olmutz, — cells which they were told that they would never leave; that they would never again hear a human voice; that their very names would never again be mentioned in their presence; that they would only be known by the numbers on their doors. A strong guard was placed on duty. The sentries had orders, on pain of a hundred lashes, to speak no word to the prisoners, and to shoot them dead if they tried to escape. Their furniture was a bed of rotten straw, a chair, and a table. Every precaution was taken; every severity employed. When it rained, water ran through the unglazed loop-holes of their dungeons, wetting them to the skin.

It is not surprising that Lafayette's health failed in such an imprisonment. In consequence of his desertion his estates in France had been confiscated, his wife's relations had been guillotined, and she herself thrown into prison.

In 1794, after the fall of Robespierre, Lally-Tollendal exerted himself to procure means of escape for one to whose services the cause of republicanism was so much indebted. Madame de Lafayette had addressed piteous appeals to Washington. It has always surprised me that no direct action on Lafayette's behalf seems to have been taken by the American government. It shows, however, how marvellous has been the change in the position of the United States within the last hundred years. Stimulated by Lally-Tollendal, Dr. Erick Bollmann, a Hanoverian, undertook the enterprise. He had first to find out the place of Lafayette's imprisonment, which had been kept as much a secret as that of Cœur de Lion.

With great difficulty he ascertained, after nearly a year's search, that a party of French prisoners at Magdeburg had been transferred to an Austrian escort, which had taken the road towards Olmutz in Moravia. He established himself at Olmutz as a traveller in search of health, and there ascertained that several state prisoners were kept in the citadel, with a degree of caution and mystery not unlike that used with the Man in the Iron Mask. He did not doubt that Lafayette must be one of them, and making himself professionally acquainted with the military surgeon of the post, he obtained leave to send some books to his prisoner, Lafayette's failing health having led to some relaxation of severity. He had been allowed light and air, the use of pen and ink, and an occasional drive through the forest of the neighborhood, accompanied by an officer and an escort.

Dr. Bollmann, through the surgeon, sent him some books with a polite note, hoping they might prove interesting. Lafayette, from the tone of the note, suspected it might mean more than it said, and, examining the books with care, discovered marks by which he could carry on a correspondence when returning them to their owner. A plan of escape having been devised, Dr. Bollmann left Olmutz, and went for a time to Vienna. There he communicated his project to Francis Key Huger, who then chanced to be in Austria. Colonel Huger was a member of one of the Huguenot families who, after the Revocation of the Edict of Nantes, settled in South Carolina. His father was a warm personal friend of Lafayette in the days of the Revolutionary War. He entered with enthusiasm into Dr. Bollmann's plot, and together they returned to Olmutz, in the autumn of 1795.

On a certain morning when Lafayette, with an officer beside him and a guard upon the driving seat, was taken out to drive in the forest, Bollmann and Huger, well mounted, followed the carriage. Their preparations had been made. A carriage was in readiness at Hoff, a small town on the frontier. Each carried a pistol, but no other weapon, thinking themselves not justified in committing murder in their attempt. About three miles from the citadel the carriage left the high-road, and passing through a less frequented country, Lafayette was permitted to get out and walk, guarded only by the officer. This was the moment seized by Dr. Bollmann and Huger. They rode up at once. Huger dismounted. "Seize this horse," he cried to Lafayette in English, "and you are free!" The officer at this drew his sword. Lafayette grappled him. The flash of the sword frightened the horse, which broke suddenly away. In a moment Lafayette was mounted on the other horse, Huger calling out to him in English, "Take the road to Hoff!" Lafayette mistook him, and thought he said, "Be off!" He delayed a moment to see if he could assist his rescuers, now striving to capture their loose horse, then went on, then rode back again and asked once more if he could be of any service, and finally, urged anew, galloped slowly away.

Meantime the horse was caught, and Huger jumped up behind Bollmann. But the animal had not been trained, like the other horse, to carry double. It had been intended for Lafayette. They had not gone far when it became restive, plunged, and threw both of them, injuring Bollmann's knee. Again Huger played the hero, remounted his friend, and trusted to his own fleetness. But he was soon captured. Dr. Bollmann easily arrived at Hoff, but there was no Lafayette there. He lingered around till the next night, when he was arrested and carried back to Olmutz. Lafayette, who had taken a wrong road, rode on and on till his horse was exhausted; then he was taken up as a suspicious person, and returned to Olmutz the following day.

All three were brought back separately to the citadel, and neither was permitted to know anything of the others' fate. Colonel Huger was chained to the floor in a small vaulted dungeon, without light, and no food but bread and water. Every six hours the guard entered with a lamp, and examined every brick in his floor and every link in his chain. He implored leave to send a letter to his mother in America, containing only the words "I am alive," but he was refused.

At the end of a year a nobleman, living near their prison, exerted himself in their behalf, and so influenced the tribunal appointed to judge them, that they were sentenced only to a fortnight's additional imprisonment, and were released before orders could arrive from Vienna annulling the proceedings of the court, and ordering a new trial. Bollmann and Huger, however, were by that time safely out of the Austrian dominions.

This account differs in some trifling particulars from

others I have read, but I had it from Mr. Ticknor, of Boston, who had heard all the particulars from Lafayette and Huger.

All former cruelties and rigors were inflicted on the unfortunate Lafayette. During the winter of 1794–95 he was reduced almost to the last extremity by violent fever, and yet was deprived of proper attendance, of air, of suitable food, and of decent clothing. He was made to believe that he was to be publicly executed, but that first Bollmann and Huger would perish on the scaffold in his sight; nor was he permitted to know if his relatives were still alive, or had fallen under the Revolutionary axe, of which, during the few days he was out of prison, he had heard such appalling accounts.

Meantime his wife and his two daughters had, after the fall of Robespierre, found their way to Vienna. There Madame de Lafayette earnestly implored the emperor to let them share her husband's imprisonment. The emperor granted her petition. For sixteen months she and her daughters endured the hardships of imprisonment at Olmutz; then her health gave way, and she asked leave to remove for a week to purer air. She was answered that she might go, but that she could not return. At once she elected at any peril to remain with her husband.

But Europe was now moving in Lafayette's favor. England discussed his imprisonment in the House of Commons, and Napoleon procured the release of the Olmutz captives by the Treaty of Campo Formio, where they were exchanged for the Princess Marie Thérèse, who, after the death of her parents and her aunt, had remained alone in the Temple.

Napoleon never liked Lafayette, who resided beyond the French frontier till 1799, when he settled on his wife's country seat at La Grange, forty miles from Paris, near the Forest of Fontainebleau. Napoleon once offered to send him as French minister to the United States, but Lafayette declined the appointment, not approving Napoleon's views of government. In 1807 he lost his wife, and mourned her deeply for the remainder of his days.

It was his voice, after Waterloo, that first publicly called upon the emperor to abdicate; but when the question arose whether France should make peace with the Allies by surrendering Napoleon's person to his enemies he nobly exclaimed, "I am surprised that in making so odious a proposition to the French Nation you should have addressed yourselves to the prisoner of Olmutz!"

After the Restoration Lafayette lived quietly at La Grange, where all young Americans of promise who visited Europe at that period were received by him. His household was patriarchal. It consisted of his son and his son's wife, his two daughters and their husbands. One daughter had married Latour Maubourg,[1] the aide-de-camp of Lafayette, who had been imprisoned, as he was, in the citadel at Olmutz. The other daughter had married M. de Lasteyrie. Eleven grandchildren were born to Lafayette. He preserved his stately presence to a good old age, but covered his white hairs with a brown wig as he grew older. About 1818 he went back to public life, and was in opposition to the Holy Alliance and the policy of the Bourbons. He actively sympathized with the constitutional revolutions in Spain, Portugal, and Piedmont. He was even deeply concerned in a Carbonaro Conspiracy. He would have been arrested for his connection with this plot had he taken a personal part in it, but, fortunately for him, the day fixed for the outbreak was the anniversary of his wife's death, and he spent it always in the seclusion of her chamber.

Soon after this, in 1824, he was overwhelmed with pressing invitations to revisit America. Congress had even voted that a United States frigate should be kept on the French coast waiting his pleasure. He was very desirous to come over to this country, and he had pecuniary affairs here which needed his attention, but he was a poor man; his patrimonial estates had been confiscated, and, as he said: "I owe debts to the amount of a hundred thousand francs (about $20,000) which must be paid before I can honorably go to another quarter of the world."

[1] Page 179

MME. DE LAFAYETTE.

This sum was accordingly raised among the general's friends in Paris, principally among Americans, at the head of whom was the founder of the great banking house of Brown, Shipley & Company. At Havre, Lafayette embarked on a packet-ship, — not on the United States frigate, — accompanied by his son George Washington Lafayette, a young man who during his father's captivity had been sheltered in the household of General Washington. His secretary was also with him, and two very ridiculous Englishwomen, who had managed to attach themselves to his party.

He happily landed, after what a contemporary calls "a short passage," that is, thirty-four days from Havre to New York. No words can describe the wild enthusiasm of his reception. He became so accustomed to raise his hat in acknowledgment of greetings, that he kept on doing it even in his dreams.

The excitement of the time, its flags, its guns, and its processions, left indelible impressions on the minds and memories of people still living, who were then young children. Here are two contemporary accounts of Lafayette's reception, one of his appearance in Boston, and at Cambridge, by Mr. Josiah Quincy; the other of how he visited New Orleans, by Vincent Nolte, the financier.

"As he proceeded on his way from New York to Boston," says Mr. Quincy, "the whole country arose to behold and welcome him. Every town and village through which he passed was ornamented and illuminated, and every testimony of gratitude and affection which imagination could devise, was offered to the nation's guest. The first sight we caught of the general was as he drove up the line in an open barouche drawn by four white horses. The enthusiasm I cannot attempt to describe. The remarkable history of the man which the events of a stirring half century have now somewhat obliterated from our memory, was then fresh and well known. He had sounded all the depths and shoals of honor. He had passed from every enjoyment that wealth and royal favor could bestow, to poverty and a dungeon.

No novelist could dare to imagine the vicissitudes of his life, since he left America.

"He went out to Cambridge, to the Harvard Commencement. There Mr. Everett pronounced an oration which moved every man to tears. . . . The weather, during his stay in Boston, was perfection. The leading men of that city made receptions for him. He met again the man whom he said of all men in America he most wished to see, though he had never seen him before for more than two minutes. This was Colonel Huger of South Carolina, who had come on to Boston to meet him. Their first meeting was unseen by any one. Colonel Huger visited him before he was up in his own chamber. The Colonel since his release from Olmutz had been living the life of a Southern planter on his farm in the uplands of South Carolina, where he had brought up a family of eleven children."

Lafayette is described by Mr. Quincy as a man of a fine portly presence, nearly six feet high, wearing lightly the three-score and ten years he had nearly completed, showing no infirmity save the slight lameness incurred at Brandywine. "His face on nearer view showed traces of the sufferings through which he had passed, but his brown wig, which sat low upon his forehead, concealed some of the wrinkles. That wig did him yeoman's service. Without it he could never have ridden with his hat off through the continual receptions and triumphal entries that were accorded him."

The next year (1825), after a triumphal tour of the United States, Lafayette returned to Boston for the ceremony of laying the corner-stone of Bunker's Hill monument, on the fiftieth anniversary of the battle of Bunker's Hill.

Declining the seat of honor prepared for him, he placed himself among the Old Defenders. Daniel Webster made the oration, Lafayette laid the corner-stone. The prayer that preceded the ceremonies was offered by an aged minister, who, fifty years before on that same spot, had offered prayer on the day of the memorable battle. Lafayette's toast at the concluding Banquet was "Bunker's Hill, and the holy resistance to oppression, which has already enfranchised the American Hemisphere. The next half century's Jubilee feast shall be to Enfranchised Europe." [1]

Vincent Nolte first saw Lafayette, whom, however, he had known before in France, on his arrival in Washington. "Henry Clay," he says, "then Speaker of the House of Representatives, introduced Lafayette Dec. 10, 1824, into the Hall of the House, and presented him to both Houses of Congress there assembled. Two thousand people were present, including all the foreign ministers, except the French one — *of the Bourbons*. Lafayette afterwards told me that though he had witnessed very many assemblies in his own country, never had he received such an impression as from this one, and that he had never been so moved by the eloquence of any man — not even by that of Mirabeau — as by the clear and spirited ring of the voice of Henry Clay. 'It was,' he said, 'the voice of a nation making itself heard by the voice of a great man.' The whole House, as if stricken by the wand of an enchanter, had risen to their feet as Clay entered leading Lafayette by the hand. Members sat down at the conclusion of the welcoming speech, but rose again at the first signs of a reply. They expected Lafayette to take his spectacles, and a written answer from his pocket, but, after a moment's pause, he spoke extemporaneously, and in English. . . . Congress voted him, as a testimony of the national gratitude, two hundred thousand dollars, and two hundred thousand acres of land, which the general chose in the newly purchased State of Florida. After this Lafayette resolved to visit all the States whose representatives had voted for this present. . . . At New Orleans, the residence of the Common Council was entirely refitted for his reception, admirably adorned, and luxuriously furnished. A table with thirty covers was set every day during the general's stay, that he might become acquainted with the principal inhab-

[1] Fifty years later the bloody scandal of the Commune had just ended, and I need not enumerate the other events which marred or impeded the "enfranchisement" of Europe as Lafayette understood that word. — E. W. L.

itants and planters." From New Orleans he ascended the Mississippi to Natchez, in a small steamboat prepared for him, accompanied by the Governor of Louisiana and delegates from among the principal politicians of the day.

All along the river, at every little town, the steamboat stopped, and delegations came on board with speeches. "I never," says Nolte, "saw a mark of impatience in his countenance. He responded to all with a few suitable and flattering words. The ease with which he performed this task greatly astonished me. I could not refrain, one day, from asking him how he managed always to reply to the most silly, idealess speeches. '*Mon ami*,' he answered, 'it is not hard. I listen with great attention till the speaker drops something which pleases me, or that gives opportunity for a repartee, and then I think about my reply, and arrange it; but of all the rest I do not hear one syllable, it blows over me.'"

Nolte elsewhere gives an anecdote illustrative of this great facility. Two young men came on board at one of the landing-places. The general addressing one of them, said: "Are you married?" The man replied: "Yes, general." "Happy man!" said Lafayette. Then turning to the other he asked the same question. The man replied he was a bachelor. "Ah!" said Lafayette, "lucky dog!"

On his return to France he visited Chavaniac, his birthplace, and during his journey through France was received everywhere with enthusiasm.

"At the first outbreak of the Revolution of July in 1830," says a writer in "Temple Bar," "Lafayette hastened back to Paris. During the night of the twenty-eighth he personally visited the barricades, directing the insurgents with all his old ardor, amidst the cheers of men, women, and children; once more he raised the tricolor upon the Hôtel de Ville, and never rested until he had not only compelled the abdication of Charles X. but had driven him from his last shelter — Rambouillet.

"But when the moment arrived to decide on the new government of France, Lafayette shrank from advising what he seemed to have been working for, and presented Louis Philippe to the populace as 'The best of Republics.' He next busied himself in the reconstruction of the National Guard, raising it to one million seven hundred thousand men. There was another grand installation, not so grand perhaps as that first one of 1790, but sufficiently imposing."

Yet no sooner was a regular government established than it dissatisfied him. He resigned his post as commander-in-chief of the National Guard, and although he retained his seat in the Chamber of Deputies, may be said to have retired into private life at La Grange.

The last great event of his life was his refusal of the crown of Belgium. He died May 20, 1834, in his seventy-seventh year. His funeral was magnificent. In the United States the Senate Chamber was hung with black for a month.

"Lafayette had every great quality," said a contemporary, "but something seemed to be wanting in each." "Popularity was the god that ruled him," said Nolte; "but so immense were his services, so ready his self-sacrifice, so amiable and honorable his private character, that this flaw (if flaw it was), as well as his political mistakes, may well be forgotten. He spoke and wrote English perfectly well, but in speaking it he had a strong French accent. In writing nothing betrayed his nationality but his French handwriting."

"He would fain be a Grandison-Cromwell," said Mirabeau, speaking of him in the early days of the Revolution. "He would coquette with the supreme authority without daring to seize it."

"There is much wit and felicity," says the writer in "Temple Bar," "in that curiously compounded epithet 'Grandison-Cromwell.' Imagine if you can, by some impossible freak of fortune, Sir Charles Grandison thrust into the position of a Cromwell, and you will understand much of Lafayette's character and actions. In America, under the influence of Washington he was admirable, but his part in the French Revolution, after it had passed its early stages, was that of a fine gentleman demagogue, who would have loved to rule over fine gentlemen republicans. . . . To stand

25

between Louis XVI. and the people; to be the protector and the master of the one, the liberator and champion of the other, and the observed of all, was to obtain the acme of his ambition. But his errors were all of the head. In his breast there beat a noble heart, in which love of liberty, and hatred of despotism, were enshrined in its highest place. . . . Above all he was generous to fallen opponents. How hardly he strove to save Napoleon from the hands of his enemies! How gratefully he remembered that to the fallen emperor, with whose acts and policy he had ever been at variance, he owed his release from the dungeons of Olmutz; and when after the accession of Louis Philippe the mob clamored for the lives of the Polignac Ministry, he stood forth to protect from public rage the men whose power he himself had worked so ardently to overthrow."

The name of Lafayette[1] was illustrious as far back as the fourteenth century. At the time of the celebration at Yorktown in 1881, the holder of the title was M. Edmond de Lafayette, a senator and president of the Conseil Général of the Upper Loire. He had succeeded his elder brother Oscar, who had died childless a few months before.

The founder of the family was a Marquis de Lafayette, who defeated the English at the battle of Baugé, shortly before the time of Joan of Arc, — a success which raised the hopes of the dauphin, who afterwards recovered the French throne.

In the seventeenth century two noble and illustrious women bore the ancient name. One of these ladies was Louise de Lafayette, maid of honor to Anne of Austria, whose husband, Louis XIII., fell so deeply in love with the young lady that he proposed to establish her in his country house at Versailles, a royal shooting box, built before the time of the great château. Alarmed by the infatuation of the king, and seeing no way to save her honor but by devoting herself to Heaven, Louise de Lafayette retired to the Convent of the Visitation, and at once took the vows. She died at the age

[1] This account of the Lafayette family is from the "Supplément Littéraire du Figaro." I translated it and republished it in the "Living Age," Sept. 17, 1881. — E. W. L.

of fifty, as Mère Angélique, Abbess of Chaillot, a convent she had founded.

Her brother, Comte Lafayette, married in 1655 Marie Madeleine Pioche de la Vergne, an intimate friend of Madame de Sévigné, and authoress of the "Princesse de Clèves," a classical romance of the old school, in many volumes.

The father of the general fell in a skirmish near Minden, April 3, 1758, at the age of twenty-five, when his son was seven months old. The name of Lafayette, through this infant, came to be worshipped by forty millions of freemen, and few American cities are without a street, a square, or an avenue, named in his honor.

All his life long nothing seems to have been able to repress his rashness. Equally in vain were the wise exhortations of Washington and the cold mockeries of Frederick the Great. Even at the age of seventy he exposed himself to great danger in a riot at the funeral of General Lamarque, and only a short time before his death he persisted in following on foot the remains of Dulong, his colleague in the Chamber of Deputies, who had been killed in a duel by General Bugeaud.

In 1778 he wanted to send a challenge to Lord Carlisle, who, in an official letter to the American Congress, had in his opinion used a phrase insulting to France. Washington at once wrote to his young friend, disapproving the challenge. "The generous spirit of chivalry," he said, "when banished from the rest of the world, has taken refuge, my dear friend, in the highly wrought feelings of your nation. But you cannot do anything if the other party will not second you; and although these feelings may have been suitable to the times to which they belonged, it is to be feared that in our day your adversary, taking shelter behind modern opinions and his public character, may even slightly ridicule so old-fashioned a virtue. Besides, even supposing his lordship should accept your challenge, experience has proved that chance, far more than bravery or justice, decides in such affairs. I therefore should be very unwilling to risk on this occasion a life which ought to be reserved for greater things. I trust that His Excellency Admiral the Count d'Estaing will agree with me in this opinion, and that as soon as he can part with you he will send you to headquarters, where I shall be truly glad to welcome you."

During the summer of 1785 Lafayette paid a visit to Germany, and particularly to Prussia. Frederick the Great received him with distinction. In his Memoirs he speaks of dining with the king at Potsdam. "Lord Cornwallis," he says, "was there. The king placed him next me at table, and on his other hand he had the Duke of York, the son of the King of England. They asked me a thousand questions on American affairs."

The wife of the general, whom he married in 1774, when he was little more than seventeen and she was three years younger, was Marie Adrienne Françoise, second daughter of the Duc d'Ayen and grand-daughter of the Maréchale de Noailles; Madame d'Ayen and the Maréchale de Noailles were guillotined during the Reign of Terror. The story of their deaths, told by their chaplain, who in lay dress followed their cart to the place of execution, will be found in the next chapter.

After three years of happy married life Lafayette quitted his young wife shortly before the birth of their first child, to hasten to the aid of the American colonies. The infant born during her father's absence became Madame Charles de Latour-Maubourg.

Madame de Lafayette, after the deaths of her grandmother, mother, and sister, languished a year longer in prison; but in 1795 she was released, and sent over the frontier of France, with her two daughters. With an American passport she reached Vienna, and there, as we have seen, implored the emperor till she obtained permission to share her husband's prison.

After three years and a half of captivity, Lafayette, with his fellow-captives, M. Charles de Maubourg and M. de Pusy, were set at liberty.

When Madame de Lafayette quitted France with her two daughters, she sent her son, with his tutor, to America. George Washington Lafayette was placed by General Washington at Harvard University. During one of his visits to

Washington in 1797, he met there a young French exile who had a project of teaching mathematics and geography for a living. It was the future King of the French, Louis Philippe d'Orléans.

Young Lafayette stayed three years in America, and when Napoleon became First Consul obtained a commission in the French army. But Napoleon, probably from motives of policy, was unwilling that the son of Lafayette should have the chance of distinction, and in 1807 the young man in disgust retired from the army.

In 1802 he had married Mademoiselle Destute de Tracy, and he had five children, two boys and three girls. The elder son, Oscar, died in 1881. His wife, a relative of M. de Pusy, one of the prisoners at Olmutz, had died after a year of married life, and Oscar never remarried. His brother, M. Edmond de Lafayette, succeeded to the title on his death, but was a bachelor. Lafayette's direct descendants in the male line are now extinct.

In the female line, through daughters and grand-daughters, he has many descendants, all of them allied with illustrious families.

Madame Charles de Latour-Maubourg had only daughters. The husband of one of them, a Piedmontese general, was killed at the battle of Novara.

Lafayette's other daughter, Madame de Lasteyrie, was named Virginia. She and her family formed part of the large household at La Grange. The Marquis de Lasteyrie died before his father-in-law, leaving four children. One daughter married the statesman, M. Charles de Rémusat, and so became daughter-in-law of the lady who has given us her Memoirs of the Court of Napoleon. The son, M. Jules de Lasteyrie, has held high positions under various French governments. Collaterally the Lafayette family is connected with other families of distinction whose names are familiar to the American public; notably with the families of De Ségur and Montalembert.

The Marquis Edmond de Lafayette attended the commemoration at Yorktown, together with his nephew, young M. de Rémusat.

CHAPTER II.

DEATHS OF THE LADIES OF MADAME DE LAFAYETTE'S FAMILY.[1]

THE old Maréchale de Noailles (Marie Antoinette's Madame l'Étiquette), her daughter the Duchesse d'Ayen, mother of Madame de Lafayette and of Louise, who had married her cousin, the Vicomte de Noailles, were imprisoned during the Reign of Terror, and were all guillotined together, July 22, 1794. Their remains shared the common lot, and were mingled with those of criminals in the cemetery of Picpus; but the story of their last hours has been preserved for us in the narrative of a priest, M. Carrichon, who had to run considerable risk in following the tumbrils to the place of execution, in order that, concealed among the crowd of spectators and carefully disguised, he might give them their last absolution. M. Carrichon wrote down his experiences immediately after they occurred, and his narrative throws a painfully vivid and personal light on events with which we are all vaguely familiar.

The old Maréchale de Noailles, her daughter and granddaughter, were imprisoned together in their own house from September, 1793 (six weeks before the queen's death), to the following April. During the whole of that time M. Carrichon, the spiritual director of the Duchesse d'Ayen and her daughter, visited them once a week; and as the Terror increased its crimes and the tale of its victims grew more and more day by day, these three friends exhorted one another to be prepared for death. One day, with a kind of presentiment, the priest said to them, "If you go to the guillotine, and God gives me strength to do it, I will accompany you."

[1] Abridged from "Macmillan's Magazine." Reprinted in "Littell's Living Age," Dec. 5, 1891.

The two women took him eagerly at his word and begged him, then and there, to promise that he would render them this last service. He avows frankly that he hesitated for a moment, more clearly conscious than they could be of the frightful risk he would run, and the possible uselessness of the sacrifice, and then he assented, adding that in order that they might not fail to recognize him, he would wear a dark blue coat and a red waistcoat. The time for redeeming a pledge of which they often reminded him came all too soon. In April, 1794, a week after Easter, the three ladies were removed to the Luxembourg, and M. Carrichon's direct communication with them ceased. But he continued to hear news of them through M. Grélet, the young tutor to whom Louise de Noailles had confided her children, two boys and a girl. Grélet's tender, faithful devotion to her and hers was the one bright spot in her fast darkening days. Hers was a singularly sweet and noble nature. One reads that clearly in her last letters to her husband and children, and every one who has ever mentioned her speaks of her as "an angel." She was beautiful as well as good and charming, and the love of her husband's family, as well as of her own, seems to have been centred on her.

What manner of man her husband, M. le Vicomte Louis de Noailles, was, we know not. He was an *émigré* with the army at Coblentz. Here is his wife's farewell letter to him, written at the Luxembourg and committed to the care of M. Grélet.

"You will find this letter from me, *mon ami*, written at different times, and very badly put together. I should like to have rewritten it and to have added many things, but that has not been possible here. I can only renew to you the assurance of that most tender feeling for you the existence of which you know already, and which will go with me beyond the grave. You will be aware in what situation I now find myself, and you will learn with consolation that God has taken care of me, that He has sustained my strength and my courage, that the hope of obtaining your salvation, your eternal happiness, and that of my children, by the sacrifice of my life, has encouraged and will encourage me in the most terrible moments. I place in your hands these dear children, who have been the consolation of my life, and who I hope will be yours. I have confidence that you will only seek to strengthen in them the principles which I have tried to inculcate; they are the only source of true happiness, and the only means of attaining to it. There remains for me, *mon ami*, one last request to make to you, which will, I believe, be superfluous when you know it. It is, I conjure you with the utmost earnestness, never to separate from these children M. Grélet, whom I leave in charge of them. There is no ease and no softening in my lot that I have not at all times owed to him, especially since I have been in prison. He has served as father and mother to those poor children. He has devoted himself and sacrificed himself for them and me in the most painful circumstances, with a tenderness and courage I shall never be able to repay. The sole consolation I carry with me is to know that my children are in his hands. You will not frustrate it, *mon ami*, and I have firm confidence you will regard this wish of mine as sacred."

Everything in the Vicomtesse de Noailles' conduct and all her utterances bear witness to the dignity and beauty of a character which, if not exceptional, at least serves to remind us that there were women at that period other in heart and soul — court ladies and *grandes dames* though they might be — from the frivolous, curious, skeptical, light-hearted beings, the minutiæ of whose dress and deportment, along with their incurable levity, live for us in De Goncourt's "Femmes du XVIIIme Siècle," and elsewhere.

But to return to M. Carrichon's narrative. In June of that terrible summer, M. Grélet came to ask him whether he would render the same service he had promised to Madame de Noailles to her grandfather and grandmother by marriage, the old Maréchal de Mouchy and his wife. The priest went immediately to the Palais de Justice (part of the Conciergerie), whither the prisoners had been moved, and succeeded in penetrating into the courtyard, where all the condemned were assembled. Those he especially sought were close to him, under his eyes, for more than a quarter of an hour, but he had only once before seen M. and. Madame de Mouchy, and, though he knew them, they were not able to distinguish him. What he could do he did for them, " by the inspiration and by the help of God ; " and he heard the brave old soldier praying aloud with all his heart, and was told by others that the evening before, as the prisoners left the Luxembourg for their trial, and their fellow-prisoners pressed round them with expressions of sympathy, the marshal made answer : " At seventeen I mounted the breach for my king ; at seventy-eight I go to the scaffold for my God. Friends, I am not unfortunate."

On this occasion, M. Carrichon thought it useless to attempt to follow the tumbrils to the guillotine, and he augured ill for the fulfilment of the promise he had made to Louise de Noailles. She and her mother had been with the De Mouchys to the last, doing their best to serve and solace them, and he knew now that their turn to go might be very near. Yet all through the dreary month that followed, the tumbrils rolled daily, and heads fell by the score, and his friends still lived.

The 22d of July fell on a Tuesday; and early in the morning, between eight and ten o'clock, just as M. Carrichon was going out, he heard a knock, and on opening his door saw the young De Noailles and their tutor. The boys were merry with the light-heartedness of their age, and from ignorance of the situation ; but the haggard sadness expressed in M. Grélet's face told the priest at once that the blow had fallen. Leaving the children, Grélet drew him into an inner room, where, flinging himself into a chair, the young man told him that the three ladies De Noailles had gone before the Revolutionary Tribunal, and that he came to summon him to keep his promise. He himself was going to take the two boys to Vincennes, where their little sister Euphémie, four years old, had been left in charge of friends, and during their walk through the woods he intended to prepare the unhappy children for their terrible loss.

Once alone with his reflections, after M. Grélet and the

boys had gone, M. Carrichon felt utterly appalled at the prospect of the task he had undertaken. Nothing gives a fresher stamp of truth and vivid reality to his simple narration than the betrayal of his own irresolution, which is more than once repeated in its pages. He was a good man, but no hero. A man of heart, but not a man of strong nerves; and having tried it once, he was keenly aware of the tremendous nature of the risk he ran, compared with the very slight chance there could be of succeeding in his mission. This psychological characteristic, which cannot fairly be called want of courage, certainly adds something to M. Carrichon's account of that day's events. It makes one feel so intensely the passionate struggle which up to the last moment went on in his mind, between the natural instinct of self-preservation and his earnest desire to do his duty by those who had confided their spiritual welfare to him while they were still at ease and in safety.

"My God!" he cried aloud in his distress of mind, "have pity alike on them and on me!"

Then the priest disguised himself as agreed, and went out. He transacted some business of his own first, carrying about with him everywhere a heart of lead, and between one and two o'clock went to the Palais de Justice. He was not allowed to enter, but he contrived to ask a few questions from some who had just come from the tribunal, and their answers dispelled the last illusions of hope. He could doubt the horrible truth no longer. His business next took him to the Faubourg St. Antoine, and it was not till nearly five o'clock that he returned with slow, lagging, irresolute steps, desiring in his heart either not to arrive in time, or else not to find there those who so much desired his presence.

When he reached the palace nothing as yet announced the departure of the prisoners. For nearly an hour he waited, at once the longest and the shortest hour of his life, pacing the great hall in an agony of anxiety, and glancing from time to time into the court below, to see what preparations were going forward. At length, about six o'clock, a noise of opening doors struck on his strained ears. He went down hurriedly and placed himself as near as possible to the grating which separated the prison from the hall of justice. For the last fortnight no one had been allowed within the courtyard on these occasions. The first cart was filled, and came slowly towards him. It contained eight ladies, all personally unknown to him; but in the ninth, the last of their number, he recognized the old Maréchale de Noailles, and the sight of her, alone, without her daughter or grand-daughter, revived within him a ray of hope. It was instantly quenched. They were together in the last cart. Madame de Noailles, girlishly young and fair, looking scarcely twenty-four, all in white, — which she had worn as mourning since the death of her grandparents, M. and Madame de Mouchy, — and Madame d'Ayen in a striped *déshabillé* of blue and white. Six men mounted the cart, and M. Carrichon noticed that the first two placed themselves at a little distance from the two ladies with an air of respect, as if with a desire to give them a brief spell of privacy.

Hardly were they seated when Madame de Noailles began to show her mother a tender, eager solicitude, which caught the attention of the bystanders. "Do you see that young one," the priest heard some one near him say, "how she moves about and talks to the other?"

Then he perceived that the prisoners' eyes were searching for him, and from their expressions he seemed to hear their whispered words: "Mother, he is not here." "Look again." "Nothing escapes me; I assure you he is not here."

They had forgotten — poor souls — in their acute anxiety a fact of which he had sent them warning, that he could not possibly enter the courtyard. The first cart remained close to him for at least a quarter of an hour. Directly it began to move on, the other started, and M. Carrichon made ready. It passed, and neither saw him. He re-entered the Palais de Justice, made a long détour, and placed himself in a conspicuous place at the opening of the Pont au Change. Madame de Noailles gazed round in all directions, but by a curious fatality missed him again. He followed them the length of the bridge, separated from them by the crowd, but still in close proximity. Madame de Noailles sought the whole time, but yet did not perceive him. Madame d'Ayen's face began to wear an extreme disquietude, and her daughter redoubled her attention, but in vain. Then the priest confesses that he felt tempted to renounce his dangerous mission. "I have done all I can," he said to himself. "Everywhere else the crowd will be still greater. It cannot be done, and I am tired to death."

He was just about to desist, and to retrace his steps, when the sky grew dark, and a distant murmur of thunder was heard. A sudden impulse made him determined to try again. By short cuts and back ways he contrived to reach the street St. Antoine before the tumbrils, at a spot nearly opposite the too famous prison La Force. And now the wind rose, and the brooding storm burst with all its fury, with lightning and thunder and torrents of rain. The priest withdrew beneath a doorway, standing on the steps of a shop, which was ever after present to his memory, and which he could never see again without emotion. In one instant the street was swept clear of all spectators; every one had run under cover, or up into the windows, and the line of march in the advancing procession became broken and disordered. The horsemen and the foot-guards moved along quicker, and the carts also. In another minute they were close to the Little St. Antoine, and M. Carrichon was still undecided what to do.

The first cart passed him, and then an uncontrollable involuntary inspiration made him hastily leave the doorway and advance toward the second. He found himself close to it, and quite alone, with Madame de Noailles smiling down on him with a radiant smile of welcome, that seemed to say, "Ah! there you are at last; how glad we are!" Then she called her mother's attention to him, and the poor woman's failing spirit revived. And with that brave action all the priest's own agony of irresolution passed away, and left him strong and peaceful. By the grace of God he felt himself filled with an extraordinary courage to do and dare the utmost. Drenched with sweat and rain, he thought no more of that, nor of any outward things, but continued to walk beside them. On the steps of the College of St. Louis he perceived a friend, — Father Brun of the Oratory, — also seeking to render them his last services of consolation, and to express his respect and attachment. The latter's face and attitude showed all he felt at seeing them on their way to death, and as M. Carrichon passed he touched Father Brun on the shoulder, saying with a thrill of inexpressible emotion, "Bon soir, mon ami!"

Here there was a square into which several streets ran, and at this point the storm was at its height, and the wind at its wildest. The ladies in the first cart were very much discomforted by it, especially the Maréchale de Noailles. Her big cap was blown off her head, and her gray hair exposed, while she and all the others swayed to and fro in the tempest, on their miserable benches without any backs, and their hands tied behind them. A number of people who had collected there in spite of the storm, recognized the well-known face of the great court lady, and fixed all their attention on her, adding to her torment by insulting cries. "There she is!" they shrieked, — "that maréchale who used to cut such a dash and drive in such a grand chariot, — there she is in the cart with all the rest!" The noise continued and followed them, while the sky grew darker and the rain more violent. They reached the square before the Faubourg St. Antoine. M. Carrichon moved on ahead to reconnoitre, and swiftly decided that here at last was the best place to accord the prisoners that which they so greatly desired. The second cart was going a little slower, and stopping short he leaned towards its occupants, making a sign which Madame de Noailles perfectly understood and communicated to her mother. Then, as the two women bent their heads "with an air of repentance, hope, and piety," the priest raised his hand, and with covered head pronounced distinctly and with concentrated attention the whole formula of absolution, and the words that follow it. All thought of self was obliterated in the solemn joy of that moment. Then the sky cleared and the rain ceased, and as the carts advanced into the faubourg, a curious mocking crowd assembled to see them pass. The ladies in the first one were heaped with insults, the maréchale especially, but no one said a word to Madame d'Ayen and her daughter.

M. Carrichon continued, sometimes beside them, sometimes a little in advance. By the Abbaye de St. Antoine he met a young man whom he knew, a priest whose integrity he had reason to suspect, and for an instant was in great fear of being recognized. But he passed without notice, and at last they arrived at the fatal spot. Then, at sight of the guillotine, — at the knowledge that in a few minutes more all these helpless victims of blind rage would, one after another, pass out of life under the pitiless stroke of the executioner, — a fresh agony of horror and despair swept over the priest's sad heart. He thought most of those he knew and loved, but he thought also of others unknown to him, men and women perishing cruelly, unavailingly, in their prime, — of the children orphaned, and the homes made desolate forever.

The carts stopped, and the guards surrounded them, with a crowd of spectators, for the most part laughing, jesting, and amusing themselves over the details of the harrowing scene. To be forced to see it all, to stand among them, and to listen to the grim ferocity of their light remarks, was an experience whose memory a man might well carry engraved on his heart to his dying day.

While the executioner was helping the ladies out of the first cart, Madame de Noailles' eyes were seeking for the priest's face, and having found it, dwelt there with looks full of sweet gratitude to him and tender farewell to all those dear ones now passed out of her sight forever. M. Carrichon drew his hat down over his eyes, so as to attract as little notice as possible, but kept them fixed on her. The mob had grown satiated with the sight of youth, beauty, and innocence mounting the scaffold, and it was not so much these characteristics of Louise de Noailles that attracted its fickle attention, as her air of radiant serenity, the expression of a soul whose triumphant faith had looked grim Death in the face and for whom its bitterness was overpast. "Ah! see that young one! how content she is! How she lifts her eyes to Heaven! How she prays! But what good will that do her?" Then, as if the sight of a spirit in that frail body which they could not break, — a fortitude and courage that they could not conquer, — a last degradation of suffering that they could not inflict, stirred them to dull fury, came savage jeers at those supposed to love their priests, "*Ah! les scélérats de calotins!*"

The last farewells were then exchanged, and the final act of the hideous drama was played out under the priest's shrinking, but yet fascinated eyes. He left the spot where he had been standing, and went round to the other side of the guillotine, where he found himself facing the rough wooden steps that led up to the scaffold. Against them leant an old man, with white hair, a *fermier général*, some one said, — a lady he did not know, — and just opposite to him the old Maréchale de Noailles, clad in black taffetas, was sitting on a block of stone, waiting, with fixed, wide open eyes, for her turn to come. All the others were ranged in two lines on the side looking toward the Faubourg St. Antoine. From where M. Carrichon now stood he could only see Madame d'Ayen. Her anxiety was at rest now, and her whole attitude expressed a simple and resigned devotion in the sacrifice she was about to offer to God through the merits of her Saviour. The Maréchale de Noailles went third to that altar of sacrifice. The executioners had to cut away part of her dress to uncover her neck sufficiently, and at this point the priest felt an intense longing to go away. But he determined now to drink the cup to its last dregs, to keep his word to the bitter end, since God had given him strength to control himself even while shuddering with dread. Six ladies followed her, and the tenth victim was Madame d'Ayen, content to die before her daughter, as the daughter was content to die after her mother. The executioner pulled off Madame d'Ayen's cap, and as there was a pin in it that she had forgotten to take out, he wrenched her hair violently, causing a sharp expression of pain to cross the calm face.

And then, with quickened poignancy of emotion, the priest watched Louise de Noailles' slender white figure mount the steps. "She looked," he says, "much younger than she really was, like a little gentle lamb, going to the slaughter." There was the same trouble with her head-dress as with her mother's, but in a moment her face recovered its sweet composure. "Oh, how happy she is now!" cried inwardly the priest, as they threw her body down into its ghastly coffin. "May the Almighty and Merciful God reunite us all in that dwelling place where there will be no more revolutions, in a country 'which,' as Saint Augustine has said, 'will have Truth for its King; Charity for its Law; and Eternity for its duration!'"

BOOK VII.

LOUIS XVII.

I. The Dauphin in the Temple.
II. Historic Doubts as to the Fate of Louis XVII.
III. The Lost Prince.

CHAPTER I.

THE DAUPHIN IN THE TEMPLE.[1]

THE interview between Marie Antoinette, M. Grandidier, and the Commissioner sent from Vienna by her nephew, the Emperor of Austria, which has been related in a previous chapter, was but a few days after her separation from her son, — that cruelest of all cruelties, — which took place July 3, 1793. No wonder that the unhappy mother was reduced to the apathy of despair; no wonder that she refused deliverance, since it would deprive her of the last sad consolation of being at least near to her son. Here is the account of the separation, as told us by the other child-captive, the future Duchesse d'Angoulême.

"The municipal officers read to us a decree of the Convention that my brother should be separated from us. As soon as he heard this, he threw himself into the arms of my mother and entreated with violent cries not to be separated from her. My mother was struck to the earth by this cruel order; she would not part with her son, and she actually defended, against the efforts of the officers, the bed on which she had placed him. My mother exclaimed that they had better kill her than tear her son from her. An hour was spent in resistance on her part, in threats and insults from the officers, and in prayers and tears on the part of us all.

1 See note to Book III., Chap. VII.

At last they threatened the lives of both him and me, and my mother's maternal tenderness at length forced her to this sacrifice. My aunt and I dressed the child, for my poor mother had no longer strength for anything. Nevertheless, when he was dressed she took him in her arms, and delivered him to the officers, bathing him with her tears and foreseeing that she should never see him again. The poor little fellow embraced us all tenderly, and was carried off in a flood of tears."

The princess then tells us that her heart-broken mother never looked up after the loss of her son. It was thus that the envoy from Austria saw her, sitting on her low stool, her face the picture of apathy. About a month after her boy had been taken away, Marie Antoinette was removed to the Conciergerie.

The two princesses, Madame Elisabeth and the princess royal, were left sad and desolate in their tower. They were kept in ignorance of the queen's condition, but knowing how much she had been accustomed to beguile her sorrows by work they sought permission to send her some materials. They collected all the silks and worsteds they could find, and also a pair of little stockings she had begun to knit for the dauphin. But these things she was not permitted to have, under pretense that she might kill herself with the knitting-needles. The queen's industry, however, overcame all impediments. She found a piece of old carpet in her cell which she unravelled, and by means of two bits of wood she contrived to knit these ravellings into garters.

Meantime the fair child, who had been torn from his mother and friends, was going through a course of misery and debasement which it makes the blood boil to read about, and its details need not be repeated here.

There has always been great doubt whether the story as told of his life in prison after the 9th Thermidor, 1794, and his death on June 8 of the succeeding year, is altogether true. Up to the 9th Thermidor there is no reason to doubt what has been told us of him. After that comes the doubt. Within the last three years especial interest has been roused

LOUIS XVII.

on the subject in France; and "Figaro" undertook an examination of the question. The date of his supposed death was June 8, 1795, a little more than one hundred years ago. The story as it has commonly been told and believed is as follows.

He was placed under the care of a fierce Jacobin cobbler and his wife. Their name was Simon. This man at once stripped the boy of the suit of mourning that had been given him for his father, and dressed him in a red cap and a coarse jacket, called a *carmagnole*, a sort of *sans-culotte* uniform. He made the boy drink intoxicating liquors; he taught him blasphemous oaths and revolutionary songs, and obliged him to repeat them at the windows, so as to be heard by the guards. Often he would rouse him in the night from sleep with a sudden cry of, *Capet! éveille-toi!* In short, no pains were spared to vitiate his character and to destroy his health. In a few months this lovely boy, who had been gifted by nature with an excellent constitution, became a miserable object, diseased and stupefied by ill treatment. He suffered, as we know from a physician's report, from tumors on his wrists and near the knees. But he must have retained a surprising degree of firmness for a child of his tender years if the following anecdote is true.

It appears that his artful keepers had drawn from him some expressions which they chose to interpret as impeaching the conduct of the queen and Madame Elisabeth, and that they compelled him to sign a deposition against them. The boy was so grieved at the use made of his words that he formed a resolution never to speak again, and this resolution he persisted in for a considerable time, although threats and promises of fruit and toys, and everything that could be most tempting to a child, were employed to make him break it.

On Jan. 19, 1794, Simon, who until then had been his companion, left him, and the princess thus continues her narrative: "Unheard of — unexampled barbarity! To leave an unhappy and sickly child of eight years old alone in a great room, locked and bolted. He had indeed a bell, which he never rang, so greatly did he dread the people whom its sound would have brought to him. He preferred wanting anything and everything to summoning his persecutors. His bed was not stirred for six months, and he had not strength to make it himself. For all that time he had no change of shirt or stockings. He might indeed have washed himself, and might have kept himself cleaner than he did, for he had a pitcher of water, but, overwhelmed by the ill-treatment he had received, he had not the resolution to do so; and his illness began to deprive him of the necessary strength. He passed his days without any occupation, and in the evening was allowed no light. His situation affected his mind as well as his body."

French historians, Lamartine among them, speak of the child as at this time reduced to imbecility.

In this pitiable condition he continued, it is said, to exist until November, 1794. three months after the 9th Thermidor, which occurred in July. Then the arrival of two new jailers of more humane dispositions brought about an amelioration of his unhappy condition. Their first care was to procure him another bed, and one of them, named Garnier,[1] would frequently sit with him whole hours to amuse him. The poor boy, who had been long unused to kindness, soon became very fond of him. But these attentions came too late to save his life, although his disease, having to contend with a naturally strong constitution, made its way by very slow degrees, and he lingered until June 8, 1795.

Such is the story generally received, and told by Garnier (*alias* Gomin) to the Duchesse d'Angoulême, who took him into her service in recognition of his kindness to the poor child. But who shall tell us that the child Garnier nursed, and whom no doubt he genuinely believed to be the son of Louis XVI., was really the little dauphin?

M. de Beauchesne has written a book on Louis XVII. which, so far as relates to the fate of the dauphin after Thermidor, was pronounced forty years ago by one who had studied the subject a "preposterous fiction."

[1] A name given in three ways, — Garnier, Gomin, and Govin.

However, the story just given is that which has been commonly received, and no doubt its details of the child's misery up to Thermidor are correct, as is De Beauchesne's narrative up to the same date. But the next chapter will show the doubts that of late have arisen in France, and give particulars of the historic doubts thrown on the same subject forty-four years ago in America. Before proceeding to detail them, I should like to give, from "Harper's Magazine," a translation that I made some years since of a noble poem by Victor Hugo, whose mother was a devout Catholic and a royalist, and who in her son's youth inspired him with some of her ideas.

LOUIS XVII.

Capet, éveille-toi!

HEAVEN'S golden gates were opened wide one day,
And through them shot a glittering, dazzling ray
  From the veiled glory, through the shining bars;
Whilst the glad armies of the ransomed stood
    Beneath the dome of stars.

From griefs untold a boy-soul took its flight;
Sorrow had dulled his eyes and quenched their light;
  Round his pale features floated golden hair!
See! virgin souls with songs of welcome stand,
With martyr palms to fill his childish hand,
  And crown him with that crown the Innocents shall wear.

Hark! hear th' angelic host their song begin:
"New angel! Heaven is open; enter in.
  Come to thy rest; thine earthly griefs are o'er.
God orders all who chant in praise of Him,
Prophets, archangels, seraphim,
  To hail thee as a king and martyr evermore."

"When did I reign?" the gentle spirit cries.
  "I am a captive, not a crownèd king.
Last night in a sad place I closed my eyes.
  When did I reign? Oh, Lord, explain this thing!
My father's death still fills my heart with fear.
  A cup of gall to me, his son, was given.
I am an orphan. Is my mother here?
  I always see her in my dreams of heaven."

The angels answered: "God, the wise and good,
Dear boy, hath called thee from an evil world.
A world that tramples on the blessed Rood,
Where regicides with ruthless hands have hurled
Kings from their thrones;
And from their very graves have tossed their mouldering bones."

"What! is my long, sad, weary waiting o'er?"
The child exclaimed. "Has all been suffered then?
Is it quite true that from this time no more
I shall be rudely waked by cruel men?
Ah! in my prison every day I prayed
'How long, O God! before some help will come?'
Oh, can this be a dream? I feel afraid.
Can I have died, and be at last at home?

"You know not half my griefs that long sad while;
Each day life seemed more terrible to bear.
I wept, but had no mother's pitying smile,
No dear caress to soften my despair.

"It seemed as if some punishment were sent
Through me some unknown sin to expiate.
I was so young; ere knowing what sin meant,
Could I have earned my fate?

"Vaguely, far off my memory half recalls
Bright, happy days before these days of fear;
Asleep, a glorious murmur seems to fall
Of cheers and plaudits on my childish ear.
Then I remember all this passed away;
Mysteriously the brightness ceased to be.
In prison a lone, friendless boy I lay,
And all men hated me.

"My young life in a living tomb they threw.
My eyes no more beheld the sun's bright beams;
But now I see you — angels — brothers! who
So often came to watch me in my dreams.
Men crushed my life in their hard, cruel hands, —
But they had wrongs. Oh, Lord, do not condemn!
Be not as deaf as they were to my prayers!
I want to pray for them."

The angels chanted: "Heaven's holiest place
Welcomes thee in. We'll crown thee with a star!
Blue wings of cherubim thy form shall grace
On which to float afar.

"Come with us: thou shalt comfort babes who weep
In unwatched cradles in the world below;
Or bear fresh light on wings of glorious sweep
To suns that burn too low."

The angels paused. The child's eyes filled with tears;
On Heaven an awful silence seemed to fall.
The Father spake; and, echoing through the spheres,
His voice was heard by all.

"My love, dear king, preserved thee from the fate
Of earth-crowned kings, whose griefs thou hast not known.
Rejoice, and join the angels' happy hymns.
Thou hast not known the trials of the great,
Thy brow was never bruised beneath a crown,
Though chains were on thy limbs.
What though life's burthen crushed thy tender frame,
Child of bright hopes — heir of a royal name?
Better to be
Child of that Blessèd One who suffered scorn,
Heir of the King who wore a Crown of Thorn,
Hated and mocked — like thee!"

CHAPTER II.

HISTORIC DOUBTS AS TO THE FATE OF LOUIS XVII.

THE story of the dauphin's imprisonment as it has been commonly received is no doubt true in its earlier part; that is, until the removal of Simon; but ever since the restoration of Louis XVIII. there have been rumors that the dauphin was secretly conveyed out of the Temple; and there have been several persons who claimed to be the dauphin, notably a man named Naundorff, calling himself by the dauphin's title of the Duke of Normandy. Recently the question has been revived in France, and has created considerable stir there.

It can easily be conceived what confusion and inconvenience it would have caused in France and in French politics, in 1814, and indeed in the politics of the whole European world, had a young man of twenty-nine suddenly been produced as the lost prince, — a man wholly untrained for his position, — and had such a man supplanted his uncle, who, in good faith (or otherwise), had called himself Louis XVIII. for nineteen years. It was far better to admit no doubt of the current story, to suppress all contradictions, to disown the pretenders as impostors, but never to investigate their tales. Nevertheless, here is the case as it at present stands, and as, during the year 1895, it has been presented to the French public.[1] Some persons have affirmed their conviction of the child's escape, and identify him with the unfortunate Naundorff. Some believe in the escape, but not in Naundorff, and say that it was a political necessity that the child whose life was saved should have remained anonymous, — lost in the world's

[1] These particulars are taken from the "Supplément Littéraire du Figaro," June 8, 1895.

crowd. Some again think that the Convention did not let its prey escape, and that the child died in the Temple.

The necessity that the Bourbons on their restoration should maintain the truth of this last story was forcibly set forth by a Prussian named Von Rochow, on the first attempt made by Naundorff to establish his identity with Louis XVII. "If this young man be the Dauphin of France," he said, "he cannot be acknowledged as such, because that acknowledgment would be to the dishonor of all the monarchies of Europe."

France, in 1794, was panting for peace. The eyes of French legitimists were fixed upon the Temple, where languished the poor child under whose ancestors France had become glorious and great. Monsieur le Comte de Provence had been accused, even in his brother's lifetime, of designs to seat himself on the French throne. His ambition and his hopes increased in proportion as the fortunes of his country grew worse and worse, and he kept up communication with some of the more prominent members of the Convention.

Barras and his party, of course, wished to retain the power that had fallen to them on the death of Robespierre. By conniving at the escape of the young boy (or even by contriving it) Barras could please Josephine de Beauharnais, who at that time had an all-powerful influence over him, and the child, should he be produced at the right moment, might checkmate the ambitious projects of Louis XVIII. and serve purposes of his own.

It is a fact that on the very night of his triumph on the 9th Thermidor, Barras went to the Temple; that he there saw the child-king; that the very next day, without any communication with the Committee of Public Safety, which, up to that time, had controlled affairs in the prison, he assigned a retainer of his own to be superintendent of the prison, Laurent, a man born in Martinique (Josephine's birthplace). Laurent turned out the people charged with the care of the child and put in a man and his wife named Liénard. During the first two months after these people came to the Temple, many persons saw the royal child, but none of them have ever described him as either dumb or scrofulous, like the prisoner who died the next year on the 8th of June. On the contrary, they all spoke of him as a somewhat delicate child, with gentle manners, who charmed all of them.

But suddenly, instead of allowing visitors to have access to him, as had been the case for two months after Thermidor, every one was forbidden to see him. This prohibition corresponds with two curious circumstances.

Madame Royale, his sister, tells us that on the last night of May, in the middle of the night, two municipal guards, much excited, forced their way into her chamber. They said nothing. All they wanted apparently was to see if she was there. No such thing happened before or after during her captivity. The second fact is that a week later another man replaced Laurent, Govin by name. Laurent had been full of kindness for the captive ; Govin ruled him by fear. About the same time there was a general impression among the underlings of the Temple that something strange had taken place. The fidelity of Laurent was called in question in the Sections. An official connected with the Temple said openly that it was hard for the guard to say if they were keeping watch over prisoners, or only over stones.

All those who served in menial capacities in the Temple were changed, some of them at the request of Laurent, who had begun his service July 27, 1794, and some afterwards by the desire of Govin. Up to this man's time there had been a daily inspection of the prison and the prisoners by members of the Council-General of the Commune. This inspection was replaced by a daily visit from a deputation from the Sections, taking the thirty-six Sections in turn, so that instead of men who had seen the prisoners only a short time before, new men came, who were not likely to take their turn again for a long while.

According to an old custom, things coming into the Temple were not examined, — only those that went out. It was easy enough therefore to bring a child into the Tower in a clothes basket, and this was done probably with two children, one after the other, while the young king was hidden in some secret corner, and waited on by the scullion Caron, Liénard, and Laurent.

This is the only way to account for the sudden dumbness of the child in prison, which took place not in consequence of remorse for having been made to malign his mother, but nine months after the Simons had been removed from him and kinder jailers had taken their place. The first child brought in to take the place of the young captive was dumb. The dauphin, up to the time when Laurent gave up his care of him, had spoken at least to twenty people. But the child committed to Govin's care on November 8, 1794, could not speak a single word. There are plenty of official documents and depositions on this subject, the most important of which is the testimony of members of the Committee of Public Safety.

By reason of the rumors afloat that the prince had disappeared, three friends of Barras, all, like him, members of the Convention, went to the Temple. They passed two hours with the child. They questioned him with the utmost persistence; but they obtained neither sign nor word. They were so much astonished at this that they decided to make no report that could be given to the public, but reported in secret to the Committee what they had seen. It is one of these men, Harmand, who tells us this.

Another curious circumstance is that Harmand, almost immediately after this visit, was sent away as delegate to the West Indies. Barras himself had some idea of accompanying him on this mission. It looks as if they were planning to secure their own safety in any event, or as if it had been intended to send the child to some French colony in America.

Both Harmand and Barras went to Brest, stayed there several weeks, and then returned to Paris.

Another series of strange events occurred between the 31st of March and the 8th of June, 1795, the date of the supposed death of the dauphin.

Laurent left the Temple. It was said that he too was going to the West Indies to attend to family affairs; but he did not leave Paris. Some time later indeed he went to the Windward Islands, on a mission for which he was well paid by government. But by that time Barras was a member of the Directory, and Laurent was sent on the mission at his recommendation. A new turnkey took his place at the Temple, Étienne Lasne, a house-painter.

Govin and Laurent had had under their care for six months a child who never spoke a word. The child confided to Lasne, he tells us himself, could chatter like a little magpie. Govin had nothing more to do with the young prince (or the child who personated him). He was transferred to the service of Madame Royale.

On June 8, 1795, the child in the Temple died. It was just then that the Committee was carrying on negotiations with Spain and with La Vendée, and it was very desirable for all parties that the child-king should be out of the way.

There is mystery even as to what this child died of. The dumb child had the rickets (*rachitis*), a disease that begins in infancy, preventing the nourishment of all the tissues affecting the spinal column and the rest of the bones. There was no mention in his case of scrofula, but the second child, the chatterbox, was eaten up by scrofula. Three doctors were sent to see him, Desault, Chopart, and Doublet. It is hinted that it proved a dangerous mission. All three shortly after died suddenly. The principal pupil of Desault, Dr. Abeille, went off to America for safety, and subsequently affirmed in an American paper ("The Bee"), that his master had been poisoned, because having seen the prince in happier times he had not recognized him in the child he was called upon to visit in the Temple, and had had the imprudence to say so. Another physician and Dr. Desault's widow have made a similar declaration.

The behavior of the Committee of Public Safety was also singular. At first it kept the death a secret. Then it caused a *post-mortem* examination to be made to satisfy those who might imagine that the dauphin had died a violent death. The Convention had every reason for wishing to establish, as a fact, the death of the young king; and yet not a single person who had ever known the dauphin living was called to identify the dead child's remains, though his sister was in the Temple and members of the Royal Household were in the power of the authorities.

The only people summoned to identify the remains were the municipal guards on duty at the Temple, about twenty men, and, according to the official document, "the greater part attested that they recognized Little Capet because they had seen him formerly at the Tuileries." The child died at the age of ten, and for five years before his death he had been little seen by the Parisians, the queen having been unwilling to present herself with her children before the public eye. If these men had indeed seen the dauphin at the Tuileries when he was five or six years old, what was the worth of their recognition of the dead body of a ten years old child worn out by suffering?

The *procès verbal* — that is, the official document concerning the death — was curiously worded. It says: "We saw on a bed the dead body of a child, who appeared to us about ten years old, which the commissioner told us was that of the deceased Louis Capet." It went on to say that the scrofula must have been of long standing, but mentions no marks about the body which all the court knew to be upon the person of the dauphin.

The man who announced the death to the Convention in the name of the Committee of Public Safety assured his hearers "that everything had been verified and all the documents placed in their archives."

This was not true. No one has ever seen the originals of these documents. A copy, on a loose sheet of paper (contrary to the law of 1792), was among the city archives, and was burnt up when the Hôtel de Ville was destroyed by the Communists in 1872. What is still more remarkable is that Govin was not called upon to sign what is called "the act of decease." It was signed by one Bigot, a man totally unknown to the public, who called himself "a friend of the King of France."

The interment was also singular. The archivist of the police affirmed that "it was secret, and in some sort clandestine." But Voisin, undertaker for the Section of the Temple, says: —

I. That the coffin was not closed in the Temple.

II. That the four men who were concerned in the burial died sudden and mysterious deaths.

The theory advanced is that while the coffin lay unclosed after official inspection of the child who died of scrofula, the real prince, who had been hidden away in some corner of the Temple, and waited on by Laurent at first, and afterwards by some other man, may have been placed in the coffin, and so carried out of the Temple. The coffin was not carried in a hearse, but in a furniture wagon. The child may have been taken out of it on the way to the cemetery, and something heavy substituted. A watch for three days was placed over the graveyard.

An old Member of the Committee of Public Safety has affirmed in writing that the boy who died of scrofula was secretly buried at the foot of one of the towers of the Temple; and General d'Andigné, seven years later, being confined in the Temple and permitted to amuse himself with gardening, testifies that he found there a small skeleton, that had been buried in quicklime.

The names of the two children substituted for the prince are known. M. Charles Tardif twice affirmed that he furnished the dumb boy. As to the scrofulous child who died June 8, 1795, his mother, Mademoiselle Lamonger, fled with another child, a daughter, to Martinique, the native island of Josephine de Beauharnais, and they did not come back to France as long as the Bourbons were in power.

All these things did not take place without rousing suspicion. Children were arrested on the roads out of Paris under the idea that they might be the dauphin. The leaders of the royalist party in La Vendée refused to believe in his death, and would not acknowledge Louis XVIII. as their king. Charette, the Vendean leader at that date, thus apostrophizes Louis XVII., in a celebrated order to his forces:

"Hardly by the fall of Robespierre wast thou delivered from the ferocity of the extreme Jacobins, when thou becamest the victim of thy natural defenders."

But what, then, became of Louis XVII.?

The political party which in 1795 succeeded the Reign of Terror, and the Provisional Government of the Commune of Paris, was willing enough to favor the child's escape. A time might come when in their hands he might be played off against Louis XVIII. But his existence and recognition were above all unwelcome to his uncle and his partisans. The Duc de Bourbon, prince of the blood, writes thus to Condé: "Rumors are becoming rife that the little king did not die in the Temple. True or false, this would be for us a serious embarrassment, if the rumors should take any consistency."

In the camp of the *émigrés* at Coblentz were numerous noblemen and gentlemen whose lands had been confiscated, and who had accustomed themselves to look to the Comte de Provence as the man who would restore them. They could make no use of a child ten years of age as an active head of their party. Far better for them that, if living, his existence should be denied. They had accustomed themselves to speak of Louis XVI. with small respect, and to place all their hopes upon his brother. Goguelat (the unlucky Goguelat of the Flight to Varennes) who had escaped to Coblentz, wrote: "I never heard Louis XVI. spoken of with so much irreverence as by these men. They call him a poor creature, a mere chip; a bigot only good to say his prayers. And their opinions, I am told, emanate from the personal followers of Monsieur, who has set them afloat."

Had Louis XVII. suddenly appeared among his supporters even in La Vendée, their first enthusiasm would soon have been damped by a feeling of his uselessness to help their cause.

The child would have been unwelcome to the Allies, even to Austria, whose ministers, as we have seen, were eager to make peace. Louis XVIII., who hated Marie Antoinette, had not scrupled long before to hint that he believed her son to be a bastard. He would certainly have treated him as such had he fallen into his hands. Clearly the best thing to be done with the poor child was to hide him away till the time came for the restoration of the monarchy, which Barras, in common with most men, believed to be at hand. Then he could be played off against Louis XVIII. Barras could not foresee the ten years of the Empire that would precede the Restoration, or imagine that his friend Josephine (in possession of his State secret, if not, indeed, his partner in it) would be seated on a throne as empress of half Europe.

The paper from which this account is copied gives a whole column to the names of persons who have testified to some knowledge of the substitution of other children for Louis XVII., and of his being spirited away from the Temple. Among these names is that of a Marquise de Broglie-Solari, attached to the household of Marie Antoinette, and to that of the Princesse de Lamballe. This lady testified that she heard it in 1803 from Barras, and in 1819 and 1820 from Queen Hortense, the daughter of Josephine.

There is reason to think that Josephine knew the story and believed it. Of late years papers have been written to attribute her sudden and somewhat mysterious death to that inconvenient knowledge.

The paper from which I have copied these details believes that Naundorff, the *soi-disant* Duke of Normandy, may have been Louis XVII.; but it owns that there are important links wanting in his story between 1795 and 1810.

The Comtesse d'Adhémar, ex-*dame du palais* of Marie Antoinette, wrote: "Assuredly I do not wish to multiply the chances of impostors, but in writing this in the month of May, 1799, I certify, on my soul and conscience, that I am positively certain that Sa Majesté Louis XVII. did not die in the Temple."

The Duchesse d'Angoulême was never convinced of her brother's death, though she was obliged, from motives of policy, to acquiesce in the view taken by the male members of her family. The Vicomte de Rochejacquelin

DUCHESSE D'ANGOULEME.

wrote to her on the subject: "Though we may believe that the unhappy child was withdrawn from the cruelty of his persecutors, and that, to save his life, he was obliged to live in obscurity, such a life would make him little suitable to be recognized as heir to the French monarchy; and, in short, in the condition of Europe, it is quite conceivable that it would have been useless to bring forward Louis XVII., and that his death, and the deaths of those that supported him, would have been the consequence."

It is said that to the Treaty of 1814 between France and the Allies, which restored Louis XVIII. to the throne, there was this secret article: —

"The contracting parties reserve their liberty to assist in mounting on the French throne him who they may conceive has the more legitimate right to it."

It is certain that Josephine said to the Emperor Alexander, "You may re-establish royalty, but you will not re-establish legitimacy." A peer of France has recorded in his souvenirs that in April, 1814, one month before the death of the Empress Josephine, he had seen documents "which contained secrets calculated to upset European diplomacy, if they ever came to light." He implored Josephine to destroy them.

"No," she said; "my resolution is fixed. I shall communicate these papers to the Emperor Alexander. He is just, I know, and will wish that everything should be put in its right place (*sera mis dans son rang*). He will look after the interests of an unfortunate young man." "I made no further objection," added the narrator. "Josephine acted as she thought best, and told what it had been better for her to have kept secret. . . . Her sudden death, a week after, took an important witness out of the way."

It may be added that on the very night of her death, which the three physicians who attended her attributed to poison, all her papers, on a frivolous pretext, were seized by the police, and the larger part of them were never restored.

As soon as the empress was dead, it was rumored in Paris that she had known the circumstances of the dauphin's disappearance from the Temple; that she had even had a hand in it; and that in a secret interview with the Emperor Alexander it had been agreed between them that the affairs of France should be provisionally settled until the son of Louis XVI. should be discovered, when the Emperor Alexander "reserved to himself the right" to do him the justice that was legitimately his due. With this the secret clause in the Treaty of 1814, already quoted, would seem to agree.

Louis Blanc says: "After the Restoration, which placed Louis XVIII. on the throne, the recovery of Louis XVII. would have caused incalculable embarrassments. This being the case, a government by no means scrupulous could very easily overlook family considerations, in virtue of reasons of state, whether it knew the truth, or preferred to ignore it."

The most remarkable proof that Louis XVIII. did not believe in his nephew's death was, that when he raised the Chapelle Expiatoire to the memory of Louis XVI. and Marie Antoinette, he took no notice of the death of Louis XVII. But the Duchesse d'Angoulême seems always to have had it in her heart that she might recover traces of her lost brother. Not that it would have been in her power to do anything to restore him to his position: and her acknowledgment of his rights would have destroyed those of her husband, her father-in-law, her uncle, and her great-nephew, the Duc de Bordeaux.

On leaving the Temple in 1796 the princess wrote to her uncle, speaking of the Jacobins, "They have compassed the deaths of my father, and my mother, and my aunt." She does not mention her brother. Again in 1801, when General d'Andigné had discovered the little skeleton in the Temple garden, and was anxious to speak of it to the Duchesse d'Angoulême, he was not permitted to have an interview with her. She told Comte de Feys when search was being made for the dauphin's body in the Cemetery of Ste. Marguerite, "that from the first she had not been sure of her brother's death in the Temple, but that she at last knew what had become of him."

There was not only no monument erected to Louis XVII. in the Chapelle Expiatoire, but a funeral service to his memory, that was to have taken place at St. Denis, was never held. The Bishop of Moulins has told us that his father (at that time Grand Master of Ceremonies), having asked Louis XVIII. the reason, received this answer, "We do not feel sure of the death of my nephew."

There was a superstition among the French clergy that all the misfortunes that fell fast on the Royal Bourbons after their restoration were a judgment upon them for the non-recognition of Louis XVII. The Secretary-General of the Diocese of Strasburg said that the certainty Monsignor Tarin had of the existence of Louis XVII. led him to give up his position as tutor to the Duc de Bordeaux. "Monsignor," said the Marquis de Nicolai, one day to him, "the royal family believes as much as you or I do that Louis XVII. is still living."

Of course many pretenders appeared after the Restoration. The most plausible one was Naundorff, — *soi-disant* Duke of Normandy, who revealed himself to Silvio Pellico in their prison at Turin, and whose history forms an interesting chapter in Pellico's sad but delightful book "Le mie Prigioni."

In the days of Louis Philippe a pale, quiet, gentleman-like man, with a somewhat Bourbon expression of countenance, might be seen in legitimist *salons*, treated with respect as the lost king. He had indeed some of the marks on his person known to have been on that of the poor little dauphin, but not on the body of the scrofulous child who represented him in the Temple. He did not attempt to conceal that he had worked at watchmaking in Switzerland, or that he had been several times in prison. He spoke French with a strong German accent, and was a Protestant. "More shame to the Church," said a French writer who believed in him, "that she had not come forward to protect him from error."

He had married the uneducated daughter of a Prussian

corporal, and had several vulgar children. He was compelled by the police to leave France, and took refuge in England.

As Duke of Normandy, he was often to be seen in Hyde Park. He pursued some scientific labors at Woolwich in shells and artillery. He got into trouble at last with the London police, and, with his family, crossed to Holland, where he died at Delft in 1841.

As I have said, I do not think that Naundorff was the dauphin, though many persons, in their certainty that the dauphin had not died in the Temple, and their uncertainty as to what had become of him, believed in him as such.

CHAPTER III.

THE LOST PRINCE.

AS preliminary to this chapter I venture to relate an experience of my own. In the autumn of 1841, when I was a young girl of nineteen, I came out to Boston to spend the winter with my father's and mother's friends, Mr. and Mrs. George Ticknor, and to go into society with their daughter, a *débutante*, somewhat younger than myself. The happiness of that delightful visit this is not the place to dwell upon.

Some weeks before Christmas it was announced that the Prince de Joinville, who, after bringing back the body of Napoleon from St. Helena a year before, had brought his ship, the "Belle Poule," to America, was coming to Boston. A great ball was to be given to him and his officers in Faneuil Hall, and the young girls in good society were much elated at the prospect. The day fixed upon drew near. The officers of the "Belle Poule" assembled in Boston, but there was no prince, — no certain news of him. Where could he be? His officers, on being questioned, could only say that they believed him to be in western New York, near the frontier of Canada. Had he gone on a hunting expedition? Very probably. But the impression left on many minds was that as the Prince de Joinville was at that day credited with being a fire-eater, and especially an enemy to John Bull, he might be making some sort of warlike reconnaissance along the Canadian border. At any rate there was mystery in his proceedings; his movements were kept secret both as regarded the public and his own officers.

The day before the ball arrived; still no prince! How could we have the ball without him? Speculation and expectation rose high among us. On the morning of the ball, however, we heard that the prince had arrived.

It was a beautiful ball, — I think the most beautiful ball I ever attended, with its chalked floor, its tricolor decorations, and its admirable music. Fifty-seven years have passed since then, but I well recall the scene, and now proceed to give an answer to the question then asked on all sides, but never answered till 1853, when the celebrated paper, "Have we a Bourbon among us?" appeared in "Putnam's Monthly," then a new magazine. Where was the prince while we were all so anxiously expecting him?

He was off at Green Bay, Wisconsin, seeking an interview with the Rev. Eleazer Williams. Here is Mr. Williams's own account of what passed between him and the Prince de Joinville: —

"In October, 1841, I was on my way from Buffalo to Green Bay, and took a steamer from the former place bound to Chicago, which touched at Mackinac and left me there to wait the arrival of the steamer from Buffalo to Green Bay. Vessels which had recently come in announced the speedy arrival of the Prince de Joinville; public expectation was on tiptoe, and crowds were on the wharves. The steamer at length came in sight, salutes were fired and answered, the colors run up, and she came into port in fine style. Immediately she touched, the prince and his retinue came on shore and went out some little distance from the town, perhaps half a mile, to visit some natural curiosities in the neighborhood, — the Sugar Loaf Rock and the Arch Rock. The steamer awaited their return. During their absence I was standing on the wharf among the crowd, when the captain, John Shook, now at Huron, Ohio, who will confirm my statement,[1] came up to me and asked whether I was going to Green Bay, adding that the Prince de Joinville had made inquiries of him concerning a Rev. Mr. Williams, and that he had told the prince he knew such a man, referring to me, who he supposed must be the man the prince meant, though he could not imagine what the prince could know or want of me. I replied to the captain in a laughing way, without having an idea of the deep meaning attached to my words: 'Oh, I

[1] And did so fully. — E. W. L.

REV. ELEAZER WILLIAMS.

am a great man, and great men will of course seek me.' Soon after this the prince and his suite arrived and went on board. I did the same, and the steamer put to sea. It was, I think, about two o'clock when we left Mackinac. When we were fairly on the water the captain came to me and said, 'The prince, Mr. Williams, requests me to say that he desires to have an interview with you, and will be happy to have you either to come to him, or allow me to introduce him to you.' 'Present my compliments to the prince,' I said, 'and say that I put myself entirely at his disposal, and will be proud to accede to whatever may be his wishes in the matter.' The captain retired, and soon returned, bringing the Prince de Joinville with him. I was sitting at the time on a barrel. The prince not only started with evident and involuntary surprise when he saw me, but there was great agitation in his face and manner, — a slight paleness and a quivering in the lip, — which I could not help remarking at the time, but which struck me more forcibly afterwards, in connection with the whole train of circumstances, and by contrast with his usual self-possessed manner. He then shook me earnestly and respectfully by the hand, and drew me immediately into conversation. The attention which he paid me seemed to astonish not only myself and the passengers, but also the prince's retinue. At dinner there was a separate table for the prince and his companions, and he invited me to sit with them, and offered me the place of honor at his side, but I begged the prince to excuse me and permit me to dine at the ordinary table with the other passengers; which accordingly I did. After dinner the conversation turned between us on the first French settlements in America, the valor and enterprise of the early adventurers, and the loss of Canada to France, of which the prince expressed deep regret. In the course of his remarks, — though in what connection I cannot now say, — he told me he had left his suite at Albany, taken a private conveyance, and gone to the head of Lake George. He was very copious and fluent in speech, and I was surprised at the good English he spoke, — a little broken, indeed, like mine, but still very intelligible. We continued talking late into the night, reclining in the cabin on the cushions at the stern end of the boat. When we retired to rest the prince lay on the locker, and I in the first berth next to it. The next day the steamer did not arrive at Green Bay till about two o'clock, and during most of that time we were in conversation. Looking back thoughtfully at what was said, I can now perceive that the prince was preparing my mind for what was to come at last, although then the different subjects seemed to arise naturally enough. At first he spoke on the condition of affairs in the United States and in the American Revolution. He expressed admiration of our institutions, and spoke at large of the assistance that had been rendered to the colonies in their struggle with the mother-country, by Louis XVI. He said that he did not think sufficient gratitude was evinced by Americans to that monarch, and that whenever his intervention was alluded to, it was attributed to selfish motives and to a desire to humble the power of England on the continent by depriving her of her fairest colonial possessions; but that in his opinion Louis XVI. felt a true regard for America, and that on every return of the Fourth of July, when throughout the United States the nation was celebrating its independence, there should be an especial salute fired to the memory of the king who had contributed so much to the result. Such was the substance of what was said by the prince on that subject. He then turned to the French Revolution, and said that Louis XVI. was innocent of any tyrannical ideas towards the people of France, and that nothing he had done personally could justify or excuse the excesses of the Revolution; that the last foundations of that event were laid in the preceding reign, and that the misconduct and misgovernment of Louis XV. were chargeable to a very great extent with the sad events that had occurred, although the storm had been slowly brewing for centuries. The people of France, though they had no just cause to complain personally of Louis XVI., had a right to do so of the oppressive institutions then existing, of the tyranny of the aristocracy, and of the burdens laid upon them by the Church. He then referred to the change that had since taken place in the form of government, and to the present amelioration of the condition of the French people, under an elective monarchy. On our arrival at Green Bay, the prince said I would oblige him by accompanying him to his hotel and taking up my quarters at the Astor House. I begged to be excused, as I wished to visit my father-in-law. He replied that he had some matters of great importance that he wished to speak to me about, and that as he could not stay long at Green Bay, but would take his departure the next day or the day after, he wished I would comply with his request. A number of persons were at the Astor House waiting to see the prince, so I declined to remain, but promised to return in the evening, when he would be more private. I did so, and on my return found the prince alone, with the exception of one attendant, whom he dismissed. The gentlemen of the party were in an adjoining room, laughing and carousing, and I could distinctly hear them during my interview with the prince. He opened the conversation by saying that he had a communication to make to me of a very serious nature as concerned himself, and of the last importance to me; that it was one in which no others were interested, and, therefore, before proceeding further he wished to obtain some pledge of secrecy, some promise that I would not reveal to any one what he was going to say. I demurred to any such conditions being imposed previous to my being made acquainted with the nature of the subject, as there might be something in it, after all, prejudicial and injurious to others, and it was at length, after some altercation, agreed that I should pledge my honor not to reveal what the prince was going to say, provided there was nothing in it prejudicial to any one; and I signed a promise to this effect on a sheet of paper. It was vague and general, for I would not tie myself down to absolute secrecy, but left the matter conditional. When this was done, the prince spoke to this effect: —

"'You have been accustomed, sir, to consider yourself a native of this country; but you are not. You are of foreign descent. You were born in Europe, sir, and, however incredible it may at first seem to you, I have to tell you that you are the son of a king. There ought to be much consolation to you to know this fact. You have suffered a great deal, and have been brought very low, but you have not suffered more, or been more degraded, than my father, who was long in exile and in poverty in this country; but there is this difference between him and you, that he was all along aware of his high birth, whereas you have been spared the knowledge of your origin.'

"When the prince had said this I was much overcome, and thrown into a state of mind which you can easily imagine. In fact, I hardly knew what to do or say, and my feelings were so much excited that I was like one in a dream, and much was said between us of which I can give but an indistinct account. However, I remember that I told him his communication was so unexpected and so startling that he must forgive me for being incredulous, and that really I was between two. 'What do you mean,' he said, 'by being "between two"?'

"I replied that, on the one hand, it seemed to me that he could scarcely believe what he said; and, on the other, I feared he might be under some mistake as to the person. He assured me, however, that he would not trifle with my feelings on such a subject, but that he spoke the simple truth, and that in regard to the identity of the person he had ample means in his possession to satisfy me that there was no mistake in that respect. I then requested him to proceed with the disclosure already partly made, and to inform me in full of the secret of my birth. He replied that in doing so it was necessary that a certain process should be gone through, in order to guard the interests of all parties concerned. I inquired what kind of process he meant? Upon this the prince rose and went to his trunk, which was in the room, and took from it a parchment, which he laid on the table, and set before me that I might read, and give him my determination with regard to it. There was also on the table pen and ink, and wax, and he placed there three governmental seals of France, — one, if I mistake not, of the old monarchy. It was of precious metal, but whether of gold or silver, or a compound of both, I cannot say, for my mind was so bewildered and agitated and engrossed with one absorbing question that things which at another time would have made a strong impression on me were scarcely noticed, though I must confess that when I knew the whole, the sight of that seal, put before me by a member of the family of Orleans, stirred my indignation.

"The document which the prince placed before me was very handsomely written in double parallel columns of French and English. I continued intently reading and considering it for a space of four or five hours. During this time the prince left me undisturbed, remaining for the most part in the room; but he went out three or four times.

"The purport of the document, which I read repeatedly word by word, comparing the French with the English, was this: it was a solemn abdication of the crown of France in favor of Louis Philippe, by Charles Louis, the son of Louis XVI., who was styled Louis XVII., King of France and Navarre, with all accompanying names and titles of honor, according to the custom of the old French monarchy, together with a minute specification in legal phraseology of the conditions, considerations, and provisos upon which the abdication was made. These conditions were, in brief, that a princely establishment should be secured to me, either in France or in this country, at my option, and that Louis Philippe would pledge himself on his part to secure the restoration, or the equivalent for it, of all the private property of the royal family, rightfully belonging to me, which had been confiscated in France during the Revolution, or in any way got into other hands. Now you may ask me why I did not retain at all hazards this document, or at any rate take a copy of it. A day or two afterwards all such points came to my mind, but at the moment I thought of nothing except the question of acceptance or rejection. And then, remember the sudden manner in which this whole affair came upon me, and the natural timidity and bashfulness of one who had always considered himself of most obscure rank, when called without preparation to discuss such topics with a man of high position like the prince. Besides which, my word of honor had been so lately pledged, and a sense of personal dignity excited by the disclosures of the prince, so that I never so much as thought of taking any advantage of the circumstances, but only whether I should sign my name and set my seal to a deliberate surrender of my rights and those of my family. It was a deeply painful and harrowing time, and I cannot describe, nor could any one imagine, how I felt when trying to decide this question. At length I made my decision and rose and told the prince that I had considered the matter fully in all its aspects, and was prepared to give him my definite answer. Then I went on to say that whatever might be the personal consequences to myself, I felt that I could not be the instrument of bartering away, with my own hand, the rights pertaining to me by my birth, and sacrificing the interests of my family, and that I could only give to him the answer made by the Comte de Provence to the ambassadors of Napoleon at Warsaw, 'Though I am in poverty and exile, I will not sacrifice my honor.'

"The prince upon this assumed a loud tone and accused me of ingratitude in trampling on the overtures of the king, his father, who, he said, in making the proposal, was actuated more by feelings of pity and kindness towards me than by any other consideration, since his claim to the French throne rested on an entirely different basis to mine, — not that of hereditary descent, but of popular election. When he spoke in this strain I spoke loud, too, and said that as he by his disclosure had put me in the position of a superior, I must assume that position, and frankly say that my indignation was stirred by the memory that one of the family of Orleans had imbrued his hands in my father's blood, and that another now wished to obtain from me an abdication of the throne.

"When I spoke of superiority the prince immediately assumed a respectful attitude, and remained silent for several minutes. It had now grown very late, and we parted with a request from him that I would reconsider the proposal of his father, and not be too hasty in my decision. I returned to my father-in-law's, and the next day saw the prince again, and on his renewal of the subject gave him a similar answer. Before he went away, he said, 'Though we part, I hope we part friends.'

"For years I said little on the subject, until I received a letter in 1848 from Mr. Kimball, dated at Baton Rouge, informing me that a Frenchman named Bellenger had made a statement on his deathbed that he had brought the dauphin, son of Louis XVI., from France, and placed him at the north among the Indians. And then when this report came from the south confirming what the prince had said, the thing seemed to me to assume a different aspect. Mr. Kimball's letter is, I think, among my papers at Green Bay; but at any rate I have for years kept a minute journal of everything that has occurred to me, and I have no doubt I have an abstract of it at Hogansburg."

Such is Mr. Williams's story, given to the Rev. Mr. Hanson in the presence of Dr. Hawks, the eloquent preacher and historian, in Dr. Hawks's study in New York, in 1852.

Of Mr. Williams, Dr. Hawks says: "I know him very well. He is a clergyman of the Protestant Episcopal Church, whose labors have been almost entirely those of a missionary among the Indians. He is of good standing as a clergyman, and is esteemed a man of truth among his acquaintance, and those with whom he has longest lived, all bearing abundant and satisfactory testimony that Mr. Williams has always been considered a worthy and truthful man. I may add to this my own statement that in all my intercourse with him I have never found reason to doubt the correctness of his neighbors and acquaintance, in their testimony to his character as stated above.

"From personal knowledge I am able to say that there is a remarkable simplicity both of manner and character in Mr. Williams. He possesses an ordinary share of intellectual power, with but little quickness, however, of grouping facts that bear on a central point, and is without much readiness in deducing conclusions from them. He is incapable of framing a mass of circumstantial testimony, made up of a combination of many isolated facts. To do this requires genius and a high inventive faculty.

"Indeed, nothing has struck me more forcibly in the conversations I have had with Mr. Williams on the facts recorded in Mr. Hanson's narrative than his seemingly entire non-perception of the bearing of many facts therein as testimony, and their coincidence with other events known to him, until these were pointed out to him. And sometimes he could not be made, even then, to comprehend readily the indicated relations. When, however, he did comprehend the relations, his countenance would light up with a smile, and he would say, 'I see it now, but I never saw it before.'

"I have found him uniformly amiable and gentle in manner, and to all appearance a truly pious man.

"In short, a knowledge of the man has seemed to me to be an important part of the story he tells; his temperament, disposition, mental operations, etc., all go to establishing one of the *facts* explanatory of some of the particulars in the narrative.

"Whether the historical problem presented by Mr. Hanson be here solved, is a matter which I will not undertake to decide. The only points on which I would speak with certainty are two: first, Mr. Williams is not an Indian, and, secondly, he is not able to invent a complicated mass of circumstantial evidence to sustain a fabricated story."

We may now ask what was the history of Mr. Williams? He was brought when a child about ten years old, by two Frenchmen, one a layman, the other apparently a Roman Catholic priest, to Ticonderoga, where was a settlement of Iroquois Indians, and he was adopted into the family of Thomas Williams, an Indian with white blood in his veins. A short time before that a Frenchman and a lady had visited Albany with a boy and girl in their company. The boy they called Monsieur Louis; and he was *non compos mentis*, as was the child shortly after confided to Thomas Williams, who in this state continued till he was thirteen or fourteen years of age.

"Have you no memory," he was asked more than fifty years later, "of what happened in Paris, or on your voyage to this country?" "Therein," he replied, "is the mystery of my life. Everything that occurred to me is blotted out, erased entirely, irretrievably gone. My mind is a blank till I was thirteen or fourteen years of age. You must imagine a child who, as far as he knows anything, was an idiot, destitute even of consciousness that can be remembered at that period. He was bathing in Lake George among a group of Indian boys. He clambered with the fearlessness of idiocy up to the top of a high rock. He plunged down head foremost into the water. He was taken up insensible and laid in an Indian hut. He was brought to life. He was conscious of blue sky, mountains, and waters. That was the first I knew of life." Still, vague dreamy memories in after years would sometimes seem to cross his mind, as when a portrait of Simon was once shown him carelessly. He became greatly excited and cried out, "My God! I know that face. It has haunted me all my life."

The story of the boy's idiocy and recovery was well known among the Indians and white men of that region, and has been corroborated abundantly.

The Williams family, with whom the boy was placed, had a singular history. In 1704 the Rev. John Williams, a Puritan minister at Deerfield, Massachusetts, was captured with all his family by French and Indians, and carried to the neighborhood of Montreal. They all returned to civilization except one daughter, Eunice, who married an Indian chief; by him she had two daughters, Mary and Catherine, and a son John. Mary married an English surgeon named Ezekiel Williams. They had one son Thomas, their only child. His parents dying when he was young, he was cared for by his aunt Catherine, and was considered an Indian of the Iroquois tribe, by virtue of his descent from his grandfather. He attached himself to the Iroquois, renouncing civilized life. He married a full-blooded Indian woman, and had eleven children besides Eleazer, who was reputed to be his son, and as such was brought up by him. All the undoubted children of Thomas Williams were strongly marked Indians, notwithstanding the white blood in their veins. They bore not the slightest resemblance to Eleazer.

After some time a proposition was made by the Williams family in Massachusetts to pay for the education of one of the boys. John was sent to Long Meadows in Massachusetts, to a certain Deacon Ely, and Eleazer went with him. Every six months the bills for Eleazer's board and tuition were promptly and punctually paid by a different agent from the one who paid the bills of John Williams.

John, Indian-like, did not take kindly to education and civilization, and was at last sent home as unmanageable; but Eleazer became a pet in the village. It was a common remark that he looked more like a Frenchman than an Indian. His skin was fair, and his eyes hazel. Though generally lively and cheerful, he was subject to fits of thoughtfulness and abstraction very unusual in a boy. He would at times sink into deep revery, and when asked the cause he would reply that there were painful ideas about his childhood which he could neither get rid of nor understand.

On one occasion, according to a certificate given by an old lady in 1853, she remarked two scars upon his face, and on saying she supposed that he had got them in his infancy, he replied that they seemed to be connected in his mind with painful images which he did not like to dwell on and could not comprehend.

Years before it had been told in an obscure book concerning the life of the dauphin in the Temple, that Simon, one day, when preparing to beat his little prisoner, snatched a towel from the wall so roughly that he pulled out a large nail. When with the towel he struck the child blows across the face, this nail inflicted two deep wounds exactly where scars remained visible on the face of Mr. Williams. It seems also that when the child was confided to the care of Thomas Williams and his wife, two boxes of clothing and other objects which might have identified him were left with them. One of these boxes was carried off by one of his reputed sisters on her marriage, and cannot be recovered. The other was removed by persons of influence to Montreal, where it is probably now in possession of the Roman Catholic authorities. In this box are known to have been three coins, — one gold, one silver, and one copper; probably coronation medals struck at the coronation of Louis XVI. and Marie Antoinette.

After Eleazer recovered his reason and before he was sent to school, two French gentlemen visited Thomas Williams at St. Regis. They sat together on a log while the boys were playing in a little canoe on the water. Attracted by the dress of the strangers, the lads landed and drew near them, when Williams called Eleazer from the group. One Frenchman and Williams got up and went away, leaving the boy with the other Frenchman, who was fondling him as he stood between his knees. The stranger wept and seemed greatly affected. He examined scars on the boy's knees and talked to him a great deal in French, of which Eleazer did not understand a word. Shortly after this interview arrangements were made for sending him to school in Massachusetts.

The Williams family and the Indians among whom they lived at St. Regis were Roman Catholics, but Eleazer's education and associations in Massachusetts made him a Protestant. It may be here remarked *en passant*, that in the Parish Register of St. Regis, where the births and baptisms of the eleven children of Thomas Williams and his wife are carefully recorded, there is no mention of Eleazer, nor is there any space between the births of boys born about 1785 for the birth of another boy to have occurred.

Eleazer's conversion to Protestantism was highly displeasing to the clergy of the Roman Catholic Diocese of Montreal, and especially to Father Marcoux, the parish priest of Caughnawaga, to which place the Williams family removed. Many efforts were made to bring him back into the fold, and promises of high and rapid preferment were made to him if he would enter the priesthood.

Caughnawaga is a straggling Indian village on the St. Lawrence within sight of Montreal.

Eleazer continued his studies until the War of 1812 broke out with England, when he was appointed confidential agent and Superintendent-General of the Northern Indian Department. During the war he continued actively employed in the service of the United States, and fought, among other places, at the battle of Plattsburg, where in 1814 he was wounded. General Cass strongly commended him to the consideration of the Hon. John Eaton, then Secretary of War, adding, "He is a gentleman of education and talents, and from his position and associations can render important services to the government and the Indians."

During the war Eleazer Williams, having had frequent occasion to visit Albany, became acquainted with Lieutenant-Governor Taylor, and with some clergymen of the Protestant Episcopal Church. On the conclusion of the war he became intimate with Bishop Hobart, who ordained him in 1826, after he had been lay reader and missionary among the Indians at Oneida and Green Bay for about ten years.

In the year 1823 he married Miss Mary Hobart Jourdan of Green Bay, a beautiful woman, a relative of Marshal Jourdan, who under the French Republic conquered Belgium, and some German possessions on the left bank of the Rhine. They had three children, but in 1853 only one of them survived.

Green Bay, where the Rev. Eleazer Williams long resided, is a small town in the wilderness, having a palisade fort. The town is surrounded by a few Indian settlements. St. Regis and Hogansburg, where Mr. Williams ministered, were both miserable, lonely spots. The missionary received no pay from the Indians, but had a small stipend from the Missionary Committee. The rigors of the climate are excessive, the thermometer being not unfrequently 30° below zero. "One can hardly fancy a situation more lonely, more unfriended, more desolate. Mr. Williams lives on the Indian reservation, a wild tract of woodland partially cleared here and there at the edges. Dead evergreen swamps, rude fences, half prostrate, surround his abode. There lives his reputed mother, whom he tenderly treats as if she were his parent. He has no church building, but is trying to erect at least a schoolroom on the Indian reservation." Thus writes one who visited the place in 1853.

In this place Mr. Williams resided, earnest in his missionary labors, but occasionally visiting Boston and New York on business connected with his mission, until Oct. 18, 1841, when his peace was broken up by his meeting with the Prince de Joinville. From 1808 Mr. Williams had been in the habit of keeping a daily journal, a practice copied from Deacon Ely. By 1853 this journal amounted to many manuscript volumes. On Oct. 18, 1841, he records his meeting with the Prince de Joinville and an interesting conversation with him about the French in America and the French Revolution. On October 19, he writes that the prince offered to take his son to Europe and provide for his education, also on hearing of a baby newly born that he proposed to give her his mother's name, Marie Amélie, and to stand her godfather. Then in the evening came the revelation, received by the astonished missionary with feelings he recorded in his journal. Here are part of the words in which he confided his thoughts to those secret pages: —

"Although the unexpected intelligence is a new source of trouble which is already working in my inward soul with inexpressible trouble, which will accompany me to my grave, yet I trust that the Almighty arm, which has hitherto sustained me, will now protect me. To the God of my salvation I fly for comfort and consolation in this hour of my distress. Let Christ be all in all. Saviour of the world, have mercy upon Thy unworthy servant, and for the glory of Thy name turn from him all those evils that he most justly has deserved, and grant that in all his troubles he may put his whole trust and confidence in Thy mercy, and evermore serve Thee in holiness and purity of living to Thine honor and glory. All that I have heard I will lay up in my heart with the utmost secrecy." And he did so, not even for a long time telling his wife.

Meantime he had an autograph letter from Louis Philippe,

thanking him for his kindness to the prince his son, and two or more letters from the prince's secretary relating to documents bearing on the French settlements in Canada, which Mr. Williams had forwarded to Europe for him. In 1848, as I have said, he was startled by receiving a letter from Baton Rouge, informing him that a Frenchman named Bellenger had just died there, confessing on his death-bed that it was he who had brought the dauphin to America and left him among the Indians, adding that he had taken the most solemn oaths not to reveal what he had done with the child, but that times were altered, he was on his death-bed, and he did not like to die with the weight of the secret he had kept for years.

In 1853 the Rev. Mr. Hanson, becoming interested in the story, which had begun to leak out in newspaper paragraphs, met Mr. Williams. He was immediately much struck by his appearance, as indeed all men were who saw him. His features were decidedly European, also his air and carriage. His face was rather heavily moulded and also characterized by the full protuberant Austrian lips. His eyes were hazel, his hair dark, soft, and tinged with gray. His eyebrows were full, and of the same color. Over the left eye was a scar. His nostrils were large and finely cut, and he was inclined to *embonpoint*, — a characteristic of the Bourbons.

My husband, Mr. Randolph B. Latimer, a few months before our marriage was introduced to the Rev. Eleazer Williams. The interview made a great impression on him; he wrote me a full account of it at the time, and has repeated what he then told me for insertion in this volume: —

"About the time that the question 'Is there a Bourbon among us?' was being discussed in this country, it was announced that the Rev. Eleazer Williams would preach on Sunday evening at Mr. Killin's Church on West Lexington Street, Baltimore. I was interested in the subject, had read a great deal about it, and determined to go and see the supposed Louis XVII. and hear him preach. In the vestibule of the church I met Mr. Killin, whom I knew personally, and he was accompanied by a tall, portly, fine-looking man in the plain costume of an Episcopalian clergyman. Instantly I recognized him as the supposed Bourbon, and made him a bow, which he returned most graciously. As he remained in the vestibule I could not take my eyes off him, and could see in his face, figure, and manner nothing of the half-breed Indian, which some claimed he was, but a very decided resemblance to the portraits of Louis XVI. and other members of the Bourbon family; in fact, I could not help thinking that had he been clad in royal robes he would have 'looked every inch a king.' His sermon was a plain, practical one, his language simple, and his pronunciation rather more French than English, such as might be expected from a man who had passed his life doing missionary work among the Indians and half-breeds along our Canadian border, where French was used quite as much as English. His apparent age corresponded with what would have been that of the unfortunate prince, and I came away satisfied that he was the real Bourbon. His claim to the throne of France might have been substantiated, but he had no desire to raise it, and preferred the simple, useful life in which he lived and died."

The publication of Mr. Hanson's article, "Have we a Bourbon among us?" in "Putnam's Magazine," February, 1853, containing Eleazer Williams' own account of the revelation of the Prince de Joinville, naturally demanded either the silence that gives consent, or some kind of denial. This the prince *himself* has never made, but he instructed one of his secretaries to write to Mr. Putnam, saying he had indeed met an Indian missionary, whose name he had forgotten, on his way to Green Bay, whither he went to make historical researches, and that they had had an interesting conversation on the boat concerning French settlements on the frontier of Canada. He remembered that the missionary had told him (as indeed Mr. Williams had done in their first day's conversation) that his mother was an Indian, but all the rest of their conversation as reported was pure fable!

And the man whose *name he had forgotten* was one to whom Louis Philippe had written with his own hand, to whom he himself had caused letters to be addressed, and about whom he had made inquiries of Mr. Ogden in New York, and of people all along his route to Green Bay, as there were many persons able and willing to testify!

A "superstitious reverence for truth," it has been said, must not be allowed to stand in the way of a satisfactory settlement of things of great importance. This probably was a lesson impressed on the Prince de Joinville when he returned disappointed to his father from his unsuccessful mission.

The subject has been thus summed up by a second writer in "Putnam's Magazine," in February, 1854, in an article on the "Problem of the Lost Prince": —

"When Louis Philippe came to the throne, he inherited the obligation of looking after his cousin, the Lost Prince. He entertains perhaps the benevolent design of calling him home and treating him like a prince, on condition that he will resign all right to the throne, and he sends his son, the Prince de Joinville (a sailor, not a diplomatist), to treat with him for this object, not doubting, from his knowledge of his position, that his proposal ought to be, and probably would be, accepted. All this was perfectly natural. It might perhaps be called generous and noble. Louis Philippe, having come to the throne by the choice of the people, could not impair his own rights or those of his family by treating with Mr. Williams; and he was of course of the opinion (from which no one would dissent) that the idea of restoring the son of Louis XVI. to the throne of his father, after all that had passed, could not be entertained for a moment in France by people of influence or by others. The mission of the Prince de Joinville, therefore, may have been prompted by humanity and benevolence. But it failed. And when the nature of it became public, the particulars concerning it being incapable on Mr. Williams' part of verification, for lack of witnesses, it would of course be denied from motives of policy."

Of course Eleazer Williams was wholly unfitted to be King of France either in 1841 or 1854. To add to his disqualifications, he was a Protestant missionary. The Rev. Father

Marcoux, whether of his own motion or prompted from without, succeeded in persuading the old Indian woman of ninety, the reputed mother of Eleazer Williams, that that unfortunate heretic might become King of France, to the destruction of many thousands of pious souls. Having thus frightened her he took her before a magistrate at Hogansburg, where she made an affidavit, speaking only Indian; this was interpreted into English by Father Marcoux, no other person understanding both English and Indian being present. It was then read over to her in Indian, and she signed it with her mark. The document was at once taken to France by a M. de Courcey. It asserted that Eleazer Williams was her own son, and had never been confided to her husband's care by any Frenchman.

When she was made subsequently to understand what she had sworn to, she went again before the same magistrate, stating the case and declaring that she had never intended to say the things to which she had signed her mark in the previous affidavit.

In the three articles published in "Putnam's Magazine," Volumes I. and III., and in Mr. Hanson's very scarce book, "The Lost Prince," there are many more particulars and much argument, which, as I hold no brief in the case, I have not repeated.

The particulars regarding the disappearance of the dauphin from the Temple are more full in the article from "Figaro," and are there based on public documents.

The idea of Mr. Hanson is that the substitution of the child who died of scrofula took place between May 31, 1795, and June 5, four days when no one saw the boy but Laurent, Lasne, Gomin (or Govin), and Bellenger, who had just been appointed Commissary at the Temple. I may here remark that neither Williams nor Mr. Hanson had ever heard the name of Bellenger in connection with the prisoner in the Temple, until after his confession on his deathbed at Baton Rouge. During the first of those days in 1795 Bellenger was a great deal with the child, trying to amuse him by pictures in a portfolio.

The impression of the writer in "Putnam's Magazine" is that the disappearance of the dauphin from the Temple and his subsequent concealment was due to the intrigues of Louis XVIII., who had long plotted for the throne of France, and who years before had not scrupled to denounce his brother's son as a bastard. It is quite true that the production of a boy-king at that crisis in French history would have damaged the slender prospects of restoring the monarchy. The "Figaro" thinks the disappearance of the dauphin was due to Barras. The two men placed over him in the spring of 1795, Lasne and Gomin (or Govin), were of different politics, though they seem to have acted together, Lasne being a republican, and Govin, so far as he dared, a royalist. Bellenger was a man trusted by Louis XVIII. (when Comte de Provence), in whose service he had been as artist and designer.

In 1795 or 1796 a French gentleman named Le Ray de Chaumont came to America from France and settled in St. Lawrence County, New York, where he lived in affluence and had much intercourse with the Indians of St. Regis and Hogansburg. In the year 1818 there was a dinner-party at the house of Dr. Hosack in New York. Among the guests were Comte Jean d'Angely, Dr. John W. Francis, and Genêt, brother of Madame Campan, ex-French ambassador to the United States. In the course of conversation the subject of the dauphin was introduced, and inquiry was started concerning his fate. Then Genêt distinctly said, "Gentlemen, the dauphin of France is not dead, but was brought to America." The conversation on this interesting subject was continued for some time, and Genêt informed the company among other things that he believed the dauphin was in Western New York, and that Le Ray de Chaumont knew all about it.

Mrs. Brown, living in New Orleans in 1854 when the subject of Eleazer Williams was attracting much attention, voluntarily testified under oath that she had been wife to the Secretary of the Comte d'Artois (Charles X.) and had resided at Holyrood from 1804 to 1810; that she was admitted to some intimacy by the Duchesse d'Angoulême, who once told her that she knew the dauphin was alive and in America. She also heard the name of Williams in that connection. She adds that the royal family, while knowing that the dauphin was alive, always asserted that he was incompetent to reign.

Another lady, wife to the secretary of the Comte de Coigny, had told Mrs. Brown, when they were speaking on the subject, that it had been much discussed in the royal palace; that it was said the elevation of such a person to the throne would only increase the difficulties of the times; that a man had come from America to confer with the family on the subject; that money had been given him, and he had returned to America.

No doubt the Duchesse d'Angoulême, while a young person, supposed her brother to have perished in the Temple, and probably took Govin's account of his last hours as fact. But anybody reading M. Beauchesne's book, with its marvellous account of the last days of the poor child's life, cannot fail to be struck with the manifest fictitiousness of the accounts given "upon their sacred honor," in 1818 by Govin and Lasne. This account answered its purpose. It was desirable to prove the dauphin dead in 1818. We have seen already that the Duchesse d'Angoulême was never satisfied about her brother's death, even after Govin and Lasne had published their story, and that every fresh report concerning him greatly excited her. But yet, as an earnest Catholic, how could she have been willing to welcome a Protestant missionary as heir to the French throne?

The Rev. Eleazer Williams died at Hogansburg, New York, August 27, 1858, aged seventy-three years.

INDEX.

A.

ABBAYE, massacre in the, 179–182.
Abeille, Dr., opinion on escape of Louis XVII., 74.
Adam, Adolphe, account of Feast of Supreme Being, *quoted*, 290–307.
Adhémar, Comtesse d', on supposed death of Louis XVII., *quoted*, 416.
Amadeus III. of Sardinia, reception of news of Louis XVI.'s execution, 220.
Andoins, Captain d', 154, 155.
Angoulême, Duchesse d', account of separation of Marie Antoinette from her son, *quoted*, 401, 402; lack of conviction as to her brother's death, 416, 418, 419; account of life in Temple, *quoted*, 233, 234, 235.
"Appleton's Journal," mentioned in note, 116.
Arras, *fête* at, in honor of Robespierre, 337, 338.
Artois, Comte d', description of, 133.
August, tenth of, insurrection, 27–29; events leading to, 176–178.
Ayen, Duchesse d', execution of, 395–400.

B.

BARRAS, 317, 409, 411, 412, 416.
Barrère, direction of *fête* to Supreme Being, 294, 295.
Bastille, celebration of taking of, 23–25; destruction of, 103–106; prisoners in when captured, 104.
Berryer, M., lieutenant of police, 74, 75, 76, 77.
Bicêtre, destruction of, 106.
Blanc, Louis, *quoted*, on Louis XVII., 418.
Blois, Henri Grégoire, Bishop of, first knowledge of, 355; political views, 356; action in the States-General, 357; appointment to bishopric, 357; public life, 357–361; death, 361.
Bois de Boulogne, appearance in 1787, 121.
Boissy d'Anglas, on Rabaut, *quoted*, 363.
Bollman, Dr. Erick, share in escape of Lafayette, 376–378.
Boufflers, Marquis de, lines on Marie Antoinette's faults, *quoted*, 137.
Bouillé, General, 151, 155, 160, 161.
Buonaparte, Napoleon, 176, 341.

C.

CALENDAR, changes in, during Revolution, 337–342.
Campan, Madame, 62.
Carlyle, Mr., 144, *quoted*, on insurrection of 10th of August, 172–175.
Carnot, Lazare, intimacy with Robespierre, 324.
Carrichon, M., *quoted*, on execution of Madame de Lafayette's family, 390–400.
Cathedral of St. Denis, description of, 122.
Charles XIII. of Sweden, 170.
Chénier, Joseph, poet, 295, 297, 300, 301, 306, 307.
Choiseul, Duc de, 151, 152, 153, 155, 157, 158.

Christian, Prince of Schleswig-Holstein, 170.
Clergy of France during Revolution, 348–372.
Cléry, valet to Louis XVI., *quoted*, murder of Princesse de Lamballe, 195–197; last hours of Louis XVI., 203–207.
Commune, sections forming, 245, 246.
Condé, Prince de, funeral services ordered by, for Louis XVI., 221.
Constitution Civile, 348–350, 357.
Convention, National, reception of king's petition, 200; orders for king's execution, 201; meeting after execution, 215, 216; recognition of Supreme Being, 294; confiscation of church property, 348–350.
Coppée, François, *quoted*, poem "Which," 342, 343.
Corday, Charlotte, birth and personal appearance, 248; education, 249, 250; resolution to destroy Marat, 251; departure for Paris, 252; letter to father, *quoted*, 253; arrival in Paris, 254; address written to Frenchmen, *quoted*, 255, 256; letter to Marat, *quoted*, 256, 257; murder of Marat and arrest, 262; imprisonment in Abbaye, 263–268; letter to Committee of Public Safety, *quoted*, 264: letter to Barbaroux, *quoted*, 264–267, 269, 270; removal to Conciergerie, 268; examination before Tribunal, 268, 271–273; letter to father, *quoted*, 271; last hours, 273, 274; execution and burial, 275.
Cordeliers, 277.

D.

D'ALÈGRE, escape from Bastille, 77–83, 97.
Danton, Revolutionary leader, departure from Paris, 277; resignation from Committee of Public Safety, 278; arrest, 279; imprisonment at the Luxembourg, 280; removal to Conciergerie, 281; trial, 281–286; execution, 287; life and character, 288, 289; alluded to, 173, 178, 244, 245.
Danton, Madame, 288.
Dauphin. *See* Louis XVII.
David, painter, 263, 275, 294, 305.
Dejean, Dr., *quoted*, letter concerning Latude, 87, 88.
De la Croix, M., 100, 101.
Desmoulins, Camille, arrest, 279; trial, 281, 285; execution, 287.
Desorgues, Chevalier, author of hymn to Supreme Being, 303, 304, 306.
Dogs in the Revolution, 343–347.
Dol, Archbishop of, epitaph to, 354.
Drouet, J. B., postmaster at Varennes, 154, 155, 158.
Duperret, friend of Charlotte Corday, 254, 255, 263.
Duplay, Eléonore, family of, 328; personal appearance and character, 332.
Duplay, Maurice, residence, 325–327; first acquaintance with Robespierre, 327; pecuniary circumstances and political views, 328.

E.

EDGEWORTH, Abbé, confessor to Louis XVI., 203, 205, 208, 213.
Églantine, Fabre d', *quoted*, description of Marat, 259.
Elisabeth, Madame, life in the Temple, 402.
Erckmann-Chatrian, "Mémoires d'un Paysan," mentioned in note, 107.

F.

FERSEN, Count Axel de, participation in flight to Varennes, 145–149; subsequent career, 164–171.
"Figaro," *quoted*, on last days of Louis XVI., 198–222; on fate of Louis XVII., 408–420; mentioned in notes, 247, 309, 344, 386.
Fouquier-Tinville, member of Revolutionary Tribunal, 240, 241, 251, 272, 284, 285, 328.
France, condition of, in 1792, 110–115; journey through, in 1787, 116–129; clergy in, during Revolution, 348–372.

G.

"GENTLEMAN'S MAGAZINE," *quoted*, on Count Fersen, 164-171; on Rabaut, 362-372.
Germany, Emperor of, reception of news of execution of Louis XVI., 221.
Goguelat, M., part in flight to Varennes, 151, 152, 157, 158, 162, 163.
Gossec, composer of hymn to Supreme Being, 295, 297, 300, 301, 302, 306.
Grandidier, M., *quoted* in Klindworth's memoirs on attempt to restore Marie Antoinette to Austria, 223-231.
Grégoire, Henri. *See* Blois.
Griffith, Thomas Waters, birth and early life, 9-17; departure for France, 18; residence in Bolbec and Havre, 19, 20; removal to Paris, 21; witness of celebration of taking of Bastille, 23, 24; public dinner given by Santerre, 25; insurrection of 10th of August, 27-30; massacres of September, 31-33; journey to Havre, 34-37; visit to London, 37, 38; return to America, 39; return to Paris and subsequent arrest, 41; imprisonment at the Madelonettes, 43-47; at Scotch College, 47-49; release, 50; efforts to obtain release of Thomas Paine, 50; visit to London, 53, 54; appointment as consul to Havre, 54; return to France, 55; life in Paris, 58-67; journey to Spain, 68; final departure for America, 69.
Guillotine, Dr., 204.
Gustavus III. of Sweden, 165, 168, 169.
Gustavus IV. of Sweden, 170.
Guyonnet, M., governor of Vincennes, 92, 93.

H.

HALLES, the, in 1789, 141, 142.
Hanson, Rev. Mr., *quoted*, description of Eleazer Williams, 436.
Hawks, Dr., *quoted*, opinion of Eleazer Williams, 429, 430.
Hébert, Revolutionary leader, 215, 246, 263, 277.
Herman, judge of Revolutionary Tribunal, 282, 283, 284, 285.
Hitchman, Francis, *quoted*, on Revolutionary Calendar, 335-342.
Huger, Colonel, share in escape of Lafayette, 377, 378.
Hugo, Victor, *quoted*, poem on Louis XVII., 405-407.

J.

JOINVILLE, Prince de, visit to America, 421-422; interview with Eleazer Williams, 422-429; subsequent conduct to Eleazer Williams, 437.
Jones, Commodore Paul, 21.
Josephine de Beauharnais, 409; action on behalf of Louis XVII., 417.
"Journal de la République," *quoted*, on execution of Louis XVI., 220.

K.

KILLARENE, Dean of, novel, mentioned in note, 365.
Klindworth, memoirs of, 223.

L.

LAFAYETTE, Marquis de, birth and early life, 373; visit to America, 374; public life on return to France, 374, 375; imprisonment, 376; escape, 377; capture and re-imprisonment, 378-379; release, 379; second visit to America, 381-383; return to France, 384; death and funeral, 385; character, 387.
Lafayette, family of, 386-389.
Lamballe, Princesse de, birth, descent, and marriage, 184; friendship with Marie Antoinette, 185; flight to England, 186; return to France, 187; imprisonment in Temple, 190; at La Force, 191-194; trial, 194; murder, 32, 195.

Larivière, account of last moments of Marie Antoinette, 241, 242.
Latimer, Mr. Randolph, *quoted*, description of Eleazer Williams, 436, 437.
Latude, Henri de, imprisonments and escapes, 72–103.
Launay, M. de, governor of the Bastille, 104.
Lebas, Philippe, friendship with Robespierre, 333.
Lebas, Madame, anecdote of, 333–335.
Lebrun, family of, friendship for Latude, 91, 92.
Legros, Madame, friendship for Latude, 99–102.
Lenfant, Abbé, murder of, 179.
Lenoir, M., lieutenant of police, 97, 99, 101.
Lettres de cachet, 95.
"Littell's Living Age," mentioned in notes, 130, 223, 290, 348, 355, 386, 390.
London, reception in, of news of Louis XVI.'s execution, 220.
"London Quarterly Review," mentioned in note, 235.
Louis XVI., description of, 131; private life in 1789, 134; seeks protection of Assembly, 189; condemned to death by National Assembly, 199; petition to above, *quoted*, 199, 200; account of imprisonment, 202; last interview with family, 203; last hours, 204–210; execution, 211, 212; burial, 214.
Louis XVII., separation from his mother, 401, 402; subsequent life in prison, 403, 404; evidence in favor of escape from Temple, 409–414; political reasons for the suppression of his escape, 415–419.
Louis XVIII., erection of Chapelle Expiatoire, 418.
Lyons, massacre at, 290.

M.

"Macmillan's Magazine," mentioned in note, 390.
Malesherbes, M. de, prime minister of France, 96, 199, 293.
Manuel, procureur of the Commune, 190–193.
Marat, Revolutionary leader, appointed President of Council of the Commune, 245; demand for heads of aristocrats, 246; political views, 247; birth and personal appearance, 257; education, 258; interest in Revolution, 258, 259; residence, 260; love-affair with Simone Evrard, 260; murder, 261; funeral, 263; honor paid to after death, 275, 276; description of, by D'Églantine, *quoted*, 259.
Marie Antoinette, description of, 132; friendship for Count Fersen, 165–167; friendship for Princesse de Lamballe, 185; letter to above, *quoted*, 187; conduct at King's death, 217; imprisonment in Temple, 233–235; in Conciergerie, 235–239; trial by Revolutionary Tribunal, 239, 240; last hours, 241, 242; execution, 41, 42, 243; lines on faults by Boufflers, *quoted*, 137.
Markham, Mrs., historian, mentioned in note, 232.
Marseilles, massacres at, 290.
Marshal Maillé, 172, 173; murder of, 182.
Maton, lawyer, *quoted*, on massacre in La Force, 179–181.
Mirabeau, Comte de, *quoted*, on Lafayette, 385.
Monroe, Mr., American minister, 52, 55, 56, 59, 61, 65.
Moore, Dr. John, letter from, *quoted*, on Marie Antoinette, 189–190.
Morris, Gouverneur, American minister, 21, 22, 31, 52, 220; letters from, to Mr. Griffith, *quoted*, 45, 46.
Motte, Madame de la, 124.
Mouchy, Maréchale de, death of, 392, 393.

N.

"National Review," mentioned in note, 348.
Naundorff, M., pretender, 408, 409, 416, 419, 420.
Necker, Madame, 98, letter from, relating to Latude, *quoted*, 101, 102.

"Nineteenth Century," mentioned in note, 355.
Noailles, Maréchale de, execution, 395–400.
Noailles, Vicomtesse de, letter to husband, *quoted*, 391, 392; execution, 395–400.
Nolte, Vincent, *quoted*, on Lafayette's visit to Washington, 383, 384, 385.
Normandie, Duc de. *See* Naundorff.

O.

OBERKIRCH, Madame d', letter from, *quoted*, 185, 186.
Orange, massacre at, 290.
Orléans, Duchesse d', 197; mentioned in note, 186.

P.

PAINE, Thomas Treat, 50, 59, 61.
Palais Royal in 1789, 139.
Paris, description of, before Revolution, 130–143; after king's execution, 219, 220; *fêtes* in, during Revolution, 291–293.
Parisians, dress of, in 1789, 140; behavior of, after execution of king, 213, 214.
Penthièvre, Duc de, 184, 191, 197.
Pétion, mayor of Paris. 172, 253.
Phalsbourg, description of town, 107–109.
Philippe, Égalité, Duc d'Orléans, 199, 218.
Polignac, Madame de, 184.
Pompadour, Madame de, 72, 74, 76, 77, 91.
Prieur, Abbé, 94.
Provence, Comte de, description of, 133; at Trianon, 136; farewell visit to king, 146; reception of news of king's death, 221; hope of crown, 409.
"Putnam's Magazine," *quoted*, on Eleazer Williams, 422–429, 438, 439.

Q.

QUINCY, Mr. Josiah, *quoted*, on Lafayette's appearance in Boston, 381, 382.

R.

RABAUT, Paul, Huguenot pastor, 362, 371.
Rabaut, Saint-Étienne, Huguenot pastor, early life, 362, 363; departure for Paris, 364; election to States-General, 365; speech against death of King, 366; downfall, 368; capture, 369; execution, 370, 371.
Recamier, Madame, 62.
Revolution, French, causes of, 70–72; episodes of, 324–347; ideas of, 335, 336; men of, 355.
Revolutionary Calendar, 335–342.
Robespierre, Revolutionary leader, as a poet, 324, 325; intimacy with Lazare Carnot, 324; verses to the Society of the Rosati, *quoted*, 324, 325: private life with the family Duplay, 325-333; Fête of the Supreme Being, 305; political views, 308; personal appearance and character, 309; love of power, 310; struggle for supremacy in Convention, 310-312; downfall, 314; arrest, 315; imprisonment and liberation, 316; attack upon by Méda, 318; capture, 319, 320; execution, 322; character, 322, 323; allusions to, 216, 237, 245, 246, 277, 278.
Rome, reception at, of news of Louis XVI.'s execution, 221.
Romme, chairman of Committee of Public Instruction, 337, 338.
Rosati, Society of the, 324.

S.

SAINT-ÉTIENNE. *See* Rabaut, Jean Paul.
Saint-Just, 278, 312, 316, 320.
Salpêtrière, description of, in 1787, 124, 125.
Sanson, executioner, 209, 210, 211, 286.

Santerre, General, commander of National Guard, 203, 206, 207, 212, 215, 344-347.
Sardou, *quoted*, on Robespierre, 325-335.
Sarrette, musical director, 290, 295, 296-304, 306, 307.
Sartine, M. de, letter of Latude to, *qucted*, 93, 95, 101.
Sauce, M., mayor of Varennes, 156, 157.
September massacres, 31-33, 178-183.
Sicard, Abbé, *quoted*, account of massacre in La Force, 181.
Supreme Being, Feast of, institution, 294; preparations for, 294-304; celebration of, 305-307.
Swiss Guard, massacre of, 174, 175.

T.

TALLIEN, Madame, 62.
Temple, the, life of royal family in, 233-235.
"Temple Bar," mentioned in note, 184.
Tourzel, Madame de, 147, 189; letter from, *quoted*, 191, 192; escape from La Force, 192, 193.
Tourzel, Mademoiselle de, 189, 190; escape from La Force, 191.
Trianon, description of, 135-138.

V.

VARENNES, flight of royal family to, 144-163.
Versailles, description of, in 1787, 125, 126; massacre at, 182, 183.

W.

WILLIAMS, Eleazer, account of interview with Prince de Joinville, *quoted*, 422-429; early history, 430-433; missionary work, 434-436; further evidence as to identity, 436-440; death, 440.
Williams, Helen Maria, *quoted*, 336.

Y.

YOUNG, Arthur, *quoted*, on condition of France, 336.